WITH RESPECT TO SEX

Worlds of Desire: The Chicago Series on Sexuality, Gender, and Culture
Edited by Gilbert Herdt

With Respect to Sex

NEGOTIATING HIJRA IDENTITY IN SOUTH INDIA

Gayatri Reddy

The University of Chicago Press / Chicago and London

Gayatri Reddy is assistant professor of anthropology and gender and women's studies at the
University of Illinois at Chicago.

The University of Chicago Press, Chicago 60637
The University of Chicago Press, Ltd., London
© 2005 by The University of Chicago
All rights reserved. Published 2005
Printed in the United States of America

14 13 12 11 10 09 08 07 06 05   1 2 3 4 5

ISBN: 0-226-70755-5 (cloth)
ISBN: 0-226-70756-3 (paper)

Library of Congress Cataloging-in-Publication Data

Reddy, Gayatri.
    With respect to sex : negotiating hijra identity in South India / Gayatri Reddy.
       p. cm. — (Worlds of desire)
    Includes bibliographical references and index.
    ISBN 0-226-70755-5 (cloth : alk. paper) — ISBN 0-226-70756-3 (pbk. : alk. paper)
    1. Transsexuals—India, South. 2. Transsexualism—Religious aspects—Islam. 3. Sex role—India,
South. 4. Sex differences—India, South. 5. Sex role—Religious aspects—Islam. 6. Gender identity—
India, South. 7. Islam and culture—India, South. 8. Transvestism—Religious aspects—Islam.
9. Prostitution—India, South. 10. Hyderabad (India)—Social life and customs. 11. Secunderabad
(India)—Social life and customs.   I. Title.   II. Series.

    HQ77.95.I4R43 2005
    305.3'0954—dc22   2004015754

IN GRATITUDE

*To the memory of my mother, who taught me to love books
and encouraged my curiosity early in life*

CONTENTS

ACKNOWLEDGMENTS

My first and greatest debt is to my *hijra* and *koti* friends and acquaintances in Hyderabad for welcoming me so openly into their lives. If it weren't for their hospitality, generosity, and warmth, not only would this book have been impossible to write, fieldwork would not have been the joy and pleasure that it was. I would especially like to thank those *hijras* and *kotis* I have referred to in this book as Munira, Surekha, Saroja, Irfan *nayak* and Amir *nayak*, Frank, Shanti, Rajeshwari, Aliya, Srilakshmi, and Nagalakshmi (all pseudonyms) for their unstinting gifts of time, patience, energy, hospitality, and friendship. I remain forever in your debt.

Research for this book was made possible by generous grants and fellowships from the National Science Foundation, the Association for Women in Science, the Mellon Foundation, and Emory University. I would also like to express my gratitude to the Sexuality Research Fellowship Program (SRFP) of the Social Science Research Foundation and its director, Diane di Mauro. Although research for this particular project was not funded by the SRFP, their subsequent support, both material and intellectual, in the form of a generous postdoctoral award and the fellowship of brilliant sexuality researchers, was crucial for my ability to clarify my analysis and crystallize my writing in the final stages of this project.

As in the case of all collective enterprises, this book could not have been written without the support and encouragement of many individuals and institutions. At Columbia University, where I began my graduate work, I am extremely grateful and will remain forever indebted to Joan Vincent and Carole Vance for their support and generous encouragement, as well as their warmth and understanding in those early years of my career.

At Emory University I would first like to thank the members of my dissertation committee, all of whom were incredibly supportive and instrumental in creating the intellectual and social environment that allowed me to complete this project. I am truly grateful and honored to have had the opportunity to work with all of you. Don Donham initially encouraged me to remain in academia and, through his insightful comments and suggestions and generous validation of my work, was also largely responsible for my growth as an intellectual over these many years. Joyce Flueckiger offered invaluable suggestions and insights on South Asian anthropology, religion, and ethnography, and always gave unstintingly of her time and energy when I needed it. Throughout my graduate career, Peter Brown has been a steadfast source of encouragement and hands-on training, as well as an example of how to be a wonderful teacher while retaining one's grounded humanity. Finally, Bruce Knauft has been an incredibly generous, profoundly insightful, and truly outstanding advisor, and has also been instrumental in my staying the course and embarking on my current academic path. I only hope I can be half as generous, supportive, intellectually stimulating, and loyal to my own advisees and students as Bruce was to me. I would also like to thank three other faculty members at Emory: Charles Nuckolls and Carol Worthman for their patience, encouragement, and support during my first couple of years at Emory, and Deborah McFarland for her enthusiasm and support of my work during my later, brief sojourn through the School of Public Health.

I owe an intellectual debt of gratitude to a number of individuals who have read this book or sections of it in manuscript form and provided me with invaluable suggestions. I am particularly grateful to Lawrence Cohen, Serena Nanda, Elena Gutierrez, Laurie Schaffner, Peg Strobel, Judy Gardiner, Biju Rao, Micaela di Leonardo, Vinay Swamy, Sylvia Vatuk, Jennifer Brier, William Wolf, Donna Murdock, and Emily Bloch, who gave generously of their time in reading, commenting on, and greatly improving parts or the whole of this manuscript. I would also like to thank Corinne Louw for her meticulous and invaluable assistance in preparing the final draft of the manuscript for publication. To the participants in my dissertation-writing seminar from 1997 to 1999, especially Holly Wardlow, Daniel Smith, and Andrew Cousins (and Don Donham for doing such a superb job of facilitating this seminar)—I could not have finished without you. Thank you for your extremely valuable critiques and suggestions, your steady encouragement and validation, and your constant presence and support—over endless shared pitchers of beer and cigarettes—through all the ups and downs of agonizing over and writing the dissertation. I thank Wendy Doniger and Kira Hall for generously making available their unpublished material. For their friendship, love, support, and encouragement over the years, I would also like to thank Edith Aubin, C. S. Balachandran,

Tassi Crabb, Beatrice Greco, Russ Hanford, Aditya Kar, Alice Long, Keith McNeal, Gowri Meda, Fabien Richards, Elaine Salo, Sumati Surya, Shauna Swartz, Deepa and Rajesh Talpade, Mayuresh Tapale and all the other wonderful Trikone folk in Atlanta, my father, Vasunder Reddy, my aunt, Jyothi Rao, Saras and G. K. Reddy, and other supportive members of my family in Hyderabad, as well as Yamini Atmavilas, Lara Deeb, Jessica Gregg, Benjamin Junge, Anil Lal, Wynne Maggi, Mark Padilla, Rebecca Seligman, Malcolm Shelley, and Anu Srinivasan.

At the University of Illinois, I would like to thank the faculty and staff of both my departments—Gender and Women's Studies as well as Anthropology—for their support and encouragement of my work. I would especially like to thank my colleagues Elena Gutierrez, Peg Strobel, Judy Gardiner, Sylvia Vatuk, and Laurie Schaffner for their extremely valuable comments on drafts of this manuscript. In addition, I would like to thank Lynette Jackson, Krista Thompson, Mark Liechty, Yasmin Nair, Javier Villa-Flores, John D'Emilio, Jim Oleson, Sandy Bartky, Beth Richie, Jennifer Langdon-Teclaw, Helen Gary, Emily LaBarbera-Twarog, Corinne Louw, and Jill Gage for making this new academic space intellectually challenging and stimulating, as well as wonderfully collegial and supportive for me. Finally, I would like to thank Ray Brod and his able assistants at the UIC Cartography Laboratory for preparing the map for this volume.

At the Press, I am profoundly grateful to series editor Gilbert Herdt, executive editor Douglas Mitchell, and editorial associate Timothy McGovern. From the very beginning, they have been enthusiastic, generous, and patient as I negotiated the various twists and turns of the publication process. I am very grateful to Nick Murray for his excellent editorial skills and for making this book more accessible to a wider audience. I am greatly indebted to the two anonymous readers of the manuscript for their incredibly careful, brilliantly critical, and constructive readings of the text. Their insightful comments and gentle efforts to push my analyses have vastly improved the manuscript. Any misinterpretations and omissions are solely my responsibility.

Perhaps my greatest personal debt is to my sister, Sita Reddy, without whose guidance, love, support, and constant encouragement I would neither have embarked on a career in anthropology nor successfully navigated graduate school, chosen the present topic, or concluded this project. To her I owe more than an intellectual debt of gratitude. It is thanks to her enduring support and belief in me—in addition to unstinting gifts of time and effort in reading multiple drafts of my chapters, often at the last minute—that this book could be written. Thank you, Sita.

NOTE ON TRANSLITERATION

For ease of reading, I have chosen not to use diacritics in transliterating non-English words in the text and have transliterated these words with appropriate diacritical marks only in the glossary. In the text, non-English words have been italicized. Those used most frequently have been italicized only the first time they appear, for example, *hijra, koti, cela, izzat,* and so forth.

1

The Ethnographic Setting

It wasn't until a few weeks after I began fieldwork among *hijras* in the South Indian twin cities of Hyderabad and Secunderabad that I had my first inkling of their perceptions of me. I was sitting on a mat, chatting with Munira, who later became one of my closest hijra friends. She was telling me proudly about her last visit to Mumbai when she had been approached by a journalist for her story, and how she had rebuffed him. Munira then turned to me and said, somewhat apologetically, "I hope you don't mind my saying this. But you know, Gayatri, when I first saw you, I thought, 'She has the body and face of a woman, she is wearing female clothing, but she has such short hair. Maybe she is a young boy of thirteen or fourteen.' That is the reason I spoke to you initially, you know. I thought maybe, maybe you were one of us at first." Then, laughing aloud, she added, "Frankly, I don't know how I thought that you might be. You are, you know, different-looking, so that is what I thought then."

I begin with this incident to highlight two issues of access and representation: First, of course, was hijras' perception of my appearance—as a young Indian, somewhat "different-looking" from them, with uncommonly short hair for a woman. Second, as I gradually learned over the course of my fieldwork, they attributed this difference not to my sexuality or sexual orientation, but to my upper-middle-class status. My short hair, my "ethnically chic" Fab India *salwar-kurta*,[1] my educational background, my status as an unmarried woman, especially given my age, and my engagement in this academic project with hijras—factors that lead to a presumption about my *sexual* identity here in the United States—were, for hijras, signs of my *class* identification.

Quite apart from privileging a particular theory, history, and politics of representation, I raise this issue to underscore a fairly simple point: the notion that sexual difference is not the only lens through which hijras perceive the world and expect in turn to be perceived. In other words, as I maintain throughout this ethnography, hijras are not *just* a sexual or gendered category, as is commonly contended in the literature (e.g., Vyas and Shingala 1987; Sharma 1989; Nanda 1990). Like the members of any other community in India, their identities are shaped by a range of other axes. Though sex/gender is perhaps the most important of these axes, hijra identity cannot be reduced to this frame of analysis.[2] Through a description of hijras' lives, this book explores the domain of sexuality as well as its articulation with broader contexts of everyday life in South Asia, including aspects of kinship, religion, class, and hierarchies of respect. Before exploring issues of representation and hijras' historical and geographic representation in particular, however, I provide a brief introductory note about hijras for those unfamiliar with these metonymic figures of Indian sexual difference.

THE HYPER (IN)VISIBILITY OF HIJRAS

For the most part, hijras are phenotypic men who wear female clothing and, ideally, renounce sexual desire and practice by undergoing a sacrificial emasculation—that is, an excision of the penis and testicles—dedicated to the goddess Bedhraj Mata. Subsequently they are believed to be endowed with the power to confer fertility on newlyweds or newborn children. They see this as their "traditional" ritual role, although at least half of the current hijra population (at least in Hyderabad) engages in prostitution, which hierarchically senior "ritual specialists" greatly disparage.[3] In recent years, hijras have emerged as perhaps the most frequently encountered figures in the narrative linking of India with sexual difference. As the quintessential "third sex" of India, they have captured the Western scholarly imagination as an ideal case in the transnational system of "alternative" gender/sexuality. In such analyses, the hijra (or Thai *kathoey* or Omani *xanith*, among others) becomes, as Rosalind Morris notes, either an "interstitial gender occupying the liminal space between male and female," or "a 'drag queen' who [is] a hero(ine) in a global sexual resistance" (1994, 16). With this specularization has come an intense gaze directed at hijras by both scholars and the press.

By their own accounts, hijras in most major cities—including the South Indian city of Hyderabad, where I did my research—have been driven crazy by foreigners or, to translate the more colorful Hindi phrase, have had their "minds eaten by foreign [*firangi*] people" desperate to capture a story for their audience. In the last decade or so, there have been at least four documentaries or news features (Kalliat 1990; Prasad and Yorke 1991;

Cooper 1999; Shiva, MacDonald, and Gucovsky 2000), four ethnographies or book-length monographs (Nanda 1990; Jaffrey 1996; Balaji and Malloy 1997; Ahmed and Singh 2002), three books of fiction (Mann 1992; Sinha 1993; Forbes 1998), at least two dissertations (Hall 1995; Reddy 2000), and several undergraduate honors theses that focus explicitly on hijras. More recently, hijras have also been "mainstreamed" into the Indian world of popular films.[4] In some ways, this is in marked contrast to the earlier ambivalent yet arguably tolerant attitude of most Indians toward them. For many Indians—both upper- and middle-class—hijras exist (and to some extent have always existed) at the periphery of their imaginaries, making themselves visible only on certain circumscribed ritual occasions. Given this history of near invisibility, the recent attention focused on hijras has been unsettling for both hijras and non-hijras.

In response to this seemingly boundless interest, hijras have become more wary of scholars and journalists alike, and this attention has also heightened scrutiny by local disciplinary regimes, including the police.[5] Just before I arrived in Hyderabad for my fieldwork, a case was registered against the senior hijras in the old city by a family that claimed their son had been abducted by the hijra community.[6] Even though the case was later dismissed, hijras told me they felt overly scrutinized for the first time in hundreds of years. Partly in response to this heightened sensitivity on the part of the hijra community, but also, I suspect, out of a patriarchal concern that this was not a "proper" topic for an Indian woman to be researching (see Jaffrey 1996), I was explicitly advised by anthropologists, several relatives, and even strangers to steer clear of hijras in Hyderabad. Needless to say, the atmosphere within the hijra community, especially with regard to interactions with non-hijras, was somewhat tense when I began my research in the fall of 1995.

For all these reasons, I was well aware that by undertaking this project I might, however unwittingly, increase hijras' visibility within disciplinary regimes in India, resulting in greater scrutiny of their lives. In recent years, with the increasing visibility of hijras in global compendia of sexuality/gender and the growth of the gay movement in India, hijras, self-identified gay men, and men cruising for sex with other men in public spaces have become increasingly visible to the police, the media, and ruffians, or *goondas*. Just in the last few years, there have been at least two dramatic disruptions and arrests of volunteers in nongovernmental organizations that work on issues relating to sexual health—and more specifically, the health of MSM, or men who have sex with men—quite apart from the innumerable incidents of everyday harassment and surveillance. Despite this greater vigilance and my anxiety on this account, however, many hijras I encountered in Hyderabad explicitly reiterated their desire to get the real story of their lives down on paper, as much in response to this scrutiny as to vindicate their life choices. Although aware of the irony of their positions and the potential for even greater vilification on account of the publicity, hijras with whom I worked most closely were eager to "tell [their] stories" so that "everyone [would] know about [their] lives."

In undertaking this project, I am also concerned that my focusing on hijras within the current frame of academic inquiry that explicitly emphasizes their sexual difference—even if my intention is expressly to refocus this gaze—inevitably privileges this mode of discourse. I grew up in India well aware of the existence of hijras, and even though I was not immersed in their lives, I have to question why my intellectual curiosity was not sufficiently piqued until I came to the United States for graduate studies. Or maybe the question should not be when and why did I remember, but when and why did I forget? What sorts of erasures—of class, caste, gender, or sexuality—were encoded in my previous silence and ongoing refraction of the hijra "category" (see Patel 1997)? More specifically, what kinds of occlusions of class and sexual privilege do these conceal/reveal in both (upper-middle-class) India and the U.S. academe? In other words, perhaps we need to be aware of the history and politics of particular discursive and theoretical lenses—the marked categories/discourses that might appear salient in one arena but less so in another (see Uberoi 1996; Thapan 1997; John and Nair 1998). This is not to imply that sex and sexuality are not important or even central to hijras' lives. It merely emphasizes the need to contextualize our analytic and personal agendas in any representational endeavor. Hence, viewing hijras solely within the framework of sex/gender difference—as the quintessential "third sex" or "neither men nor women"—ultimately might be a disservice to the complexity of their lives and their embeddedness within the social fabric of India.

Further, although this project explicitly attempts to subvert the reification or commodification of a third category—making hijras' lives *count* as much as it addresses various "categories" of sexual thirdness—to the extent that it multiplies rather than dismantles third genders/categories, I am somewhat uneasy that it might reaffirm as much as it subverts, nominalizing, numericalizing, and naturalizing embodied difference in its wake. There is, after all, as Kath Weston notes, "a relationship of longstanding [*sic*] between counting and commodification" that one must be aware of when embarking on such a project as this (2002, 41).

Finally, my ambivalence in undertaking this research also relates to the exclusions sustained (or produced) by such a project. To what extent does the focus on hijras as *male*-to-hijra subject-positions contribute, even unintentionally, to the continuing discursive and systemic violence against women? As Lawrence Cohen (1995b) observes, highlighting shifts from *male* (rather than female) to a third-gender identity erases the political differences between male and female experiences and, ultimately, works within a two-gendered system—male and third—in which the female position has been virtually erased. In a somewhat similar vein, speaking for the Thai context, Rosalind Morris (1994) points out that patriarchal narratives seem to have "effaced [if it ever existed] any expression of female sexual identity that could not be subsumed under a reproductive mandate" (1994, 26). In this ideology, femaleness is thoroughly naturalized as reproductive capacity. Only in the recent past, with the emergence of sexualities defined in terms of object choice, has the category of woman been differentiated into hetero- and homosexual identities. Perhaps the important historical and empirical question (as Morris asks with respect to the *kathoeys* of Thailand) is "[H]ow have sex/gender systems [in both Thailand and India, apparently] organized the somatic economy in such a way as to render both 'female' and 'male' bodies as media of masculine subjectivities?" (1994, 25). While this is not the question I explore in this book, I argue that it is an important one to keep in mind—along with the other issues of ambivalence and (inadvertent) silencing noted above—as one explores issues of sexual difference and the place of hijras within that context.

FRAMING THE SETTING: THE TWIN CITIES OF HYDERABAD AND SECUNDERABAD

On the flight from Frankfurt to Delhi on my way to begin fieldwork, I was sitting next to a British art historian who was a frequent traveler to India. In the course of conversation, he asked me what I did for a living and whether Delhi was my final destination in India. "I'm an anthropologist and I'm going to [the South Indian city of] Hyderabad to do an ethnographic study of this one community—hijras—now fairly well-known as the 'third sex' of India," I replied, expecting to expand on this theme.[7] Instead, he appeared far more curious about the city of Hyderabad, having heard it was "different" from other Indian cities on account of its Muslim influence.[8] By way of an initial response to his questions about the city, I told him the classic tale of the founder of the city, Muhammad Quli Qutb Shah,[9] and his love for his wife, Hyder Begum, after whom the city was named, a story that in many ways captures the issues central to Hyderabadi hijra identity—love or desire, religious pluralism, and the history of Muslim influence in the city.

As the popular legend goes, before his ascension to the throne, Muhammad Quli Qutb Shah, an excellent equestrian, often exercised his horse in the area surrounding the fort of Golconda. One day, on one of his extended rides, he stopped at the village of Chichlam for a drink of water.[10] Passing by at that moment on her way to the temple was Bhagmati, the daughter of Lingayya, a relatively poor Hindu resident of Chichlam village. Muhammad Quli was immediately taken by her beauty and grace, and began to visit the spot frequently, incognito, to catch a glimpse of Bhagmati and win her affections. When Muhammad Quli ascended the throne as the ruler of Golconda a few years later, he sent for Bhagmati's father and asked for her hand in marriage. Muhammad Quli Qutb Shah and Bhagmati were married in 1596 CE and, as the legend goes, lived happily together until Muhammad Quli's untimely death in 1612.

During his reign, Muhammad Quli founded a new city ten miles east of Golconda on the southern bank of the Musi River in order to ease the congestion and shortage of water in the crowded city of Golconda and, as folk wisdom has it, to commemorate his love for his wife. The city was initially called Bhagnagar for Bhagmati, but its name was later changed to Hyderabad following Bhagmati's conversion to Islam and adoption of the title Hyder Begum. Hyderabad quickly became an important and bustling city. After the fall of Golconda to the Mughal emperor Aurangzeb in 1687 and the subsequent dissolution of the Mughal Empire, the first Nizam (as subsequent rulers of Hyderabad were known), Asaf Jah I, chose this city rather than the walled fort of Golconda for his capital, with Charminar serving as the heart of the city. Charminar, which literally means "four minarets," continues to symbolize and function as the center of what is known as the "old city" of Hyderabad.

Quite apart from the documented antiquity of hijras in this city (Lynton and Rajan 1974; Jaffrey 1996), the reasons I chose this city as the locus of my study are captured in some measure by this origin myth/historical folktale. Two issues are worth mentioning here: The first relates to the importance of Islam for the larger part of Hyderabad's history, although this influence has always been balanced by a significant Hindu counterinfluence. The mutual engagement and tension between the Muslim and Hindu presence in this region is unique in the South Indian experience. Hyderabad and its

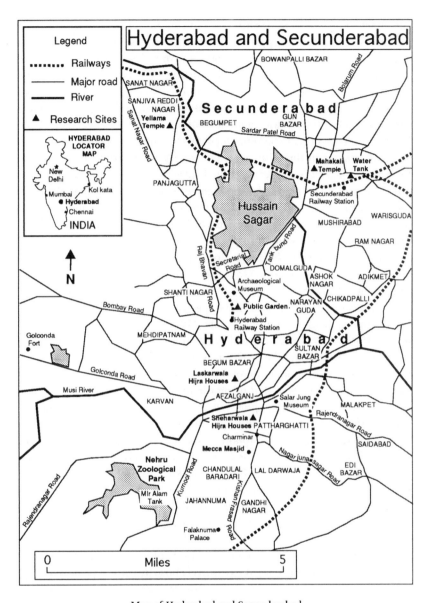

Map of Hyderabad and Secunderabad

surrounding region have constituted the only continuously Muslim-ruled area in South India for the past five centuries, and this influence is apparent even today. More important for the current context was my interest in the relation between present-day hijra identity and the history of Muslim patronage, given the recorded history of eunuchs in the Islamic royal courts of the Mamluk Sultanate and in the Byzantine and Ottoman empires (Peirce 1993; Marmon 1995; Ayalon 1999) in addition to their presence in medieval Indian history. As several authors have noted, eunuchs in India were often accorded respect in the Delhi Sultanate and Mughal courts, holding positions of eminence especially under the Khiljis of Delhi in the thirteenth and fourteenth centuries and under the Mughals from the sixteenth to the nineteenth centuries. Although many eunuchs were initially brought as slaves into the houses of Muslim nobility in principalities such as Awadh and Hyderabad, they were accorded respect and trusted with sensitive positions, including guarding the *harim*, or inner/female spaces within the palace (Knighton 1855; Bernier 1891; Manucci 1907; Saletore 1974; Kidwai 1985; Chatterjee 1999, 2002).

With respect to the second issue, perhaps as a legacy of Muhammad Quli's love for Hyder Begum, Hyderabad is also popularly known in some tourist brochures as India's "city of love," complete with the local version of the Pont Neuf spanning the Musi River. Interestingly, some tension exists between this idealized love and other contemporary images of Hyderabad, as captured by the adage that a hijra laughingly related to me. She said, *"Delhi dilwalon ka, Bombay paisewalon ka, aur Hyderabad randiyon ka"* (Delhi stands for those who have love, Bombay for those with money; and Hyderabad for whores). As I explain in the following pages, these idioms of "romantic" and "modern" love, or desire if you will, played out in interesting ways in the lives of the hijras I came to know, not only in terms of their occupation, their position in the hijra kinship hierarchy, their dis/avowal of sexual desire, and their degree of respect, but also in terms of their spatial location in the twin cities of Hyderabad and Secunderabad.

THE SPATIAL HISTORY OF HYDERABADI HIJRAS

The actual number of hijras in India is in dispute, ranging from ten thousand to two million (Bobb and Patel 1982; Jaffrey 1996). The popular belief is that hijras live primarily in northern cities, especially those with a history of Muslim rule, such as Delhi and Lucknow. However, Hyderabad has been and continues to be a "traditional center of hijra culture" (Lynton and Rajan

1974), although, currently, no more than a few hundred hijras live there at any given time, owing primarily to hijra migration to the larger metropolitan cities in India.[11]

The fact that hijras—or *kojjas* as they are also known in Telugu[12]—have existed in Hyderabad at least since the birth of the city seems indisputable, given the seventeenth-century accounts by such travelers as Francois Bernier (1891) and Jean Baptiste Tavernier (1995 [1676]). The story of the hijras' vacillating fortunes, intertwined with those of their Muslim patrons over the four-hundred-year history of this city, is just as interesting as those of the Qutb Shahi and Asaf Jahi dynasties. As hijras tell the story today, although they explicitly date their origin to the pre-Muslim period—in fact to the mythical/historical days of Rama, the hero of the pan-Indian epic *Ramayana*[13]—they believe, as one hijra told me, that "the Muslims brought us closer to them instead of pushing us away."

This is particularly true of the sixth Nizam of Hyderabad, Mir Mahbub Ali Khan Asaf Jah VI, or Mahbub Ali Pasha, as he is more affectionately called, during whose reign at the turn of the twentieth century hijras claim they attained their greatest glory (Lynton and Rajan 1974). They mark their decline in status from the time his successor, Osman Ali, became the Nizam. During Mahbub Pasha's reign, hijras were granted a tract of land close to Charminar at the center of what is now the old city of Hyderabad. This area—between the Madina hotel and *Mahbub ki Mehndi*—is the site of the largest hijra residences, or *hijron ka allawahs*.

Most hijras live together in residences that serve as both physical and social units of identity or lineage affiliation. There are seven hijra houses or "lineages" in India. Only two of these are represented in Hyderabad, namely, Lashkarwala and Sheharwala,[14] of which the latter appears to have the most members. While I am not sure of the actual figures, given the hyperbolic accounts of hijras in both lineages, Lashkarwala hijras are always bemoaning their frequent intimidation by Sheharwala hijras on account of the latter's greater numeric strength. Furthermore, the *ilakas*, or prescribed territorial boundaries for their ritual practice, also appear to be skewed in favor of the Sheharwala lineage.[15]

Each of the two lineages occupies three individual households, all six of which are located within a few miles of each other in the old city of Hyderabad. Each has a separate, independent household structure. The individual households of each lineage are closer to each other than to those of the other lineage, but they are independent of each other as far as social organization, food preparation, and sleeping arrangements are concerned. Each household includes a *nayak*, the head of that household, her *celas*, or disciples, and the *cela's celas—nati celas*. On average, between ten and fifteen people are permanent residents in each of these six households (three belonging to the Sheharwala lineage, and three to Lashkarwala). While there is only one nayak per household, two or three of her celas and many more nati celas might live under the same roof. The status hierarchy (nayak, followed by her celas, and then her nati celas) is evident in all respects; the nayak is always accorded due respect by those below her in the hierarchy. Not only do the nayaks serve as the heads of their respective households, together they constitute a council for the arbitration of disputes, the conferring of titles, and the representation of their lineage in any interregional hijra event. The line of descent for this title follows the cela genealogy, with the most respected, just, and capable among a nayak's celas inheriting the responsibility after her death.

Originally, the "two [lineage] houses were one," according to Hyderabadi hijras. Whether this means that there was only one lineage in the past or that the two lineages merely lived together in the same area or household is not absolutely clear from the historical record and hijras' statements to me. What is well known, however, is that the land allotted to hijras by the Nizam was in one specific area near Charminar. At some point in the twentieth century, there was a major disagreement between the two hijra lineages, after which the Lashkarwala lineage moved across the Musi River to the area of the Churi Bazaar. When asked, Lashkarwala hijras claimed that the government needed their property in order to build a low-income housing project and, after compensating them monetarily, took over their land. With the money received from this transaction, they bought property "across the [Musi River] bridge" and have been there ever since. While they acknowledge that the largest of the current Sheharwala hijras' houses was the original structure given by the Nizam, they claim that the only reason they do not live in a similar structure is that the government took it over for public housing. Sheharwala hijras, on the other hand, derive symbolic capital from the antiquity of their residence and claim greater importance on that basis. Quite apart from their spatial separation, the two lineages have also been feuding with each other for years, largely over territorial sovereignty, or the right to perform in particular localities, as well as over disputed claims to individual celas. Only in the last year of my fieldwork, following the death of one of the Lashkarwala nayaks, did members of the two houses attempt to overcome their differences and retract the prohibitions on visiting each other.

When I first arrived in Hyderabad, like the majority of the city's inhabitants, I believed that hijras lived only in the "old city" of Hyderabad—in the *hijron ka allawahs* (hijra houses) I have described above—and I assumed this site would be the primary locus of my fieldwork. In fact, I had approached hijras living in these houses on a previous trip to Hyderabad, and although I was not summarily dismissed, neither were those I met particularly forthcoming about their lives. Given their increasing wariness of non-hijras (Jaffrey 1996), I have to admit that I was apprehensive about how to reintroduce myself and my project so as not to incur their displeasure. At that point I found out about the hijras living "under the water *tanki*" in Secunderabad. They turned out to be more marginal in some respects within the hijra hierarchy but also more central to the larger homoerotic universe of Hyderabad. These hijras became my closest friends, and it is their life stories that constitute the bulk of this book; thus, Secunderabad in some ways became my primary field site.[16]

The city of Secunderabad has a more recent history than its twin, Hyderabad, and owes its origin to the British in the early part of the nineteenth century. In the latter part of the eighteenth century, the Nizams of Hyderabad were forced to involve themselves in the Anglo-French wars in South India (the Deccan), and in the ongoing struggles for power between the British forces and those of the Marathas on the one hand and Tippu Sultan of Mysore on the other. To protect his dominions, Nizam Ali Khan Asaf Jah II signed a treaty with the British in 1768 pledging mutual support. This pact culminated finally in the treaty of 1802 signed by his successor, which provided for the permanent establishment of a subsidiary British force in the region located in present-day Secunderabad (Ali Khan 1991).

Physically, the twin cities of Hyderabad and Secunderabad are separated by a man-made reservoir known as Hussain Sagar (more commonly called Tank Bund for the bridge spanning its length) after Hussain Wali Khan, the son-in-law of the fourth Qutb Shahi ruler, Ibrahim Quli Qutb Shah, who had this tank built in 1562. But it was not until 1806, when Colonel Lang established the regional headquarters of the British Subsidiary Force in what was to become one of the largest British cantonments in India, that Secunderabad was formally founded and named after the ruler at the time, Sikander Jah Asaf Jah III (Seshan 1993).

Although traffic is increasing between the two cities, each still retains its particular flavor and identity: Hyderabad, a city that was established by the Muslim rulers four centuries ago, still retains a distinctly Hyderabadi Muslim and old-world flavor. Secunderabad, on the other hand, indicates its more recent and colonial vintage with its clock towers, churches, and such symbols of the British legacy as the Secunderabad railway station, which is one of the main hubs for people arriving and leaving the twin cities.

HIJRAS UNDER THE WATER TANKI

Less than a mile from the Secunderabad railway station lives a fairly large group of hijras, whom I refer to as those living under the water tanki.[17] This group of Secunderabad hijras, all of whom are affiliated with the Lashkar-wala lineage, is the largest single group living together outside the hijra houses in Hyderabad. Numbering approximately thirty-five, these hijras live in makeshift tents or shacks under a triple-storied concrete water tank. Five independent tents are set up in this area. Each one belongs to three or four hijras, often a guru and her celas, who sleep, store their belongings, and cook together on a hearth just outside the shack. While there is some give and take among these units, they are virtually independent as far as finances, food, and sleeping arrangements are concerned.

The seven or eight hundred square meters of land occupied by these hijras is government property, directly adjacent to the railway tracks on one side and bordered on the other by a low-income housing colony for railway employees. Since hijras do not own this land, they cannot build permanent structures on it, and they are subject to eviction at any time by the government. For this reason, they take pains to maintain relatively smooth ties with their neighbors, the residents of the railway colony. Despite their efforts, hijras' primary occupation—commercial sex work—caused constant friction between them and their neighbors, resulting ultimately in the hijras' eviction in the autumn of 1999. This study, then, is probably the only one of this particular group, given their recent eviction and their increasing vulnerability to AIDS. Since 1997, at least six members of the original group have died, most of them from AIDS, though the more proximate reasons are their ignorance about this debilitating syndrome and its modes of transmission, the stigma attached to it and to the person affected, their lack of access to health care, and the poverty that helps to reproduce these patterns of structural violence, affliction, and suffering (Farmer 1992, 1998; Farmer, Connors, and Simmons 1996; Kleinman, Das, and Lock 1996).

Ironically, it was a policeman, Venkatesh, working as a part-time cleaner in my father's apartment, who facilitated my initial access to hijras living in Secunderabad. As noted earlier, I was apprehensive about approaching hijras and possibly contributing to further sensationalism. Especially in the initial stages of my research, I talked to a number of my friends and family in Hyderabad about this apprehension. Needless to say, none of my relatives or the upper-middle-class folk I encountered knew anything about hijras in Hyderabad other than the ubiquitous urban myths; for the most part, hijras were accused of being "dirty," "shameless," and "aggressive people

Hijras who live under the water tank

who live in the old city," with whom I ought not to have any dealings. Although some people believed they had "special powers to bless and curse," even these reactions were mixed at best, combining respect in particular, circumscribed contexts (such as during their "ritual" or *badhai* performances), with outright derision or stigma in most other social contexts.

Venkatesh arrived every morning to sweep and mop the house and to clean the dishes. He also worked as a police officer. As soon as he finished his work in my father's apartment, he would change into his uniform and get ready to go to the Ramgopalpet police station—one of the main police stations in Secunderabad—which was a ten-minute walk from the apartment. Overhearing my conversation on the phone one day, Venkatesh somewhat hesitantly told me that because of his police work, he knew exactly where hijras lived in Secunderabad. He once again emphasized that he knew this because of his police "duty" before agreeing to take me there or at least to point the location out to me on his way to work. So, one morning in September 1995, Venkatesh and I set out together from the apartment toward the Secunderabad railway station. We passed by the main road near the Secunderabad bus station, a mile or so from the railway station, and Venkatesh pointed out the water tank under which the hijras lived.

The following day at around ten thirty in the morning, armed with Serena Nanda's book on hijras,[18] I finally marched into what would be "the field" for me—a world that was very different from the one I was familiar with, even if it was in the same city and just a ten-minute drive from where I was living with my father in his upper-middle-class apartment. I took an auto-rickshaw to the Secunderabad bus station and walked along the path from the main road toward the water tank. Unfamiliar with the area, I wandered along the path somewhat aimlessly, peering into an empty shed next to the tracks that served as a railway office. A few men walking by glanced at me curiously but did not stop to speak to me. Not seeing anyone, I followed the dirt path from the main road through a metal gate as it sloped up toward the railway tracks.

As I walked through the gate, with the railway tracks directly in front of me, I saw a hijra sitting alone and smoking a *bidi*.[19] She had her back to me and I had a moment to observe her before she saw me walking up.[20] She was wearing a bright red, printed synthetic sari and was squatting on her haunches with her arms draped over her knees. I could see her face in profile. She was very dark-complexioned, and her features were distinctly masculine. Her hair, which seemed to be about shoulder length, was pulled back untidily into a ponytail with a rubber band. She was smoking her *bidi* and staring out over the tracks in apparent peace with the world.

I took a deep breath and walked up to her. She looked a little surprised when I began speaking to her, not so much because of how I looked but more, as she later informed me, because of how respectfully I spoke to her. I spoke to her in Telugu, introducing myself and asking if I could speak to her and the other hijras, or kojjas, living in the area.[21] She smiled shyly and said she would lead me to the others. After taking a last drag, she threw her *bidi* down and got up. I followed her as she walked down a path on the other side of the gate I had walked through, toward the water tank that towered over the railway tracks about fifty yards away.

She led me directly under the water tank, where a group of five hijras were sitting on a straw mat, casually chatting in the sun. As we walked up to them, I glanced around, not seeing any permanent structure that could house hijras. I remember wondering where these hijras slept at night. Meanwhile the hijras sitting on the mat had stopped talking and were glancing curiously at me. I repeated what I had said to Jyotsna, my guide, introducing myself, positioning myself as a student who was interested in understanding their way of life. After answering all their questions about my parents and siblings—the fact that I had only one sister (the number as much as the fact that I didn't have any brothers) eliciting much tut-tutting and exclamations of regret—it was my turn to ask questions. I was told that there were about thirty hijras living under the tank, all of whom had gone out to sing and dance at weddings and births in the neighborhood, accounting for their absence at the moment. The five of them had stayed back only to protect everyone's belongings. "We are all *asli* [real] hijras here. We don't fight with anyone. We all have *izzat* [respect] here," one of them (an older hijra to whom the others present appeared to defer) told me proudly. As I later discovered, these particular hijras were involved in sex work, a practice that earned them the active denigration of the senior hijras in the old city, who explicitly accused them of being inauthentic and lacking izzat.[22]

Not surprisingly then, precisely these issues—their "realness," or authenticity, and their claim to izzat (respect)—constituted central tropes in hijras' constructions of identity across the various domains of their lives. Hijras were actively striving to authenticate themselves within the parameters of a local economy of izzat through the commission (or omission) of various practices, including physical emasculation, engaging in sex work or any display of sexual desire, displaying markers of religion and class status, adopting gendered modes of sartorial practice, and maintaining formal kinship links. Further, it was precisely these axes—sexuality, religion, gender, kinship, and class—that hijras employed to distinguish themselves from the wider community of *kotis* in Hyderabad, an issue I explore in the remainder of the book.

Through hijras—and especially those living under the water tank—I gradually discovered a social universe that I never knew existed in the twin cities, one that had its own social categories, idiomatic terminology, and rules of membership. Hijras situated themselves within this universe, in which the central axes of sexual and gender identity were the act of penetration in sexual intercourse and the performance of "women's work." In this performative understanding, the gender system appeared to be divided into, on the one hand, *pantis*, behavioral and biological "men," and, on the other, *kotis*, very loosely translated as effeminate men, or behavioral "not-men," to use Don Kulick's (1998) phrase, and *narans*, or all women. Hijras saw themselves as one among a range of koti identities—their wider koti "family," as they referred to this group. As I gradually discovered, all of these kotis, who for the most part dressed and looked to me like most other middle-class Hyderabadi men, differentiated themselves along axes that included genital excision, religion, clothing, kinship, and class. I map this spectrum of differentiation and its production in the next chapter. It includes self-identities such as *catla kotis* (hijras), *zenana kotis*, *kada-catla kotis*, *jogins*, and *siva-satis*. Here, as in the rest of the book, I use the feminine gender to refer to hijras following their own usage, and the masculine gender to refer to all other kotis, unless otherwise indicated.

In my interactions with all of these kotis, and especially hijras, perhaps the most common phrase that I heard, repeated over and over again in different contexts, was, "[It is] a question of izzat" (*izzat ka sawal hai*). Izzat appeared to be one of the most important criteria by which most kotis evaluated behavior, constructed identity, and were motivated to act. Such constructions of izzat, both within the koti community and in relation to wider societal evaluations across various domains of identity constitute an important theme in this book. I argue that while hijras (and kotis) are constituted in part by their sexual differences, this very domain in turn is constituted by and cuts across various other axes of difference within which hijras and kotis situate themselves and through which they evaluate their moral differences and construct their authenticity.

2

Hijras, Individuality, and Izzat

This book complicates our understanding of the so-called third sex in India and unpacks the category "hijra." It does so by focusing on the active contestation of authenticity and respect that occurs between various sexual categories in Hyderabad and by arguing that the axis of sexual difference through which hijras have traditionally been understood is intersected by a variety of other axes of identity, including religion, gender, kinship, and class. Further, in each of these interconnected domains, hijras, I argue, are deeply implicated in the local moral economy of izzat, or respect, a value that provides the primary impetus for the construction of their identities. In other words, this book questions representations of hijras as *the* personification of a third sex while also challenging the sufficiency of sexual politics and gender performativity as adequate glosses on hijra identification and practice. Ultimately, it endeavors to show how hijras (and kotis more generally) are coherent identities crafted by diverse ethical practices; practices which do not construct them merely as *sexual* identities, but identities articulated by and through a multiplicity of morally evaluated differences.

In contrast to chapter 1, which focused primarily on the study's ethnographic contexts, this chapter focuses on delineating the theoretical frames within which this analysis of hijra identity locates itself.[1] This process requires, first, an excursion into the varied historical and cultural representations of hijras, each representation—whether in the ancient, medieval, colonial, or contemporary context—reflecting its own particular ideological agenda and framing premise. In charting the history of these representations, perhaps the most noticeable feature is the silence of the people who are so represented. Although this ethnography could be seen as contributing to such hijra marginalization, it is important to note that hijras' own accounts of their individuality and their crafting of personhood are central to the analysis here. In this regard, an important icon around which they configure their identity is that of the renouncer, or *sannyasi*, a figure with an extensive and complicated lineage in Indian religion, mythology, and history. I contextualize hijras' narratives within the vast body of South Asian literature relating to renunciation, focusing on the relationship between the symbols and practices of renunciation and individuality. Finally, this construction of individuality is fundamentally moral, intricately bound up with a local economy of respect. Given their stigma in Indian society, it is perhaps no surprise that hijras emphasized ways to assert and maintain their izzat, a term often translated as "honor" in the South Asian and anthropological literature. I argue, however, that hijras use the term with a more individualized and less "libidinized" understanding than that in much of the anthropological literature, leading me to translate the term as "respect," rather than "honor." In this chapter therefore, I contextualize hijras' accounts of their lives by sketching the contours of three frameworks: historical representations of hijras, South Asian constructions of individuality and renunciation, and analyses of izzat, or respect.

INTERROGATING CONSTRUCTIONS OF THE "THIRD" SEX

Four somewhat distinct constructions of the third sex dominate the existing literature, which I broadly characterize as the ancient, medieval, colonial, and contemporary anthropological, each representing both a chronological moment and an analytic concern in the representations of hijras. I address each of these representations not as they were produced chronologically but, instead, as they analyze hijras in different epochs, each with its own particular critical agenda. I start with the relatively recent secondary literature that represents the historiography of the third sex in what can be termed the ancient Indian philosophical and liturgical texts. I then examine the medieval Perso-Urdu secondary literature, which highlights the history of eunuchs—as political actors, as religious figures, and as slaves. Next I look at the largely British colonial literature, which focuses on the classification of hijras and the "criminal" nature of their activities. Finally, I address the recent anthropological body of literature that situates hijras explicitly within the larger framework of sexual difference.

Historiography and "Ancient" Texts

The first domain of literature about hijras relates to the analysis of ancient Indian texts[2] (Brahmanical, Buddhist, and Jain) and addresses the ostensible history of the third sex and sexuality in India (see Meyer 1971; Artola 1975;

O'Flaherty 1980; Dundas 1992; Zwilling 1992; Goldman 1993; Sweet and Zwilling 1993; Zwilling and Sweet 1996; Vatsyayana 2002). Starting from the premise that "the category of a third sex has been a part of the Indian worldview for nearly three thousand years" (Zwilling and Sweet 1996, 362), these authors set out to elucidate this category—variously referred to in Sanskrit (Hindu) and Pali (Buddhist) texts as *kliba, pandaka, trtiyaprakrti,* or more commonly as *napumsaka*—providing historical evidence for a premodern (and pre-Islamic) concept of sexuality and the category of sexual thirdness in India.[3]

While shifting forms, third-natured individuals, transposed genders, sexual masquerades, and same-sex procreation abound in the Hindu mythological, folkloric, epic, and early Vedic/Puranic literatures (Doniger 1999; Vanita and Kidwai 2000; Doniger and Kakar 2002),[4] according to Zwilling and Sweet (1996), it is among the Jains, a minority religious community with an ancient history and a distinct corpus of literature, that speculations on the nature of third-sexed individuals were the most elaborated and thorough, constituting perhaps "the single richest source for knowledge of the third sex, as well as for speculations on sex and gender, to be found in India from the ancient to medieval periods" (363). By virtue of a "pan-Indian acceptance of a third sex," they argue, this category has "served as a focal point for speculations that ultimately resulted in the formation of an autonomous idea of sexuality" for the Jains, much like that postulated by sexual historians for the modern, nineteenth-century West (365).

As Sweet and Zwilling (1993; see also Zwilling and Sweet 1996), Goldman (1993), and others contend, speculation by religious scholars on the characteristics attributable to the different sexes arose in the context of examining the relationship between natural gender and grammatical gender. Such a relationship was premised on the assumption that "objects, as well as people, are gendered by the presence or absence of certain defining characteristics," and expressed through a single term for both natural and grammatical gender, that is, the *linga*.[5] By the third century CE, there were three distinct views on the essential characteristics by which a person could be assigned to one of the three genders (*purusa, stri,* and *napumsaka*). The first (Brahmanical) view characterized gender by the presence or absence of certain primary and secondary characteristics, a doctrine that was also endorsed by the Buddhists.[6] The second, Buddhist, position (which was also a Brahmanical belief elaborated most clearly in Indian medical literature) assigned gender by the presence or absence of procreative ability, with impotence signifying membership in the third, or *napumsaka*, category (Filliozat 1964; Zysk 1991; Sweet and Zwilling 1993).

The Jains, however, rejected both these Brahmanical and Buddhist bases for differentiating masculine and feminine markers. As Zwilling and Sweet (1996) contend, the Jain system of thought is the only Indian system to differentiate between what they term "biological sex," or *dravyalinga* (material [sexual] mark), distinguished by primary and secondary sexual characteristics, and "psychological gender," or *bhavalinga* (mental [sexual] mark), referring to the psychic makeup of a particular individual. Given this additional marker of gender assignment in the Jain exegetical literature, determinations based on primary and secondary sexual characteristics alone (as in the Brahmanical and Buddhist systems) were deemed insufficient. After the fifth century CE, Jains rejected the second marker of Brahmanical/Buddhist gender assignment—the criterion of reproductive capacity—because prepubescent and postmenopausal women would not be characterized as women by this criterion. Instead, what was deemed important as a distinguishing characteristic was sexual behavior, or the role (receptive or penetrative) adopted in sexual intercourse. In the late canonical as well as the early exegetical Jain literature (from approximately the fifth century CE), there appeared a fourth sex (the masculine *napumsaka* or *purusanapumsaka*). What distinguished the feminine *napumsaka* from the masculine *napumsaka*, given their similar physical appearance, was their sexual practice—whether they were merely receptive partners in sexual intercourse (feminine), or both penetrative and receptive (masculine), with the penetrative behavior determining their masculine characterization.

In debating the definitions of the sexes, Jains had an overriding theoretical and pragmatic interest. On the one hand, given the relatively recent formation of their canon and their heterodox nature, they were actively debating the issue of whether or not women could attain spiritual liberation (*moksa*), which led them to examine what it meant to be a man, woman, or neither man nor woman.[7] On the other hand, they had inherited the conception and terminology of a third sex from classical (Vedic) schools of thought but were still in the process of identifying and marking this category. While they concurred with contemporary Brahmanical scholars and texts that male sexual desire for a man formed one aspect of third-sex sexuality, Jain texts of the time also emphasized the *hyperlibidinous* nature of third-sex persons. Aside from this hyperlibidinous aspect, however, third-sex sexuality was largely unexamined in the Jain canonical literature.

One of the more striking innovations of exegetical Jain literature after the fifth century, was a theorization of this sexuality and an explanation postulated for the hyperlibidinal nature of *napumsakas* in terms of bisexuality—a solution to their ordainment dilemma that allowed for the spiritual liberation of these individuals (and thus their ordainment). According to Zwilling and Sweet (1996), *napumsakas* in Jain texts went from being characterized by and through their desire *exclusively* for men in the early canonical period (fourth century to the fifth century), to being characterized by their desire for *either* men or women (i.e., a differentiation was made between masculine *napumsakas* [*purusanapumsaka*] and feminine *napumsakas* [*pandaka* or *kliba*]) in the late canonical period, to ultimately being characterized by desire for *both* men and women in the exegetical literature (what the authors of the article refer to as bisexuality). In postulating this schema, and through its various manifestations and theoretical forms, Jains maintained the separation of sexuality and sexual object choice from biological sex and gender, and identified third-sex sexuality as primarily hyperlibidinal and bisexual.[8] Ultimately, whatever the differences between the Brahmanical, Buddhist, and Jain texts, there was certainly an extensive debate and literature on the concept of sexuality, differentiations between biological and grammatical gender, elaborations on sexual object choice, and the notion of a third nature in India, dating back to at least the third century, if not before.

Despite the existence of this vast corpus of literature, however, contemporary sexual identities/categories are by no means unproblematic extensions or instantiations of these figures or early debates as Zwilling and Sweet (1996) seem to suggest when they state, "the class of transvestite singers, dancers, and prostitutes known as hijras are the contemporary representatives of the unmales and third sex of earlier times" (363). Given that the term *hijra* is believed to be an Urdu word, used widely in the subcontinent only after the arrival of the Mughals in the sixteenth century, it is difficult to see this term in explicit relation to the terms used in the Sanskrit and Pali texts to refer to "unmales and the third sex" prior to this period, namely, *trtiyaprakrti*, *kliba*, and *napumsaka*. In fact, as Wendy Doniger notes, the term *kliba* is explicitly *not* the same as "third nature" or *trtiyaprakrti*, notwithstanding Richard Burton's elision of this difference in his (infamous) translation of the *Kamasutra* (Doniger 2003). Further, the meanings of the Sanskrit/Pali terms themselves vary widely; the term *kliba* ranges in meaning from "eunuch" (a translation that, as Doniger notes, possibly dates only from the Turko-Persian influence of the ninth century) to someone "who was sterile, impotent, castrated, a transvestite, a man who had oral sex with other men, who had anal sex, a man with mutilated or defective sexual organs, a hermaphrodite, or finally, a man who produced only female children" (11). Given this wide range of meanings, Zwilling and Sweet's assertion that hijras are the contemporary representations of the ancient *napumsakas* would be difficult to defend. Whatever the veracity of their characterization, however, it is significant that there was an extensive debate and a body of literature in India devoted to delineating the nature of sexuality and erotic interactions with people of a "third nature" in texts even prior to the fifth century CE.

"Medieval" References

References to individuals of a third nature, other than commentaries on the earlier texts (see Vanita and Kidwai 2000), are harder to find during the medieval period of Indian history, from the eighth to the eighteenth centuries. Explicit references to *eunuchs* in South Asia, however, increase dramatically with the arrival of Muslim rulers in the eleventh and twelfth centuries.[9] As several scholars have noted, the courtly traditions of eunuchs in the Islamic world, especially in the Mamluk Sultanate and Ottoman empires, as well as in the (non-Islamic) Roman, Byzantine, and Chinese empires, have been well documented (Mitamura 1970; Anderson 1990; Peirce 1993; Ringrose 1994; Marmon 1995; Ayalon 1999; Gaul 2002; Sideris 2002; Tougher 1999, 2002; Tsai 2002). In much of this secondary literature, the overarching framework for the social history of eunuchs emphasizes one (or more) of three aspects—eunuchs' political, religious, or slave status.

As historian Shaun Tougher notes, the predominant focus in the historical study of eunuchs has tended to be "their place and function at royal and imperial courts," despite, as he notes, "other interesting and fertile topics of study" (2002, 143). Medieval European travelers and recent social historians alike have been fascinated by the vibrancy and longevity of the eunuchs' presence and their increasingly prominent role in the court systems of various empires as political advisors, powerful administrators, and "chamberlains," as well as trusted generals and guardians of the *harim*, or inner/ female domain.

The fundamental concern guiding these accounts was to explain *why* eunuchs became so valued an instrument of imperial power—a focus that perhaps reveals as much about the authors and their frames of reference as about the courtly traditions of eunuchs. The answers to this question are fascinating and center explicitly on eunuchs' social and embodied difference. At times, their difference stemmed from their origin as outsiders, often as slaves imported from outside the boundaries of the (Roman, Ottoman) empire (Hopkins 1978; cf. Ayalon 1999; Tougher 2002), and thereby spatially bound to their owners.[10] Or their difference derived from the "physical nature of eunuchs" (Tougher 2002, 144) that allowed their bodies to be imbued with moral worth—the ultimately trustworthy and loyal subjects in a (gendered) world often full of intrigue, shifting loyalties, nepotism, and violence. As gender-neutral, non-"testiculated" individuals (Ringrose 1994), eunuchs were incapable of impregnating women and directly perpetuating their lineage and yet capable of "manly" protection. As Shaun Tougher notes, the "condition of the eunuch as a castrated *man*" (2002, 152; emphasis added) is what made them valuable (slave) commodities in the politics of empire building.

Although many analyses of the early Roman, Byzantine, and Chinese empires do exist, much of the literature focuses on the role of eunuchs in *Islamic* empires, including the Mamluk Sultanate in what is now Egypt (Marmon 1995; Ayalon 1999) and the Delhi Sultanate and Mughal empire in present-day India and Pakistan (Kidwai 1985; Chatterjee 1999, 2002). In these analyses, the question of why eunuchs were able to rise to such prominence was an explicit focus of inquiry. According to David Ayalon (1999), their prominence owes as much to Islamic gender segregation in the social sphere and to the "special character of the Muslim slave institution" that was dominated by people of non-Arab, slave origin who were thus bound to their owners/patrons, as to the stereotypic perception of eunuchs as clever, loyal, and trustworthy servants who had free access to all spatial domains and segments of the population (15). Whatever the reason for their prominence, during the medieval period of history, eunuchs certainly existed in large numbers in most Islamic (and many non-Islamic) empires and rose to positions of significance and affluence in the royal courts.

Eunuchs were significant not only as political actors. Shaun Marmon gives a fascinating and detailed account of the position of eunuchs in the Islamic religious sphere, focusing on the sacred societies of eunuchs at the tomb of the Prophet Muhammad in Madina and at the Ka'ba in Mecca— societies that have endured from the mid-twelfth century to the present day.[11] One of the most interesting aspects of this account for the present context is the apparent discomfort engendered by these holy eunuchs and the shift in explanations of their presence over the course of time. While thirteenth-century accounts were hagiographic treatises by pious scholars, later works by travelers such as Ibn Jubayr and Ibn Batutta in the fourteenth century, as well as those by Mamluk historians such as al-Sakhawi in the fifteenth century, emphasize the history of the eunuch societies and their traditional occupation as the guardians of the Prophet's sanctuary in Madina. These accounts primarily debate the *origin* of their royal patronage, rather than the incongruity of their occupation as powerful and venerated figures whose presence requires a "reasonable" explanation (Marmon 1995).

The extraordinary prestige of eunuchs in the holy cities, however, greatly disturbed the imagination of European travelers from the eighteenth century onward, who could not comprehend the veneration accorded these eunuchs. The very sight of "whole men" kissing the hands of these "repulsively ugly . . . startlingly emaciated," sexless creatures (Rutter 1928, quoted in Marmon 1995, 95) clearly upset the Europeans. The only plausible explanation for this abomination was a functional one that highlighted a sexual or gendered purpose: "that in the event of a disturbance occurring [in the *harim* of Mecca] in which women are concerned, or in the event of a woman appearing on the Mataf in unseemly attire or in a state of uncleanness, they may handle such offenders and expel them without impropriety, as they are not really men in the full sense of the word" (96). While European explanations prior to the eighteenth century were also functional, they did not have a sexual focus. In these earlier accounts, the reason eunuchs were appointed to their high office in the mosque was to guard the treasures stored there, their lack of progeny guaranteeing their honesty and fiscal responsibility.[12] However, as Marmon notes, by the late eighteenth century, this account was generally supplanted by the sexual interpretation of "the eunuchs' role as guards not of the treasures of the mosque but of the women who visited it" (Marmon 1995, 97). Interestingly, in these later accounts (including that by the well-known traveler, Richard Burton), it is apparently the racial element—most of these eunuchs were of African origin and therefore "not just a non-man but a 'black' non-man" (Marmon 1995, 100)—as much as the sexual aspect that causes their discomfort. Through all of these accounts, eunuchs themselves are never given a voice, their history and representation becoming as much a chronicle of the authors' preoccupations and anxieties as a historical account of their lives.

In almost all of the abovementioned contexts, however, one issue is indisputable: Most eunuchs began their careers as slaves.[13] As Indrani Chatterjee notes, however, slavery in many of these contexts—and certainly in precolonial India—should not be understood as the kind of servitude intrinsic to eighteenth- and nineteenth-century plantation economies, but as resulting from a more peaceful commerce that highlights the tropes (and dialectic) of "alienation and intimacy," rather than violence (Chatterjee 2002, 61). Slavery, Chatterjee argues, is central to the historical understanding not only of social hierarchy, but also of same-sex desire in the Indian past. In much of the Perso-Urdu poetry of medieval India, the paradoxical relations inherent in the linguistic trope of slavery serve as the normative framework for the language of desire more generally. In such poetry, the "free" author/lover speaks as the "slave" of his beloved, who is in fact often an "idealized" slave, much as the author is always a "free" adult male. As long as representations of desire did not subvert the social order, that is, "threaten a reversal of real power relations (the slave controlling the 'slave of love,' his master)" (61), this trope was the normative lens through which relations of love, both within and outside of the formal slave topos, were depicted (see Naim 1979; Rahman 1990; Chatterjee 1999; Kidwai 2000).

By the eighteenth century, however, this framework had been transformed by the European colonial encounter. Colonial accounts henceforth rendered all homosexual relations as "criminal" and also consistently omitted any allusions to a slave topos from their accounts of a hierarchical Indian society. *All* sexual acts between men were henceforth coded in the idiom of gender and sexuality. Previous discourses of "active" and "passive" sexual activities that accorded with free and slave status, respectively, were uniformly reinterpreted as masculine and feminine or "natural" and "unnatural" (collective) propensities. Gradually, the lens of gender or sexuality "displace[d] the lens of slavery in the language of the colonized" (Chatterjee 2002, 67). This sexualization of the discourse of love—with slaves (including eunuchs) as the silent subjects of this "unnatural" transformation—resulted in an epistemic shift in the discursive understanding of homoeroticism, social hierarchy, and embodied difference in eighteenth- and nineteenth-century India. Eunuchs and hijras, it would seem, were central to this colonial (mis)representation.

Classification in Colonial Literature

Interestingly, the colonial literature that explicitly spotlights hijras focuses less on their status as slaves or as a third sex than on their status as one among the scores of castes/tribes in India that were stratified according to gender and religion. These accounts primarily emphasize the classification and reproduction of this community, rather than its ambiguous gender or slave status.

Hijras find a place in several compendia and glossaries of castes and tribes of India, including one compiled in the 1880s by E. J. Kitts, which claims to be "a list of all castes and tribes as returned by the people themselves and entered by the census enumerators" (1885, v). Several other colonial accounts also reinforce this view of hijras as a distinct caste or community in different regions of the country (Crooke 1896; Bhimbai 1901; Thurston 1909; Ibbetson 1911; Russell 1916; Rose 1919; Enthoven 1922; see also Preston 1987). William Crooke, basing his observations on the 1891 census, classifies hijras into Muhammadans and Hindus as well as males and females (1896, 495). In enumerating hijras in thirty-eight districts of contemporary Uttar Pradesh, Crooke lists twenty-one as having both male and female hijras, with one district even having more female than male hijras (Crooke 1896; Agrawal 1997). In total, Crooke lists 372 female hijras out of 1,125 hijras listed in the 1891 census. Similarly, Enthoven (1922), referring to the 1901 census, notes that there were 138 eunuchs in certain regions of northwest India, including "eight females who appear to be prostitutes" (quoted in Agrawal 1997, 282). It is not clear from these colonial and census records whether this classification refers to an internal organization of the hijra community in terms of masculine and feminine roles or, as some accounts indicate, to the large number of women who were dependent on the hijra community. As several census enumerators and scholars have noted (Gait 1911; Hutton 1931; Agrawal 1997), the census frame for the data on sex was (and continues to be) essentially binary, perhaps accounting for the classification of "female" hijras. Nevertheless, this classificatory information is interesting as much for what it reveals about colonial categories and frames of reference as for what it reveals about the reality of hijras' lives during British rule (Srinivasan 1984; Cohn 1987).

Colonialism and "Criminal Castes"   While caste was undoubtedly the primary social category in the colonial imagination, hijras, as the proverbial "eunuchs," were not just *any* one of the several hundred castes and tribes of India. Rather, they were classified and registered along with other "criminal castes," a new category of being in the discourse and polity of colonial India (Arnold 1985; Freitag 1985; Yang 1985; Radhakrishna 1989; Nigam 1990; Tolen 1991). Following the promulgation of the Criminal Tribes Act (Act 27) of 1871, which called for the "registration, surveillance and control of certain tribes and eunuchs," hijras were officially included under this rubric of dangerous outlaws (Ayres 1992; Srivastava 2001).[14] Although initially applicable only in the Northwest Provinces, Awadh and Punjab, by the early twentieth century, many sections of this act were extended to the whole of British India.

Under this act, the term *eunuch* was "deemed to include all persons of the male sex who admit themselves, or on medical inspection clearly appear to be impotent," a classification that then allowed for the registration, surveillance, and ability to arrest all such individuals. This category included individuals who (*a*) "are reasonably suspected of kidnapping or castrating children, or of committing offenses under section 377 of the Indian Penal Code, or of abetting the commission of any of the said offenses"; (*b*) "appear, dressed or ornamented like a woman, in a public street or place, or in any other place, with the intention of being seen from a public street or place";

or (c) "dance or play music, or take part in any public exhibition, in a public street or place or for hire in a private house" (Collection of Acts Passed by the Governor-General of India in Council of the Year 1871).

The constitution of this colonial category—a "criminal caste"—involved the construction and detailed elaboration of "a body of knowledge defining the nature, habits, and characteristics" of individuals so classified (Tolen 1991, 106). This knowledge base was premised not only on prevailing understandings of the nature of *Indian* society (and caste in particular), but also on constructions of crime, deviance, and vagrancy in Victorian *England* (Yang 1985). As Tolen (1991) notes,

By the mid-nineteenth century, the idea of the "dangerous classes"—who were composed of the unemployed, vagrants, the poor, criminals, drunkards and prostitutes—was firmly ensconced in Victorian thought, and a common discourse identified their physical characteristics, habits and locale. Various causes were proposed to explain the criminality of the dangerous classes: strong drink, ignorance, poor upbringing, indigence, character defects, and hereditary predisposition. The theory that certain people had an inborn propensity for crime implied that nothing, other than overt control, could prevent them from acting on such propensities. (108)

Embedded in this construction was the notion that crime was an inborn, hereditary propensity, passed on to succeeding generations as was caste affiliation. The propensity for crime and its subsequent codification was, in essence, written onto the bodies of the so-called criminal castes. In addition to this literal embodiment, colonial control/reform efforts were also directed at the *labor* that these bodies performed. In the case of hijras, as the Criminal Tribes Act indicates, this labor was both sexual (Article 377 of the Penal Code, which prohibits sodomy), and asexual or work/occupation-related, that is, dancing, singing, and relating to public rules of habiliment (see Cohn 1989).[15] Most important, this knowledge also legitimized the moral condemnation and subsequent subjugation of these criminal subjects. As hereditary castes, their bodies and their labor were to be regulated, surveilled, and controlled; in effect made into "docile bodies" (Foucault 1995). To this end, laws were passed criminalizing their bodies and proscribing their labor. Further, their lands, granted to them by previous rulers (*inam* lands, or lands granted by royal decree), were confiscated because hijras could not demonstrate legitimate heritage (Revenue Department correspondence, 1844, as referenced in Ayres 1992).

Supporting this British obsession with classification and regulation was an elaborate discourse on the nature of hijras and the recruitment patterns of this caste/community, a narrative that obliquely acknowledged the inability of hijras to reproduce themselves in the manner of other castes and tribes. There appear to have been three (British) views regarding the "naturalness" of hijras and their subsequent status as potential recruits to the community. The first focused on hijras as "naturally" impotent men (Bhimbai 1901; Thurston 1909; Enthoven 1922). However, it is not clear from these accounts whether this condition was sufficient for recruitment, or whether it merely signaled the necessary prior condition for the emasculation operation that signified real membership in the hijra community.

The second and perhaps more prevalent view relates to those "males born with congenital malformation" (Preston 1987). While opinions apparently differed regarding the manner in which "malformed" men became members of the community, that is, whether parents gave them to the community when they were born (Russell 1916), hijras claimed them (Crooke 1896; Faridi 1899; Bhimbai 1901), or they joined voluntarily at a later age (Thurston 1909), malformation or genital deformity itself was perhaps the most common and natural reason for recruitment to the hijra community.[16]

The last category of individuals seen as potential recruits were those characterized as "artificial eunuchs." This label included those who "usually mutilate themselves in the performance of a religious vow, sometimes taken by the mother as a means of obtaining children" (Russell 1916, 207). In all of these colonial accounts, the "regularity with which the British concerned themselves with the hijra body" (Agrawal 1997, 285) is noteworthy, signifying not only the binary sex/gender frame of reference within which colonial officials were operating, but also the naturalization of sexual difference and the centrality of the "deficient" body in such constructions of identity.

Colonialism and Sexuality   As several scholars have noted with respect to the politics of European colonial rule, sexual prescriptions along the lines of race, class, and gender have often been the linchpin of colonial ideologies (Ballhatchet 1980; Nandy 1983; Hyam 1990; Stoler 1995, 1997; see also Manderson and Jolly 1997). In fact, as John and Nair (1998) contend with regard to British imperial ideology, the "concepts of 'private' and 'public,' moral and scandalous have hinged ... decisively on questions of sexuality" (12–13; see also Sarkar 1995; Engels 1996).[17] In particular, sexual lack or inadequacy on the part of the natives became the premise for a colonial characterization of the entire community and way of life in India. Fundamental to British colonial constructions of power and subjectivity was the homology they drew between sexual and political dominance; their masculinity legitimized their colonization, which in turn proved their superior masculine prowess and the dominance of (British) masculinity over (Indian) femininity (Nandy 1983; Chatterjee 1989). In such an imperial ideology, all Indians—women *and* men—were feminized vis-à-vis the British. In fact, as Mrinalini Sinha (1995) and Indira Chowdhury (2001) suggest, the hypermasculinity, or "manliness," of the British colonialists was seemingly *contingent* on the "effeminacy" and contemptible weakness of colonized Indian men (see also Nandy 1983; Krishnaswamy 1998).

Quite apart from characterizing and representing a way of life for both the colonized as well as the colonizers, this preoccupation with Indian effeminacy as a foil for British masculinity also prefigured Indian nationalist responses to colonialism. Indian nationalists explicitly responded to this discourse of colonial masculinity and drew on the tremendous iconic value and moral force of renunciation, both material and sexual (Caplan 1989; Kakar 1989; Basu 1995; John and Nair 1998; Srivastava 2001). They sought to construct a new masculinity for the colonized in terms of the "political *sannyasi*," or renouncer (Nikhilananda 1953; John and Nair 1998; Roy 1998; Chowdhury 2001). While earlier nationalists emphasized the virility of *kshatriya*, or warrior castes, a construction that ultimately reproduced the categories of imperial ideology (see Nandy 1983), later nationalists redefined masculinity not in terms of proving one's militant virility but by indicating the superiority of indigenous "spiritual" worth. Drawing on the work of figures such as Swami Vivekananda, these nationalists revisioned masculinity in terms of the elevation of Indian spiritual strength as opposed to Western bodily or physical strength (see Chatterjee 1989; Chowdhury 2001).

A somewhat more radical repudiation of colonial masculinity was Gandhi's nationalist call to what Leela Gandhi calls "dissident androgyny" (Gandhi 1998, 100). As Ashis Nandy (1983) notes, Gandhi's was a two-pronged strategy: First, he critiqued the elevation of male sexuality and its equation of hypermasculinity with authentic Indianness. Second, drawing on several of the ascetic traditions of India, he posited the ability to transcend the man-woman dichotomy through a self-conscious aspiration for androgyny. The desire to become "God's eunuch," as he put it (Mehta 1977, 194), was superior to both the essence of masculinity and femininity. Together, these principles not only questioned the colonial homology of sexual and political dominance but also provided a nonviolent means for combining activism and courage, the courage to "rise above cowardice or *kapurusatva* (failure of masculinity) and become a 'man,' on the way to becoming the authentic man who admits his drive to become both sexes" (Nandy 1983, 54; see also Kakar 1989; Parekh 1989). In this characterization, Gandhi creatively disables the logic of colonial sexual binaries by inverting the terms of the nationalist debate and elevating femaleness to an equal footing with maleness in the crafting of anticolonial subjectivity.[18]

Despite their different political agendas, both Vivekananda's and Gandhi's formulations can be interpreted as attempts to elevate celibacy, or explicit sexual renunciation, as an ideological challenge to colonial constructions of masculinity/dominance. If, for Vivekananda, celibacy was what built real (spiritual) masculinity, for Gandhi, celibacy served as the ultimate means through which politics could be domesticated. In both of these elaborations, the embodied transformation of (male) sexual energy into a higher spiritual power through the disciplining of the body and, most importantly, the renunciation of sexual desire can be read as a protest against colonial masculinity. In other words, following Nandy's (1983) and Chowdhury's (2001) characterizations, Gandhi's and Vivekananda's repudiation of virile masculinity as the means by which to protest colonial orderings of the (Indian) self highlights sexuality—or its active renunciation—as the transcendent solution to the "problem" of re-masculinizing the nation. This power—the power of sexual renunciation—is a powerful moral force in hijra conceptualizations, one they explicitly draw on in their elaborations of authenticity, izzat, and identity.

Contemporary Third-Sex Analyses

The third, more recent literature on hijras returns to issues of their sex/gender ambiguity, engaging hijras in debates relating to binary gender categorization, cross-cultural understandings of gender fluidity, and the construction of sexual categories. The earliest sociological debates focusing on hijras in the postcolonial period set the stage in this regard. While not explicitly detailing the issue of hijras' sexual ambiguity, this body of literature highlighted the role of hijras as sexual performers and, perhaps for the first time, created a separate domain for the analysis of hijra sexual practice as distinct from their religious/ritual practice. Such analyses find their most explicit expression in the 1950s Carstairs/Opler debate that questioned the sexual and "professional" identity of hijras, categorically opposing the realms of homosexuality and ritual practice by way of an answer (Carstairs 1956; Opler 1960; Shah 1961; see also Sinha 1967; Freeman 1979; Bobb and Patel 1982; Claiborne 1983; Sanghvi 1984; Vyas and Shingala 1987; Sharma 1989).

The vast majority of subsequent (largely anthropological) literature addressing hijras in the past ten or twelve years situates them explicitly within the realm of sexual difference, implicating them in the debate on Western

versus non-Western tolerance for sexual ambiguity and binary gender categorization (Nanda 1990, 1994; Jaffrey 1996; Balaji and Malloy 1997). In
addition, this literature enlists the hijra as one more actor in the global
drama of subversive sexuality. Along with the *kathoey* of Thailand, *xanith*
of Oman, *berdache*/two-spirit of Native North America, and *f'afafine* of
Polynesia, among a host of other third genders, these "institutionalized"
categories (often standing in for each other) represent an alternative to the
duality of the Anglo-European two-gender system (cf. Epple 1998).

Perhaps the best-known work on hijras in recent years, especially in academic and popular circles in the United States, is Serena Nanda's ethnography *Neither Man nor Woman: The Hijras of India*. Originally published in
1990, Nanda's was one of the first ethnographies to represent hijras outside
the framework of deviance, as "full human beings." It was also the first
book-length monograph on hijras published in the United States. Through
contextual chapters and personal narratives, this book, richly configured
around hijras' institutionalization of a third role, conveys an empathetic
and humanistic understanding of the lives of the hijras with whom Nanda
interacted. Despite its nuanced understanding, however, Nanda's analysis
remains enmeshed within the limits of what, for lack of another phrase,
can perhaps be termed a "third-sex" analysis. That is, the general aim is to
dispel the "Western belief that there are only two sexes and two genders,
each naturally and permanently biologically determined and each exclusive
of the meanings and characteristics of the other" (1990, xi). This emphasis
is signaled by the choice of John Money, best known for his controversial
work on intersexed children and his role in promoting a "healthy" dual
gender system in the United States (see Colapinto 2000), as the author of
the preface to the book. Given this analytic agenda, hijras, who occupy, according to Nanda, one of the few contemporary "alternative gender roles,"
are framed in this ethnography as the quintessential third category that is
rooted in "Indian culture's" implicit accommodation of gender fluidity.

The most representative of what I am referring to as a third-sex analysis is
the volume edited by Gilbert Herdt, *Third Sex, Third Gender: Beyond Sexual
Dimorphism in Culture and History* (1994). In the preface, Herdt asks, "Is
sexual dimorphism inevitable in human affairs?" The answer, a resounding
no, is the substance of this book. Drawing on the disciplines of anthropology and social history, the articles—including a chapter by Serena Nanda
on hijras in India—not only describe the "cultural and historical contexts in
which [third] sex/gender schemata have evolved, become institutionalized,
changed and matured" (Herdt 1994, 18), but also address the relationships

between the third sex and erotic desire/practice and, more generally, between "cultural processes and the historical production of third-sex roles and categories" in different regions of the world (19).

Although Herdt and the other contributors do an admirable job of sketching the particular contexts of third-sex elaboration in India, the Balkans, eighteenth-century Holland, Papua New Guinea, and during the Byzantine Empire, to name just a few places, by delimiting sexual categories of analysis, their project overly reifies the domain of sexuality, merely adding another block to the edifice of sexual studies. Despite the caveat that the emphasis on the *third* category is merely a heuristic device that stands in for the possibility of multiple categories, many of the chapters—including Nanda's on hijras—emphasize the code of thirdness as *the* transcendent solution to the sexual dimorphism question. Clearly, *Third Sex, Third Gender* is noteworthy for its deconstruction of sexual dimorphism, which many earlier studies were predicated upon, as well as its marshaling of a wealth of interdisciplinary and cross-cultural data on systems of sex and gender. Nevertheless, it tends to effectively separate the domain of sexuality from that of political economy and the analysis of other axes of identity, thereby limiting its usefulness as an articulation of the complexity of everyday life. Ultimately, the emphasis on alternative sexualities in different cross-cultural contexts unwittingly encourages the delineation of yet another distinct subfield of study. Rather than prying open the sex/gender arena, third-sex studies have reiterated the somewhat tautological and static terms of the debate by reinscribing the division of Western (historicized) versus non-Western (somewhat ahistorical) sex/gender systems, and reified the study of sexuality rather than emphasizing its articulation with other axes of identity and modes of practice.

Serena Nanda's early work, although exemplary in the richness of its ethnographic detail, can be criticized on this count. Given the third-sex framework of the analysis, Nanda's early work inadvertently reinforces a division between Western dual gender systems and Indian accommodations of gender variation outside this binary framework.[19] As I learned during my fieldwork, hijras in Hyderabad did not always identify themselves as third-sex individuals in opposition to a binary framework. Instead, they sometimes adopted cultural symbols that were either feminine or a combination of masculine and feminine, rather than defining themselves categorically as "neither man nor woman," a point that other scholars make as well (Cohen 1995b; Agrawal 1997). Further, hijras do not see themselves or others solely through the lens of sexuality; they argue explicitly for the roles of kinship, religion, and class, among others, in their constructions of self-identity. In other words, hijras cannot be reduced to merely metonymic, non-Western figures for an analysis of gender fluidity; rather, they provide a lens through which to examine the embeddedness of sexuality within other arenas of everyday life.

However—and this is particularly germane to my characterization of changing representations of hijras in the literature—Nanda's own thinking and work on hijras appears to have shifted during the last decade. In the second edition of her ethnography, published in 1999, not only has Nanda omitted the preface by Money, she has also reframed her analysis in line with recent developments in gender theory and anthropological modes of inquiry and representation, paying greater attention to the historico-political contexts of current scholarship (Nanda, pers. comm.). Perhaps, in addition to signifying changes in hijras' lives over the course of this past decade, these shifts in analytic frameworks and ideologies of representation are a testimony to changing theoretical winds and modes of ethnographic crafting.

Axiomatic of recent shifts in anthropological knowledge and modes of presentation is the work by Lawrence Cohen. Although his primary research does not focus on hijras (see Cohen 1999), Cohen has presented several papers and written at least two articles relating to hijras and other "sexual" categories in the north Indian city of Banaras (Cohen 1993, 1995b, 2002). In all of these works, he explicitly calls for a more contextualized account that does not essentialize hijras as a third sex/gender. Cohen's insightful critique of the essentialized vision of third-sexed hijras, favoring an "analysis which locates the body within a multiplicity of differences, . . . [thereby] defer[ring] efforts to read the etiology of the sexed body in terms of the primacy of either cultural system or political economy or to reduce it to biology or psychology [alone]" (1995b, 295), has been influential in the development of my own larger theoretical agenda.[20]

In this book I focus on hijras and also explore their localization within the wider (male) social universe of kotis in Hyderabad. Despite the exis-tence of this wider community and social/linguistic category of kotis in India and other parts of the subcontinent for at least the past decade, and the sometimes acrimonious on-line debates relating to their politics of iden-tity, relatively few analyses of kotis have been published in the literature (Khan 1999, 2000). One of the only book-length monographs on the subject is Jeremy Seabrook's *Love in a Different Climate* (1999). In this account of "men who have sex with men" (hereafter referred to as MSM) in India,

Seabrook provides data from conversations with seventy-five MSM, most of whom he met in the parks of Delhi. The author's agenda appears to be twofold. On the one hand, by explicitly highlighting the expression "MSM" rather than "gay" or "bisexual," he seeks to "avoid projecting Western preoccupations ... and ways of structuring same-sex contact ... onto other cultures" (1999, 1). Instead, he allows the social categories that constitute local same-sex cultures to speak for themselves. On the other hand, inspired by the work of the NAZ Foundation, a sexual health project based in south Delhi, his agenda is at least partly pragmatic: to gain a better understanding of this community so as to limit the spread of HIV/AIDS in the country. While noteworthy for its attempts at relativism and its explication of the koti/panti same-sex classificatory grid in India, Seabrook's analysis is limited as a nuanced cultural account precisely because of its form—it is less ethnography than a detailed journalistic account—and its practical agenda. Although he attempts to avoid Western categorical imperatives, by using the label "MSM," Seabrook inadvertently deploys the constellation of meanings attached to a term that has its own history and moral trajectory, entrenched as it is within specific public health agendas (often derived from or mediated by a Western context). An important corrective to such an account, therefore, is to look precisely at the historical and cultural contexts of koti-panti symbolic elaboration, expressly addressing their links with hijras (including the political history of koti-hijra relationships) over the course of the past decade.

Given all of these various analyses, why do we need yet another book on hijras and kotis? Clearly an extensive corpus of literature on this subject exists, ranging from analyses of "deviance," through exotic parables and relativistic formulations, to "normative" accounts of their role, alongside academics, as gatekeepers of the truth of sexual difference. Almost all of these accounts, however, situate hijras and kotis explicitly within the frame of *sexual* difference, thereby obscuring the multiplicity of differences that construct and mediate their lives. Lawrence Cohen's work explicitly attempts to redress this emphasis, but it remains insufficiently detailed in its ethnographic specificities. The aim of this book, therefore, is to delineate "what it means to make sexual difference matter ... in terms of other forms of social difference" (Cohen 1995b, 277), not only for hijras and kotis themselves, but more broadly for the analysis of everyday life in South Asia. This study ethnographically re-theorizes an out-of-the-way people (to paraphrase Tsing 1994), arguing not only for their relevance in understanding gender and sexuality, but also, and more important, for the inextricable articulation of these axes with other domains of life in South Asia.

SOUTH ASIAN RENUNCIATION AND INDIVIDUALITY

An analysis that embeds sexuality in other forms of social difference high-lights the manner in which claims to hijra/koti identities are negotiated, contested, and refuted, and implicitly engages the vast literature on con-structions of renunciation, personhood, and individuality in South Asia. Starting with the classic work of Louis Dumont, a recurring theme in much of the social science literature on India in the last half century is the emer-gence of Hinduism and notions of South Asian individuality through the dialogue between the householder (*grhasta*) and the renouncer (*sannyasi*), between what Dumont terms the "*man*-in-the-world" and the "*individual*-outside-the-world" (1960; emphasis added)—a dialogue that assumes par-ticular significance for hijra constructions of self and society.

In one of his earliest and best-known articles on the subject, Dumont (1960) maintains that in the relation between these categories—that of the world-renouncing sannyasi, whose religion is based on individuality, and the worldly householder, who is enmeshed in (non-individuated) caste society—we can find the "secret of Hinduism" (Dumont 1960, 37). In this ideological framework, the individual does not exist in the domain of worldly Hinduism, and any discussion of individuality in (Hindu) India can occur only under the terms of other-worldly renunciation.

As Mattison Mines (1994) notes, although Dumont's views on the place of the individual in Indian society build on other scholars' ideas, namely those of Marcel Mauss (1985) and Max Weber (1958), it was Dumont's views that "initiated the debate on individualism among South Asian scholars [that] has held center-stage" since he first set them out in the 1960s and 1970s (Mines 1994, 4). In his best-known work, *Homo Hierarchicus* (1970), Dumont con-tends that, at an ideological level, Indians value collective identities such as that of caste more than the identities of individuals, so that the individual cannot be the unit of analysis in such cultures. Dumont distinguishes two meanings of the term *individual*: first, the "empirical individual," or the self-conscious, physical entity that is postulated as an unproblematic and universal feature of being; and second, the *idea* of the individual as a cul-tural value (Mines 1994, 4). For Dumont, only the second sense of the term should be used (by anthropologists/scholars) in characterizing and analyz-ing societies, in order to "avoid inadvertently attributing the presence of the individual to societies in which he is not recognized" (Dumont 1970, 9). In this context, he surmises that "it is immediately obvious that there are two mutually opposed notions of the person: one is characteristic of traditional societies and the other of modern society." In "traditional societies" such as

India, rather than valuing the life of each individual, "the stress is placed on the society as a whole, as collective Man...[where] each particular man in his place must contribute to the global order [of society]" (9). For Dumont, the Indian collectivity par excellence is defined by the caste system. In Dumont's view, this collectivity—an interdependent division of labor, which is generated by the all-encompassing religious notion of hierarchy— represents the country's societal solidarity and its history.

For Dumont, at the level of ideology, "homo hierarchicus" of Indian society is opposed in some measure to "homo equalis" of the modern West. The context, as Oyvind Jaer notes, is given: "[O]n the one side is hierarchy, on the other equality" (1987, 357; see also Béteille 1986, 1987; Khare 1984; Srinivas 1987). Within Indian or Hindu society in this framework, "on the level of life in the world, the individual is not," whereas for the modern West, "ontologically, the society no longer exists" (Dumont 1970, 9).

One of the most trenchant critiques of Dumont's analysis of Indian individualism (or its lack) is Mattison Mines's *Public Faces, Private Voices: Community and Individuality in South India* (1994), wherein Mines argues for the centrality of individuality to Tamil society. Not only is individuality recognized as "an essential feature of ordinary life" (3), he argues, but "it is absolutely central to how South Indian Tamils explain who they are, understand others, and conceive of their society" (10).

In Mines's view however, this Tamil individuality is somewhat different from Western understandings of the individual. In contrast to the autonomous, independent nature of the individual in the West, the individual in South India is believed to exist in relation to others and derives distinctiveness precisely from these particular and contextual relationships. In some respects, this is similar to Ramanujan's (1990) characterization of the Indians' "overall tendency to think in terms of...context-sensitive kinds of rules" (47). As Mines (1994), Ramanujan (1990), and other scholars contend (Singer 1972; Roland 1979; Shweder and Bourne 1984), Indians employ a "cognitive style that is relationally conceived and contextually appraised" (Shweder and Bourne 1984, 189) rather than the abstract, context-free model of the autonomous individual that characterizes Western modes of social thought (Shweder and Bourne 1984; Mackie 1977; cf. Inden 1990 for a critique of the dangers of such essentializing tendencies). In such a framework, contexts are clearly specified, and behavior is enacted and interpreted according to these circumscribed contexts and relationships rather than according to universal rules governing all conduct. What defines the individual in such a scheme are "the particulars of who s/he is, including his/her relations, and what s/he does to whom" (Mines 1994, 212)—evaluations that are contextual, spatially defined, ranked, and unequal in regard to political status as well as moral values such as generosity, honor, dignity, trust, intelligence, and wisdom. A person's identity is critical to how one interacts with that individual, and, significantly, assessments of such personhood are based not only on character, but also on gender and caste status, family background, education, and position in life, including eminence, occupation, office, influence, relationships, and status within one's family.

Mines's account is an important elaboration of Indian individuality at an ideological *and* empirical level. In order to make his point, however, he constructs an overly rigid and somewhat caricaturized version of Dumont's thesis. Whatever one's disagreement with Dumont's formulations—and there are several critiques, constituting a veritable cottage industry within South Asian studies[21]—he does not suggest that there are no practices of individualism in everyday life or symbolically elaborated in Indian society. As he cautions, the "man-in-the-world's adoption of notions which are essentially those of the renouncer should not conceal from us the difference between the two conditions and the two kinds of thought" (1960, 46). Rather, Dumont suggests that the dominant *ideological* structure of self and society in India is radically different when compared to Western society. While Mines argues, correctly in my opinion, for a theorization of individuality that takes into account the *relationship between the ideological and empirical* bases of self-crafting, in debunking Dumont's construction of the individual, he appears to read Dumont as making a cultural as opposed to a structuralist argument about ideology.[22]

Even within the terms set by the Dumontian framework, the *idea* of the individual in the sense of a non-empirical, "normative subject of institutions," is not entirely absent in (Hindu) India. According to Dumont, whereas the caste Hindu is absorbed in the collective world of relations, a world in which he has no "reality in thought, no Being" (Dumont 1960, 42), there *is* a "thinking creature" comparable to the "modern" idea of the individual in Hindu India. Such a "creature" exists outside caste society as an individual-outside-the-world, a renouncer, or sannyasi (Dumont 1960). For Dumont, renouncers *are* individuals, and in the present context, hijras are also renouncers in their ideological self-structuring (L. Cohen, pers. comm.).

Renunciation—and the figure of the sannyasi—has been given much attention by scholars of South Asia, especially after Dumont's conceptualization of the sannyasi as the arch "creator of values" in the structural logic of Hinduism (Dumont 1960).[23] In this formulation, *sannyasa*, the fourth and last stage of the Hindu fourfold life cycle, is in complementary opposition to the second, householder, stage (*grhastya*). According to Dumont, it is this ideological opposition—between *sannyasa* and the values of renunciation (including especially sexual renunciation), and *grhastya* as the householder stage that emphasizes social/material/sexual reproduction and well-being—that structures the principles of identity. However, while the sannyasi, or "individual," in this Dumontian value system is outside the social framework, his/her position is ultimately defined in explicit opposition to a caste- and often *brahman*-centered logic; eventually, even if only by opposition, the sannyasi's individuality is subsumed within the logic of caste holism.[24]

An interesting exception to this holistic, caste-driven logic is the ideology of the Lucknow Chamars (low-caste "untouchables") outlined by Ravindra Khare in his book, *Untouchable as Himself* (1984). Delineating a non-*brahmanic* interpretation of *sannyas*, these low-caste Chamars manipulate the terms of the debate in a way that undermines the principle of hierarchy and caste holism and disengages it from its Dumontian mooring in other-worldly asceticism. In the process they articulate an anticaste ascetic identity that is focused on *this*-worldly moral values. As Joseph Alter notes, "the Chamar gives a 'protohumanist' interpretation to the *sannyasi's* individuality by inscribing notions of freedom and equality onto the extant concept of yogic self-realization" (1992, 318). In this manner, Khare's Lucknow Chamars recraft notions of *sannyas* and individuality in India, providing a powerful critique of social hierarchy and caste inequality along the way. However, as Alter (1992) and others point out, despite its radical potential, this ideology does not really "dismantle the master's house," to paraphrase Audre Lorde's well-known maxim, ultimately reifying the structural position of the sannyasi in Hindu India, while the transposition of the category (sannyasi) onto a sectarian group ultimately allows for its incorporation into the larger, predominant social framework of caste hierarchy (see Dumont 1960; Das 1977).

Similar to this Chamar ideology, but different in their particular reformulation of "what it means to be ascetic-like," are the interpretations of wrestlers in northern India (Alter 1992, 295; 1997). As Alter notes, "unlike the Chamar, who actually becomes a *sannyasi*—albeit a reformed and non-brahmanic one—the wrestler psychosomatically reconstitutes himself and his worldview by manipulating *sannyas* categories in order to become a different kind of person altogether" (1992, 319). In this reformulation, it is not merely anticaste sentiments that orient this individuality (although it incorporates an implicit caste critique) but a moral self-definition that derives its ultimate value from somatic discipline—in effect, a fundamentally embodied notion of moral individuality. To quote Alter, "[I]t is by virtue of the fact that the practice of *sannyas* has such profound spiritual, other-worldly significance that the practice of wrestling is meaningful as an ethical ideology with worldly implications. The agency through which one point of reference is translated into another is body discipline" (1992, 223).

Much like Alter's wrestlers, hijras in Hyderabad are not themselves sannyasis, but are merely "like sannyasis" as Amir nayak, one of the senior hijra leaders, told me in no uncertain terms. While they are not mendicants in the strict sense of the term and do not completely separate themselves from the social world, they do in fact demarcate their social world from that in which they grew up, are dependent to some extent on "people-of-this-world" (*duniyadari*) for their livelihood, and, what is perhaps most important, they are enjoined to renounce or abstain from sexual intercourse (the practice of *brahmacarya*), the quintessential lay and theological marker of *sannyas*— a marker that is embodied in the most radical manner for hijras through a complete excision of the genitalia.[25] "Real hijras," I was repeatedly told, do not "have [any] mental or physical desire for [sex with] men."

How then do hijras reconcile their ethic of renunciation with their everyday sexual practice? What meanings do *sannyas* and *brahmacarya* encode for hijras, and how are they expressed in their lives? As several scholars have pointed out, with a few notable exceptions (Ojha 1981; Raheja and Gold 1994; Basu 1995; Khandelwal 1997, 2001), discussions of sexuality and renunciation in South Asia have remarkably focused on men's preoccupation with what is now commonly referred to as "semen anxiety"—where "a 'loss' of semen is equated with a loss of masculine strength and 'life-force'" (Srivastava 2001, 2; see also Alter 1992; John and Nair 1998). Celibacy in this regard is often understood in hydraulic terms as a retention or accumulation of semen; a process that essentially accounts for the "creative" power of male ascetics.

Countering this androcentric narrative, Meena Khandelwal's research on female sannyasinis argues for a "more expansive" understanding of the term *brahmacarya*, its ideologies and practices (2001, 167). Rather than restricting its meaning to semen retention—an anxiety over which pervades Banaras wrestlers' articulations of *brahmacarya*—the sannyasinis' accounts highlight a more egalitarian model that emphasizes "moral purity, a lifestyle of self-control or self-restraint, and emotional detachment" rather than the androcentric focus on "semen obsession" (Khandelwal 2001, 173).

Hijras seem to employ just such a model. Despite their radically corporeal enactment of *brahmacarya*, the logic underlying Hyderabadi hijras' ethic of *sannyas* is not dictated *solely* by a physiological model of semen anxiety but by a more egalitarian ethic of spiritual strength, emotional detachment, and moral self-control—much like that of Khandelwal's sannyasinis.

After all, as Irfan and Amir nayak told me repeatedly, not only is the "male body [penis]...useless" for hijras, its excision merely underscores their (ontologically prior) asexuality rather than delineating the centrality of semen retention and power stemming from such control. Instead, as many hijras emphasized, it is the emotional detachment and possession of *himmat*, or courage/strength—emotional, psychological, and physical—to undergo this commitment to permanent sexual abstinence that reveals hijras' greater authenticity and ultimately, their greater izzat. "Having nothing there," as one hijra phrased it, serves as a corporeal symbol that inscribes and reveals hijras' superior agency, authenticity, and izzat, constituting in itself their heightened "reputation...responsibility...control, agency, and eminence"—factors that explicitly construct "individuality" in Mattison Mines's sense of the term (1994, 23). In other words, among hijras, the relationship between izzat and individuality is dialectical—hijras gain izzat through constructing their individuality as renouncers, and the medium or currency through which they construct their individuality is izzat. Izzat, therefore, emerges through this process as a central authenticating trope in hijra constructions of self and society.[26]

THE IDIOM OF HONOR AND ITS RELATION TO IZZAT IN SOUTH ASIA

A Farsi word originally, the term *izzat* refers most closely to the constellation of meanings glossed in English as "honor" or "respect." In this book I use it to imply the term *respect*, a wider, more inclusive term than *honor*. In the primarily anthropological literature that explores this issue, *honor* signifies a more communal as well as more circumscribed, erotic dimension—a meaning that I contend is narrower than hijras' usage of it.

In the anthropological literature, the paradigm of "honor and shame" is most indelibly associated with cultures in the circum-Mediterranean basin (Abu-Zeid 1966; Bourdieu 1966, 1977; Peristiany 1966; Schneider 1971; Davis 1977; Pitt-Rivers 1977; Meeker 1979; Brandes 1980; Herzfeld 1980, 1984; Gilmore 1980, 1982, 1987; Blok 1981; Wikan 1984; Abu-Lughod 1985, 1986). Starting with the British structuralists, most notably Julian Pitt-Rivers and Jean Peristiany, a cultural archetype of Mediterranean peoples was constructed, based on the complementary codes of honor and shame that were believed to constitute a "supreme" and uniform value system. More recent accounts not only problematize the supreme and premature nominalism of this value syndrome (Herzfeld 1984), but also question its internal cohesiveness (Davis 1977; Herzfeld 1984; Wikan 1984; Marcus 1987;

Stewart 1994) and, most relevant to this discussion, its confinement to circum-Mediterranean cultures (cf. Mauss 1967; Wyatt-Brown 1982; Asano-Tamanoi 1987; Gilmore 1987; Pastner 1988; McHugh 1998). As Appadurai notes, "[I]deas that claim to represent the 'essences' of particular places reflect the temporary localization of ideas from many places" (1988, 46). In this brief introduction, rather than trace the genealogy of honor and shame in the Mediterranean region, I address the issue of localization by examining constructions of this value syndrome in South Asia.[27]

As some historians have suggested, Mediterranean honor and shame codes may be just one variant of a more universal moral system pertaining to the "Indo-European agrarian civilizations" (Wyatt-Brown 1982, xiii). Although this line of reasoning has not been taken up very seriously, its underlying logic—that the honor/shame code is not restricted to the Mediterranean region but has a wider valence (including the regions of South Asia)—has been widely addressed in recent studies.

Most accounts of honor—those focusing on the circum-Mediterranean region as well as on South Asia—emphasize the regulation of female sexuality; that is, the analysis is located squarely within the framework of sexual control and gender relations (Pitt-Rivers 1963; Jeffery 1979; Papanek and Minault 1982; Nandy and Das 1985; Gilmore 1987; Mandelbaum 1988; Pastner 1988; Sharma 1990; Das 1990, 1995; Menon 1997; Butalia 1998; Menon and Bhasin 1998). Extending Pitt-River's original contention that "everywhere honor is closely associated with sex," recent South Asian analyses undertaken to reclaim the histories of women who survived the partition of India and Pakistan reiterate the indelible connection between women's sexuality and honor. As Ritu Menon and Kamla Bhasin (1998) state in one the first feminist histories of the partition of India, "There was clearly some degree of consensus in the patriarchal notion of safeguarding honour (male as well as community honour) through a control of women's sexuality. Most men and women we spoke to were agreed that honour—for losing or preserving—is located in the body of the woman" (58). Chronicling the horrific violence inflicted on the bodies of women—both Indian and Pakistani, Hindu and Muslim—during this turbulent time, these authors contend that

the preoccupation with women's sexuality...was of an even greater order of magnitude than circumcision or forcible conversion and marriage. So powerful and general was the belief that safe-guarding a woman's honor is essential to upholding male and community honor that a whole new order of violence came into play, by men against their own kinsmen, and by women against their daughters or sisters and their own selves. (45)

To preserve their chastity and protect their individual, family, and community honor, thousands of women chose, or were forced into "real but honourable death" rather than face the "symbolic death" that sexual violence and subsequent marriage and conversion entailed. As these authors note, "It was made abundantly clear [to women] that death was preferable to 'dishonour,' that in the absence of their men the only choice available to them was to take their own lives" (45). Many women recounted stories of other women killing themselves, and men recounted with pride how their women "preferred to commit suicide" rather than lose their honor (45). In this and other analyses in which "honor" plays a significant role (Das 1995; Menon 1997; see also Zajovic 1994), it is particularly interesting that women's bodies are chosen as the singular locus that mark and are imprinted with these "other"—in this case ethnic or religious—divisions.[28] The woman's body *becomes* "other," the honor of which must be preserved and the dishonor, avenged. Honor in these analyses is always already "libidinized," to use David Gilmore's (1987) term.

In one of the few South Asian accounts of *ijjat* (or "honor," as McHugh translates the Nepali term)[29] in a non-libidinized context, Ernestine McHugh (1998) addresses this value as an "organizing principle" by which Nepali Gurungs are situated in social space and through which they "apprehend their own significance" (1998, 155). McHugh's article examines honor as a cultural model, taking into account not just Gurung ideational schemas, but also their instantiation in practice. Honor in such a schema is "a code for both interpretation and action: in other words with both cognitive and pragmatic components," to use Paul Friedrich's definition (1977, 284). In particular, McHugh argues that honor, a widely held and important motivating force in Gurung life, is tightly bound to both social and personal integration or identity. Framing her argument within the wider social contexts of caste, gender, religion, and urban/rural space, McHugh indicates that honor provides the model in reference to which "the self [is] situated and defined." The constituent features of honor, in this model, include status, wealth, lineage, and the demonstration of "appropriate moral behavior," such as graciousness, generosity, and evenness of temper. Given the interconnections between sociality, "personal wholeness," and honor in the Gurung schema, this value is not only vital to the integrity of the self but also important for the construction of social stature, both attributes that not only reflect but also constitute honor in Gurung society (see Mines 1994). Ultimately, as McHugh argues, "the idea of honor [for the Gurungs] reflects a larger configuration: through this concept one's place in a given social world is defined, and one's character as a moral person is assessed" (1998, 165).

Although McHugh uses the term *honor* rather than *respect* to refer to the constellation of meanings characterized above, I prefer the term *respect*. Given the strong association of the term *honor* with the circum-Mediterranean societies in the anthropological literature, it is perhaps inevitable that residual meanings from that context will spill over when the term is used outside of it. As David Gilmore states, "Mediterranean honor...is a 'libidinized' social reputation; it is this eroticized aspect of honor—albeit unconscious or implicit—that seems to make the Mediterranean variant distinctive" (1987, 11). Contrary to this statement, I argue that the notion of honor in South Asian contexts also has an "eroticized" element; thus, I prefer to restrict the usage of this term only to such communal, explicitly gendered, and "libidinized" contexts.

By contrast, in hijras' use of the term *izzat* (and in the Gurungs' apparent interpretation of the concept), the referent is not restricted to an eroticized dimension. Instead, the concept of izzat among hijras has a moral valence that derives strength precisely from its diffusion beyond the axis of sex/gender to encompass a range of other hierarchical domains, including kinship, religion, and class. Rather than restrict its meaning to "honor," therefore, I translate the term *izzat* as "respect," an interpretation that is reflected in the title of this ethnography. It is in relation to the centrality of izzat to hijras' and kotis' lives that I problematize current understandings of the third sex in India.

The themes outlined above are explicated in the following chapters to make a relatively simple point: Against an overly essentialized vision of the third sex, hijras and kotis construct, experience, and enact their individuality through a *multiplicity* of social differences in addition to that of sexuality. Each of the chapters focuses on a separate domain or axis of identity, including corporeality (chapters 3 and 4), religion (chapters 4 and 5), gender and dress (chapter 6), kinship (chapter 7), and class (chapter 9), arguing for their embodied manifestation through praxis, and for the motivational imperative of izzat in constructing hijra and koti identity in Hyderabad. The chapters focus on three aspects of hijra and koti identity construction: first, the use of each of these axes of identity—namely, gender and corporeality, religion, choice of clothing, kinship, and class—to craft more than merely sexual difference; second, the centrality of embodied practice and ambiguity in constructing identity; and third, the importance of izzat as the currency through which hijras and kotis craft their identities and negotiate their relative status.

3

Cartographies of Sex/Gender

In July of 1996, I was sitting under the tank in Secunderabad with a group of hijras, sharing their roasted peanuts. It was a hot, sultry afternoon, and most hijras were asleep in their huts. Surekha and Sushmita were lying down next to me in the shade of their hut, reading about the latest escapades of Saundarya and Mohan Babu (film actors) in a Telugu film magazine they had just bought. Lekha had just woken up and had sauntered over with her bowl of rice and lentils. Nobody felt compelled to talk until two men appeared on the scene. I noticed them standing a short distance away and staring at us, but didn't pay them too much attention. As soon as Lekha noticed them, however, she started abusing them loudly: "You *gandus* [faggots]! Why don't you come closer! I'll show you how it is done properly. Radhika, give me that knife." The few hijras who were within hearing distance laughed aloud when she said that, and the men promptly left. Lekha didn't stop there but, making a disgusted face, went on to complain to me about "Those 'double-trick' *gandus*! I know those two people. They are not pantis or kotis, but AC/DCs."

Drawing on such hijra categories, I chart a sexual "cartography," if you will, of Hyderabad. This cartography introduces the actors in my story—pantis, kotis, and AC/DCs among them—giving some understanding of the complexity of sexual and gender configurations in this region. As a point of departure, I contend that bodily practice is an important axis of difference in this system, with sex/gender performativity rather than anatomy being the salient marker of difference (see Kulick 1997, 1998).[1] Specifically, I argue that the act of penetration in sexual intercourse and "doing [gendered] work," serve as central axes around which hijras and other kotis configure their identities. In this praxis-based understanding, the gender system appears to be divided into pantis (penetrative, "masculine" men) on the one hand, and both kotis (receptive, "effeminate" men) and narans (all women), on the other. But while performative aspects of bodily praxis are extremely important in theorizations of gender difference, the criteria of difference in identity configuration and their salience in an individual's life can vary depending on the temporal, spatial, and life-historical positioning of the actors. In other words, the differential axes of koti identity(s) preclude an easy understanding of gender difference in terms of sexual performance *alone*. By delineating this system and unpacking koti identities, this cartography questions the common understanding of hijras as *the* personifications of third-sexed individuals in India. More generally, it challenges hermetically sealed theorizations of sexual/gender difference by showing their embeddedness in other forms of difference as well as the manner in which claims to identity are negotiated, contested, and refuted by these individuals.

CARTOGRAPHIES THROUGH THE HIJRA LENS

When I first got to Hyderabad, my intention was to do a wide-ranging ethnography of hijras, or kojjas, in Hyderabad, and my initial interactions were primarily with this community of individuals.[2] In my conversations with them, depending on the particular language we were speaking in— either Hindi or Telugu—one or the other of these terms would be used, much as I expected. I soon found, however, that quite apart from the use of *hijra* (Hindi) and *kojja* (Telugu) depending on linguistic context, they used other self-referential terms that cut across both Hindi and Telugu linguistic contexts, namely the terms *koti, panti,* and *naran.*

In my early interactions with hijras, I had a difficult time understanding these terms when they were first used. I initially thought it might be my unfamiliarity with the specific and to some extent class-based vocabulary that hijras used most often—curse-words and colloquial abuses—even though Telugu is my native language. While I recognized some words in a sentence, they would frequently use an unfamiliar word that made the sentence unintelligible. I soon realized, however, that they used these same words even when speaking Hindi, and I started paying closer attention to the specific vocabulary. Two words that were commonly used—the first two words I learned in this vocabulary—were koti and panti.[3] I had never heard these words before with reference to a person in either Telugu or Hindi,[4] and none of my non-hijra friends or family were aware of them either. The terms were employed in various situations and clearly referred to a person of some sort. If a non-hijra male walked into their living area,

I would invariably hear one of the hijras ask another, "Is that a koti or a panti?" Or if a man walked up and asked for a specific hijra with whom he appeared to share some relationship, the hijra in question would be told that her panti was here.[5] Obviously, there was a connection between the term *panti* and a "man," but they did not seem to be synonymous, because some people who dressed and looked to me like men were referred to as kotis. When asked explicitly, the only explanation initially provided was: "All of us are kotis, and our husbands are pantis." Following hijras' own cartographic understandings and self-definitions, my frame of reference thus expanded from that of hijras alone to the whole of the koti-panti spectrum of identities that they both identified with and seemingly positioned themselves against.

"ALL OF US ARE KOTIS": MAPPING SEX/GENDER AXES OF DIFFERENTIATION

As I gradually discovered, by "all of us," hijras were referring to their identity as kotis, explicitly opposing this term to pantis, or "men." What differentiated pantis from kotis appeared to be defined not so much sartorially as performatively in a sexual encounter. Pantis were individuals who looked like men and dressed and acted like men, as did some kotis; but only pantis were the penetrators in sexual encounters. Kotis on the other hand, claimed to be more "like women" in the things they desired and engaged in, defining this construct both in terms of sexual (receptive) performance and in terms of gendered acts outside the sexual realm. As one hijra said, echoing many others, "From birth, I always liked to put *moggus* [rice-flour designs drawn on the ground, typically by women], play with girls, and help with the cooking and cleaning. I liked only men and was spoiled by them early in life. I used to make up games where I was the wife, and this boy I liked was my husband, and I would make him spoil me."

The "spoiling" (*cedu* or *cedugottu* in Telugu) referred to the sexual experiences of many hijras and other kotis when they were either receptive partners in their sexual relationships with men or, as they indicated in a few instances, "raped" by them. Most of these kotis said they were "spoiled" by these men *because* they were kotis, that is, they actively desired receptive, anal intercourse, and the men they had sex with knew kotis enjoyed this sexual practice. Others however said that it was this first sexual experience that "spoiled" them for future penetrative/heterosexual intercourse, "weakening [their] organ" and subsequently making them either impotent or able to "enjoy only 'homosex.'" Whatever their causal attribution, as they categorically stated, "Now [we] are kotis and there is nothing [we] can do about it."

Apparently, as several hijras and other self-identified kotis informed me, one can easily identify a koti on the street. When I took bus trips with some of the kotis, they would take great pleasure in identifying fellow kotis for me from among the general public. Individuals who looked to me like men, wearing pants and shirts and sometimes sporting mustaches and beards were immediately identified by the kotis as "belonging to [our] family." They told me, "You have to look at their hands." "Kotis can be easily identified by the way their joints move, especially their wrist joints," according to Salman. "If a man's hand appears to flop about seemingly unhinged at the wrist, then that is as good an indication as any that the individual in question is a koti," he said. "Then there is the way they move their heads and hands when they talk, the way they look other men up and down. And then of course, there are those obvious people who are *lacak-matak* [hip-swinging] kinds, who are the most easily identified as kotis," Jaipal said to a chorus of nods from other kotis sitting there.

My persistent questions about the criteria for differentiating kotis from other men almost always elicited the following answer: "All kotis desire pantis." While the various kinds of kotis might differ in their manner of attracting and interacting with pantis as well as in their investments in the rhetoric of asexuality, kotis were generally represented as people "who desire pantis." For the present purposes, I accept this axis as central to their gendered identity, but I explore in the following chapters the ways in which this so-called thirdness is repositioned and complicated in different contexts.

Koti numbers in Hyderabad have apparently grown exponentially in the past couple of years. "Earlier, one knew all the kotis in Hyderabad, and we could all trust each other. But now there are so many that we cannot possibly get to know all of them. And some of them are real thieves," Suresh, a koti, told me, in a disgusted tone. He had recently gone on a trip to Vijayawada (a city about two hundred kilometers from Hyderabad) with some kotis whom he thought he could trust. On arriving, however, he realized that one of the kotis he was traveling with had stolen his watch and a nice pearl necklace he was going to wear for a party there.[6] "This would never have happened even just a few years ago," he complained. Earlier, there were a few "secret" spots in the city where kotis hung out. Today, these spots "have become 'public' and all kinds of ruffians [*goondas*] roam around there." Also, with the number of kotis having increased, "it is impossible to really know all the people who come there, unlike how it was in the past," said Jaipal. He and other older kotis formed their closest friendships from among their neighborhood koti gang, a pattern that is difficult if not impossible to emulate in the current alienating circumstances. Most of the kotis who have been in Hyderabad for the past eight to ten years confirm Suresh and Jaipal's statements. Commenting on the numbers alone, Saroja, one of my hijra friends, said proudly but with some hyperbole, "Today, every single household in Hyderabad has at least one koti," a sentiment that was echoed by many other hijras and kotis in Hyderabad. While an accurate numerical estimate is difficult, when I pressed the kotis, Prasad told me that there "must be at least twenty-five to thirty thousand kotis in Hyderabad," and other kotis present concurred.

Unlike kotis, pantis were "real men," as one koti stated categorically.[7] They were men who desired and engaged in sex with women or with kotis. Though many kotis were married and had children, they and other kotis saw this as merely a social obligation that apparently had no significance for their identity as kotis.[8] Pantis, on the other hand, were men who either *only* engaged in heterosexual intercourse or, as was more often the case with the hijra's pantis, performed the role of the penetrator in male same-sexed interactions ("homosexuals" in the Euro-American context).[9] Most of the hijras' pantis had their own "families" or a female wife and children, and had an "alternative," heterosexual life outside of their interactions with hijras or other kotis.

In the koti cartography, then, all "men" (defined as performing the act of penetration in sexual intercourse) were pantis. Although this label included hijras' sexual clients, they typically differentiated between their pantis and sexual clients by referring to the latter as *girakis* (customers). Even the older, supposedly asexual hijras either currently have or definitely have had pantis when they were younger. "All hijras do it, otherwise why are they hijras? They all have pantis, and if they say they don't, then they are lying," Aliya said quite assertively. So even though it is not the *only* definition of a hijra,[10] for some, being the receptive sexual partner of a panti did constitute an extremely important aspect of their identity.

Interestingly, the reality of having a panti as a "husband" and sexual partner was an important dimension of hijra identity for many of the junior sex workers, but this was denied by senior hijra leaders or nayaks who epitomized the hijra ritual/asexual role. The nayaks I spoke to categorically denied the assertion that "*all* hijras have pantis," and reiterated their own and other hijras' asexuality. However, some of the older kotis who used to cruise the neighborhood along with hijra nayaks in their youth told stories about their sexual escapades when they were younger (although not in the presence of these nayaks). On one occasion, Arif Khan, a respected and elderly koti reminisced about the "number of pantis they [the nayaks and he] used to have," somewhat contradicting the nayaks' own statements in this regard. In addition, some of the hijra sex workers also told me of having met their nayaks' pantis on occasion in the recent past, indicating that the lived experience regarding this issue differs somewhat from the articulated ideal.

So who were these men who chose to have sex with hijras? For several reasons, both ethical and practical, I did not interact as extensively as I would have liked with many of the pantis. First, I was inhibited from getting to know pantis as well as I would have liked by my status as a "respectable," middle-class, Indian woman and by my own fears and inhibitions associated with normative gender and class prescriptions (cf. Kumar 1992). Further, given the emotional polarization of the koti-panti relationships, I felt morally bound to kotis' points of view. Finally, to some extent, the hijras' monopolization of what little time they got to spend with their pantis also restricted the opportunities for interaction between us. Gradually, however, some of the hijras' pantis acknowledged my presence and even interacted with me to some extent. Surekha's "husband," Rajesh, in particular, made it a point to greet me every time he saw me, even if he was with his non-hijra friends on the street. I had many conversations with him regarding his relationship with his "wife," Surekha, and other hijras. Rajesh is what many hijras described as "a real *badmas*" (a wretched fellow), even though they did not always feel this way about him. In fact, earlier he was one panti who seemed completely accepted by the community of hijras living under the water tank, and he used to come and go more freely than any of the others.

Rajesh's relationship with hijras illustrated, in some respects, the general tension between hijras and their pantis. Rajesh is a handsome, well-built man in his late twenties. He is not from Hyderabad but had come to this city at about the same time his hijra "wife," Surekha, had arrived from her village in Warangal district, eight years ago. Rajesh was born and had grown up in a village in the neighboring state of Karnataka and therefore spoke no Telugu when he first arrived here in pursuit of a job. He knew a smattering of Hindi and otherwise spoke only Kannada, the language spoken in Karnataka. He used to do odd jobs and sleep on the street until he met Surekha. Apparently, he thought Surekha was a woman when he first saw her, which is why he approached her. He was her first customer, or *giraki*, Surekha said. He claimed that until he actually had sex with her, he did not know that she was a hijra. After realizing that she was a hijra, he told her that he couldn't pay the agreed upon rate of twenty rupees but instead would pay only ten rupees.[11] They haggled over the price for a while, but when he told her in his broken Telugu-Hindi-Kannada that he was new here, didn't know anyone, and was feeling very lonely, she "felt very bad," and instead of accepting the money, she treated him to a decent meal in the local restaurant. Ever since then, they have "been together, through good [times] and bad." Soon after, they were married to each other in a ceremony performed by other hijras. At the same time, he was also made "[an adoptive] son and brother" of other hijras among the tank group.[12] His kin links with this group of hijras were undisputed. Although he disappeared for most of the day to hang out with his male friends, he would show up when he was hungry, needed money, had to have a bath, or needed his clothes washed, all of which Surekha would willingly and gladly do for him, "as a good wife would." During their time together, she said (and he agreed), she must have spent hundreds of thousands of rupees on him.[13]

Recently however, Rajesh did something that, while it did not alter the perception of him as a panti, clearly changed his status among the rest of the hijras. Toward the end of my fieldwork period, he did not frequent the tank as much and was verbally abused every time another hijra saw him there. I was told in no uncertain terms, "[H]e is a bad man. He has not acted correctly." What did he do to deserve this disapprobation? Rajesh had sex with Shakuntala, another hijra from this group—in fact, Surekha's "grandmother" in the hijra kinship hierarchy. While Shakuntala was held somewhat accountable, the derision for this act was directed almost completely at Rajesh. The magnitude and direction of the derision could have something to do with Shakuntala's being a senior member of the community in terms of age and especially in terms of the number of years she had been here. In addition, she was Rajesh's grandmother, which invoked kin and age (sex) taboos rather than any gendered understanding of responsibility. But as some of the hijras said to me, "*He* is the one who did the act, and [while] she could have refused, it was what *he* did that defined this as a bad act." Penetrating and penetrated sexual roles appear to take on different significance here with different perceptions of personhood and responsibility attached to them. A panti is a "man," and not only did sexual intercourse with a hijra *not* threaten or prejudice a panti's masculinity, in some ways it reinforced the behavioral definition of sexuality and male-gendered identity, accentuating the difference between a panti and a koti.

While they are not pantis, kotis are also "not narans"; they are only "like narans." This term as I soon learned, referred to a woman.[14] They would always use it when I arrived on the scene, usually in the context of curbing their abusive speech because "a naran was present." *Naran* was a generic term that encompassed all women, whether married, single, widowed, young, or old. While narans were clearly different from them—the ability to bear children being the single and most potent marker of difference—hijras felt comfortable interacting with women, chatting about important issues such as where to get the best deals for saris, new styles of stitching blouses, discussing which design one should use for making jewelry, complaining about the price of vegetables, and exchanging recipes. Women from the neighborhood would occasionally come to the tank and chat with them or, as happened more often, would call them to their homes during the day when their husbands were away at work. It was considered somewhat inappropriate for a woman to interact extensively with hijras,[15] perhaps not so much because hijras were *sexually* threatening in any way, but primarily because of their profession (sex work) and the kind of men they subsequently attracted. Nevertheless, interactions between specific hijras and neighborhood women seemed to be not only acceptable, but quite common. The women would send their children to call hijras to their houses sometimes just to watch television or to chat with them. At times, hijras would wander over to help the women with their everyday tasks, such as cutting vegetables or cooking, and exchange gossip for a while before returning to the tank.

Not only did hijras share tastes in clothing, jewelry, and everyday "domestic" concerns, such as the escalating costs of vegetables and oil, with narans, but, like them, they also suffered physical abuse at the hands of their "husbands," a topic that they often discussed in these interactions. While hijras have the reputation of being overly aggressive with most people, especially men, they appeared extremely "docile" with their husbands and were apparently beaten up by them almost daily. Any suggestion that they should or could resist this behavior and retaliate was greeted with the overt statement "Tcha! That is wrong. We cannot do that."

At first glance, hijras appear to resemble men—they are big and muscular. Most people fear hijras as much for their belligerent, aggressive style as for their inauspicious potential. However, hijras identify with women on the issue of "domestic" abuse and see themselves as relatively helpless when faced with violence from their putative husbands, although they probably would not hesitate to lash out if other, unrelated men were to behave in a similar manner.

Despite hijras' potential for aggression, sexual and otherwise, with men, the only aggression they directed toward women was in the context of extracting money and almost never in a sexual context. In fact, an insinuation of *heterosexuality* ("having been married and fathered children") prior to formal hijra membership was among the worst accusations in the community—one that occasioned the highly disparaged label *berupia* and virtual ostracism by other hijras. In my own experience with hijras, far from feeling sexually threatened, in virtually every interaction with them, I felt extremely safe because of how explicitly protective hijras were of all narans.

Men, on the other hand, seemed to have an ambivalent relationship with hijras: they seemed attracted to them in some measure but at the same time scared of them. Unless explicitly invited by hijras, men were afraid to walk into their living space because hijras could get quite abusive with them, both verbally and physically. It was much safer (if morally suspect in the eyes of respectable society) for women to interact with the hijras. Clearly, the object of hijras' sexual desire was men or, as they said, "We are kotis. We are like women and do everything like them, so how can our love be for women?" On the few occasions that I mentioned lesbianism, they found it too ludicrous to be possible. "How can two women be together? How do they have 'sex'? What can they do? I mean . . . It is not possible!" Munira said, her face mirroring the incredulous expressions on the faces of the other hijras sitting there. Female same-sex desire and especially sexual *practice* were apparently dismissed as an impossible "habit" because there was no prospect of penetration. A woman could only be the receptive partner, and any other sexual or gender configuration was outside the realm of possibility.[16]

THE KOTI "FAMILY"

The koti "family" referred not just to hijras but a whole range of koti identities. In addition to hijras—otherwise referred to as *catla* (sari-wearing) kotis—there were *kada-catla* (non-sari-wearing) kotis, *zenana* kotis, *jogins*, and *siva-satis*, all of whom looked like men to me but self identified as kotis. Not only was koti sexual identity configured against panti identity, but this "koti family" as it were, had several distinct members with marked differences among them. The analogy of the "family" was commonly used to describe their relationships: "Like in any family, there are different children who do different things, it is like that with us. All kotis belong to one family, but we are also each of us different at the same time," Shanti said.

The koti "family" has at least five members, or identities, that I know of—hijra, zenana, jogin, siva-sati, kada-catla koti—differentiated on the basis of idealized asexuality, dress, kinship patterns, religion, respectability, and the centrality of the body to their understanding of self (see table 1). While there is clearly interaction and even dual membership across these subgroups,

Table 1 / Schematic of koti variation

Kotis	Asexuality	Operated status	Women's dress (sari)	Kinship ritual (*rit/man-pan*)	Shared living space	Hindu	Muslim	Work
Hijra								
Kandra hijra		X	X	X	X		X	Sex worker
Badhai hijra	X	X	X	X	X		X	Ritual worker
Zenana			*	X	*		X	Dancer
Kada-catla koti						X	X	Various occupations
Jogin	X		X	X	◆	X		Ritual (temple) worker
Siva-sati			*		◆	X		Various occupations
AC/DC						X	X	Various occupations
Berupia			X			X	X	Ritual workers impersonating hijras

X = the ideal, often the norm; * = possible but not necessary/universal identification or practice; ◆ = temporary or periodic (e.g., during pilgrimages, or *jatras*) there was some degree of closure in their interactions with each other. This separation involved different evaluations of authenticity and bases of hierarchy along the axes listed above, as well as socioeconomic and class differences.

A brief description of each of these koti "categories" follows,[17] starting with hijras, followed by zenanas, kada-catla kotis, jogins, and siva-satis. I also refer to local categories that blur the koti/panti axis, such as AC/DCs, or "alternating" koti/pantis, as well as *berupias*, or hijra-impersonators. As the opening vignette of this chapter indicated, AC/DCs are clearly disparaged by hijras on account of their "alternating" receptive/penetrative practice, accounting for their label. *Berupias*—men who impersonate hijras for a living—are perhaps the most disparaged by hijras, primarily because they are members of one sexual identity by behavioral definition (panti), and imitate another in their gendered role (koti). By crossing this invisible divide, they (along with AC/DCs to some extent) are considered the most "deviant" individuals in the hijra cartography of sexual identity.

Hijras: Operational "Men Minus Men"

I was buying vegetables in the marketplace, completely engrossed in bargaining for eggplant, when I heard sounds of an altercation to my left. The friend who had accompanied me to the market poked me in the ribs and said, "There are your friends—the hijras—creating a commotion, as usual." Sure enough, it was a group of hijras who had come to demand money from the shopkeepers in return for a "divine blessing." Apparently one of the owners had refused to pay up, and, predictably, the hijras were reacting loudly. I recognized the group of four hijras as ritual practitioners belonging to the Sheharwala house in Hyderabad. They started by clapping their hands loudly and yelling abusive curses. The motive was to attract attention, and they were succeeding. When the offending shopkeeper still refused to give them any money, one of the hijras made as if to lift her sari and expose her lack of genitalia to him. Afraid of being further shamed, he quickly handed over twenty rupees and, folding his hands to them in supplication, asked them to please leave. Laughing, the four hijras moved on to accost another shopkeeper.

Hijras or kojjas of India are often described in the literature as "eunuch-transvestites" (Vyas and Shingala 1987), or "institutionalized third-gendered" individuals (Nanda 1990), or, in O'Flaherty's (1980) phrase, "men minus men." For the most part, they look like men, wear saris, grow their hair long, and generally enact a "feminine" performance. Hjiras are easily identified in public places. Their choice of dress (sari) and their loud,

Tank hijras posing for the camera

aggressive behavior clearly mark them in the eyes of an onlooker. Not only are they "essentially just men who wear saris" as a non-hijra neighbor (who had recently had money "extorted" from him by hijras) somewhat disparagingly described them, but they draw attention to themselves by their exaggerated femininity and, above all, by their marker of identity—the hijra hand-clap. This distinctive gesture—a loud clap made with the flats of the two hands—is a clear statement signifying hijra allegiance. Any parody of hijra behavior includes an exaggerated, hip-swinging movement and this distinctive clapping. I remember occasions during my school years when hijra impersonations (always by boys or men) drew a great deal of applause and much laughter. These performances usually included the following: a loud, overly aggressive manner of speech, exaggerated "feminine" gestures and movements, the loud clapping of hands, and demonstrations of "shamelessness" signified by the potential exposure of (mutilated) genitalia. Hijras are stigmatized figures, marginal mockeries of a "normal" Indian man (and woman). But, like many other marginalized cultural identities, they embody and engender much of the ambivalence that surrounds issues of Indian sexuality and, for that reason, remain a potent and enduring cultural identity in the Indian universe.

Badhai hijras singing at a wedding

A "real hijra" is said to be like an ascetic or sannyasi—completely free of sexual desire. Many hijras undergo a complete emasculation—the *nirvan* operation, in which the penis and testes are excised—and are subsequently believed to be endowed with the power to confer fertility on newlyweds. They see this conferral of blessings as their traditional ritual role, and hijras who earn their living in this manner are referred to as *badhai* hijras (*badhai* being the term for their payment for these services). Another primary occupation of some hijras is sex work, and hijras engaging in this work are referred to as *kandra* hijras.

Traditionally, hijras did not engage in prostitution, I was told. When they were described to me as part of the koti hierarchy, hijras were "those who sang/danced for a living," surviving primarily on "badhai earnings." Only when I probed was sex work mentioned, even by kandra hijras themselves. Both of these occupational identities seem to be mutually exclusive and appear to operate on distinct status levels. Badhai hijras, or ritual practitioners, consider themselves (and are generally considered by most hijra sex workers as well) to be the more respected hijras—those with izzat. However, kandra hijras see a common trajectory for *all* hijras: everyone starts out as a sex worker, and when their bodies or desires change, they become "ascetic" badhai hijras. This trajectory, of course, was disputed by the badhai hijras, who see the two paths as necessarily independent, reflecting the difference between "real" and "false" hijras.

Related to this issue of ideal asexuality is another hijra criterion of authenticity, namely sexual "dysfunction." All hijras claim to be impotent, or physically impaired, or both. Munira, among others, said, "The body—I mean, you know what I mean right? A *man's* body—that should not be functional. Only then can we say that that person is a hijra."[18] In recent years, as Munira informed me, this criterion is being increasingly mentioned as the most necessary and important criterion for recruitment. Further, many hijras undergo complete physical emasculation: they become *nirvan sultans*. This operation is clearly the recommended act, and while non-operated hijras experience pressure to undergo *nirvan* (become operated), having this operation does not seem to be an absolute rule for membership; in fact, some relatively senior individuals in the community do not have the operation—but they must be circumcised (the *khatna* operation) in accordance with Muslim rules.[19] This is an absolute must, because, as they say, "We become Musalmans after joining the hijras." Despite the avowed Muslim identity of Hyderabadi hijras, many of whom perform Islamic rites and rituals (including going on the Hajj in some instances), *all* hijras are enjoined to worship a Hindu goddess, Bahuchara or Bedhraj Mata, from whom they are believed to get their power to confer fertility (I explore these issues in the next two chapters).

Hijras have extensive kin ties with each other and a nationwide network that gathers on occasion for special events, funerals (*rotis*), and commemorations. While the actual numbers of hijras in India are in dispute, every time I met hijras and kotis in Hyderabad, they loved to give me (often inflated) estimates of their numbers. "In every single village in India, there is at least one hijra," Shanti told me categorically when I first met her, a somewhat hyperbolic but nevertheless telling assertion. The community has been extremely hard to enumerate because of its highly secretive as well as migratory lifestyle and because hijra identity is not recognized legally and legislatively.[20]

The popular, and to some extent mistaken, belief is that hijras live primarily in northern cities such as Delhi, Banaras, Lucknow, and, more recently, Bombay, among others.[21] However, as the literature indicates, the South Indian city of Hyderabad has been and continues to be a "traditional center of hijra culture" (Lynton and Rajan 1974, 52; cf. Jaffrey 1996) and, along with other South Indian cities such as Bangalore, currently boasts a significant hijra community (Nanda 1990). While the degree of connection among the communities in these cities appears to vary, the fact that they exist is not disputed.

All hijras in India seem to belong to one of seven primary (social and physical) houses.[22] Membership is conferred through and symbolized by "putting a *rit*." The literal meaning of the term is "custom," but in this instance it signifies a symbolic kinship link with a particular hijra house. All real hijras are expected to "put a *rit*" in one of these houses. This process involves a specific ritual involving the elders of the particular house, the aspiring hijra, and her guru, or immediate superior (see chapter 7 for details of this ritual and hierarchy). Almost the first question asked of all hijras is "[In] which house did you put the *rit*?" Each city might have one or more of these houses represented; all hijras from that city would then be members of those houses. Each of these lineage houses have several, separate households that they subsume, each with its own hierarchy.

This hierarchy includes a nayak (senior leader), gurus (teacher/leader), and celas (disciples), with the former being the most senior member, followed by her celas, who are in turn the gurus of other hijras who serve as their celas in an iterative pattern of relatedness. While there is only one nayak per household, there might be two or three of her celas, and many more of her nati celas (grand-celas) living under the same roof. The status hierarchy (nayak, followed by her celas, and then her nati celas) is evident in all respects, with the nayak being accorded due respect by those lower than her in the hierarchy. Nayaks serve not only as the heads of their respective households, but together constitute a council for the arbitration of disputes, the conferring of titles, and the representation of their symbolic house in any interregional hijra event. The line of descent for this title follows the cela genealogy, with the most respected, just, and capable of a nayak's celas being given the responsibility after her death.

Hijras occupy the most strikingly visible dimension of koti identity. For this reason they have come to embody the quintessential third-gendered role in India, and any attempt (including mine in some respects) to theorize sexual and gender difference in this part of the world has invariably come to start from this locus of identity. In popular understandings as well, any and every "cross-dressed" man on the street is identified as a hijra. This simple reductionism does not really reflect the range of identities that crosscuts this space and the plurality of differences that go into constructing these individuals' lives. While hijras may be the most dramatic, the differences they embody clearly do not serve as the only axes of identity in the sexual or social universe of Hyderabad.

Zenana Kotis: Blurring the Gender Domain

The first time I heard the term *zenana*, it was mentioned by Munira, my hijra friend, in the context of outlining the difference between "us" (hijras), and a pant-and-shirt-wearing koti who had just walked up to chat with another hijra: "[He] has a *rit* in the zenana," she said. The term *zenana* refers specifically to the female domain and was (and still is) used to refer to that part of the Muslim household that was set off for women, as opposed to the *mardana*, or the area for *mard* (men). In addition to a spatial connotation, it also refers to the collective of women (*zenana*) as opposed to men (*mardana*). In the present context though, this term was used specifically with reference to an individual or group of individuals, different from but "related" to hijras—part of their koti family.

Journal entry, June 22, 1997: Finally, BR took me to meet "one of the zenana nayaks," or leaders. It was three o'clock in the afternoon and very hot. I was doubtful that anyone would be sitting around in the middle of PG (Public Garden) in this heat, but BR was sure she would find him here.[23] She took me to a particular spot toward the western corner of the garden, and sure enough, there he was—Zarina, the zenana nayak. I had heard his name mentioned before, usually in the context of my learning more about zenana kotis, but had never actually met him. He is a big, imposing man with a thick bushy beard. He was dressed in a white *pathan* suit and had a cloth folded over his head.[24] He had a skullcap under this cloth, such as that worn by all devout Muslim men, though he might have had the cloth on primarily because of the heat. Given the other kotis I had met, he struck me as looking somewhat incongruous as a koti. He told me that he was a zenana *baiji*, the equivalent of a hijra senior leader or nayak "in this line."[25] He had a number of celas in his name. He seemed extremely suspicious of me and refused to say anything substantial until he had "checked with the hijra nayaks and got their permission" to speak to me. He was also somewhat drunk or at least was reeking of alcohol, as were the four other kotis (also zenana kotis as I discovered later) who were with him.

As it turned out, Zarina was a somewhat atypical zenana koti. It was true that he had been a zenana *baiji*, but, as I later found out, he had been removed from that position largely because of his nonconformity to the ideal zenana mould. He looked unabashedly masculine with his heavy beard, large build, his clothing, general bearing and demeanor, and, as another zenana told me disparagingly, "Just like a man, he [openly] drank alcohol." In addition, not only was he married (to a woman), his exploits "chasing pantis" were well known in koti lore. Some time during 1996 he apparently set himself on fire in a jealous rage over his panti's philandering, a fact that apparently contributed further to his vilification. According to Iqbal, another zenana *baiji*, Zarina was a "*randi* [a crude word for a female prostitute], a garden koti." By this, he was referring specifically to the koti cruising area, the Public Garden or "garden" as it was commonly called, where I actually met Zarina. More important, Iqbal was denigrating the public enactment of koti desire, "chasing pantis," likening it to (female) prostitution. As he stated categorically with respect to these zenanas:

There are different *pes's* [lifestyles] in this "line." If one marries, has children, leaves them and comes, sitting in the garden, eating, drinking, fighting with one another, chasing pantis. Those are different. They are living like *berupias*. If they come into this line, then they should forget other things. That is not there with these people. That is all the work that these people do. That is why [we] do not make these people *baijis* [leaders]. There are these types also: those who are married and live at home. When they come to the zenana, they sing and dance, play, talk, and things. They have a different *pes*. Then there is me. I have no father, no children, and I am not married. I'm living like a *bal-kumari* [young, chaste girl].

What this statement reveals apart from the criteria of zenana authenticity, are hierarchies of gendered valuation. The last *pes*—Iqbal's lifestyle—is clearly the most highly valued, followed by the married-but-still-dancer zenanas. The "garden" zenanas are the most disparaged, not only on account of their having left the "dance line" but also by virtue of their apparent sexual desire. Both hijras and zenanas used an idealized rhetoric of asexuality; in reality, however, there were different sexual arrangements. This apparent ambivalence regarding their engagement in sexual practice is an issue I return to in the next chapter. For the present purposes, it appeared that almost all zenanas had pantis, but some were more willing than others to confess that fact.

Unlike hijras, however, zenanas do not openly present themselves as visibly "othered" to the general public. More often than not they wear pants and a shirt or a *pathan* suit (kada-catla clothes in their vocabulary) and cannot be sartorially identified as kotis. Most of them are clean-shaven, but unlike hijras, they do not necessarily pluck out their facial hair in an attempt to reduce hair growth. Their gestures and movements (*cal-calan*) are virtually indistinguishable from those of pantis. However, this masculine performance is often restricted to particular social contexts. When they get together with other zenanas, their speech patterns and hand gestures appear to undergo a marked change. They "are kotis now," as one of them stated,

A zenana koti dancer

and mark this identity by "performing" the hijra hand-clapping gesture and engaging in exaggerated feminine gestures and styles of speech. Contrary to their individual presentations of self (see Goffman 1973), as a group they do not appear to fear being identified as kotis or teased and harassed by the non-koti public.

Another factor that contributes to their "passing" is the zenanas' living arrangement. Unlike hijras, they do not all live together. Each has his own family and physical dwelling, and they only get together for special occasions or to cruise for sex at night in the garden. For the most part, they live with their natal families, who might guess but do not often publicly acknowledge their alternate lifestyle. While zenanas are not a "community" in the spatial sense of the term, their perception of commonality with respect to aspects of identity creates a shared space in their imaginations (Anderson 1983). Two such criteria of similarity are their occupation and the *rit*.

Zenana kotis do not physically emasculate themselves; that is, they are not *nirvan sultans* and therefore do not see themselves as necessarily having recourse to divine power. Their occupation, at least historically, was restricted to entertainment. As they describe it, they and not the hijras, were the traditional "singers and dancers," an occupation that hijras apparently "stole from [them]" (see also Cohen 1995b; Jaffrey 1996; Hall n.d.) "Everyone used to come to us and ask us to sing for them. Everyday we used to give performances. And the dances, don't even ask me about the dances! Now, everything has changed. The primary goal is to have fun with men rather than perpetuate the singing/dancing tradition," lamented Arif Khan, one of the oldest and most respected zenanas in Hyderabad. Although many individuals "in the dance line" are zenanas, this does not amount to more than about sixty or seventy "real" zenanas living in Hyderabad today according to Jamaluddin, a well-known zenana dancer.

The zenanas' training in dance appears to be tied to a tradition of urban, lower-caste/class burlesque performance with elements of various Indian classical dance styles such as *bharatnatyam*, *kathak*, and *kuchipudi*. They still give public performances, but in addition to classical elements, their programs incorporate modern dance styles and are set to the latest hits from Hindi movies, with vigorous hip-thrusting and overt sexual gestures, even though many of the dancers have been or claim to be classically trained. The dancers are usually invited or commissioned to perform for specific functions, mostly for male audiences at secular celebrations, such as a party to celebrate a promotion. Obviously this form of entertainment is still quite popular, because it appears to be the sole means of support for zenana dancers.

The single most important criterion for belonging to the zenana community, apart from an ostensible dancing tradition, is that of having a *rit*. When differentiating themselves (and being differentiated by hijras), zenanas are referred to as "those kada-catla kotis [non-sari-wearing kotis] who have a *rit*." While zenanas have their own system of establishing kinship within the zenana community (what they refer to as *man-pan*), almost all zenanas have a *rit* in a hijra house. They become the disciple, or cela, of one of the hijras in that house and claim authenticity and izzat by virtue of this kinship link. This is their marker of difference from other kada-catla kotis and *berupias*, and one that garners them considerable respect in the eyes of hijras.

In addition to their *rit*, zenanas also have their own structural community, complete with hierarchical positions, initiation rituals, rules of comportment, and specific kin alignments. Like hijras, zenanas also have houses that are both social/symbolic structures and physically existing households, even if zenanas do not necessarily *live* there together. The leader or head of all zenanas in Hyderabad is known as the *caudhary*, and below him in importance each zenana house has its head of household, known as *baiji*. Currently, there is only one zenana leader and four heads of household for the remaining houses in Hyderabad. Earlier, some of the zenanas contended, there were at least fourteen houses in the city, each with its own head, or *baiji*, and his numerous disciples.

Of late, the numbers have dwindled because the primary goal today is to "have fun with men" rather than perpetuate the zenana tradition of singing and dancing, as Arif Khan and others lamented. Not only has the demand for their traditional occupation declined, but zenanas do not see the benefits, either material or symbolic, as sufficient for the trouble necessitated in becoming a *baiji* and maintaining a zenana house. Salman, one of the few remaining zenana dancers, could have become the head of one of the houses, he said. In fact, he did consider taking over leadership of one house after the death of the previous *baiji*. But he soon decided that "becoming a *baiji* and running a house is not worth the effort any more," and he "declined" the honor. "It is too expensive, because you have to pay for all your celas' functions, and nobody gives you respect [izzat] for all the trouble you take," he said. To date, there is no *baiji* in this house, and it is widely believed that, like other such houses, this house too will rapidly fall into disrepair and eventually be lost forever.

Given their present living arrangements and solitary performative genre, estimates of zenana numbers are extremely problematic. But according to some old-timers, there may be two or three hundred zenanas in Hyderabad alone. Accurate assessments are complicated by the fact that there is much slippage between the various "identities" within the koti family, with individuals claiming more than one at any given time (see chapter 8, where I explore the range of individuals who shift and negotiate their identities along this spectrum).

Kada-Catla Kotis: "Kings by Day, Queens by Night"
It was six o'clock in the evening. Kandra hijras (sex workers) at the tank were getting ready for their evening's activities. They were bustling about,

tying on their false hair, getting their saris ironed by the neighborhood *istriwala* (person who irons clothes for a living), and borrowing eyeliner and talcum powder from each other, all of these activities accompanied by loud, contentious negotiations and frequent fights. In the midst of this activity, a person wearing pants and a shirt and carrying a cloth bag, his shoulder-length hair bundled into a cap, walked into this area. As soon as he walked in, he touched the elders' feet, repeating the requisite hijra greeting, "I touch your feet." He then proceeded to "get ready." He changed into a blouse that he pulled out of his bag and quickly tied on a borrowed sari, obviously adept at this task. He then patted some "phanking," or pancake/foundation, onto his clean-shaven face and finished up by applying bright red lipstick. Puzzled, I inquired about him and was told, somewhat disparagingly, "He is a kada-catla koti. But he comes here in the evening every day for [sex] work. He is a king by day, and queen by night."[26]

"Are *gandus* and kada-catla kotis the same?" I asked my hijra friend Munira one day, a few months after I started fieldwork. "Yes, they are the same," she replied, without any hesitation. "We call those [kotis] who do not have a *rit, gandus*. You know what the term means, don't you?" she added, somewhat hesitantly. The term *gandu*, derived from *gand*, or ass, literally means "one who uses his ass." It is a highly pejorative term and used by hijras only in either abusive, derogatory contexts, or humorous, self-denigratory ones. It is the more pejorative term to refer to kada-catla kotis. Although anal sex is an important aspect of their sexual repertoire, hijras never refer to themselves in a self-aggrandizing way as *gandus*. Hijras are the more respected, sari-wearing (catla) kotis who sing and dance for a living and share kinship bonds with each other. *Gandus*, on the other hand, are the kada-catla men who enjoy "homosex." Their sexual desire—the *degree* of desire as much as object choice—seems to be the most salient identifying criteria, at least in the eyes of hijras. Kada-catla kotis appear to agree with this characterization, stating that they "are in this line for the sex and excitement." While this may be universally acknowledged, there are clearly differences between kada-catla kotis in terms of class, upbringing, means of livelihood, and especially the degree to which they associate their identity with transnational idioms and therefore see themselves as part of the "global gay" community.[27]

Kada-catla kotis seemed to be the most numerous of the various kotis in Hyderabad. For the most part, they are only recipients in a (male-male) sexual relationship. By contrast, the few who said they "were both active and passive" tended to identify themselves as "gays" or "homosexuals" (mentioning the English terms explicitly).[28] For the most part, these self-identified

Kotis in the Public Garden

gay men were wealthier, more educated, and often English-speaking, al-though this was by no means true of all kada-catla kotis or gay men. This difference was marked by language use (English versus Telugu or Hindi) and, more importantly, by knowledge and use of the Farsi or koti vocabulary (Hall 1995), regarding which many self-identified gay men in Hyderabad professed their ignorance. In addition, gay men's terms of self-reference and their unwillingness to acknowledge and enact a consciously feminine public presentation of self set them apart in certain respects from other kada-catla kotis. In the Public Garden (the public space that many kotis fre-quented in a bid to find partners), they had their own group. While there was some acknowledgment of koti membership among the various subgroups, they often socialized separately. Some of the gay men had started their own organization, Sathi (meaning "companion" in Hindi), and they held support-group meetings twice a month in a specific corner of the garden.[29] The meetings did not seem to be very well attended by the larger kada-catla koti population, who often denigrated these upper-class enactments of same-sex desire.[30]

In their conversations with me, gay-identified kotis, in turn, would often disparage other kotis and hijras for their perceived lack of global awareness and their traditional ways, including undergoing the *nirvan* operation and institutionalizing kinship links. Part of the self-identified gay group's agenda was "educating these people" about safe sex and HIV/AIDS, a task that they found extremely frustrating because "these people just do not want to listen to anything like this. They are only interested in having fun and don't care about the consequences," said Pratap, an active Sathi member. He acted as a liaison between the gay group and the other kada-catla koti groups, distributing condoms and selling copies of *Bombay Dost*, the most popular English-language gay magazine, to those who could both read it and afford to buy it.[31] Apparently Pratap was the ex-panti of Bala Rao, one of the kada-catla kotis who had recently joined the hijra community. According to Bala Rao, it was because "she" started wearing saris that Pratap left her. As Bala Rao informed me, she was the fourth in the line of Pratap's kotis that he had left because of their preference for female clothing. Apparently Pratap (like other gay men, according to Bala Rao) did not want his sexual partners to dress like women, thereby indexing *one* construction of gay identity—to include (male) dress as a criterion of difference. Clearly a multiplicity of differences (even within each so-called category) go into constructing "sexual difference."

The other (not gay-identified) kada-catla kotis were more numerous than the gay men I met in Hyderabad. They appeared to have closer ties to zenanas and hijras, and self-consciously used the koti vocabulary in conversations with each other. Often it was these individuals who "became" zenanas or hijras later in their lives. As mentioned above, they wore pants and shirts (kada-catla clothes) and were virtually indistinguishable sartorially from pantis. While this was true of the majority of kada-catla kotis, some of them, such as the person mentioned in the opening vignette of this section, wore a sari or some other feminine attire for some part of the day. As this koti told me later, however, he would never be caught in women's clothes outside the spatial and temporal context of the water tank.

Like zenanas, kada-catla kotis do not have the operation, and most of them are married to women and have children. They did not see this as detracting from their koti identity. Given their alternative life, however, some of them were more wary of speaking to me than others. Kada-catla kotis often refused to be photographed, and many of them were scared to talk to me for fear that their secret, "homosex" lifestyle would be revealed.

Other kada-catla kotis, often those who had long-standing, exclusive relationships with men or their "husbands," were quite comfortable speaking to me about their lives and lovers. One such koti was Frank, a self-identified

"Anglo-Indian," middle-aged man who had been married to her husband for a little over twelve years. She always referred to herself and to other kotis in the feminine gender and to her panti as her "husband."[32] Her husband also had a female wife and two children. This fact, however, did not seem to affect Frank's relationship with him. Frank was "crazy about [her] husband," as indicated by her willingness to sell her kidney in order to raise money for this man, much to the chagrin of many of Frank's koti friends. They repeatedly told Frank to "forget this man before he kills you," but Frank was in "no mood" to heed these statements. Despite virtual abandonment and calculated extractions of money by her husband, as well as chronic back pain following her kidney donation, Frank continued to maintain that she was "married to this man, and will always love him till I die."

Kada-catla kotis do not have a *rit* with hijras. They are widely disparaged because of this by hijras and zenanas, who often refer to them pejoratively as *gandus*. Their lack of a *rit* separates them from the hijras and zenanas to some degree and emphasizes the latter's hierarchical evaluations, wherein sexual desire is invested with less importance than other criteria in axes of identity.

Although kada-catla kotis were defined as "those without the *rit*," all of their celebrations, or *dawats*, included many of the other kotis *with rits*, especially zenanas. Kada-catla kotis almost always had their *dawats* in what they now consider "their" space, an open-air spot in a tourist area about fifteen kilometers from Hyderabad, where they have been hosting their *dawats* for over ten years. On the four occasions that I attended their *dawats*, I met people who clearly identified themselves as either zenanas or kotis with *rits*, although hijras themselves almost never attended these functions. Nevertheless, there were definite links between kada-catla kotis and hijras (especially the hijras who engaged in sex work, kandra hijras), evidenced through occasional visits and, as in the case of Bala Rao, temporary switches in identity. These undeniable links and the degree of overlap among these various identities reflect the apparent mobility across categories, an issue I address in greater detail in chapter 8. Such connections index the range of differences that crosscut "sexual" categories, problematizing the positing of sexual difference as independent of and separate from other axes of difference that make up an individual's identity.

Jogins and Siva-Satis: Kotis of the Turmeric Lineage
As I walked into the (Hindu) Goddess Yellamma temple in Hyderabad with one of the hijra sex workers (a former siva-sati), I saw two big-boned,

muscular individuals standing on either side of the main door. The one on the left seemed older. He was wearing a *dhoti* (lower garment worn by older men) and a long shirt, with a scarf draped across his shoulder and head.[33] His forehead had turmeric smeared across it. On the right was another person, wearing a sari and heavy makeup. Both of them were clean-shaven. In front of each was a basket filled with turmeric, vermilion, and what looked like a curled-up snake but was actually a dirty rope with shells tied onto it. They would stop worshippers who passed them on their way out of the temple and, for a token fee, would bless them. They would place the rope over the head of the male or female devotee, recite a little blessing, and smear a pinch of the turmeric and vermilion on his or her forehead. These two individuals did not present themselves as typical men, but they did not seem to be acknowledged as hijras either. On meeting them, the hijra with me did not use the standard hijra greeting, the Muslim *salam aleikum*, but said *kshenarti* instead.[34] When I asked her why, she explained, "These people are not kojjas. They are *jogollu*.[35] That is why I said *kshenarti*."

Every July, the Goddess Yellamma temple in Hyderabad bustles with activity. The occasion is an important Hindu festival in the region—the *bonalu panduga* (literally, the "pot festival," in Telugu). Near the temple premises, one invariably sees a number of sari-clad men (and women), their foreheads smeared with turmeric, dancing as if possessed. These individuals are jogins and siva-satis, still other self- (and hijra-) identified members of the koti family. While they acknowledge this (koti) aspect of their identity, they differentiate themselves from hijras and zenanas on account of their religious affiliation. "We are all Hindus, unlike those [hijra] people, who are Muslims," Lakshmana, the dhoti-clad jogin I saw at the temple, said. "We don't have the *khatna-watna* [circumcision] done, like those people. We are Hindus," Madhava, the other jogin, added. These individuals highlight their Hindu identity by smearing turmeric on their foreheads, and they refer to themselves as belonging to the *bandaram vamsam*, the lineage of those who apply *bandaram* (turmeric). The absence of this marker is considered a transgression of their community rules and occasions a fine. Interestingly though, while their greeting is different from the hijras' (*kshenarti* as opposed to *salam aleikum* or *paon padti hu*), the jogins and siva-satis embrace each other three times on alternate shoulders, a practice often associated with Muslim forms of greeting.

The term *jogin* is often translated as "female ascetic" (Bradford 1983), which indexes not only their gendered role but also their (ideally) asexual lifestyle. *Puttu jogin* refers to the fact that these individuals "are born this

Jogins at the Goddess Yellamma temple

way."[36] The "real" *puttu jogins* are those men who wear female clothing, that is, a sari and blouse, and, what is more important, do not get married except to the goddess. This renunciatory, apparently asexual aspect of their lives is what differentiates jogins from siva-satis. The latter share many of the attributes outlined for jogins, but they also marry women and father children. The marital status of siva-satis does not necessarily mean they do not like to engage in homosexual acts. They "are all kotis, after all," as Shahbaz (an ex-siva-sati who is now a hijra) stated, proceeding to tell me about the previous night's activities. The night before the *bonalu* festival, according to Shahbaz, there was a veritable sexual orgy among siva-satis and their pantis who had gathered for this event.

Jogins too are part of this community, and, despite their asexual rhetoric, they also have pantis, as Shahbaz as well as other siva-satis informed me. Jogins, of course, denied this categorically and positioned themselves as morally superior to siva-satis "who did all these things, chased pantis and everything," as Lakshmana stated. "Siva-satis also have izzat, but we [jogins] have more izzat because we are like this from birth, we wear saris, and we don't get married," said Arjuna, another jogin.

Most jogins (and some siva-satis) wear female clothing, and like hijras, are recognizable on the streets as female-garbed men. Unlike other kotis, however, they do not appear to face as much stigma, perhaps on account of their ostensible connection to the goddess. Almost all these individuals began their stories to me by saying, "We were born this way. When we were very young itself, we used to get possessed by the goddess [literally, "the goddess used to come onto our bodies"], and we have been like this ever since." They emphasized this aspect of jogin identity, their divine possession, in their accounts of their lives, and so did their families, friends, and neighbors. Hijras, on the other hand, do not claim this particular performative aspect of identity. Jogins and siva-satis are usually Hindu men who get possessed by a goddess (Yellamma, one of several meat-eating, single, mother goddesses, is the most important of these), often in early childhood, between the ages of six and twelve or fourteen.[37] Once they know that they are vehicles of the goddess, they apprentice themselves to a member of this community, who then teaches them the ways of jogins or siva-satis.

In terms of the broader koti hierarchy, jogins claimed a status, respectability, and historical authenticity that placed them "maybe a little lower than badhai hijras but for the most part at the same level," and definitely higher than either zenanas or kandra hijras. Siva-satis, they said, had less izzat than they did but potentially had the same amount of izzat as kandra hijras. Siva-satis, on the other hand, did not acknowledge the status differential between jogins and themselves, saying that they were fundamentally the same except that jogins, unlike themselves, "were not given permission by the goddess to get married." Criteria for authenticity and izzat shift, depending on the perspective of the particular person.

Although the two jogins I first met, Lakshmana and Madhava, initially denied their association with hijras, they later acknowledged that they did have a definite kinship link with the badhai or ritual kojjas. Lakshmana is the contemporary, or *gurubhai*, of the present head (Irfan) of one of the

Sheharwala houses, and Madhava is currently Irfan's disciple, or cela. Other jogins I met corroborated this link; many of them had official (if informal) *rits* in the various hijra houses. While they did not visit often, on special occasions such as the Muslim festival of Muharram, jogins were invited to socialize with hijras and even received gifts from the latter. The senior hijra leaders, on the other hand, never openly acknowledged this kin tie. In fact, attending the *bonalu* festival is considered a crime among hijras, incurring a stiff fine. Last year, Rani, an ex-jogin who is now a badhai hijra (and Irfan's cela), had to pay eleven hundred rupees because word got back to her nayak that she had danced along with other jogins at the Yellamma temple during the festival. Clearly, there is some ambivalence regarding kinship relations between these various gender categories.

Like zenanas and kada-catla kotis, jogins and siva-satis too do not live together as one community in the spatial sense of the term. They each have their own homes, living either with their parents, wives and families, or alone. The only time all of them meet as a group is during the pilgrimages, or *jatras*, they undertake as part of their ritual identity (cf. Handelman 1995; J. Flueckiger, pers. comm.). There are five *jatras* that are of primary importance to them, each to a specific temple site in Andhra Pradesh. These *jatras* occur at various times of the year, and sometimes only once in two or three years. Some individuals may go on other *jatras*, but these five are the most important, and jogins are encouraged to attend all of them if possible. It is on these *jatras* that they socialize as kotis most extensively. Many of the jogins I met attending the festival at the temple in Hyderabad had come specifically for this purpose and were returning to their native places as soon as the festivities were concluded.

While there appeared to be a definite structure to their community—a hierarchy of leaders and disciples and possibly a grand leader, or *caudhary*—I could not obtain categorical, unambiguous information regarding this issue. Not only did I encounter these kotis only toward the end of my period of fieldwork, but since they only come together as a community for pilgrimages or festivals I found it difficult to meet them on an everyday basis. Many of them live with their natal families or affinal kin in one of the several middle-class neighborhoods in the city, only meeting infrequently with their other koti friends. Nevertheless, I was also told by some jogins that they did have a head, or *caudhary*, named Muthamma, who had several celas, both men *and* women (Bradford 1983). This does appear to be one group of kotis where extensive commingling between men and women occurs. Unlike other kotis, gender does not seem to interfere in the establishment of relationships among jogins such as guru and cela. As one (female) jogin said to me, "We are all the same; some are women and others are kotis, but we are all jogins in the end."

BEYOND THE KOTI/PANTI AXIS: "ALTERNATING" AC/DCS

As the opening vignette of this chapter indicated, in addition to pantis, kotis, and narans, there appeared to be another group, AC/DCs, that hijras (and most kotis) defined themselves against. AC/DCs, or "double-trick *gandus*," were highly disparaged characters in the hijras' universe. Other colloquial terms for these individuals were "double-deckers," or the Telugu phrase *esudu-theesudu*, "putting in and taking out." An AC/DC was one who both "took and gave" (*lete bhi, dete bhi* [see Cohen 1995a, 1995b]) and could be either a penetrating or penetrated partner in a sexual encounter. These individuals seemed particularly vilified by hijras, and my efforts to learn more about them were either ignored or treated with outright disbelief: "What do you need to know about those people for? They are not good people, and we [hijras] do not go with them. It is only these *gandus* who encourage them," I was repeatedly told, in a contemptuous tone of voice.

AC/DCs or double-trick *gandus* were *especially* disparaged by hijras who were *nirvan sultans* and therefore saw themselves (and were seen by most other hijras/kotis) as being of higher status. They claimed to have nothing whatsoever to do with AC/DCs. They did, however, mention that non-operated, or *akkva*, hijras occasionally had sex with them. As one of the *nirvan* hijras told me, "I don't know what they do with each other, but *chi!* It's disgusting." Given the disapprobation surrounding sex with an AC/DC, the *akkva* hijras were not enthusiastic about acknowledging their "disgusting" sexual proclivities. Thus it was difficult for me to get any systematic and substantive information on this other sexual identity, but their disparagement makes this identity particularly interesting for the way it reflects and refracts constructions of hijra/koti authenticity.

HIJRA-IMPERSONATING *BERUPIAS*: DOUBLE MIMESIS

"Those damn *berupia* people! They are *men*. They just wear a sari and steal our money," Lata, a badhai hijra said extremely contemptuously to me one day. She was referring to those who apparently "impersonate" hijras and "steal" their rightful earnings by singing and dancing in their place (*berupias*, literally, people of a "different form/face"). According to hijras, *berupias* are essentially men who pass as hijras by wearing female clothing and adopting exaggerated feminine gestures and movements. They travel around the city in groups and engage with or force their presence on the families of newlyweds, much as hijras do. They sing and dance on these occasions and, like hijras, end by blessing the couple (or a child) with fertility. Almost every time *berupias* roamed a neighborhood in search of houses where there was a newlywed couple or a newborn child, it was when hijras were unable to be there. During the Muslim festival of Muharram or when one of the hijra nayaks in Hyderabad died, for instance, *berupias* reaped the benefits of the hijras' absence by passing themselves off as a hijra group. On the one occasion that they were caught by hijras, they were severely beaten up, as Lata told me proudly.[38] Unfortunately, I only learned of their activities after they had occurred, so I never did encounter a *berupia* troupe. Since their identity is based on hijra *impersonation*, they would not publicly confess to being *berupias*, presuming, of course, that this does function as a self-referential label. Nevertheless, like AC/DCs, *berupias* are interesting largely because of hijras' intense condemnation of this identity and for what it reveals about constructions of masculinity and hijra authenticity. Not only do *berupias* transgress the primary axis of sexual differentiation— that is, they are men, or pantis, and not kotis (like AC/DCs)—but they also transgress the secondary performative gender boundary: They are men who impersonate women without any of the feminine behavioral attributes that supposedly justify this gender crossing, as in the case of hijras.[39] According to hijras, *berupias* are men, anatomically, chromosomally, hormonally, and more important, in terms of behavior or practice. Most of them are married men with children who do not engage in homosexual acts or have the embodied "desires and habits of a woman." For hijras, this transgression is apparently greater than that of AC/DCs, who, after all, only blur the sexual axis of difference.

Against this hijra accusation of spurious identity, the narratives of all such supposedly mimetic and "false" hijras—*berupias* in Hyderabadi hijras' accounts as well as *jankhas* in Lawrence Cohen's (1995a) work in Banaras, zenanas in Lynton and Rajan's (1974) earlier account in Hyderabad, and kotis in Kira Hall's (n.d.) work in Delhi—challenge this assertion of inauthenticity. Whatever the veracity of these accounts—a question that I contend is neither interesting nor productive to explore in this context— the very fact that they differ highlights the contextual nature of "authentic" third-sex identity. As Cohen notes, the very existence of such challenges "pushes us to avoid enlisting groups like hijras or *jankhas* [or *berupias*, zenanas, and kotis] in grand touristics of gender difference without challenging what is at stake for each gender" (1995b, 278). All thirdness, as he states, is not alike.

RE-THEORIZING SEXUALITY AND GENDER DIFFERENCE: A FEW PRELIMINARY COMMENTS

In his article and subsequent book on Brazilian *travestis*, or "transgendered prostitutes," Don Kulick argues for a re-theorization of gender difference, grounded "not so much on sex (as in modern northern European and North American cultures) as on sexuality" (1997, 575), where "sex" refers to the anatomy or genitals, and "sexuality" refers to "the role the genitals perform in sexual encounters" (579). Based on research among *travestis* in Salvador, Brazil, Kulick argues that these individuals, as effeminate, penetrated partners (as opposed to the men who penetrate them) reconfigure the gender system from the categories men and women, to that of men and not-men. In this schema, men are those who are the penetrators, and the latter—not-men—is a category "into which both biological females and males who enjoy anal penetration are culturally situated" (Kulick 1997, 1998; for elaborations on *activo-passivo* distinctions and Latino/Mexican/Chicano male sexualities, see Almaguer 1994; Carrier 1995; Lancaster 1995; Murray 1995; Green 1999; Parker 1999; Carillo 2002).

As with Kulick's *travestis*, the locus of gender difference among kotis in Hyderabad does appear at first glance to be the act of penetration. Kotis differentiate between themselves as effeminate, penetrated partners in a male, same-sex encounter, and pantis, or the "men" who penetrate them. In other respects too, kotis see themselves as aligned with women, or narans, in their relationships with men. The gendering of the panti/koti divide is evident in the latter's terms of self-reference, their performance of "women's work" (cooking, sewing, and cleaning for their husbands), gendered patterns of abuse, and sartorial/presentational inclinations, among other factors.

While the act of penetration is a relevant axis of gender difference for kotis in Hyderabad, it is clearly just that—*one* axis of difference, making it inadequate to completely understand and theorize difference. This act is not only insufficient as the only marker of sexual/gender difference, but, on a broader level, sexuality itself is not the only axis around which these individuals configure their identities. Five issues present themselves here to complicate one's understanding in this respect: (*a*) using the axis of penetration, some kotis can be defined as pantis; (b) the criterion of sexual difference aside, kotis and pantis share other axes of sameness that they consider integral to their identity; (c) fluidity in identity means that individuals have shifting and multiple nodes in their self-crafting; (d) hijra and koti constructions of ideal (companionate) marriages emphasize emotional intimacy rather than sexual intimacy as the "tie that binds"; and (e) perhaps the greater disparagement of *berupias* in relation to AC/DCs indicates that it is not merely the axis of sexual performance that accounts for the existing differences in status and identity across the koti continuum.

What happens to those among the kotis who are married and have children? If penetration is in fact the sole axis of difference, those who "penetrate" women would be categorized as pantis rather than kotis in this schema. Most of the zenanas and kada-catla kotis and some siva-satis had wives and children, yet still described themselves as kotis. How does one account for this divergence? Obviously, seeing sexuality as the only baseline of difference does not result in a complete understanding of sexual/ gender difference. Only by analyzing the radically different desires, choices, and lived experiences of these individuals—by "engaging the body in the gender . . . [and] locating it within a multiplicity of differences" (Cohen 1995b, 295)—can one begin to understand the various and at times conflicting axes that construct identity for these individuals.

Linked to the above is another confounding and potentially destabilizing factor: individuals who occupy different ends of the sexual spectrum along the axis of penetration, can and do share axes of sameness that they consider fundamentally important to their construction of themselves. Munira sees herself as a Muslim not so much by virtue of her "hijra-ness," as by the religion of her "husband," Zahid. "I became a Muslim because of Zahid. Otherwise, how could I cook beef for him," she said. Place of birth is an important criterion of identity for others, who choose not only their husbands on this basis, but also their koti identity. Surekha became a hijra (as opposed to another koti identity) primarily because the only koti she knew in Hyderabad was a hijra from her village, leading her to choose this identity. Language, class, and age also serve as important axes of identity, along with shared everyday practices such as drinking. While the act of sexual penetration is clearly an important axis of difference, it conceals both the range of competing, intersecting axes and the embeddedness of sexual/ gender difference in other forms of difference.

Further, although hijras and kotis are officially located outside the bounds of a legal (same-sex) marriage, a long-lasting and emotionally intimate relationship with a man is perhaps their most longed-for relationship, serving as a powerful motivating factor in their everyday lives. In their ideal constructions of this "companionate marriage," kotis and especially hijras appear to differentiate between sexual desire and emotional intimacy. As I explain in chapters 7 and 8, sexual desire/pleasure was not the only basis of their relationships with their "husbands"; companionship, caring, and emotional intimacy were the preeminent ideals desired. While sexual desire and practice were important, they were not the most important elements in their constructions of themselves and of their desires and practices as kotis/hijras.

In addition, a qualitative difference was apparent in the way hijras reacted to *berupias* as opposed to AC/DCs that was not entirely subsumable under potential economic threat. While AC/DCs did evoke exclamations of disapproval and were stigmatized by hijras, it was *berupias* who garnered virtual disgust and ostracism. *Berupias* were "men," I was repeatedly told, without any of the female-gendered, etiological referents that hijras and other kotis invoked in their constructions of identity. The reiteration by hijras and kotis of the differences between *berupias* and AC/DCs in this manner supports the argument that it is not *merely* sexual performance—or "sexuality" in Kulick's terminology—that accounts for hijra/koti identity.

Finally, quite apart from the complexity derived from intersecting axes of difference is that complexity resulting from the relative fluidity of boundaries across these divides. Individuals who identified themselves as kada-catla kotis for instance, did not necessarily perceive axes of hijra identity as beyond their range of identification. Bala Rao, for example, identified herself as a kada-catla koti, or as "homosex," or "gay" on some occasions, and yet she lived, acted out, and enjoyed the identity of a hijra without apparent dissonance. Nagesh was a self-identified kada-catla koti as well as the "daughter" of one of the hijras. Similarly, Iqbal clearly saw himself as a zenana *baiji*, but at times he went and stayed with his guru, the hijra nayak, and performed his role as a hijra cela. Srinivas was a siva-sati before he became a hijra, a fact that results in his practice of both identities in different spatial and situational contexts. Most of these people recognize differences among these identities, but that does not appear to preclude the enactment of two or more of them.

Significantly, the negotiation of identity appeared to occur primarily among kotis rather than across the koti/panti divide, which seemed to be relatively less permeable. Although there were instances of a married man "becoming" a hijra, these were few and occasioned much derision on the part of other hijras. "Ruining a woman's life by marrying and then becoming a hijra is the biggest sin," Shanti told me. As this indicates, different valences may be attributed to varied axes of identity. However, the fluidity of perceived self-representation among kotis clearly precludes any easy reading of difference as merely sexual or gendered. Axes of identity and their salience in an individual's life shift, not just spatially, but categorically and temporally as well, with different configurations of identity emerging at different points in the life course.

4

Sacred Legitimization, Corporeal Practice

HINDU ICONOGRAPHY AND HIJRA RENUNCIATION

Madhavi was one of the first hijras I met in Hyderabad. She was living under the water tank at the time, along with other hijra sex workers.[1] From the beginning, she was extremely warm and friendly, talking openly and easily to me about her desires, frustrations, and life as a hijra. In one of our first interactions, she told me the following as an account of one part of her life.

Journal entry: Madhavi was born in a village in the Nizamabad District of Andhra Pradesh. Her name at birth was Madan. She used to "really like doing women's work," such as cooking, sweeping, cleaning, and playing with girls as a child. She also loved to dance, and, having "trained" herself in Bharatanatyam (a classical form of Indian dance), she used to work as a dance instructor in her local school. When she was eighteen or nineteen, one of her male friends brought her to Hyderabad and, for a measly sum of fifteen hundred rupees, "left" her in the care of senior hijras in the Sheharwala house in Hyderabad.[2] She was imprisoned in this hijra house for five years, not being allowed out at all lest she run away. Her family, not knowing her whereabouts, presumed she was dead and hung a garland on her photograph at home. Two years after she came to Hyderabad, she had her *nirvan* (physical genital excision) operation. Following this radical surgery, she had no choice but to join the community forever, wear female attire, and engage in badhai work (singing and dancing at marriage/birth ceremonies). She underlined the fact that she was not involved in prostitution when she first joined the hijra community. In answer to my question, she said she could not go back home because that would have been shameful, given that she had had the *nirvan* operation and was a "real" hijra. Madhavi is now twenty-six years old and has been an "official" hijra for seven years.

This account is interesting for a number of reasons. First, in substantive terms, it focuses attention on one of the most ubiquitous myths surrounding hijras, namely, their recruitment patterns (i.e., whether hijra membership is a voluntary act or one of forced conversion). Second, it refers to some of the important criteria of membership within the hijra community, such as the dress code and *nirvan* operation, as well as highlighting the stigmatized nature of this conversion in the eyes of "normative" Indian society. Third, and perhaps most interestingly, this construction of her life turned out to be just that—a fabrication concocted by Madhavi for my benefit. She had not had the operation at the time she told this story, nor had she ever engaged in the ritual practices of singing and dancing, hijras' badhai work.

Significantly, the use of their bodies for purposes of sex work or badhai work and their status as *nirvan sultans* (operated hijras) were the only two issues that some of the other hijras also seemed to consistently fabricate in their constructions of self and authenticity. These two issues appear to be highly salient markers of identity and izzat for hijras. In this chapter, I focus on these issues and the corporeal nature of hijra identity in terms of the hierarchy of the roles of (asexual) ritual performer and (sexual) prostitute; the idealization of asexuality; and, finally, the necessity of corporeal transformation as a criterion of asexuality/authenticity.

THE PRAGMATICS OF EROTIC ASCETICISM: HIJRA SEXUAL HIERARCHIES

AMIR NAYAK: Real hijras are those whose bodies [sexual organs] have no strength and who should have no mental or physical desire for men whatsoever. We are like sannyasis. This is what is important.
ALIYA: All hijras desire men. Otherwise why do they become hijras? Those who say, "We do not do this," they are lying.

Interestingly, both of these statements were made by hijras. The former was made by one of the senior leaders or nayaks, and the latter was made by one of the much-disparaged hijra sex workers. How does one reconcile these apparently conflicting statements made by individuals who occupy the same cultural universe? Three issues seem to be involved here: At one level, these statements reference the izzat hierarchy within the hijra community wherein the sex workers (kandra hijras) have lower respect than the non–sex workers (badhai hijras). To some extent, this hierarchy appears to reflect a life-historical course, with the supposedly asexual senior nayaks and badhai hijras having "had fun with pantis" when they were younger. This contention was made by younger, sexually active hijras but was reiterated by older zenana kotis as well, although it was loudly denied by badhai hijras themselves. At a broader level, these statements reflect the privileging of asceticism and the tension between (Hindu) sexual and asexual principles and lifestyles, both mythological and "real." Finally, they focus attention on the role of anatomy in inscribing these differences. There appears to be a distinct privileging of bodily enactment in instantiating hijra identity and reinforcing the disjuncture between the asexual sannyasi (ascetic/renouncer) lifestyle of older hijras and the sexually promiscuous, sex-worker lifestyle of younger hijras.[3] Any legitimizing historiography or myth provided by hijras necessarily referenced genital absence as "proof" of authentic asexuality/hijra identity. In this chapter, I examine all three of these issues, namely, the process of traversing the sexual/asexual trajectory from sex worker to sex renouncer, the idealization of asexuality and patterns of sexual ambivalence in (Hindu) myth and life, and the relationship between hijra transformations of the body and the notions of authenticity and identity that they connote.

One day, a week or so after I had started fieldwork in Hyderabad, I was walking home from the bus stop, which was about a mile or so from my father's apartment. About halfway home, I saw three hijras sitting by the road. I still had not met very many hijras and was delighted by this chance encounter. I walked up to them and, after saluting them with the customary respectful *namaste*, asked if I could talk to them. I explained who I was, where I lived, what I wanted to do and answered all their questions about my family and their whereabouts. They told me that they were waiting for a few other hijras who had said they would meet them at this spot at 2:00 P.M., before going on for a badhai (ritual) performance together. I sat and waited with them. At 2:30 P.M., when there was still no sign of the others, the eldest of the three hijras indicated her weariness and left with one of the other hijras, her cela (disciple) as I later learned. I sat and waited with the last of the hijras, Basanti, or Aijaz—a male, Muslim name—as the other hijra slyly suggested I call her before running off to catch up with her guru. In the course of conversation, Basanti asked me whom among the other hijras in Hyderabad I had met. I had only just met the kandra (sex worker) hijras living under the water tank in Secunderabad and told her so. Immediately she said, "*Chi!* Those people. They are very bad people. They do this bad work, and they are not real hijras. Don't go to see them again. Really, I am telling you for your own sake."

A few days later, when I went to see the kandra hijras again, I told them I had met this hijra, describing Basanti, and asked them if they knew her. All of them recognized the name Aijaz, but not Basanti, which I later learned was the name she had acquired after putting the *rit* in the Sheharwala house. Apparently, until just a few months ago, Aijaz used to come to the tank almost every other day "for kandra" with them. They had not seen her in a while, they said, and seemed very surprised when I said she was now performing at badhai ceremonies. "Now that she has become a *pedda manisi* [big/respected] person, I guess she won't be coming here any more for kandra then. I should tell that *bhadva* [pimp] who keeps asking for her," Aliya said, half-jokingly.

Within this frame of reference, the two hijra occupations of kandra and badhai appeared to be ideologically exclusive domains of practice. I was told explicitly that a hijra who engaged in one practice did not under any circumstances engage the other simultaneously. There were a few hijras who might change from one to the other temporarily, but both practices were never engaged in by the same hijra at the same time. In addition, there appeared to be a moral hierarchy between the two occupations, with badhai work and its practitioners being more highly respected than kandra hijras. This hierarchy of respect was explicitly stated by several hijras. With respect to her own nati celas (grand-disciples), Amir nayak had this to say:

Like ascetics [sannyasis], among whom there are real ascetics [*asli* sannyasis] and false ascetics [*naqli* sannyasis] or devils [*saitans*], among the hijras too there are *asli* and *naqli*, good [*accha*] and bad [*bura*] hijras. The good ones are those who live a life of izzat; they look after their guru, they go and ask for badhai and are happy with whatever is given to them by the people. Most important, they do not associate with men and have desire for them. The bad hijras are like these "tanki" hijras. They don't come and live in the nayak's house and continue to do things that are bad and lose their izzat. How many times I have told them. Come and live a life of izzat here in this house, but they do not listen. What can I do?

Surekha, one of the "bad hijras," herself explicitly acknowledged the greater izzat in badhai work when she said, "Here [at the water tank], what izzat do we have? The hijras who do badhai work, those people have more izzat than us." The fact that almost all kandra hijras at the tank initially claimed to be doing badhai work also suggests that they recognize the two occupations as unequal in terms of respect. In answer to an explicit question when I first met her, Munira, a hijra sex worker said, "Why should I lie? In other places they do that [prostitution], but not here. We all go to the *basti* [neighborhood] to sing and dance." Other hijras reiterated Munira's statement, explicitly deriding hijra sex workers in other cities and disclaiming any connection with this occupation. In fact, a few weeks later, during the Hindu festival of Dussehra, hijra sex workers invited me to their village a couple of hours distant from Hyderabad. Here, as "proof" of their statements, the whole group put on a performance wherein they enacted a "badhai scene," from the moment a household was marked for its newborn child to the final payment of the badhai at the end of their performance. At the end of this "play," although it was evident that almost none of the hijra actors knew any of the songs and did not know what to do or say, Munira turned triumphantly to me and said, "*This* is what we do for a living."

Not until a few weeks later did Madhavi tell me that in fact a few hijras living under the water tank were involved in sex work. Even then, she claimed that it was celas (like herself) who were involved in prostitution, while gurus "went to the *basti*" for badhai work. When Munira finally acknowledged their involvement in sex work almost a month after I met her, she still did not admit that it was their current occupation. Instead, she constructed it as a progressive, life-historical process: "I will not lie, Gayatri. We all used to be involved in prostitution before, but now we go to the *basti*," she said.[4]

This construction—that all hijras start out as sex workers and only later in their developmental history do they become badhai hijras—was one that hijra sex workers subscribed to, a construction that Robert Merton refers to, in another context, as a "status-sequence" (1957, 370). These hijras claim that *all* hijras are defined by their desire (for men) and the subsequent enactment of this desire.[5] As Aliya's statement at the beginning of this section attests, hijras who do not acknowledge their desire are believed to be lying. Munira made a similar claim (later in my fieldwork) when she said, "If everyone does not do it [with reference to sex work], then why are they hijras? Some do it for money; some do it for desire. Everyone does it. I don't lie. I washed my hands in the water of the Ganga [the holy river in north India]."

Interestingly, despite their recognition of both the prevailing same-sex desire of all hijras and the lower izzat accruing to kandra vis-à-vis badhai hijras, none of the kandra hijras claimed to be engaged in both occupations simultaneously. When asked, Rajeshwari, a kandra hijra, said, "Are we born knowing how to sing and dance or what? We have to learn gradually, and only then can we do it. That is why we start by doing this work and then slowly, as we learn, we do badhai work." The two activities were always constructed as mutually exclusive, but as kandra hijras contended, they were merely developmental stages, with prostitution, which "all hijras engaged in" early in their lives, leading gradually to the more respected badhai activities. Referring to this temporal and developmental perspective, Munira said, "We haven't seen our *nana-dadis* [grand-gurus] doing it [prostitution]. Us, our *nana-dadis* are seeing, our *gurubhais* [contemporaries] are seeing us do it, but our nati celas will not. Like that. What those people ate, drank, and did we haven't seen. What we are eating, drinking, and doing they are seeing. That is all."

Needless to say, "that" was not "all" for the senior hijras, who did not share this life-historical construction. According to them, the existing occupational variance signaled the difference between real/good hijras and false/bad hijras, as Amir nayak stated. Vanitha, one of the badhai hijras, affirmed the nayak's contention when she said, "It is not like we don't have the opportunity, because there are men around all the time. We rent out these two rooms, so there are men living close by. But we just don't have any desire for men. That is the mark of a real hijra. Not like these 'tanki' people who have husbands and what not around them all the time. *Chi*, that is not good." Rather than signaling "true" hijra identity, as some kandra hijras contended, for the badhai hijras sexual desire implied the opposite—inauthentic hijra identity. "Real" hijras were those who had no sexual desire; by extension, hijras who not only acknowledged their desire but also acted on it were not real or good hijras.

Further, senior badhai hijras used history and the patronage of the Nizam as legitimizing factors in their reiteration of real hijra identity and work. Recounting their days of glory during the "Nizam's *zamana* [period]," that is, from the mid-eighteenth to the mid-twentieth century, many of the more senior badhai hijras and nayaks told me that they had a tremendous amount of izzat at that time, izzat that has been lost in recent years. As Irfan nayak told me,

Every time there was a birth in the royal palace, we used to be called. And during that period, all hijras used to dance and sing so well, I cannot tell you [how well]. And even the Nizam gave us izzat! If a child was born, we were called immediately to bless him. In that period, we hijras had izzat. Nowadays what is it? Nobody knows how to dance, and all these younger hijras want to do is run after men. They have spoiled the name of hijras. *Chi!*

Amir nayak affirmed this sentiment. "It is only in the last twenty-five or thirty years that hijras have started doing this bad work," she said.[6] During the Nizam's rule, *all* hijras were badhai hijras, she claimed, and hijras were highly respected on this account.

However, this (re)construction was not entirely accurate. Sex work as a commodified, economic transaction might be a somewhat recent occurrence, but hijras' enactment of sexual desire is clearly not a "new" practice. Some of the senior-most zenanas, who had cruised with the current hijra nayaks during their youth, explicitly contradicted badhai hijras' version of history. Chuckling at the memory, Arif Khan, one of the zenana leaders, recounted a few of his escapades with two of the current hijra nayaks or leaders. In one instance, one of these nayaks desired a young man in her neighborhood. Dragging her *sahelis* (girlfriends) with her, this nayak used to walk up and down the street outside this man's house, adopting an exaggerated hip-swinging walk and a coquettish manner until, after a week, she had successfully seduced this man.[7] Apparently, the present nayaks had neither been immune to sexual desire, nor had they abstained from acting on it. Perhaps the fact that badhai hijras neither denied that those currently engaged in prostitution were hijras nor refused to allow them to put a *rit* in their house and acknowledge them as celas suggests their acceptance, however reluctant, of both the reality of sexual desire and hijras' engagement in sex work.[8] Nevertheless, it is apparent that badhai work was and still is the more respected, "authentic" hijra practice. It is badhai work that both defines *asli* (real) hijras and gives them izzat, as both badhai and kandra hijras acknowledge. Moreover, it is the asexuality implied by badhai work that is important in defining a real hijra. To quote Amir nayak again, "Real hijras . . . go ask for badhai . . . and live with izzat . . . [They] do not have any desire for men . . . Real hijras are like ascetics. This is what is important."

HINDU IDEALS OF CREATIVE ASCETICISM

Why is asexuality revered as one of the most important aspects of hijra authenticity? What place does this ideal have in the Indian public imaginary? And how does it legitimize hijra identity and practice? Perhaps, in part, the answer to these questions is reflected in the centrality and ubiquity of the ascetic or renunciant ideal in the various epics and tales of Hindu mythology and folklore.[9] As Madeleine Biardeau states in her treatise on Hinduism,

For all religions which contain some form of renunciation of the world, human love and the pursuit of an Absolute situated somewhere beyond the world have been felt to be antagonistic. However, whereas the Gospel is content to oppose God and Mammon, Brahmanic orthodoxy is more radical in opposing *kama* [love/desire] and *moksa* [liberation from the cycle of rebirth], one being solely of this world, the other outside the world. But Hinduism was to rework these elements in all directions, bringing *moksa* into this world by making it possible to live there without *kama* and, conversely, seeking *moksa* in *kama*. (1994, 68)

The two paths within Hinduism that Biardeau references above can be interpreted as *tapas* (asceticism)[10] and *tantra* (or its practice, *tantrism*), respectively. Both seek to attain the final goal of *moksa* but do so through different paths. While the ascetic achieves liberation by renouncing all material goods and worldly ties (i.e., *kama* or desire in all its forms), the tantric achieves liberation through engaging the senses with the material and physical world, placing *kama* at the service of *moksa*. While the path of tantrism was eventually marginalized in the service of post-Buddhist Hinduism, the former path of *tapas* received primary attention in the Vedas and subsequent literature. This is the path with which I concern myself in this chapter, given its salience to hijra ascetic rhetoric and practice.[11]

"Of the variegated connotations of *tapas*, the most significant is that of asceticism," Patrick Olivelle states (1993, 3). This term, deriving from its Sanskrit root *tap*, refers to heat or "ascetic heat," as he translates it. As Olivelle comments, *tapas* refers not only to the process of generating heat (asceticism), but also to the product of that process, namely "magical heat."[12] This "magical heat" possesses a creative, sacred quality from which it derives its power. As such, asceticism is also that process which produces this sacred heat/energy, inextricably associated with fertility and productivity.

"Although in human terms asceticism is opposed to sexuality and fertility, in mythological terms *tapas* is itself a powerful creative force, a generative power of ascetic heat," O'Flaherty notes (1973, 41). In fact, the fertile creative power of ascetic heat is the starting point of many cosmogonic myths. In a creation hymn from the *Rig Veda*, as well as in the *Atharva Veda*, it is from *tapas* that the "One is born" (Blair 1961). Similarly, in the Brahmanas, it is through his *tapas* that Prajapati, the Creator, "creates" fire, air, the sun, and the moon (O'Flaherty 1973). The key to this creative power, however, lies in chastity—an ascetic must remain chaste and renounce sexual desire and practice to generate *tapas*.

The various myths that feature the ascetic who is seduced by a courtesan underline the salience of this belief. One such myth is that of the ascetic Rsysrnga, which appears in several different versions in the sacred texts. In its basic form, the story is as follows. The ascetic Rsysrnga practiced such fierce asceticism that the god Indra, fearing that the sage would depose him through the power of his *tapas*, sent an *apsara* (celestial courtesan) to seduce him.[13] When Rsysrnga saw her, he immediately desired her. She embraced him, and his chastity was destroyed. This theme—the seduction of an ascetic on account of the potential for excess power through his (and less frequently, her) *tapas*—is repeated in several of the Vedic texts (O'Flaherty 1973, 2000;

cf. Khandelwal 1996, 2001). A similar theme appears in the myth in which Kama, the god of love, is burnt to ashes by the wrath of Siva for daring to distract him from the pursuit of asceticism (O'Flaherty 1973; Das 1977; see also Knipe 1975). All of these myths emphasize two basic points: the role of *tapas* in generating sacred (creative) power, and the potential opposition between *tapas* and *kama* or asceticism/renunciation and desire/eroticism.

The creative power of *tapas* is well demonstrated in the early cosmogonic myths whereby Prajapati creates the world. As Wendy O'Flaherty notes, the Brahmanas clearly set out this creative process: "Prajapati was alone here in the beginning. He wished, 'May I exist, may I reproduce myself.' He exerted himself and performed *tapas,* and when he was exhausted and heated, the waters were created from him, for waters are born from the heated man. The waters said, 'What is to become of us?' He said, 'You shall be heated.' They were heated and created foam," and so on in the creative process (quoted in O'Flaherty 1973, 41).

A related form of creation resulting from *tapas* and chastity is the production of rain. In the myth of Rsysrnga noted above, his chastity gives him the power to produce rain. Similarly, in the *Mahabharata,* the sage Agastya uses his *tapas* to cause the god Indra to send rain. Indra in turn is said to "derive his cosmic forces from rain" (O'Flaherty 1973, 22). In these as well as other myths in the Vedas and the epics, *tapas* is clearly associated with various forms of creation—of water, of organic life, and paradoxically, of erotic/procreative power. *Tapas,* in all of these formulations, provides the ascetic or renouncer with greater sexual power—the power that gives him the potential for (pro)creative abilities as well as the right to use such power to good effect. As Siva says to Parvati, "By *tapas* one wins *kama*" (O'Flaherty 1973). Even in the *Kamasutra,* that renowned textbook of eroticism, this concept, "so basic to *all* Hindu thought, emerges: the successful lover . . . obtains his powers by great meditation" (quoted in O'Flaherty 1973, 55; emphasis in original).

Not surprisingly, this paradoxical source of (male) sexual power was commented upon both by colonial officers as well as missionaries in India. As Abbe Dubois noted with distaste at the turn of the century, "By one of those contradictions which abound in Hindu books, side by side with the account of the punishments inflicted on a hermit for his inability to conquer his sensual passions, we find, related with expressions of enthusiasm and admiration, the feats of debauchery ascribed to some of their *munis* [ascetic sages] . . . and (burlesque idea!), it is to their pious asceticism that they are said to owe this unquenchable virility" (1959 [1918], 508). As O'Flaherty notes, it is "this very burlesque idea [that] is the core of the nature of Siva, the god of ascetics [who is] permanently ithyphallic, yet perpetually chaste" (1973, 5). This central paradox of Siva as the erotic ascetic is ubiquitous in all Saiva mythology and, despite its apparent logical contradiction, is accepted as a unified if ambiguous concept in Indian thought. As O'Flaherty contends, "the ambiguity of ithyphallicism is possible because, although the erect phallus is of course a sign of priapism, in Indian culture it is a symbol of chastity as well" (1973, 9; cf. Trawick 1990). At the mythological and iconic level, Siva is the god of both ascetics and erotics, giving form to the tension and potential textual resolutions of the paradoxical relationship between *tapas* and *kama*.

Despite the mythological existence of such erotic ascetic figures as Siva, the paradox remains, with *kama* and *tapas* being described in much of the literature as mutually exclusive states or processes. The power derived from *tapas* is sustained by its separation from *kama* through the maintenance of chastity. Chastity or renunciation of sexual activity results in power, but this power is always at the risk of being lost if one is not chaste. It is precisely the tension between *tapas* and *kama* that fuels these myths. How is this paradoxical relation between asceticism and eroticism, which is so prevalent in early Vedic literature, to be explained or resolved? Various solutions were offered in the later Brahmanic texts, although none of them were entirely satisfactory, all of them "suspending" rather than "resolving" the tension between the two poles (O'Flaherty 1973). The two primary mythological and social/practical solutions[14] were the alternating cyclical patterns of asceticism and eroticism evident in Saiva mythology and the proposition of the four-fold *asrama* system.

As O'Flaherty states with respect to the first solution, the alternating cycles of asceticism and eroticism in the myths of Siva do not really provide a solution to the paradox. But, as she adds, "Hindu mythology does not seek any true synthesis. Where Western thought insists on forcing a compromise or synthesis of opposites, Hinduism is content to keep each as it is; one might say that the conflicting elements are resolved into a suspension rather than a resolution" (1973, 318). The second solution, although equally "suspended" in some respects, was the practical/social resolution of the paradox that the creative ascetic posed for Vedic scholars.

As initially conceived, the sannyasin, or renouncer, was a threat to ortho-dox Brahmanical value and practice, insofar as the ideals of renunciation questioned the value of major Brahmanic values and institutions such as marriage, ritual obligation, and the social hierarchy of castes (Olivelle 1993). Ultimately, however, this religious tradition assimilated the role of the san-nyasin into its fold. Attempts were made to find theoretical limitations for the lifestyles of both the renouncer and the householder, the most significant of which was the system of the four *asramas*.[15] Simply stated, the ideal life, according to Vedic scripture, consists of four *asramas*, or stages of life,[16] namely, *brahmacarya*, the period of education and discipleship; *grhastya*, the life of the householder; *vanaprasta*, the life of a hermit, preparatory to the last stage; and *sannyasa* or the life of an ascetic.

In its early (Upanishadic) articulation, given that the renouncer was one who had already extricated himself from the confines of obligation, or *dharma*, the *sannyasa* stage in this conceptualization was not a fourth *asrama* complementing the first three, but a rejection of this-worldly life (Olivelle 1993). In the later Vedic literature, however, this threat was creatively assimilated into the orthodox fold. As Walter Kaelber states, "The fourth *asrama* came to be seen not as a place for those who *have already attained* liberation, but rather as a place in which one *seeks* liberation" (1989, 120; emphasis in original). Asceticism or *tapas* was now prescribed as a means, often the most significant means, of attaining *moksa*.

Commenting on this resolution of the paradox in his influential essay on renunciation in Indian religions, Louis Dumont stated that "the secret of Hinduism may be found in the dialogue between the renouncer and the man-in-the-world" (1960, 37). While Dumont was not the first person to draw attention to these Hindu life-stages, it was his essay that refocused attention on the inherent tension between these ideals as well as their complementarity. Although not every theorist agrees with Dumont's hierarchical articulations, several scholars followed his lead in focusing their attentions on this central tension in myth, in philosophy, and in life (see Khare 1984 for a different reading of this tension). As Romila Thapar was to echo more than twenty years after the publication of Dumont's article, "The essential dichotomy is the opposition between the *grhasta* and the *sannyasin*" (1982, 281), a comment wherein she notes the salience of procreation/celibacy and the nature of social obligations as the defining principles of this dialogue.[17] The central tension in this dialectic then, is that between desire, or *kama*, and its renunciation, or *tapas*, a tension that is reflected in hijra mythology and lived experience.

As O'Flaherty states, "The interrelation of asceticism and desire . . . must be accepted as a unified concept which has been central to Indian thought from prehistoric times" (1973, 9). This tension has fueled not only the *asrama* (life-stages) system, but is also manifestly elaborated in various myths, legends, and folktales throughout India for thousands of years. If "Indian myths constitute a cultural idiom that aids in the construction and integration of one's inner world," as Sudhir Kakar (1989, 135) contends, then the elaboration of the tension between asceticism and eroticism in Indian myth and life is central to the construction of self in this region of the world, for both hijras and non-hijras. Not only are these images available for active constructions of value and practice, but they also serve as a ready resource for historical legitimacy.

Situated as they are in this cultural universe, hijras also use these mythical and iconographic images to legitimize their lives and practices. They explicitly reiterate their ascetic identity and emphasize their affinity with mythological asexual figures. As Amir nayak said to me, "We are like sannyasis. . . . Real hijras . . . have no mental or physical desire for men . . . This is what is important." Further, they see their lifestyle ("going to the *basti* and asking for badhai") as similar in some respects to the ideal life of an ascetic. As Lata told me one day, "We [badhai hijras], we go and ask for money from *duniyadari* [householder] people like you. How much we get depends on their goodness. That is how we make a living," emphasizing in this dialectic the essential complementarity between the householder and the renouncer in the idealized *asrama* system (see Kaelber 1989).

In addition, hijras articulate their affinity with divine figures such as Siva, especially in his *ardhanarisvara* (half man/half woman) form, and the Pandava brother Arjuna in his disguise as Brhannala, the dance teacher/ eunuch in the court of King Virata (van Buitenen 1973).[18] In the course of conversation with me, both Shakuntala and Shanti, tank hijras who prided themselves on having the greatest knowledge of hijra beliefs and customs among hijra sex workers, invoked these connections. Shakuntala said, "We are like Arjuna in his Brhannala incarnation. Some hijras may say, 'not the Brhannala incarnation because that was because of a curse.' But our life is also a curse isn't it?" she added, half-jokingly.

As Alf Hiltebeitel argues, "Arjuna-Brhannala is inescapably the foremost representative of Siva" (1980, 153), revealing through his name, occupation, and physical appearance unambiguous hints of identification with Siva. "As a dancer-musician and eunuch-transvestite [Arjuna/Brhannala] evokes Siva," Hiltebeitel contends (167). Siva, as already mentioned, is the foremost "creative ascetic" (O'Flaherty 1973, 5) or the "eunuch of the firm phallus" (Hiltebeitel 1980, 155). Having established the symbolic connection between Arjuna/Brhannala and Siva, Hiltebeitel goes on to articulate the explicit resonance between these images and those of eunuchs both past and present. "The theme of eunuch-hood resonates throughout the *Mahabharata*," Hiltebeitel claims, "but it is Arjuna as eunuch-transvestite who brings this theme to central stage" (161). After surveying the historical literature regarding hijras/eunuchs, Hiltebeitel states that, like contemporary

Hijras worshipping the Goddess Bedhraj Mata at the tank

hijras, "Arjuna is a eunuch who presides over both a marriage and a birth," that is, the birth of Uttara during the period of his disguise as Brhannala (166). Hiltebeitel concludes by stating that "when eunuchs dance and sing at births and weddings, they mark by their presence the ambiguity of those moments where the non-differentiation of the male and the female is most filled with promise and uncertainty: in the mystery that surrounds the sexual identity of the still unborn child, and in that which anticipates the re-union of the male and the female in marital sex" (168).

Echoing this theme of the eunuchs' auspicious potential stemming from their undifferentiated nature, Shakuntala and Shanti also likened themselves to Sikhandi, another figure in the *Mahabharata* who is a man/woman.[19] These mythical images, as well as that of Arjuna/Brhannala/Siva, serve as important figures that reference not just the implicit asexuality or non-differentiation of "eunuchs," but also their power to bless and their historical/mythical association with the occupation of dancing and singing. By aligning themselves with these mythological figures, hijras not only emphasize these aspects of their lives, but also actively construct themselves through these images, deriving legitimacy from such an association. As Margaret Trawick (1990) eloquently points out, there is a fluid relationship between ideals and experiences, myths and praxis in India. As she reminds us, "[W]hen you are trying to understand a story told in India it becomes important to consider the life of the person telling the story, and when you are trying to understand a person it becomes important to listen to the stories that that person tells." In India, texts and myths are therefore like "spirits out of bodies," because people, including hijras, "live these texts" (24).

I have elucidated some of the potential sources of legitimacy that hijras can and do deploy in constructing both their individual selves and the hijra institution. First, hijras liken themselves to sannyasis, or ascetics, figures who are clearly ubiquitous and central to much of the Vedic and post-Vedic literature. Second, the tension between asceticism and eroticism or *tapas/kama*, which plays out in hijras' lives as the tension between badhai hijras and kandra hijras, runs through the Vedas and is resolved in the later texts by the *asrama* system, a solution that is readily extended to hijras' contemporary understanding of their life cycle. Third, hijras invoke non-differentiated images such as the *ardhanarisvara* form of Siva, Arjuna as Brhannala, Sikhandi, and Vishnu as Mohini both to legitimize the sacred nature of their gender-ambiguous form and to validate their occupation of singing and dancing at festive and liminal occasions. In other words, Hindu mythology and iconography play an important part in hijras' constructions of their identities, serving as one important legitimizing discourse of hijra history and ontology, and demonstrating the significance of religious symbols in everyday life.

PRACTICES OF CREATIVE ASCETICISM: *NIRVAN* AND THE EMBODIMENTS OF DIFFERENCE

In addition to mythological bases of legitimacy, hijras also invoke the more pragmatic logic of the *nirvan* operation as proof of asexuality. It is through this more profane evidence of nonreproductive potential that disembodiment, or the excision of the "useless" sexual organ, provides ritual power, authenticity, and izzat. On one occasion when I went to visit Amir nayak, she told me the following story.

There was a hijra who lived in a king's court from childhood. From when she was very young, she used to go to the zenana [the area reserved for women] and help the women there with their tasks. This practice continued even after she had grown up. One day, the king, who didn't know that this person was a hijra, got suspicious of her activities and asked her to leave the palace. The hijra did not know what had occasioned this change of heart but packed her things and started to leave. As she was walking out a big storm began to rage through the area. For safety the hijra climbed a nearby tree. On the way up, however, her clothes got snagged on a branch and her genitalia—or lack thereof—were exposed. On seeing this, the king realized his folly and asked the hijra to return to his kingdom with him. "Then he understood that this was a real hijra because she had nothing there," the nayak concluded triumphantly.

Clearly, "having nothing there" was an important marker of authenticity, proof that the individual in question was a "real hijra." Ideally, a hijra should be "born like this," that is, lacking male genitalia from birth (in Telugu, a *puttuka* kojja—a kojja or hijra from birth). Although this was an ideal that few hijras lived up to, many of the individuals I interacted with claimed to have been impotent or sexually "dysfunctional" before having their *nirvan* operation. When I asked Shanti, in the context of our conversation, what the criteria of hijra authenticity were, without hesitation she said, "The most important [criterion] is that the [male] organ should not be functional. [Earlier] they used to check all the individuals who wanted to become hijras very carefully. They used to make them take off all their clothes and then see their bodies or touch their penis to make sure that it was really not working. Only then were these people allowed to join the hijra community. Nowadays, things are very different, and anyone who wants can join," she added distastefully.

Bala nayak, one of the senior Sheharwala hijras, echoed this sentiment: "From my childhood I have been like this. From birth, my organ has not been there. My mother took me to many doctors, but they said medicine would do no good because I was not a man. From that time, my mother would dress me like a girl. But when she knew it was of no use, she sent me to live with the hijras. I am a real hijra, not like some of these others." Munira, too, indicated both her authenticity and the apparent logic of this criterion when she said, "If I had a little 'tenkson' [tension] in my penis, if I had some faith in my body, then why would I spoil my name this way? Far from my mother, father, far from my brothers, I came and joined the hijras. Why Gayatri? In my house I could have lived well. My fate was written that way; that is why I became [like this]. I was born this way. Some children are born correctly from the womb; some are born as hijras." Apparently, sexual impotence or "incorrectness," whether physical or functional, is a necessary criterion for hijra-ness, current infractions notwithstanding.

Nevertheless, sexual impotence/dysfunction was not a sufficient condition for authenticity among hijras. In the event that one was not born "with nothing there," an impotent hijra was expected to undergo the *nirvan* operation. In fact, they used their impotence to legitimize their decision to have the operation. As Amir nayak said, "This man's *sarir* [body/organ] is of no use, so why keep it. Cut it off and throw it! That is why we have this operation." The *nirvan* operation served as ultimate proof of the asexuality of hijras, important in guaranteeing their authenticity and izzat.

However, despite this obvious valorization of the operation, its importance as a marker of hijra authenticity sometimes seemed to be denied. Significantly, this denial of its importance only served to further naturalize embodied difference; rather than diminishing the importance of the body, these disavowals merely highlighted the hierarchy of embodied enactments, from "natural" birth, through impotence, to reconstructive surgery. For instance, when I first met Irfan nayak and asked her about the *nirvan* operation, she said emphatically, "Here [in Hyderabad], nobody does that. We are all born this way and we don't have to have any 'operation-shoperation.'" Similarly, although both Shanti and Rajeshwari had undergone the *nirvan* operation, the first time I met them, they both told me that they had not had any need to on account of being "born this way."

In actual fact, almost all hijras in Hyderabad have had, are going to have, or express a desire to have the *nirvan* operation. Although being "born this way" did bring the most respect, the rarity of that occurrence made the *nirvan* operation necessary. Some of those who were *not* operated, like Madhavi and Sati, also felt compelled to lie to me, initially saying that they had undergone this procedure. As Srilakshmi told me about a month before having her operation, "We all want to become *nirvan sultans* because that is what gives you *paruvu* ["respect" in Telugu]." When we had this conversation, I was sitting in one of the huts under the tank with her and Nagalakshmi. The latter had just had her operation about a week before and was in obvious pain and discomfort. Despite the reality of Nagalakshmi's suffering, there was absolutely no doubt in Srilakshmi's mind that this was what she wanted to do. "Once you get it done, you have some *paruvu*, some izzat, when you go out on the street," she said. In response to the question of whether Nagalakshmi's experience—her obvious pain and discomfort—dissuaded her at all, Srilakshmi replied, "Now, in fact, there is a line waiting to go get it done. There are five of us who are ready. First there is me, then Aliya, Sati, Radhika, and Kajal. We will all get it done. You see. One by one, we will go and get it done." Nagalakshmi reiterated this sentiment, stating that despite the incredible pain she had to suffer, she was glad because now she was reborn as "a real hijra." The rewards of achieving this marker of authenticity appear to outweigh the cost for many hijras.

What exactly does this process of "rebirth," or *nirvan*, involve?[20] Given its elaboration in Serena Nanda's work, I will not provide a detailed description of the operation here except to say that it involves a radical penectomy and orchiectomy; that is, both the penis and the testicles are entirely removed.[21] "Traditionally," this ritual was performed by hijras known as *daiammas* (midwives), but most hijras now go to biomedical doctors to have it performed. However, a *daiamma*-performed operation is still considered to garner far more izzat than a biomedical procedure. Saroja, the only hijra sex worker who had had her operation performed by a *daiamma*, was clearly perceived as having more izzat than the others. Whether performed by a doctor or a *daiamma*, however, this operation is currently illegal in India. And yet, for the right fee, there appear to any number of local doctors who are willing to perform it. As a result, the rate of postoperative infections is high, and at least one in ten patients dies, one hijra estimated.

As the opening vignette of this chapter indicated, sometimes a boy or young man is forcibly kidnapped and made to undergo this procedure against his will. Popular magazines and especially tabloid newspapers love to report any instance of such "evil-doing." One particularly badly written article in *Crime and Detective*, "Producing Third Sex Was His Business," recounted the following story.[22] Shiv Prasad, a poor, fourteen-year-old "vagrant boy," met hijras for the first time at one of their big feasts while serving as a maid in place of his sick mother. These hijras were "very kind to him," and he was persuaded to stay on in the house of Rekha, one of the senior hijras. Gradually, tempting him with money and food, Rekha and her fellow hijras convinced him to pierce his nose and ear lobes. He didn't object. But when they asked him "to get operated," he flatly refused, realizing that it meant "loss of manhood forever." Unable to convince him otherwise, Rekha and the other hijras drugged him and forcibly emasculated him. According to the story,

[Following Shiv Prasad's adamant refusal] Rekha and her accomplices carried out their predetermined conspiracy. Special *suji-ka-halwa* [sweet pudding] was prepared and distributed among all the housemates. Shiv Prasad was given his share in a separate plate, because it had been drugged. He soon fell down unconscious. After long hours when he regained consciousness, he felt excruciating pain in his groin. When he touched his private parts, he found that his male organ had been cut off and the wound bandaged crudely from which blood was still oozing. The realization of this big loss and sense of betrayal made Shiv shriek violently. Then he lost consciousness again. When Shiv regained consciousness, he was surrounded by a large group of hijras. Rekha was there too. Her face was lit with a smile of triumph. . . . Writhing in pain (for which he was denied painkillers as atonement for his defiance) Shiv Prasad remorsefully cursed his fate and the day he came to work for these evil creatures. (*Crime and Detective*, July 1996, 16)

A somewhat more credible and widely read news magazine, *India Today* (1982), reported a similar incident in which a fifteen-year-old boy was forcibly kidnapped and operated upon. Under the heading "Behaviour," this article recounted Mohammad Hanif Vora's "horror story" after "he broke out of the half-world of eunuchs" with "a first person account of their lives, their brutal tribal rites, and the hierarchical system under which they ply their bizarre trade" (84–85; see also Allahbadia and Shah 1992).[23]

That instances such as these occur is well known, though they are highly exaggerated in popular conceptions. In fact, hijras serve as the quintessential bogeymen of India; children are threatened with potential kidnapping by hijras if they do not behave themselves. However, forcible conversions appear to be less common than such articles suggest, especially in South India. By reporting only on this feature of hijras' "bizarre" or "evil" lives, the media both vilify hijras' current existence, and more important, reinforce the strictly corporeal basis of hijra identity and thereby perpetuate the stereotype and, subsequently, the very practice they condemn. It is embodied conversion as it were, that defines hijras, simultaneously stigmatizing and highlighting such identifications in the public imaginary.

Of the hijras I met in Hyderabad, only one, Madhavi, mentioned physical coercion as a potential scenario. And ultimately, as the opening vignette points out, she was not forced into having her operation (see also the first section of chapter 7 for an elaboration of Madhavi's story). All other hijras in Hyderabad who underwent this process either during or just prior to my fieldwork did so voluntarily—in order to gain izzat, as many of them attested. Apparently, being a *nirvan sultan* not only signals respect within the community and indicates the possession of *himmat* (strength), which is necessary to acquire seniority, but it also provides a measure of izzat in the outside world, according to hijras. One is not liminal but resolutely and irrevocably a "real hijra" following this operation. Srilakshmi's statement that as a *nirvan sultan*, one "can have *paruvu* [or] izzat in the street" echoes this sentiment.

Surekha's motivation for her *nirvan* operation arose from just such an incident when she "lost her respect" in public. This is the story she told me:

I had gone to the market to buy some things. When I was there, I decided to earn some extra money, so I went to the shopkeepers to ask for money,[24] even though it was not the Lashkarwala *ilaka* [territorial boundary; see chapter 7 for an elaboration of hijra houses and their territorial boundaries]. When I walked up to one shopkeeper, maybe because he had not seen me before, he said "Show me that you are a real hijra." I was still *akkva* [not operated] then. Having completely lost respect, I quietly came back. After that, I decided to become *cibri* [operated] and after a few months I went for my *nirvan* [operation].

Paradoxically, the *nirvan* operation serves to increase hijras' izzat at the very moment that categorical identification with this label stigmatizes them in the eyes of the mainstream public. While physical emasculation serves as the absolute marker of stigmatized hijra identity, evoking horror and fear for the public, this very condition simultaneously symbolizes hijras' power and increases their izzat.

How and why does this paradoxical transposition occur? The primary reason is the association of *nirvan* with the creative power of (Hindu) sexual renunciation. While hijras obviously perceive and understand the stigmatization of impotence in normative Indian conceptualizations, the *nirvan* operation serves to elevate them beyond this vilified state to the realm of asexual sacredness. At one level, the operation is proof of a hijra's impotence/asexuality, while at another (derived from the first), it is the source of ritual power and sacred legitimacy.

SEXUAL RENUNCIATION, CREATIVE POWER

In Hindu myth and folklore, sexual abstinence can be transformed into potent strength and the power of generativity through *tapas*, the practice of asceticism. The renunciation of sex and the suppression of sexual desires (among others) is crucial to the practice of *tapas* and the acquisition of generative power. Not only does *tapas* permit the acquisition of immense power even when practiced by the evil *asuras*—for example, in the well-known myths of Hiranyakasipu, Mahishasura, and Bhasmasura (see Doniger 1999)—but it is also associated with the process of creation.

In one Hindu creation myth, as noted by O'Flaherty (1973), Siva, the preeminent "creative ascetic," is asked to create the world. He agrees and disappears for a thousand years in preparation for this task. Meanwhile, Vishnu and Brahma, worried and impatient, create all the gods and other beings during Siva's period of *tapas*. When Siva reappears and is ready to begin the process of creation, he realizes that the act has already begun. He then breaks off his *linga* (phallus) and throws it onto the earth. As O'Flaherty states, "[The *linga*] becomes a source of universal fertility as soon as it has ceased to be a source of individual fertility" (1973, 135). Likewise, hijras undergo the *nirvan* operation and bury their severed organ in the ground, following which they believe they have the power to confer fertility on others. Sacrificing their "individual fertility," they are then given "universal" (pro)creative power. Hijras derive both legitimacy and power from such myths and explicitly use these sources as affirmation of their special status with respect to creativity and fertility.

One of the most commonly expressed stories in this vein invokes hijras' power to produce rain. Given that "in the philosophy of Hindu asceticism, chastity [which generates *tapas*] in turn generates the power to produce rain" (O'Flaherty 1973, 42), hijras' ability to do so is significant. Shanti told me the following mythical story to highlight the creative power of the hijras:

Once, during the Nizam's rule, there was a big drought in Hyderabad. There was no water at all, and people were dying. The Nizam did not know what to do. Finally, he went to the hijras and told them that it was in their hands to save the city. The Nizam had come to them and asked for their help. So, breaking a thorn from a plant nearby, one of the hijras cut off her organ [penis] and made herself *nirvan*. She then threw the organ on the ground, and the minute it touched the ground, there was rain.[25]

In addition to its connection with general productivity/creativity, hijras see their *nirvan* operation as linked to their subsequent power to confer fertility. Despite the Muslim allegiance of many of the hijras—including the Hyderabadi hijras—all hijras in the country worship an incarnation of the Hindu goddess Bahuchara Mata or Bedhraj Mata. They worship this goddess especially (and necessarily) at the time of their *nirvan* operation. Following the prescribed period of postoperative recovery, it is to Bedhraj Mata that the subsequent *puja* (ceremony of worship) is dedicated, with the *nirvan sultan* asking for her explicit blessings. It is as vehicles of her power that hijras derive their "symbolic capital," translated into the blessings that they in turn bestow on newly married couples or newborn children. As part of the badhai performance, hijras bless the couple or child with good health and fertility, that is, the ability to produce many children, ideally sons. Their *nirvan* status allows hijras to serve as conduits of the goddess; by virtue of sacrificing their potential reproductivity to the goddess, they are blessed with the power to confer fertility. As a Sindhi neighbor of mine told me on the occasion of a badhai performance at his house, "Hijras are really blessed by the goddess. It is very auspicious and lucky to have them come and bless your child. Every time there is a wedding or a birth in our family, we always call hijras to bless the child because they have the power to do that." Although not everyone shares such a benevolent perception, whether out of fear or respect, hijras are widely believed to have auspicious power (or inauspicious potential) with respect to fertility. Hence, the *nirvan* operation serves as the means for ritual legitimization through recourse to myth, as well as facilitating the transformation of asexuality/impotence to (pro)creative potential.

Ultimately, the *nirvan* operation is a corporeal marker that instantiates hijra identity. This focus on the body as the site of difference is explicitly deployed by hijras in articulating their identity. Why, one might ask, this emphasis on the body? As Veena Das says in an interesting if somewhat dramatic statement, "The body occupies an essentially ambivalent position in social discourse, for it is the only object which can be subjectively experienced and conversely, the only subject that has an existence in the world of objects" (Das 1977, 193). Given the ambiguous nature of this subject/object both discursively and at the level of pragmatic reality, it appears to be the ideal vehicle of hijra identity. The dramatically embodied negotiations between their ideals and lived experiences both define hijras and serve as the medium through which they affirm their authenticity and izzat within Indian society. But while Hindu mythology and iconography provide one important node in this embodied crafting of hijra identity, their engagement with the practice of Islam constitutes another vital element of the hijra body's sociality in Hyderabad, an issue I explore in the next chapter.

5

"We Are All Musalmans Now"

RELIGIOUS PRACTICE, POSITIONALITY, AND

HIJRA/MUSLIM IDENTIFICATION

It was May 19, 1996. I was sitting in the shade of Munira's hut, chatting with Gopalamma, Surekha, and Savita. In the course of conversation, I asked them about their celebration of *Pir panduga* (the Shi'a Muslim festival of Muharram), which was only a week away. Savita looked a little surprised and, turning to the others, asked in all seriousness, "Do we celebrate *Pir panduga*?" In reply, Gopalamma snorted and said, "Soon she will be asking if we have to wear saris!" Surekha in turn gave Savita a scornful look and said, "Hey *gandu*, what is the matter with you? Who do you think we are? We are all Musalmans now. Don't you even know that? *Pir panduga* is very important for us. The older hijras say *namaz* [prayers], they go on the Hajj; we are all Musalmans now. What do you think!"[1]

This vignette highlights two issues that I focus on in this chapter. First, the rather extraordinary observation that hijras in Hyderabad see themselves, generically, as Musalmans, or Muslims, despite their recourse to Hindu mythology in constructing their histories; and, second, that claims to this religious identity appear to be constructed primarily through practice. Not only does one perform certain actions because of who one is, but one is who one is by virtue of what one does. In other words, hijras in Hyderabad identify as Muslims, and it is practice—through the various acts that they employ, the proscriptions they are subjected to, and the festivals they celebrate—that facilitates hijras' claims to Islamic identification.[2]

In reading the literature on hijras before I left for the field, nothing prepared me for the statements that Hyderabadi hijras made regarding their religious affiliation. Although the literature does mention the fact that some hijras identify as Muslim (e.g., Preston 1987; Nanda 1990; Hall 1997), nowhere does it mention that they believe that *all* hijras are Muslim, as the statement above indicates.[3] In fact, a direct question in the initial period of my fieldwork did not elicit such a reaction either. When I first began fieldwork in Hyderabad and had an opportunity to ask hijras about religion, Amir nayak had this to say: "Religion does not matter for hijras. Hindus, Muslims, Christians, anyone can join."[4] While this is certainly true, once an individual joins the community, as Surekha stated, they "are Musalmans now," enjoined to practice all that such an identity entails. In this chapter, I examine what it means for hijras to "become Musalmans." I argue that an integral element of hijra identity is constructed through and by their religious affiliation, which in turn is understood and mediated primarily by their practice of Islam. The various Muslim-identified rituals that they perform, festivals that they celebrate, and commensal and sartorial rules that they subscribe to inform hijra identity as Hyderabadi Muslims.[5]

As scholars have noted, Islamic doctrine is best captured by the term "orthopraxy" rather than "orthodoxy," highlighting the importance of practice rather than belief (Smith 1957). In this context, hijras, too, could be characterized as orthoprax religious practitioners. In their orthopraxy, however, hijras not only blur the gender boundary in their practice of Islam, following rules of comportment specified by the *shari'at* (Islamic law) for *both* men and women, but they also practice a form of religion wherein they identify and practice (for the most part) as Muslims but simultaneously derive their power and social legitimacy from a Hindu goddess, Bedhraj Mata. After describing hijra religious practices in the first two sections of this chapter, I explore in the penultimate section the apparent contradiction of these practices. Such dissonance is situated within the framework of religious pluralism in India and involves an ability, as several scholars have noted, to contextualize or "compartmentalize" potentially conflictual beliefs and practices (Singer 1972; Shweder and Bourne 1984; Ramanujan 1990), allowing for a continuum rather than a dichotomy of religious thought. Understanding religious practice to be contextual, however, does not necessarily explain what Muslim positionality *does* for hijras, that is, what it means for hijras to identify—generically—as Muslim. The final section of this chapter engages the system of positions and meanings within which we can place hijra/Muslim identification. Drawing on the historiography of the Deccan Sultanates as well as the subalternity of Islamic identification, this section explores the historical and symbolic implications of hijra positionality in contemporary India, arguing for its potential significance as a supralocal node in the wider cultural politics of Hindu nationalism.[6]

"ALL HIJRAS ARE MUSALMANS": PRACTICE AND IDENTITY
IN THE HYDERABADI CONTEXT

GAYATRI: What does it mean when you say "I am a Musalman"? How do you know that you are a Musalman?

MUNIRA: See, once you become a hijra—I am talking about Lashkarwala hijras—then you become a Musalman. [You] say *salam aleikum* when you meet other hijras, wear a green sari for special occasions, do not wear a *bindi*, eat *halal* meat, have the *khatna* [circumcision], you say *namaz*, older people go on the Hajj. It is like that. That is why we say "now we are Musalmans."

Although South Asian Islamic beliefs and practices are pluralistic and heterodox (Ewing 1988; Hassan 1997), at least theoretically, many Muslims and scholars believe one can start with any Islamic tenet or body of religious literature or ritual practice and be led unerringly to the same fundamental teachings of Islam (Metcalf 1984). "This cohesion and replication is one dimension of the unity that is the fundamental symbol of Islam," Barbara Metcalf notes in the introduction to her edited volume on the concept of *adab* (discipline/training, or proper behavior) in South Asia (1984, 3). There are common moral expectations for all Muslims, whatever their class or occupational position, and these expectations exemplify the moral qualities and behavior represented by the life of the Prophet Muhammad (Metcalf 1984). Given this fundamental unity, Muslim identity in South Asia—in effect, the answer to the question what makes a Muslim Muslim?—entails a certain belief in and practice of a character and way of life referred to as *sunna*, involving certain ritual observances and a programmatic code of behavior that approximates the Prophet Muhammad's. Although there is an inherent ambiguity both in the interpretation and practice of *shari'at*, or Islam-derived codes of conduct (Schact 1974), and in the relationship between Islam-derived and alternative codes (Ewing 1988; Pastner 1988), as well as between Sunni and Shi'a Islam (Ewing 1988; Pinault 1992; Minault 1998), most Hyderabadis could (and often did) speak of an ideal approximation of Prophet Muhammad's life in terms of specific behavioral attributes or practices that included prayer, the ritual observance of particular festivals and life-cycle ceremonies, and the adherence to prescribed rules of everyday behavior.

As the basis of Muslim identity in South Asia, these practices were also adhered to by hijras in Hyderabad. The approximation of the "ideal life," in their perspective, translated in practical terms to the custom of praying,

or saying *namaz*, undertaking the pilgrimage to Mecca (the Hajj), the celebration of Muharram, and the observance of commensal practices, sartorial
prescriptions, circumcision rites, and Muslim burial practices, among other
customary rules of practice. The hijras' answer to the question "What makes
a Muslim Muslim?" appears unequivocally to be the *practice* of Islam—a
practice shaped and conditioned by the particular spatial, historical, and
cultural context of the region. Ernest Gellner wrote the following about the
Berber tribes of Morocco: "Koranic propriety emanates from their essence,
as it were. Islam is what they *do*. They *are* Islam" (Gellner 1969, 149; emphasis in original). Likewise, in many respects, for the hijras of Hyderabad,
a hijra is a Muslim because what she does (or is required to do) is what a Hyderabadi Muslim does (or is required to do). Religious practice or knowledge
of prescribed practice becomes (religious) identity in this instance.

However, while hijras identified as Muslim, this was by no means an
unambiguous affiliation. For one thing, hijras, as "neither men nor women"
in Serena Nanda's (1990) words, did not see themselves as restricted to performing *only* (Muslim) men's or *only* (Muslim) women's practices. Instead
hijras practiced a combination of *both* men's and women's (Muslim) rituals and customs. In addition, despite their self-professed Muslim affiliation, hijras did not restrict themselves to an orthodox, Quranic practice of
Islam; instead, they assimilated Hindu elements into their religious practice. In the following sections, in addition to addressing the issue of what
in their opinion makes a hijra Muslim, I also focus on their blurring of gender and religious boundaries in their everyday practice as Muslim/Hindu
men/women.

BLURRED GENDERS AND THE PRACTICE OF ISLAM

One rainy afternoon during the monsoon season, I sat huddled together
with Aliya, Nagalakshmi, Rajeshwari, and two or three other kandra hijras
under a plastic sheet near the tank. Nagalakshmi and Aliya were having an
argument, in the course of which the former cursed Aliya, using profanity.
Immediately Rajeshwari, one of the senior hijras in this group piped up and
said, reprimanding Nagalakshmi, "That is wrong. You should not curse Aliya
like that. She has more izzat than you. She is *sunnat*.[7] Do not forget that."

As I later learned, Aliya was born a Muslim. In her village of Chandrapet,[8]
she was and still is known as Aziz (a male Muslim name). As a child, Aliya
had been circumcised, as were all Muslim boys. She was thereby *sunnat* and
thus had more izzat within the hijra community. Ideally, all hijras who join

the community are required to undergo the *khatna* operation.[9] Although circumcision was not strictly enforced among kandra hijras (even though it was recognized as accruing greater izzat), I was told that it was a fairly strict rule among badhai hijras. Both celas of Irfan nayak, Rani and Shahbaz, were circumcised almost as soon as they formally joined the community, even though they planned to undergo the *nirvan* operation a few years later. In fact both these individuals had been devout Hindus prior to their becoming hijras. More specifically, they identified as siva-satis, individuals who presumably had been "visited by" or "chosen" by a (Hindu) god/goddess, before joining the hijra community. On becoming hijras, however, they were required to undergo circumcision, which they accepted without demurral. As one of the quintessential markers of a male Muslim identity, circumcision was one of the first practices required of aspiring hijras. As an extension of this logic, hijras saw the *nirvan* operation as further evidence of their Muslim identity, as an exaggerated (Muslim) ritual of circumcision. As Munira once said to me, only half-joking, "We are even more Muslim than Muslims. They cut off only so much, and we cut off the whole thing." Clearly, corporeal symbols of identity are enlisted in crafting more than merely hijras' sexual identity.

Further, when joining the hijra community, initiates, or more commonly their gurus, were allowed to choose a name for themselves (often female and Hindu). In addition, however, they were given male Muslim names, which were their official names entered in the hijra register maintained by the nayaks. For instance, although she was commonly referred to as Shanti or Bijli, Shanti's "official" name was Kabir Baksh.[10] Likewise, her guru's "official" name was Rahim Baksh in the hijra roster, although she preferred the Hindu (female) name Lekha. Although many of the senior hijras (including badhai hijras) continued to refer to themselves by their Hindu names, all of the nayaks in Hyderabad were addressed by their (male) Muslim names, whatever their prior religious affiliation. Hence, although their names used to be Narayan and Rohini (both Hindu names), they were now referred to as Irfan nayak, and Amir nayak (male Muslim names), respectively.

In yet another gendered component of their religious identity, I was told that many of the senior hijras went on the Hajj, the holy pilgrimage to Karbala or Mecca and Medina.[11] Amir nayak's predecessor in the Lashkarwala house had apparently been on the Hajj and was therefore referred to with some respect as Salmanhaji nayak, as her celas and nati celas told me with much veneration and pride.

More common than going on the Hajj was the Muslim practice of saying *namaz*.[12] Although most hijras did not go to the mosque for this purpose (except those who had gone on the Hajj), many of them did make an explicit effort to say their prayers at least every Friday. Amir nayak told me that she did not get a chance to pray five times every day, but made sure that she said *namaz* at least every Friday. All the nayaks' houses had at least one poster or scroll with Quranic verses on their Mecca-facing walls, to which they turned when saying their prayers.

Hijras not only performed many of these nominally "male" religious practices, they simultaneously enacted "female" Muslim practices such as wearing a *burqa*, or black robe and veil, that many Muslim women wear. Especially when going out alone or with their pantis, some of the hijras (mostly the kandra hijras rather than badhai hijras) wore *burqas* over their saris. Munira told me that whenever she went out with her husband, Zahid, she "always [wore] a *burqa*," which she didn't take off "until [they] return[ed] home." She felt shy and awkward if she did not have a *burqa* on, Munira said, and Zahid echoed her sentiments approvingly.

However, when hijras went out as a group either for badhai purposes or to go shopping, there was absolutely no question of wearing a *burqa*. On these occasions, hijras intend to attract greater attention to themselves as hijras, rather than attempting to conceal their identity and appear as "good" Muslim women. Thus, rather than invoking an explicitly feminine religious self-image, the *burqa* could potentially be used just as a means of conceal-ment, a cloak of anonymity. Nevertheless, the fact that hijras adopted this explicitly Muslim practice rather than other forms of (Hindu) veiling is perhaps significant (Raheja and Gold 1994).

Further, like other Indian women, whether Muslim or Hindu, hijras wore saris. While these saris were usually variously designed and colored, on certain special occasions their color was specified: green, the color most indelibly associated with Islam.[13] On one special occasion I witnessed, dur-ing the *puja* (ritual worship) to Bahuchara Mata on the fortieth day after Nagalakshmi's *nirvan* operation, she was required to wear a plain green sari. "A green sari is absolutely necessary at this time," Munira said. When I asked why, Munira looked perplexed and said, "*Arre*. We are Musalmans, aren't we," in a tone that implied this was a really silly question. Nagalakshmi had to change into this sari just prior to the *puja* that marked the end of her confinement and the official beginning of her status as a *nirvan sultan*; it was only after her ritual bath following the *puja* that she was allowed to take this sari off.

Much like other Muslim women, hijras were also officially not allowed to wear *bindis* (marks traditionally symbolic of Hindu marital status) on their foreheads. While kandra hijras (like many Muslim women) frequently transgressed this rule for aesthetic reasons, they always made sure they had removed all traces of the *bindi* when they visited with their nayaks. If the nayaks saw any trace of a *bindi*, they immediately imposed a fine on the transgressors, as Saroja told me, relating the story of her friend who was fined five hundred rupees.

Further, although emphasizing the importance of saying prayers every Friday, hijras made a point of telling me that, unlike Muslim men, they did not go to the mosque for this prayer. I was told that only hijras who had gone on the Hajj could go to the mosque. On their return from this pilgrimage, these hijras were also the only ones permitted to wear male clothing on an everyday basis, that is, a *lungi* (wrap-around cloth) and a shirt, rather than a sari. As these shifting markers of identity in hijras' lives show, axes of religion and gender mutually constitute each other in interesting and complex ways. Ultimately, whatever their parents' religious affiliation, on joining the hijra community in Hyderabad, these individuals identified generically as Muslims, adopting many of the practices of an "orthoprax" religious practitioner (Smith 1957). Although there was no explicit discourse, ritual, or injunction to give up their Hindu/Christian identity—perhaps partly because the ideals were not very strictly enforced—Hyderabadi hijras identified for the most part as Muslims.

CROSSING RELIGIOUS BORDERS

Not only do hijras adopt the gendered Hyderabadi Muslim practices detailed above, they also diligently follow other, more general Muslim rules and prescriptions. For instance, the greeting reserved for fellow hijras of equal rank is *salam aleikum*, the same as that used by Muslims. This form of greeting is one of the first rules a hijra learns; one that separates her from other kotis such as jogins and siva-satis. The latter have their own form of greeting—*kshenarti*—a term that both marks their identity and signals their difference from hijras. Likewise, kada-catla kotis do not use these terms of greeting, using instead the more generic Telugu/Indian greeting, *namaskaram*, or (more commonly nowadays), "Hi" or "Hello," a linguistic marker of aspiring modernity and a potential path by which to access the gay lexicon. Among non-hijra kotis, only zenanas, fellow-Muslims for the most part, used the greeting *salam aleikum*.

Like many zenanas and other Muslims in Hyderabad, most hijras eat only *halal* meat, that is, goat or chicken meat that is specially cleansed and prepared by ritually sacrificing the animal and allowing it to bleed to death.

As Akbar, my zenana friend, said, that was one of the reasons neither hijras nor zenanas could attend the feasts (*dawats*) hosted by siva-satis and jogins: "The food would not be *halal*, no? That is why we cannot go," he said by way of explanation.

Even the somewhat unorthodox hijra sex workers made sure that the chickens or goats they prepared were at least sacrificed by Aliya, the only Muslim (by birth) in the group, if not by a Muslim butcher. For Naga-lakshmi's *nirvan dawat*, hijras bought two live goats that were ritually sacrificed by a Muslim butcher just before the *puja* to the goddess. In fact, the heads of these goats were placed before the image of the goddess, and, as part of the ritual, Nagalakshmi had to dip her hands in the goat's blood and smear her prints on the wall—a literal imprinting of genealogy on the walls of the house. It was unthinkable not to get *halal* meat for this occasion. "Haw, *tauba*! It has to be *halal*," Kajal said, crossing herself on each cheek in reaction to my question on this issue. "The meat has to be *halal*, Gayatri. We are Muslims, no? So we cannot eat non-*halal* meat," she repeated patiently.

The celebration of Hyderabadi Muslim festivals was another marker of hijras' professed religious identity. One of the only occasions when hijras from across the country got together (apart from death ceremonies) was during Muharram, or the *Pir panduga*, as it is known in Hyderabad. A ten-day mourning ritual, Muharram is the annual commemoration of the seventh-century martyrdom of the two saints Hussain and Hassan (sons of Ali and grandsons of the Prophet Muhammad) who were killed at the battle of Karbala (Fruzzetti 1981). It also marks the split between Shi'as and Sunnis in Islam: this event is primarily celebrated by Shi'as. For Hyderabadi Muslims, it is one of the principal public events of their calendar.[14]

The last day of Muharram is marked by a procession through the streets, headed by men who mourn the death of these saints by beating themselves with chains and other men who carry *taziyas*, or symbolic representations of the tombs of Hassan and Hussein. The procession winds its way through the streets, past the central mosque in old Hyderabad, to the Muslim cemetery. Although I did not witness this myself, I was told by some hijras that senior hijras who lived in the old city of Hyderabad through which the procession marches sometimes accompany these fellow-Shi'ite mourners, visiting the *asurkhana* at the shrine of Hazrat Abbas for the annual *matam* devotions (Pinault 1992).[15] However, other hijras contradicted this account, stating that hijras never actually accompany the procession but do in fact mark this mourning period and perform a ritual at the mosque on this day. Whatever their actual public performance, hijras do mark this event in their calendar and, much like other Muslims in the city, commemorate the death of these brothers through commensal rituals and religious worship in the mosque and in their respective houses.[16]

Perhaps the most marked symbol of hijras' Muslim identity is the ritual that accompanies the death of a hijra. Whatever their natal religion, hijras are buried rather than cremated. Further, all the rituals prior to this event replicate those performed at the death of a Muslim man in Hyderabad. Given the inauspiciousness of even speaking about death, hijras were extremely reluctant to talk to me about their rituals surrounding this event, even if only in the abstract. Not until an actual death occurred in Hyderabad while I was there, was I able to get any information on this issue.

In June of 1997, toward the end of my period of fieldwork, one of the nayaks of the Lashkarwala house, Ijaz nayak, passed away. I was not allowed to witness the rituals that followed this death, but I did get to hear about the ceremonies and practices engaged in on this occasion, as related to me by Amir nayak's cela, Vanitha, and a Muslim neighbor, Abbas, who regularly called the faithful to prayer at the local neighborhood mosque. The day a hijra dies, her body is thoroughly washed, along with the area around it, by a man referred to as *ghasl*—a hereditary caste/occupational position in the Muslim community. All ornaments are removed from the body, and the *ghasl* is given one half of these, that is, all the ornaments from one side of the body including one earring, the bangles, nose-ring, toe-ring and anklet, as well as a tablet of silver with which he has to apply *surma* (kohl) under his eyes. The body is now ready for the *mayyat*, or viewing. People who wish to pay their last respects—in this case primarily other hijras—can come and view the body at this time. As they file past, each person usually puts a little money in a bag left there for this purpose. The money is given to the *ghasl* before he leaves. At the end of the day, specific prayers from the Quran are read over the body before it is moved onto a stretcher, and only non-hijra Muslim men (usually from the neighborhood) then carry it to the Muslim cemetery. The body is placed in the grave on a north-south axis with the feet facing south and the head turned west, in the direction of Mecca.

On the third day the *ziyarat* is performed. Fruits, lentils, and *paan* leaves are laid out in the house, specific payers are read, and forgiveness is asked for all sins. Then all the hijras go to the cemetery to pay their respects, after which they are all fed by the members of the deceased hijra's family, which in this case was the Lashkarwala house. A similar ritual is performed on the tenth day, the *dasva*; the twentieth day, *bisva*; and the thirtieth day, *tisva*.

On the fortieth day, there is a big ceremony and feast to which everyone is invited, that is, hijras from all across the country. This *roti*, or death ceremony, is one of the only occasions, apart from Muharram, when hijras from across the country get together. For Ijaz nayak's *roti*, Lashkarwala hijras to whom I spoke expected at least four or five hundred hijras to come from different corners of the country. At such times policy decisions are made and interregional or interhouse disputes are settled.[17] On this occasion, an entire hall was rented, and special cooks were employed. All the visiting hijras were housed and fed in this hall at the expense of the Lashkarwala house.

The rituals performed on the death of a hijra are not Hindu or Christian, but Muslim. Irrespective of the natal religion of the hijra concerned, the same practices and rituals are employed to bury them (although with less pomp and expenditure for non-nayaks). As Abbas told me, "It is like for any Muslim man in our *mohalla* [neighborhood]. The same things are done, except hijras invite their people for the *roti*."

And yet despite these explicitly Muslim religious customs and rituals, hijras simultaneously incorporated explicitly Hindu practices in their construction of religious and gendered selves. Perhaps the most marked of these practices was their worship of Bedhraj Mata, an incarnation of Devi (goddess) or Mata (mother), as they refer to her.[18] Very soon after I began fieldwork, I was categorically informed, "All hijras throughout the country worship Bedhraj Mata." When questioned in detail about this goddess, most hijras were unable or unwilling to give me any details, but referred me instead to the *bare hijre-log* (the older, respected hijras) who live in the only temple dedicated to this goddess in Gujarat. However, none of the hijras I spoke to in Hyderabad had been to this temple. In fact, none of them planned to go in the near future either, although many hijras frequently visited or at least intended to visit various Muslim *dargahs* (mausoleums) across the country. And yet, Bedhraj Mata was "extremely important . . . the most important for hijras," I was told.

"You have to get Mata's blessings before you become *nirvan* and before the *dawat* on the fortieth day after *nirvan*," Madhavi informed me. "Otherwise what happens?" I asked. "Otherwise, you will die," Madhavi replied in all seriousness. Other hijras reiterated this sentiment, stating that it was imperative to ask for the goddess's blessings, especially if (as was often true nowadays) she did not "call you" for the operation. Earlier, most hijras were "called" by the goddess, either by a dream or some other omen that clearly signified the desire of the goddess for the person to "become a hijra" and undergo the *nirvan* operation.

Every time the issue of the goddess's "calling you" was raised, I was told a version of the following myth:[19] There was once a prince. His parents really wanted him to get married, so they found this extremely beautiful goddess and got them married to each other. But the marriage was never consummated. Every night the prince would go away somewhere. One day, the princess/goddess followed him and saw him enjoy himself with other men. She got very angry and stated categorically that henceforth, "people like that" should be reborn (*nirvan*) as neither men nor women, and so saying, she cut off his genitalia. Recognizing that it was not the prince's fault, however, she also stated that if such people worshipped her at this point, she would help them to recover quickly and bless them with her power. Hence the importance of worshipping the Mata before the *nirvan* operation, I was told.

The mainstream public (or at least those who invited hijras to bless their children), believed hijras derived their power and efficacy from being vehicles of this (Hindu) goddess. "It is very lucky to call them when a child is born, because they are blessed by Mata," Mr. Mamdani told me. Mr. Mirchandani told me on a different occasion, "It is very auspicious you know, to call hijras to your house. They have the power of the Mata to either bless you or curse you." Clearly social and sacred legitimacy for hijras derives from this Hindu goddess, at least among the Hindu community, which forms the bulk of their badhai clientele.[20]

In yet another instance of blurred religious boundaries, hijras behave in many ways as Hindu widows on the death of their gurus. Like traditional Hindu widows, they break all their bangles, remove all their jewelry, and wear a simple, white sari for the period of mourning following the death of their guru. Ideally hijras are permitted to start wearing colored clothes only after they have acquired another guru or teacher.

Further, although categorically proscribed, many hijras—especially sex workers and former siva-satis—celebrate Hindu festivals such as the *bonalu panduga*, one of the most important and popular festivals in Hyderabad. Literally, the term refers to the "festival of pots." As its title indicates, the goddess Mahakali (or one of her several sisters, including Yellamma), an incarnation of Devi to whom this festival is dedicated, is worshipped—mostly by women—by the carrying of elaborately decorated pots, which are then ceremoniously broken at the goddess's temple. This public event is one of the most popular and important of the Hyderabadi (and Telangana) Hindu festivals. As Musalmans, however, hijras are officially forbidden to participate in this celebration, and a stiff fine is imposed for this transgression if senior hijras get to know of it. Rani, one of the badhai hijras, had to pay eleven hundred rupees last year she said, because someone had told her guru that she was present at the Yellamma temple during these festivities.

In 1997, when I attended the festival at the Yellamma and Mahakali temples, I was implored not to tell the nayaks about the presence of at least four or five badhai hijras (including Rani again), and almost all the kandra hijras at the temple. In fact, for the kandra hijras from the tank, this was the one annual festival for which they spent the largest amount of money and celebrated with the most pomp and enthusiasm. Every year, they pool their financial resources and employ a band to accompany them as they dance with the *bonalu* (pots) on their heads, all the way from the tank to the Mahakali temple, about two or three miles away. This procession is followed by a big feast, which they prepare for themselves, their "husbands," and some of their koti friends. Although it is a Hindu festival, the *bonalu panduga* is also a popular Hyderabadi festival, perhaps highlighting hijras' affiliation with place rather than religion in particular contexts.

RELIGIOUS PLURALISM IN THE INDIAN CONTEXT

At first glance, hijras appear to celebrate a pluralistic form of religion, combining elements of Islam and Hinduism. But how unusual is this in the Indian context? Despite the apparent doctrinal uniformity of Islam (Metcalf 1984) and Hyderabadi Muslims' articulation of identifiable "Muslim" practices, Islam in India is characterized by a bewildering diversity of communities, traditions, and customs (Misra 1964; Mujeeb 1967; Ahmad 1976, 1980; Engineer 1980, 1989; Madan 1995). Islam came to the subcontinent over a succession of periods, conquests, and immigrant waves, resulting in manifest differences in peoples' experiences and practices of it, depending on class, region, and manner of diffusion. Over the years, Muslim traditions evolved markedly pluralistic forms to coexist peacefully with Hindu and Jain religio-cultural beliefs and practices in different parts of the country (Roy 1983).

Several scholars and travelers over the past century, including British civil servants, have noted this pattern of pluralism. For instance, Charles Elliot, writing from Uttar Pradesh in north India a century ago, noted the "strong tendency among Muslims to assimilate with their Hindu neighbors... [with many of them] wearing *dhotis* and using *Ram-Ram* as [their] mode of salutation" (1892, 28). In a similar vein, Bampfylde Fuller wrote about the "Hindu influences" on the Muslims: In agricultural districts, the people "not only understand each other's systems, but the systems often seem to overlap," he observed (1910, 130), with Hindus and Muslims attending each other's festivals and singing each other's songs. Almost a century later, an editorial in the daily newspaper reported that in villages in north India, Muslims celebrate the Hindu festival of Diwali, including the elaborate ritual of Goddess Lekha *puja* (worship) in their celebration (*Times of India*, September 10, 1995). On the other hand, many Hindus venerate the martyrdom of Imam Hussain along with their Muslim neighbors (Fuller 1910; Reeves 1971; Blunt 1909; Lawrence 1928; Pinault 1992) and regularly attend the annual commemoration of several Sufi *pirs*, or saints, in Delhi, Agra, and Ajmer (Lopez 1995; van der Veer 1998). On another performative level, the Muslim *shahnai*, a string instrument, is used in the *arti* (invocation) of Hindu temples in Benares, including the Vishvanath temple (Pugh 1988).[21] Islam in India (especially in southern India, which was less subject to repeated conquest and upheaval) is obviously a pluralistic tradition, incorporating several beliefs, rituals, and practices of neighboring religions and cultural traditions, including Hinduism and Jainism. Commenting on the inappropriateness of comparing Islam in India with that in other countries, Maulvi Zakaullah noted that "for a thousand years, [the] religion of Islam has been intimately bound up with India; and in India, Islam has won some of its greatest triumphs for its own popular form of civilization" (quoted in Schimmel 1980, 14).

Given this pluralistic context in India, it is not surprising that hijras adopted both Hindu and Muslim rituals. While they employed Muslim commensal, sartorial, purificatory, and burial customs, they simultaneously worshipped a Hindu goddess through whom they derived their divine power to confer fertility and thus obtained social legitimacy. Further, even though they practiced and identified as Muslims, when asked directly, they would answer, "hijras have no *jati* [caste/class] or *dharm* [religion]." Hijras did not see a disjuncture or conflict in either the "consistency" of their religious identities as Hindu or Muslim, or in their religious orthopraxy in the face of an apparently secular ideology.

As some scholars have suggested, this way of thinking may be explained by Indians' reported ability to "compartmentalize" potentially conflictual beliefs and practices. Over the years, Indologists and scholars have noted the particular Indian ability for "multiple diglossia"—the ability for one person to hold multiple, potentially "inconsistent" ideas and beliefs—as Ramanujan characterizes it (1990, 57). In an article intriguingly titled "Is There an Indian Way of Thinking?" A. K. Ramanujan extends linguistic references to the study of cultures and concludes that it is possible to identify those cultures that have "overall tendencies—tendencies to idealize and think in terms of either the context-free or the context-sensitive kinds of rules." He then states, "In cultures like India's, the context-sensitive kind of rule is the preferred formulation" (1990, 47). In such a formulation, "consistency is the hob-goblin of foolish minds," as Gandhi is reputed to have said, paraphrasing Emerson (quoted in Ramanujan 1990, 55). "When Indians learn, quite expertly, modern science, business, or technology, they 'compartmentalize' these interests; the new ways of thought and behavior do not replace, but live along with older 'religious' ways. The 'modern,' the context-free, becomes just one more context," Ramanujan notes (57).

The anthropologist Milton Singer also commented upon this characteristic more than two decades ago. He introduced the concept of "compartmentalization" in his book *When a Great Tradition Modernizes* to account for the particular relationship between "tradition" and "modernization" that he observed in the South Indian city of Madras. As he states, the "relationship of modernization (and of Westernization) to tradition is neither one of deep antagonism and struggle for dominance nor one of harmony and mutual support. It is rather a historical process in which the new and the foreign are culturally differentiated as such from the indigenous traditions, then tried out in a 'neutral' area, and eventually selectively integrated into an 'essential' core of indigenous traditions, which has itself changed in order to incorporate the new items" (1972, 387). This is possible because of the adaptive strategy wherein "those who simultaneously modernize and 'Sanskritize'...tend to compartmentalize their lives, following a 'modern' model in a ritually neutralized work sphere and a 'traditional' one in their domestic and social life" (Singer 1972, 387). While this formulation of the problem might be somewhat artificial and essentializing in many respects, especially in its stark juxtaposition of "modernity" and "tradition," the proposed solution of "a cognitive compartmentalization of the conflicting spheres of activity" remains an important avenue of research pursued by several scholars (Roland 1979; Shweder and Bourne 1984; Ramanujan 1990).

As Ramanujan (1990) notes, three cultural traits have been attributed to Indians (primarily, it should be noted, by British colonial officers), two of which are potentially relevant for this discussion, namely, inconsistency and the lack of universality. The former, as noted above, is apparent in such instances as the simultaneous use of "inconsistent" concepts such as *karma* and *talaividi/talavrata* (Daniel 1983; Keyes and Daniel 1983),[22] or the "holding together in one brain both astronomy and astrology" as Ramanujan's father did (Ramanujan 1990, 43). The latter trait—the lack of universality—is perhaps best captured by Hegel's statement: "While we [Europeans] say 'Bravery is a virtue,' the Hindoos say, on the contrary, 'Bravery is a virtue of the Cshatriyas'" (quoted in Ramanujan 1990, 44). There are specifications not only for moral conduct according to one's stage of life (*asramadharma*) and class/caste (*svadharma*), but also for one's individual nature (*svabhava*) and the place of one's birth or one's spatial orientation (*des/ur*), as well as conduct that is specified for an emergency (*apadharma*) (see Beck 1972; Lingat 1973; Daniel 1984; Ramanujan 1990). The determination of a uniform set of rules for moral self-crafting becomes even more complicated when we take into account the belief that differentially valued and ranked "substances" underlie all systems, individuals, and objects, all of which have "the ability to mix and separate, to transform and be transformed, to establish intersubstantial relationships of compatibility and incompatibility, to be in states of equilibrium and disequilibrium, and to possess variable degrees of fluidity and combinability" (Daniel 1984, 3; cf. Marriott 1976). Specifying a universal rule or context-free interpretation of an action becomes extremely difficult if not impossible in such a framework.

In this interpretation, like other Indians, hijras too may lack this so-called trait of universality and are apparently "inconsistent," employing a cognitive style that is "relationally conceived and contextually appraised" (Shweder and Bourne 1984, 189), rather than deploying the abstract, context-free model of the autonomous individual that characterizes so-called Western modes of social thought (Shweder and Bourne 1984; cf. Mackie 1977). For hijras, contexts are clearly specified, and behavior is enacted and interpreted according to these circumscribed contexts, rather than according to universal rules governing all conduct. Hence, for instance, although seemingly disjunctive to a visiting anthropologist, hijras' worship of both Hindu and Muslim gods/goddesses is explainable on the basis of demarcated contexts for the worship of each. While Bedhraj Mata is worshipped prior to their *nirvan* operation, Allah is the god invoked at other times, and especially on Fridays. Likewise, while burial customs might be Muslim-oriented, the social practices imposed on celas at this time, including sartorial rules and death rituals such as breaking one's bangles, are "Hindu" customs.[23]

HIJRA POSITIONALITY AND THE MEANINGS OF MUSLIM IDENTIFICATION

And yet, apart from being an essentializing and potentially orientalizing characterization that displaces the agency of Indians (see Inden 1986, 1990), this contextually dependent frame of reference does not necessarily explicate Hyderabadi hijras' generic identification as Muslim. What does it imply for hijras to state that their very identity as hijras necessitates their Islamic identification? What does this pluralistic practice *mean* for hijra identity in the present context? While historians and secularists have long pointed to the "ancient" history of religious pluralism in the subcontinent, hijras' generic identification as Muslim militates against such a simple answer. Their simultaneous incorporation of Hindu and Muslim rituals could (and possibly does) indicate religious pluralism in practice, but their subsequent identification is not reducible, as Lawrence Cohen notes (pers. comm.), to *just* a question of pluralism or fluidity. What it *does* mean, however, is a more complex question with no clear-cut answers. Two potential avenues of analysis suggest themselves, however, one historical and the other cultural, deriving from representational modalities, or the system of positions within which hijra identification can be located.[24]

Historical Basis of Hijra Identification

Perhaps we can understand Hyderabadi hijras' Islamic identification—as Muslims, generically, and as Shi'as secondarily—through a historical lens, as a consequence of the cultural and religious history of the Deccan. Since its establishment over four hundred years ago, the Deccan kingdom of Golconda (of which Hyderabad became the capital) was a Muslim principality. Following the disintegration of the Bahmani kingdom, Golconda was founded in the early sixteenth century by the Qutb Shahi dynasty, a dynasty of Shi'a rulers with close ties to the (Shi'ite) Safavid rulers in Persia.[25] Given the predominance of the (largely Sunni) Mughal dynasty to the north, the Bahmani kingdom and its successor, the kingdom of Golconda, were among the few Shi'a refuges in the vast sea of Sunni influence outside of Persia, accounting for the close relations between Persia and Golconda and the subsequent influx of Persians into the city of Hyderabad (Hollister 1989; Pinault 1992). As a result, there was a significant Perso-Islamic domination of the cultural, religious, and political life of Hyderabad. This influence was apparent in all respects, from the layout of the city and the architecture of the buildings to the art and literature of this period, as well as in the changing religious affiliation of the city's inhabitants as more Turks, Arabs, and especially Persians streamed into the city and were appointed to important administrative positions in the royal court.[26]

Although a definitive history of the hijras in Hyderabad remains elusive, their own accounts, as well as the sparse historical literature available attests to the existence of "eunuchs" in this region since the birth of the city. At least one account mentions their having accompanied the original founders of the kingdom, as slaves, on the journey south from Delhi (Kidwai 1985).[27] Slavery or bondage was by no means a medieval (Islamic) invention (Kosambi 1975; Chakravarti 1985). But unlike earlier periods of Indian history, the medieval era saw slavery begin to radically influence the social and political structure of society, with *domestic* slavery becoming especially significant. Not only were the rulers themselves products of a very different history (often, as with the founders of Golconda, themselves being descendents of slaves who had risen to occupy prominent positions in the military and administration), but rapid urbanization brought a dramatic increase in domestic slavery as more and more cosmopolitan rulers and nobles employed slaves to cater to their personal needs (Kidwai 1985). Especially in the early medieval period, these slaves, both domestic and especially "elite" slave troops, were for the most part foreigners, although often Muslim foreigners (or recent converts to Islam)—Turkish in the north, and African in the South and in Bengal. Further, the laws of slave ownership during this period stipulated that non-Muslims could not own Muslim slaves and were obligated either to sell them to Muslims or to emancipate them. Hence, many of these domestic slaves and their descendants owned by the ruling (Muslim) families apparently were themselves of the Islamic faith (and were probably, although not necessarily, Shi'a Muslims), including the eunuch slaves through whom contemporary Hyderabadi hijras derive their historical legitimacy (Kidwai 1985; Chatterjee 2002).

Islamic affiliation and, more specifically, identification as either Sunni or Shi'a, appear to have played a fairly significant role in the historiography of the Deccan and the lives of the Hyderabadi people. It was Shi'ism—especially the close ties between the two Shi'ite kingdoms of Persia and Golconda—that provided the excuse for the Mughal (orthoprax Sunni) emperor Aurangzeb to invade the Deccan in the seventeenth century. He is reputed to have labeled the reigning Qutb Shahi ruler "an oppressor against whom the people were invoking the heavens, a heretic who had perverted the subjects from the pure Sunni faith, and lastly an ally and financial supporter of the king of Persia. Not to punish such a heretical ruler would be failure of duty on the part of an orthodox Islamic emperor" (Hollister 1989, 124).

The Mughal invasion of Golconda in 1687 ended the reign of the Qutb Shahi dynasty, and not until the death of Aurangzeb in 1707 did the kingdom of Golconda begin a new chapter in its history with the establishment of the Asaf Jahi dynasty in 1724, a dynasty better known as the Nizams of Hyderabad. Although the Asaf Jahis were Sunni Muslims, unlike Aurangzeb, they continued the Qutb Shahi legacy of religious tolerance through their patronage of Shi'a shrines and the sponsorship of (and even participation in) the Muharram processions that made up such a large part of Hyderabadi religious culture. In fact, the Nizams at this time were renowned for their religious pluralism and appointment of people of all faiths, including Hinduism, to important and powerful positions in the royal court (Lynton and Rajan 1974; Leonard 1978; Austin 1992; Lynton 1993; Kakar 1995).

In addition to their pluralism in matters of the state, the Nizams also actively maintained in their households a large retinue of eunuch slaves who were given diverse responsibilities, ranging from menial tasks to supervising the zenana and managing the household. In addition, these eunuch slaves also served as confidantes and advisors to the rulers, often entrusted with the keys to the royal treasury. The *khwajasara,* or "chief eunuch," held a prominent and important position in the royal household and the political hierarchy of the court (Jaffrey 1996; cf. Manucci 1907; Chatterjee 2002).

Eunuchs have existed in large numbers in Hyderabad since the establishment of the kingdom of Golconda by the Qutb Shahis, and they almost certainly lived in the city during the tenure of the Asaf Jahi Nizams. In addition to their renown as trusted servants and slaves, there is also explicit reference during this latter period to hijras as public performers at the birth of a (male) child. As Hyderabadi hijras' accounts to me attest, and as Lynton and Rajan (1974) and Jaffrey (1996) indicate, the Nizams of Hyderabad also served as patrons of badhai hijras. As legend has it, the decline of hijras' preeminence in the city is attributable explicitly to one such badhai performance: It was 1908, and the wives of both the reigning Nizam, Mahbub Ali Pasha, and his son and heir, Osman Ali Khan, had given birth to sons within a couple of days of each other. Rejoicing, Mahbub Ali Pasha summoned the hijras to his palace, Purani Haveli. In his exuberance at the birth of his son *and* grandson, he kept the hijras there for eight days and nights as he celebrated this joyous occasion. Meanwhile, his son, Osman Ali Khan, had also summoned the hijras to his own palace, King Kothi, to bless his child. But having received his father's summons earlier, all the hijras had gone to Purani Haveli, so they did not receive Osman Ali Khan's request. Feeling personally slighted by their absence, Osman Ali Khan never again summoned hijras to celebrate the birth of his children and, on becoming the Nizam after his father's death, he issued a law curtailing hijras' activities, especially their recruitment patterns (Lynton and Rajan 1974; cf. Kakar 1995; Jaffrey 1996).[28]

Whatever the truth of this story, the fact that at least until the reign of Osman Ali Khan, the Nizams were patrons of badhai hijras is indisputable. If, as some hijras and scholars maintain, hijras' legacy extends back to the (Hindu) Ramayan and the Vedic era, predating the Muslim presence in the subcontinent, "it was during the rule of the Qutb Shahis and the Nizams, that hijras attained their greatest [glory] in Hyderabad, ... bringing [hijras] closer to them rather than pushing [them] away," as Shanti, one of the tank hijras maintained, perhaps accounting in part for their current Islamic identification (see Lynton and Rajan 1974; Jaffrey 1996).

Cultural Representations and the Muslim Other

As noted, hijras identified generically as Muslim; that is, by virtue of being hijra they are, by that token, Muslim. In reading previous accounts of hijras in Hyderabad, however, nowhere does one come across this generic identification. In Harriet Lynton and Mohini Rajan's ethnohistorical account written in the mid-1970s and Zia Jaffrey's narrative of her encounters with hijras in the late 1980s, there is no mention of a Muslim hijra identity. Is this, then, a recent identification? What is the context within which we can place this identification? And how can we understand this issue in a way that does not dissolve into a polarized and somewhat reductive history of religious "pluralism" in the Indian context, one that posits either an "ancient" or a "modern," colonial legacy of intolerance in the Indian subcontinent and places hijra identity explicitly within this framework of communal history?

Although definitive answers to these questions are difficult to generate at this time without further research, at least two potential avenues of inquiry suggest themselves. First, we may see hijras' Islamic identification not through the present lens of religious conflict but as a context-specific, *nonstrategic* positioning; and, second, that we embrace the potential subalternity of Islamic identification and examine the intrinsic connections between religious identification, nationalism, and hijras' supralocality in contemporary India.

While hijras' Muslim identification is obviously important for everyday practice, perhaps reading it in terms of the contemporary political context imbues it with subaltern significance that hijras themselves might not attribute to it. To what extent might hijras' identification (or non-identification) as Muslim be a reflection of the *researcher's* frameworks or the contexts of such inquiry rather than a statement about the significance of Islam in hijras' lives? In both of the analyses mentioned above, Lynton and Rajan (1974) and Jaffrey (1996) were exploring hijra identity through the lens of social marginality, representing them as "unworldly" and "invisible" outcasts, respectively. In that context, perhaps hijras were invested in articulating their position to these researchers as individuals located outside the bounds of social, gendered, *and religious* markers of society, thereby refraining from invoking their religious identification.

By articulating this position, I do not mean to indicate a hierarchy of authentic fieldwork practices or methodology but merely to highlight the contextual nature of such research. As this ethnography shows, on several occasions in my conversations with them as well, hijras explicitly emphasized their lack of caste, class, gender, *and* religious affiliations. One way to address this issue is to ask how the contexts of these elicitations were different from each other. Could there have been differences in the contextual milieus and the representational agendas of fieldwork/fieldworkers that elicited these differential identifications? In line with my broader argument that representations of hijras in the literature have often depended on the particular agendas of their interlocutors—hijras themselves often being silent bystanders in these portrayals[29]—this line of inquiry serves to introduce a note of caution in attributing meanings to hijras' religious identification, meanings that might inadvertently negate the very agency, or "voice," that writers/ethnographers seek to provide.

However, having said that the meanings attributed to hijras' Muslim identification might not be the same for hijras as for their interlocutors in the current context, the reality is that the hijras I spoke with *did* in fact identify generically as Muslim, an issue that has significant implications for a politics of identity, religion, and nationalism in the late twentieth-century context of religious or communal violence in India.[30] Hence, putting aside the potential for nonstrategic agency, it is important to address the system of positions within which we can place hijras' Muslim identification and understand the significance of this act.

In the current context of academic debate and everyday practice in the Indian subcontinent, the question of the historical relationship between Hindus and Muslims is an emotional one, often resulting in polarized conclusions deriving from differential investments in nationalism, religion, and politics. The two most prominent stances on this issue can be characterized as "nationalist" and "secularist," with the "Muslim fundamentalist and the Hindu revivalist on the sidelines, trying to interject their particular brand of venom in the proceedings" as Sudhir Kakar notes (1995, 13). On the one hand, religious (in this context, Hindu) nationalists stress the deep historical antipathy between Hindus and Muslims, stretching back to the "invasion" of Muslims in the eleventh and twelfth centuries CE. This antipathy, they argue, derives from theological as well as so-called civilizational differences stemming from Muslims' inability to "adjust" to a non-Muslim nation.

On the other hand, secularists point to the recent history of the Hindu-Muslim conflict. The antipathy between these communities, they argue, is attributable in part to the colonial policies of divide-and-rule, in part to the backlash of Hindu revivalism and Pan-Islamism this gave rise to, and in part a result of the declining importance of the religiously syncretic

(Hindu and Muslim) army, made up of soldiers for hire who commingled in the armies of the independent principalities and kingdoms (Kakar 1995).[31] In the secularist view, rather than being a strictly religious or theological matter, the tension revolves around the sectarian or communal sentiments fostered by the colonial state (Pandey 1989; Ludden 1996; van der Veer 1998).[32] In this view, Hindus and Muslims coexisted peacefully prior to the nineteenth century, evolving a harmonious and "syncretic" practice with mutual borrowing in the realms not only of religion, but also of art, architecture, literature, and philosophy. In this context, secularists emphasize the importance and popularity of Sufism, the mystical component of Islam, whose practitioners are held up as the ultimate "examples of 'composite culture' [and as] syncretic Muslims par excellence" (Kakar 1995, 17).

Clearly, as with any issue that excites political passion, the truth lies somewhere in between, neither underestimating the historical rift between Hindus and Muslims nor overestimating the symbolism of the Muslim as the quintessential Other in India. While there is historical evidence of antipathy and violence between Hindus and Muslims prior to the colonial presence in the subcontinent, these differences were undoubtedly fueled and exacerbated by the British colonizers who constructed religion as the preeminent "moving force of all Indian politics," thereby laying the foundation for a communal narrative of Indian history (Pandey 1989, 132). Religion—specifically, allegiance to Hinduism or Islam—emerged for the colonizers as well as early nationalists as the basis for a politics of difference, a politics that was mapped onto bodies and nations to tell the definitive story of Indian history.

According to Peter van der Veer, "from its very beginning in the nineteenth century, nationalism in India has fed upon religious identifications ... [leading] at Independence ... to the most important political event of twentieth-century South Asian history—the formation of Pakistan as a homeland for Indian Muslims" (1998, 2). It is this history that provides a backdrop to the homogenization of a "national" Hinduism in India today— the ideology of Hindutva—that is increasingly deployed by the ruling Bharatiya Janata Party government and its right-wing *parivar* (family) compatriots. Drawing on the work of V. D. Savarkar, a prominent 1920s Hindu nationalist, the ideology of Hindutva explicitly "equates religious and national identity: an Indian is a Hindu," an equation that necessarily locates other Indian religious communities such as Muslims outside the nation (van der Veer 1998, 1). It is this story, then, of the historical and political *utilization* of such antagonism in the service of a "religious nationalism" within and against which we must read the narrative of contemporary India.

But what do hijras have to do with all of this? How is their Muslim positionality related to the ideology of religious nationalism in India? Perhaps, as I indicated earlier, it is not, any attempt to see the connection being spurious, a manifestation of a secularist's contemporary understanding of the significance of religious difference and its relation to nationalism. On the other hand, especially given this Hindu nationalist context, maybe it is imbued with even *greater* significance as a subaltern statement about religion, identity, and citizenship. Perhaps, as Lawrence Cohen suggests (pers. comm.), in this particular context, Muslim identification can be seen as potentially translocal, or transnational even, in a way that various Hindu identifications cannot. Could it be hijras' very supralocality, their ability to cross borders—of gender, religion, and nation—that allows for their Muslim positionality? After all, the very sign of hijras' apparent authenticity— the mark of the absent phallus—serves simultaneously as a signifier of super-Muslim identity in Munira's statement to me,[33] at the same time as it symbolizes a supralocal transnationality—an "all-India pass" that permits hijras to travel on public transportation, free of charge, anywhere in the subcontinent, including Pakistan (see Cohen 1995a, 1995b). In the current context of Hindu nationalism in India, perhaps it is hijras' Muslim translocality that positions them as "authentic" subaltern citizens of the Indian nation—the ultimate metasignifiers of the potential for a genuinely transnational and transcultural citizenship.

I conclude this chapter by drawing on a vignette from Mani Ratnam's popular Hindi/Tamil film, *Bombay*, which narrativizes the communal riots of 1993 in the Indian city of Bombay, or Mumbai, as it is currently known. Through the eyes of a couple—the husband Hindu, the wife, Muslim— and their twin sons, this film portrays the insanity of a city torn apart by (putative) religious difference. In one scene, as a communal riot breaks out, the two boys get separated from their mother in the marketplace. In the ensuing battle between the marauding crowds of Hindus and Muslims (all men, one might add) out to avenge their "honor," the young twins are buffered from this violence by a hijra who harbors the boys till the riot expends itself—seemingly the only representative who is, or can be, situated outside of the madness and cacophony of such violent communal difference. In one reading of this representation, perhaps hijras, whether "real" or symbolic, are not only *constituted* by the axis of religion but also embody the only transcendent position in a world of categorical absolutes in contemporary (Hindu) India—the very violence of their becoming locating them indelibly as the ultimate border agents of humanity in contemporary South Asia.

6

(Per)Formative Selves

THE PRODUCTION OF GENDER

I had gone to visit my hijra friend Madhavi one day and was sitting outside her shack, chatting with her. It was lunchtime. Out of the general bustle and noise on the street, I heard someone—a man—call Madhavi's name and greet her familiarly. On seeing just the two of us, this man walked up and sat down next to Madhavi. He was sitting opposite me and as we talked, I could see him darting furtive glances toward me. Finally, after about ten minutes, he turned to me and blurted out, "When did you become *nirvan*?[1] Is that how you do not have any hair on your face? I have never seen a hijra who looks so much like a woman before!" in an incredulous tone. Madhavi of course promptly burst out laughing and, winking at me, continued this fiction for the next ten minutes. She informed this koti that I was a senior hijra because I had put the *rit* (kinship marker) when I was very young, and was highly respected because I had become a *nirvan sultan* (person who has undergone *nirvan*) at that early age. He bought the story immediately, even though we were both grinning broadly. Looking enviously at me, he said, "I wish I had done the same; then I would also look just like a woman—really beautiful."

In addition to authenticating hijra asexuality and their identity, the *nirvan* operation is also believed to make a hijra more beautiful, more feminine—"just like a woman." In this chapter, I address this aspect of hijra/koti identity, namely, their gendered performance both in terms of the ideals subscribed to and the practices deployed to enact these gendered ideals. I address the emphasis on practice in hijras' enactment of gender, including the sartorial marker of their identity, the performance of "women's tasks," and the various methods of beautification employed, such as the use of hormones. However, in addition to the resignification of normative gender aspirations and practices that hijra performances evoke, there is another facet to their performativity that suggests a more subversive role.

In particular, the flamboyant and markedly hijra practices of hand-clapping and flashing of their genitalia, by focusing attention on their sexual ambiguity as opposed to their femininity, makes it difficult to interpret their identity as *either* merely reinscribing gender norms, *or* purely as subverting gender in the Indian cultural context.

PRACTICE MAKES THE PERFECT WOMAN: MARKERS AND METHODS OF GENDER ENACTMENT

"When I was very young, I used to love going to my uncle's shop. He was a tailor. All the little bits of cloth that were lying around, I used to gather all of them and tie them on my head like I had long braids. Then I would use other bits to make a sort of midi [skirt] and go hide under the bed. My uncle used to have a radio in his shop. He used to love old film songs. I used to sit under the bed and listen to these songs, [flick] my long hair, and feel really happy. The only person who knew [that I used to do this] was my sister, but she didn't tell anyone because I would have been thrashed by my father and brothers if anyone knew."

Kajal, one of the hijra sex workers living under the water tank, related this incident about her childhood to me, her eyes shining at the memory. I had asked her how and when she first knew she was a hijra. In response, she said this to me, following which she narrated the incident above: "From when I was very young, I used to like wearing my sister's clothes, combing her hair, playing with girls—everything that a girl would do. That is how I knew I was a hijra." This theme—the realization of hijra identity by way of sartorial desire and gendered (female) practice—was one that recurred over and over again throughout my fieldwork. In addition to stating that they were "born this way," almost all hijras would add sartorial and performative elements to their (re)constructions of identity. Shakuntala, another hijra sex worker, said almost the same thing: "I knew I was a hijra because I always liked to wear women's clothes, do women's work, and dance and sing." Similarly, Surekha provided a version of the same story: "From birth, I always liked to put *moggus* [designs made on the ground with colored powder, primarily by women], play with girls, dress like them, and help with the cooking and cleaning." In hijra conceptualizations, constructing a feminine appearance and enacting gendered practices were some of the foremost determining criteria of gender and sexuality; to a certain extent, such performative (gendered) attributes defined hijras' sense of self.

This gendered component is evident in their delight at passing as women, an ability that was highly valued in the community and was explicitly articulated by hijras as a positive attribute. For instance, when Munira returned after a month-long trip to Delhi, the first thing she told me was how she was mistaken for a woman on the journey to Delhi a month ago. She was sleeping in the "ladies compartment"[2] along with her cela, Aliya. "I always travel in the ladies compartment. If I cannot get a reservation in the ladies compartment, then I don't go," Munira said with respect to this issue. There were three other women in the compartment, and a small child, the daughter of one of these women. Because Aliya looked "exactly like a man," everyone knew she was a hijra, "but they were not sure about me," Munira said. Soon, it was night and everyone got ready to sleep. Munira had the lower berth. Because they had closed the door to the compartment, Munira kept her window half-open. In the middle of the night, when they had stopped at a station, she felt a movement and woke up with a start. A man had put his hands through the bars of the window and was going to snatch her gold necklace from around her throat. She was too scared to shout, but the woman in the berth across from her saw his hand and started screaming. The man hastily withdrew his hand and ran away. Everyone in the compartment had woken up in the meantime and began to inquire after Munira. "They called me *behenji* [sister] and asked if I was all right. Then they started cursing men and saying that nowadays it was impossible for women to get out of their house and feel safe with these ruffian men everywhere. Obviously, they thought I was a woman," Munira concluded with pride.

Likewise, Surekha told me proudly of the time she was mistaken for a woman in the market when she went to buy some jewelry. "They thought I was a woman! They spoke to me really politely and gave me a seat to sit in. I was scared to open my mouth because then they would know. I came away without buying anything because of that," she said. In a similar incident, Saroja asked me to accompany her to the market to get her eyes tested and get a new pair of glasses. In the shop, the salesmen obviously thought we were both women. As a result Saroja would not open her mouth to say anything while we were in there, even when I asked her a direct question, nodding and shaking her head to indicate her preference. "Once we speak, then people know we are hijras because of our voices. That is why I did not want to talk in the shop," Saroja told me as we were on our way home. Clearly, there is some pleasure and izzat associated with passing as a woman.

While looking like a woman is not a necessary criterion of hijra authenticity, it is valued and contributes significantly to their sense of self and identity. In fact, the physical appearance of a hijra and the degree to which she looked (or did not look) like a woman was a common topic of conversation within the group, often being the subject of their jokes when teasing one another. For instance, Saroja had nicknamed Surekha *kukka sandlu* (dog-breasts) on account of her flat chest, an epithet that was invoked gleefully by all the other hijras whenever they wanted to make fun of Surekha. Despite popping "Sunday-Monday *golis* [pills]"—oral contraceptives that contain estrogen and progesterone—by the dozen, much to her frustration, Surekha's breasts did not grow.

In contrast, Saroja was much respected for her ability to pass. She was the only hijra among the sex workers under the tank who was a *daiamma cibri*, that is, one who had been operated on by a hijra *daiamma* or midwife. This practice—of having a *daiamma* perform the operation—although considered significantly more dangerous to one's life than a "doctor *cibri*," and perhaps because of it, was more respected than the latter. It was also believed to produce a more feminine and therefore coveted appearance. *Daiamma cibris* have significantly less facial and body hair growth, and their skin is believed to become softer after their operation—"just like a woman's." As Surekha restated, "their bodies become more rounded, more like a woman's body." This construction of femininity—rounded, voluptuous bodies, absence of body hair, smooth, soft skin, and, they would add, long, thick hair that could be braided without any need to attach false hair—is also hijras' ideal of beauty and the goal toward which they all strived.

Erasing "Masculinity"

Apart from undergoing the *nirvan* operation and ingesting dozens of Sunday-Monday *golis* among other hormonal substances (see Kulick 1998), hijras also engage in several less harmful practices to erase vestiges of masculinity and enhance their femininity.[3] One of the most common of these is the use of tweezers (*cimte*) to pluck out their facial hair. All hijras are required to tweeze their facial hair. The leaders impose a fine on those who disregard this rule. The reason for this painful practice is that facial hair does not grow back as quickly and coarsely as it would if shaved. Hijras willingly undergo the torturous practice largely because they want to look as much like women as possible. "If someone uses a razor, then we can make out immediately. The face gets all black and the hair grows thicker and more quickly. It looks like a man's face; it does not look good at all," Munira informed me when I asked initially. As a result whenever I went to visit the hijras, I would invariably find at least one of them sitting and plucking out her beard, holding a mirror to her face so she could get at every hair. If possible, hijras would get another to do it for them, lying in her lap while their hair was systematically plucked out with a special pair of tweezers. These tweezers have a large, flat blade, wider than I've ever seen in regular shops in India. I was told that this was a special *cimte* made by hijras for the use of other hijras. It was not available in any store and therefore was a prized possession.

There were frequent fights over *cimtes*, with accusations of stealing and unsolicited use being common causes for violent arguments and even physical fights. Not everyone appeared to own a *cimte*, especially not the younger hijras. They were therefore highly valued and could be used to garner favors and to barter for goods and services. Although it was rare for a guru to deny permission to use one of her *cimtes*, the owner of a *cimte* would sometimes demand a service for the use of it. Often, Munira or one of the older hijras would tell a younger one that she would lend her her *cimte* if she ran an errand for her—usually something easy like getting her a cold drink from the stall a couple of hundred meters away. In addition, the possession of a *cimte* was also used to garner affection and support from other hijras. For instance, Madhavi gave her *cimte* to Munira, her *nani* (grandmother), to demonstrate her affection for her and possibly to curry Munira's favor. The tweezers were also used for profit. Sati had bought her *cimte* in another city, while on a *jatra* (pilgrimage) with other siva-sati kotis a few years ago.[4] She said she bought two, but used only one. When the blade of this *cimte* became somewhat blunt, she sold it to one of her fellow hijras for substantially more than she paid for it.

While most kotis know about this hijra possession, and some of them had bought *cimtes* from hijras, its use was not as wide and strictly enforced in other koti communities. However, given its potential for creating a more "feminine" appearance, many kotis would come to the tank to use hijras' *cimtes*. In fact, this was how I met the first kada-catla koti to whom I was introduced. He told me he had come to visit his "mother," as he referred to a senior hijra—a kinship link born "out of affection" rather than any formal, recognized ceremony—and to use her *cimte*. He was a "kada-catla koti, a *paonbattawala*," that is, an ostensibly "heterosexual," married, non-sari-wearing man in koti terminology, as one of the hijras told another disparagingly, in response to the latter's question.[5] He stayed only a few hours chatting with his mother while she "removed his *darsan*," or beard, before leaving.

The term *darsan* was used by all kotis to refer both to the beard and to the act of plucking out one's beard (see Bradford 1983). If someone asked where another hijra was, the answer was often "She is doing [her] *darsan*." Interestingly, this term is one of the most ubiquitous in Hindu religious

Hijras tweezing their beards

worship, and refers in that context to the ritual viewing of the god/goddess and the receiving of his/her blessing in return (Eck 1981). Lawrence Babb (1981) has noted that for Hindus, vision is the cosmologically crucial sense, and being seen is "not just . . . a passive product of sensory data originating in the outer world," but a constant flow of energy emanating from "the inner person, outward through eyes to engage directly with objects seen, and to bring something of these objects back to the seer" (396). In this substantive sense, as Bernard Cohn notes, the concept of *darsan* operates both at the sacred and profane levels: "Indians wish to see and be seen, to be in the sight of, to have the glance of, not only their deities, but persons of power . . . [such as] . . . a movie star or the Prime Minister" (1989, 346). In the context of this chapter, perhaps the hijras' act of *darsan*—a performative act of desirous sight/agency—indexes the importance of praxis as well as the significance of the desire to see and be seen in the everyday world as nonmasculine (see also Cohen 1995b).

When I asked hijras about this meaning of the term in connection with their usage, however, they just laughed and did not elaborate on its etymology. For the most part, hijras under the tank did not know the etymological significance of many of their terms and seemed to use them without any *explicit* subversive intent. As many of them stated, they used the *cimte* so that "they would look more like a woman." While this act could be read at a broader level as a potentially subversive one, this did not appear to be the manifest intent of hijras/kotis. For them the *cimte* was a means to approach their beauty ideal, and thus it was an important and highly coveted object in their eyes.

Hijras also sometimes underwent an "operation" to remove facial hair. On one occasion when I was visiting Irfan nayak, another hijra from Delhi, Nagma, was lying down in an inner room, her face completely swathed in bandages. She could hardly speak, and Irfan told me in very disapproving terms that she had just spent "thousands and thousands of rupees" on an operation to permanently remove her facial hair. Apparently, another hijra in Delhi had had this same operation and "it was a success." Despite the pain, discomfort and expense, therefore, Nagma thought it well worth the effort because then she "could look just like a woman [and] not have to use the *cimte* every day."

Hijras also used facial bleach for a more feminine appearance. Senior hijras frowned on the practice, but some of the younger hijras I knew (especially the sex workers under the tank) used this method to "make [their] faces whiter, more like a woman's, [and] the hair less visible."[6] This was an "unconventional," recently adopted method, one which Surekha had "discovered" when leafing through a magazine. It was advertised for women who wanted to conceal their facial hair, and once tried, was enthusiastically adopted by some of the other hijras at the tank. It was not a common hijra practice, and I was told, if somewhat sheepishly, not to let the senior nayaks know that they were adopting such practices, even though the nayaks themselves were aware of and clearly disapproved of this activity. Obviously, hijras were inclined to use whatever methods worked in terms of their beautification. For instance, having explained the process of electrolysis to these hijras—a process I presumed hijras had not heard about, given their polite and curious expressions—I called an electrolysis center in Hyderabad on their behalf to ask if hijras could use this method. Before I could ask a question about hijras' eligibility, I was told brusquely that it was "only for women, not men." As the receptionist then explained, some hijras had apparently called and asked about this process, necessitating their prefatory remarks.

Augmenting "Femininity"

In contrast to methods of erasure such as the use of the tweezers and the bleaching of their faces, hijras also adopt more additive methods of beautification, namely, the use of makeup, jewelry, and the growing of their hair, to approximate a "female" appearance. At least once a week, I was asked by hijras if I knew of any "foreign" medicine that "made people white [fair], like those people in Amrika." One of the essential items for hijras was a tube of Fair and Lovely cream, a moisturizing cream sold widely in Indian markets that they applied liberally on their faces in an attempt to make themselves look "fair and lovely." This desire for whiteness, while it may not have the same racial undertones that it might have in the United States, is nevertheless widespread in India, especially in South India, where people are often darker than in the north.[7] Almost the first comment about a newborn is about the child's coloring. "Oh! Look how dark she is. That is too bad," or "She has nice eyes, even though she is so dark," might be common statements at the birth of a child, particularly a daughter. In this sociocultural context, whiteness or being fair is beautiful, especially for women. Hijras appear to subscribe to this belief too. Not only do many of them use Fair and Lovely cream, but they also apply "phanking" (pancake, or foundation makeup) fairly liberally on their faces to achieve this effect. Every evening, when hijra sex workers under the tank were getting ready for work, they invariably fought over accusations of excessive use of one another's "cream" or "phanking." Dressing up invariably involved whitening one's face to look beautiful. Since I was fairer than most hijras under the tank and supposedly had access to all the "special creams and medicines [that were] 'foreign,'" I was constantly asked to get them miracle cures so all of them could become "whiter" (fairer) and thereby "more beautiful."

In addition to skin color, another gendered aspect of hijras' beauty ideal was the use of jewelry, which accentuated their femininity as well as their hijra identity. In all the time I was in Hyderabad, the only hijras I saw without any jewelry were those who were *munda*, or widowed (see chapter 7), a stigmatized and temporary condition that hijras attempted to alleviate as soon as possible. Other than a *munda* hijra, all others, however poor, wore at least some jewelry, if only plastic earrings or a fake pearl necklace. Richer hijras, including some of the older hijra sex workers, possessed and often wore solid gold jewelry. Gold was most often the first substantial purchase that hijras made, and most of the hijras I knew in Hyderabad had at least one or two items of gold jewelry.

Another marker of beauty was the length of a hijra's hair. All hijras were required to grow their hair once they joined the community. This rule was obligatory; any infraction brought a fine (*dand*). Although not all hijras followed the rule, especially the younger hijra sex workers who wanted to experiment with different hairstyles, they tried to conceal from the senior nayaks the fact that they had cut their hair, primarily by using false hair

Hijras bleaching their faces

attachments (*saurams*). Almost all hijras I knew had *saurams* that they braided into their hair. These *saurams* were not cheap, each one costing from two to five hundred rupees, yet almost all the hijras had their own *sauram*, and some of the older ones had two or three each.

The first time I approached hijras under the tank, they thought I was a young boy, despite my wearing a *salwar-kurta* a dress worn by young women, primarily because of the length of my hair, as Munira told me later. At first we thought, "She has the body and face of a woman, she is wearing female clothing, but she has such short hair. Maybe she is a young boy of thirteen or fourteen.... Your hair was so short that we thought, 'It cannot be a woman.'" Hijras repeatedly urged me to grow my hair long. Apart from one's dress, lack of facial hair, and vocal timbre, the length of one's hair was used to gauge and mark gender. Hijras could not understand why I *wanted* to keep my hair short. "You would look so nice if you grew your hair," Lekha told me. "Nicely you could braid it. You wouldn't need a *sauram* or anything. It is so funny. You are a woman, and you have short hair and don't want to grow your hair long, and we are men and we want nice long hair," she added, with a grin. Obviously the irony was not lost on her.

Given its gendered associations, this marker was greatly coveted by hijras. They would take pains to oil their hair, wash it "with Clinic shampoo only, not Shikakai," so that their hair would be thick and shiny, "just like the woman on TV who uses this shampoo," they said, referring to the advertisement for this product. They would constantly compare the length and thickness of their hair and poke fun at those who had less luxuriant hair. Shanti in particular, being bald, was the butt of these jokes because she was most insecure about this issue. Her baldness was attributed to her age and especially to the age at which she had undergone the *nirvan* operation.[8] Although Shanti claimed otherwise, she looked to be almost forty years old and had become a *nirvan sultan* only three years ago. Especially because it irritated her so much, the other hijras called her *bodi* (bald). When I first asked her name, she said "Shanti," but all those around her grinned and said, "You can also call her Kabir-*bodi* [bald Kabir]." Both Shanti and another hijra who was balding wore wigs every evening when they dressed up to solicit clients.

Having long hair was not only desirable, it was also required. A hijra had to grow her hair long or incur a stiff fine. Hijra sex workers told me that every time they went to see their *dadi* (paternal grandmother), the nayak, they would make sure they attached their *saurams* to conceal the fact that they might have cut or trimmed their hair. Saroja told me that on one occasion when she visited her *dadi*, she had just cut her hair because of lice infestation. She could not tie a *sauram* properly because her hair was too short, and the nayak discovered her infraction. She was immediately made to pay five hundred rupees for breaking this rule.

Further, the length of one's hair is used as a marker of izzat or status within the community. As some of the badhai hijras insinuated, hijra sex workers are "marked" by their propensity to cut their hair, and consequently have lower izzat than them. When I first visited Lata, a badhai hijra, she said, "We don't cut our hair like those people there [under the tank], and that is why we have izzat," distancing herself from hijra sex workers. Quite apart from the desire to pass as a woman, or perhaps because of it, a koti's hairstyle and length is of primary significance in marking both identity and status (Obeyesekere 1981; Zwilling and Sweet 1996; Hiltebeitel and Miller 1998).

TAILORED IDENTITIES: SARTORIAL MARKERS AND GENDER HIERARCHIES

Perhaps the single most important marker of hijra identity and femininity/beauty, however, is their clothing. As Umberto Eco said more than twenty-five years ago, "[I] speak through my clothes" (1975, 57). Although he was alluding more generally to the semiotic potential of all objects, Eco's statement could be referring directly to hijras' emphatic use of clothing style. Hijras are identified by society, and often identify themselves as hijras, through and by their adoption of women's clothing. Such clothing is the single most visible marker of their identity and sets them apart both from heterosexual men and pantis as well as most other kotis.

Hijras are identifiable on the streets by their explicitly gender-ambiguous appearance. Most hijras have a fairly masculine musculature and physique, have deep, baritone voices, and despite their attempts to temper its growth, have at least the basic rudiments of facial hair; for the most part, they are physically distinguishable from women. Further, many hijras adopt an exaggerated feminine hip-swaying walk, grow their hair long, and most important, *all* of them wear saris. This latter attribute is what distinguishes hijras most visibly in public arenas.

Not only does their sartorial style differ from mainstream male attire, it also sets them apart from other kotis in Hyderabad. In fact, the catla (sari) serves as an important axis of koti identity and hierarchy. The only other kotis who also wear saris are jogins, and for this reason, jogins are also believed to "have izzat" according to hijras. Kada-catla kotis, who do not wear saris, are spoken of extremely disparagingly by hijras, who explicitly indicate that sartorial preference/performance accounts for such differences in izzat. "Among regular people, they [kada-catla kotis] might have more izzat because they dress like men and act like them. But among kotis, we have more izzat. We don't try to hide anything. We wear saris openly and throughout the day, unlike these 'king by day, queen by night' people," Munira told me in no uncertain terms. Female attire (saris in this context) serves as a marker of (public) recognition, and for hijras it is the quintessential symbol of izzat. Those who are "out" on this scale of sartorial identity (like hijras) might be more stigmatized by the wider community, but they have greater respect within their community precisely because of their sartorial practices.

Moreover, this symbol of difference apparently distinguishes hijras, in their conceptualizations, from zenanas and kada-catla kotis. My questions regarding the differences between themselves and these kotis were invariably answered by pointing to the fact that "those people are kada-catla people. They don't wear saris like us. And they have less izzat." In hijra terms this was the single most important marker of difference among kotis, in addition to the *nirvan* operation and *rit.* Clearly, "clothing matters" (Tarlo 1996; cf. Barthes 1972; Bean 1989; Cohn 1989; Hebdige 1991).

Although signification need not be intentional, as semioticians have noted, there is an identifiable difference between "intentional" and "innocent" signification, to echo Roland Barthes (1972). While the latter is "expressive of normality as opposed to deviance, i.e., [ensembles which] are distinguished by their relative invisibility, their appropriateness, their 'naturalness,'... intentional communication is of a different order.... It is a visible construction, a loaded choice. It directs attention to itself; it gives itself to be read" (Hebdige 1991, 101). As such, the "visual ensembles of spectacular subcultures," by being "obviously fabricated," go against the grain of a mainstream culture whose principle defining feature according to Barthes, is "a tendency to masquerade as nature,... to translate the reality of the world into an image of the world which in turn presents itself as if composed according to the evident laws of the natural order" (1972, 54). Hijras' intentional choice of an "unnatural" sartorial style, in this context, appears to signify difference from the "innocent" mode of mainstream society.[9] And yet, hijras strive to elide precisely this difference between intentional and innocent signification. Their obviously intentional choice of dress is accompanied by explicit efforts to craft *other* aspects of their "inappropriate" significations in line with this (intentional) mode. Significant among these efforts is the use of hormones to sculpt a more "natural" female body.

HORMONE USE AND THE SCULPTING OF "FEMALE" BODIES

"See, Gayatri, I am more like a woman than any of these other hijras here. Only I can produce milk from my breasts. None of these people can. See, I'll show you. Do you know what this means? Of all the hijras here, I am most like a woman," Lekha told me proudly, while demonstrating her femininity for my benefit. One of the most commonly expressed desires on the part of hijras I met in Hyderabad was their desire for a *chati* (bosom). Over and over again, I heard hijras wish for this symbol of femininity and attempt to translate this desire into practice. Despite repeated sermons on my part about the deleterious effects of drugs on their bodies, almost all hijras I knew injected or ingested female hormones in order to develop a *chati* (cf. Kulick 1998).

The most common of these hormonal products are oral contraceptives for women, commonly referred to as "Sunday-Monday *golis*," which are sold across the counter in all pharmacies. The one most commonly used is sold under the brand name Lyndiol, which contains primarily estrogen/progesterone compounds. While the normal dosage for ovulating *women* is one pill a day, hijras would take as many as nine to twelve pills a day, believing in their cumulative effects to produce the "biggest breasts in the shortest time." Hijras would frequently compare their breasts, commenting on their shape, size, and lactating potential. Even though many of them knew that these "*golis* were not good for the body," they continued to take them in alarming dosages. "We want a *chati*, Gayatri. If you want us to stop taking these pills, then tell us what to do to get a *chati*," Sati responded angrily one day, when I told her, somewhat moralistically, that such excessive use of these *golis* was not good for her. Similarly, Surekha said, "So what if it is bad for you? Anyway we all die. But this way we will have a *chati* and look just like women. Look at Lekha and those other hijras anyway. They take at least fifteen *golis* a day, and nothing has happened to them. No illness, no nothing. They sleep well, eat like buffaloes, and have a nice *chati* and everything! She even gets milk from her *chati*, do you know?" she added enviously.

Perhaps more deleterious to their health than this unrestricted use of oral contraceptives is hijras' recent habit of injecting themselves with estrogen and progesterone concentrates, bought illegally from the local pharmacies. Not only were they completely unaware of exactly how these products affected their hormone levels and more generally their bodies, none of them would go to a doctor or nurse either to get a prescription or in order to be injected. Shanti claimed to know how to give an injection, having "watched a doctor many times," and it was to her that hijras under the tank went for their weekly injections. Shanti not only had no training, but she used the same needle for multiple injections, facilitating the transmission of HIV (among other infections). Although hijras had heard that these *golis* and *sudis* (injections) were bad for them, they also knew that these substances produced results. Given their strong desire for a *chati*, they felt this risk was worth taking. The yearning to possess womanly attributes—breasts being one of the most visible and significant of these—was an extremely important motive for such practices.

The other corporeal symbol of femininity for hijras was the vagina, or *sipo* as they called it in their (Farsi) vocabulary (Hall 1995, 1997).[10] As some of the hijras told me, they had repeated operations to construct a vagina after their *nirvan* operation. Significantly, only the kandra hijras and only those among them who had had the *nirvan* operation expressed the desire for and subjected themselves to this operation. This procedure does not approximate a transsexual operation, but it does result in the semblance of a vagina, if only just "for show." Munira told me very proudly that her husband, Zahid, thought she had a "real" vagina immediately after her operation. Apparently, hijras ask the doctor who performs the (illegal) *nirvan* operation to stitch up the flap of skin immediately below the urethra to give the appearance of a "woman's body." Vasundara told me she had had as many as three operations because the skin had not been stitched up properly. Although the practice is not essential for constructing hijra authenticity, this corporeal symbol does assume some significance in hijras' mimetic production of female gender.

In addition to harboring the desire for breasts, a vagina, and the fantasy of nursing a child, *cibri* (operated) hijras also informed me that they had periodic discharges every month, "just like a woman's menstrual period." While it is not blood that is discharged, it is not seminal fluid either, they stated, a claim with substantial medical and symbolic significance. "It is a white discharge, but not thick like semen [*nirji* in koti vocabulary or *intiriam* in Telugu]. It is watery, and once every few weeks we have to have it, otherwise we get headaches and back pain," Madhavi informed me. Munira echoed this statement, stating that it was only operated hijras who had this periodic discharge "just like it is for a woman." I was told repeatedly that this fluid was not semen, like "what the *akkva* [non-operated] hijras discharge."

THE MIMESIS OF FEMININITY AND PARODIC GENDER SUBVERSION

Despite all these accoutrements of femininity, hijras and other kotis did not unequivocally think of themselves as women. Whenever I asked a question regarding their gender affiliation, hijras would laugh and say, "We are neither men nor women; we are hijras" (Nanda 1990). As Amir nayak stated categorically, "there are three *jatis* [castes] in this world—men, women, and hijras." Hijras are "born this way," a result of the "different mixing of 'creams' in the mother's womb," as Madhavi believed. Although they are "more like women than like men [and] can talk and behave more freely with women," hijras are not women. The most explicit proof of this is their inability to produce children. Almost all the hijras I interacted with appeared to love children, and many harbored a fantasy of giving birth and nursing a child. They often insisted on my photographing them while they "nursed" a child in their laps, but as they themselves indicated, "hijras cannot give birth to a child themselves." As evidence of this, I was told the story of Tarabai:[11]

There was once a hijra named Tarabai who desperately wanted children of her own. So she went to Ajmer Baba and asked for this wish to be granted.[12] Only, she said, "I want a child to be produced in my womb," and did not explicitly ask for it to be born. So her pregnancy continued for several months and finally, unable to bear the pain and burden any longer, Tarabai slit her stomach and removed the baby, killing herself and the baby. But to this day, hijras who go to Ajmer Baba's *dargah* [tomb] inevitably pay homage to Tarabai as well.

This story was recounted by hijras as "proof" that they "cannot have children," and by virtue of this fact "are not women" (Nanda 1990). At least a few of the hijras see themselves as neither men nor women but as hijras. As Munira said to me in unequivocal terms, "I was born a hijra, I am a hijra, and I will always be a hijra."

In one of the most widely read treatises on the production of gender in recent years, Judith Butler outlines a genealogical critique, arguing for the understanding of (all) gender as "performance" and, relatedly, for parody as the most effective strategy for subverting the fixed "binary frame" of gender. For Butler, as for Erving Goffman, "Our identities, gendered and otherwise, do not express some authentic inner 'core' self but are the dramatic *effect* (rather than the cause) of our performances" (Bordo 1992, 168; see also Butler 1990; Goffman 1973). In such a framework, all identities are performative, and conscious parody of such performance is what subverts both the category and lived reality of gender. But who or what decides the parodic nature of a performance? In some of Butler's early work, discourse is viewed as foundational; the body, in many ways, is seen as thoroughly "text."[13] Hence, in a Butlerian reading, determinations of the parodic or subversive nature of a particular act or performance can presumably be "read" from the "textual surface" of the body, without a necessary contextualization of such meanings through history, lived experience, materiality, and cultural or institutional context.

In the case of hijras, for instance, does their gendered performance constitute parodic subversion, or does it merely constitute a resignification of normative gender ideals and practices? Hijras clearly express an overwhelming desire for the accoutrements of femininity. Does this imply that hijras are merely reinscribing given, normative patterns of gender ascription and aspiration? Equally clearly in many contexts, hijras appear to perceive their identities as outside the binary frame of gendered reference. Given hijras' realization of the constructed nature of their (gendered) identities, does this in itself constitute their performance as parody and therefore as potentially subversive? What constitutes resistance in such a scenario? In other words, are hijras primary agents of gender subversion in the Indian cultural context, or are they uncritically reinscribing gendered categories through their desires and practices?

While hijras' sartorial preferences, cosmetic practices, and excessive hormone use seem to favor the latter interpretation, that is, an uncritical reinscription of normative gender ideals, other hijra performances problematize such an easy characterization. Not only do hijras explicitly locate themselves outside the binary frame of reference, they also deploy specific practices that appear to focus attention explicitly on their gender liminality rather than accentuate their femininity. Two such practices are their distinctive hand-clap and the lifting of their saris to expose their genitalia (or lack thereof). These practices serve as performative correctives to an easy understanding of their identity as merely embodying a resignification of existing gender patterns. Instead, these dramatic hijra performances necessitate critical reflection on hijras' role in this debate and indicate that they are neither *only* subversive agents of resistance nor simply particularly flamboyant feminine surrogates. Hijras appear to embody both these images/ideals, and their gender performances instantiate their "inherently ambiguous" and axial position in the Indian imaginary (see Trawick 1990, 242).

"TROUBLING" PERFORMANCES: HIJRA HAND-CLAPPING

Scene 1: When I was in the marketplace one day, I saw a group of four hijras who had come to ask for money from the shop owners. On being refused payment by a shop owner, all four hijras began to clap loudly, hurling abusive epithets at the shopkeeper. *Scene 2:* "*Arre*, what kind of hijra are you?" Munira asked Gopalamma half-jokingly, clapping her hands together vigorously when the latter informed her that she was going to cut her hair (a transgression of hijra rules) because of lice infestation. *Scene 3:* A knife-sharpener had come to the tank at the beckoning of one of the hijras. On being flirted with and teased mercilessly by them, the distinctly uncomfortable man started to slap his thighs like a wrestler and say repeatedly, "I am a man, I am a man." Sati, a hijra who was one of the chief provocateurs, started clapping her hands in response and saying defiantly, "We are hijras, we are hijras. What do you think, *re?*" *Scene 4:* A group of zenana kotis was sitting in a circle on the central lawn of the Public Garden. One of the newcomers to their fold turned to his neighbor and asked him if he had a *rit* (kinship marker). The latter, apparently offended, promptly started clapping his hands and said in reply, "What do you think? We have izzat. We are *rit-riwaz* people [people with a kinship custom/tradition]."

In all of the above scenes, the distinctive clapping of hands served as an unambiguous marker of hijra/zenana identity. All four individuals used it self-consciously both to signal their allegiance to these identities and to be marked as such by the audience(s) in question. More than any other gesture or movement, this loud clapping of hands is indelibly associated with hijras. Any parodic imitation of hijras would need to include only this gesture to be recognizable as such.

In scene 4 above, the group of zenanas looked like any group of men sitting on the lawns of the garden until Arif began to clap. Automatically, all those in their immediate vicinity cast them as hijras. As I was walking out of the garden on my way home a short while later, a man who identified himself as a (plain clothes) policeman followed me to the gate and asked me what I was doing with those *hijre-log* (hijra people). Even when hijras could have passed as women, the minute they started clapping their hands they were marked unambiguously as hijras. On one occasion, I had gone to the market with Surekha because I wanted her help in buying a sari. Apparently the salesmen in the two shops we went to thought she was a woman too. We bought the sari and had just stepped out of the shop when two junior hijras from the Sheharwala house walked up to Surekha and extremely belligerently asked her to pass on a threat to Rajeshwari, another hijra in the tank group. There had been a recent flare-up in antagonism between these two groups (the Lashkarwala hijras under the tank and another, smaller group of Sheharwala hijras engaging in sex work close by), with each being accused of sending ruffians to beat the other. Surekha reacted immediately and, clapping her hands loudly, said, "We are not scared of you. What are you going to do?" The shop owner who was standing next to me was extremely surprised and said, "I didn't realize that was a hijra! What are you doing with people like that?" The clapping of hands, more than any other embodied performance, publicly identifies a hijra.

Hijras know that better than anyone else and consciously use this act to mark their identity and negotiate the sentiments at play. In scene 1 above, the hijras wanted to attract attention to themselves *as hijras*. The clapping served to mark them as hijras in this public space, an identity they then levered to their advantage by signaling their difference and disruptive potential, both social/symbolic and physical. They played on their potential for shaming the shop owner to get what they wanted: once they start their performance, the owner usually pays up quickly to get rid of them.[14] Hijras, perhaps even more than others, recognize their marginality as nonprocreative, disfigured people who are "neither men nor women." But rather than acquiesce in this marginalization, they proclaim their status publicly, acknowledging their stigma and playing on it. They draw attention to themselves with their hand-clapping, recognizing its potential both to label them and to threaten the public. While marking them as hijras, the clapping gesture also symbolizes their potential, precisely because of their acknowledged marginality, to shame the public and make them lose their respect. Hence, although it is often a double-edged sword, hijras use this clapping gesture to mark their identity and to deploy this identity to their advantage.

Clapping, however, is not merely a *public* hijra practice; it is used even within the hijra community to symbolize both identity and relative izzat. In scene 2, for instance, Munira's clapping was meant to signal to Gopalamma not only the inappropriateness of her action according to hijra rules, but also Munira's self-proclaimed superiority on account of this transgression: Munira, in contrast to Gopalamma, was a "real hijra" who did not commit such infractions. The hand-clapping served to reinforce this sentiment, signaling its specific use as a hijra marker of identity and authenticity. Similarly, when Arif, the self-identified zenana, clapped in the garden in response to his fellow koti's remark, he was doing so to indicate his greater izzat in this relationship. Although it marks him as a hijra in the public eye, this practice also signifies his allegiance to this community and his voluntary subjection to its rules and regulations. Having a *rit* in a hijra house serves to elevate the status of a koti (at least according to hijras and zenanas), and by clapping like a hijra, Arif is acknowledging his acceptance of this fact and his greater izzat on account of it.

Further, this practice is also utilized as an explicit means of distancing in-group from out-group and signaling solidarity within the community. As Kira Hall (1997) notes, hijras have a special clap—what they refer to as *dedh tali*, or one-and-a-half clap—that signals the onset of a particular discursive performance for the benefit of the public. As she states, "When in the presence of non-hijras,...hijras create scripted quarrels amongst themselves to shock and embarrass their eavesdropping bystanders, [with] some hijra communities having a special *tali* [clap] used expressly for signaling the onset of this discursive strategy" (448). Clapping, in other words, explicitly marks the liminality of hijra identity and is explicitly deployed to indicate both solidarity and authenticity within this marked category.

(DIS)EMBODIED EXPOSURES, REVEALING PRACTICES

Yet another performance that focuses attention explicitly on hijra sex/ gender ambiguity is the practice long associated with the hijra community of lifting their saris to expose their lack of genitalia (Bhimbai 1901; Russell, Bahadur, and Lal 1916; Preston 1987; Ayres 1992). This action, more than the hand-clapping, is threatening to the public on account of its potential for shaming them. Hijras' lifting of their saris is embarrassing and even shameful not only because many people find exposing oneself distasteful, but because it is especially so when "there is nothing there"—a fact, however, that makes the act potentially empowering for hijras. The absence of genitalia signals a paradoxical inversion of power in favor of hijras, both by exposing the mutilation of the body and by implicitly incorporating a potential curse, as if to say, "By exposing myself to you, I curse you with such a fate."

To a large extent, hijras are constructed as people without *sarm* (shame). "[Hijras] are shameless. They have no honour. They are answerable to no one," Ved Vatuk contends (quoted in Hall 1997, 446). By rejecting the centrality of procreation—"the question of progeny" (Balse 1976)—hijras are perceived to be outside the social order. As Kira Hall notes, they are "a people freed from the constraints of decency that regulate the rest of society" (1997, 445). Quoting a hijra in Benares, she adds, "Hijras are just hijras, and women are just women. If there's a woman, she'll at least have a little *sarm*. But hijras are just hijras. They have no *sarm*" (445). As Satish Sharma and other anthropologists maintain, it is by virtue of their impotence/sexual dysfunctionality and gender ambiguity that hijras are considered to be outside the social mainstream and thus to have "no *sarm*" (Pimpley and Sharma 1985; Vyas and Shingala 1987; Sharma 1989). Hijras serve as potential repositories of shamelessness, and by exposing that by which they are construed as shameless, they serve as purveyors of this stigma to the public. Given their perception as *besarm* (without shame) and knowing their potential to invoke shame in others, people are afraid of provoking them. As Morris Carstairs states, "[Hijras'] shamelessness [makes] people reluctant to provoke their obscene retaliation in public." Serena Nanda (1990) echoes this statement when she notes that "hijras know that their shamelessness makes most people reluctant to provoke them in a public confrontation" (51). Hijras in turn use this knowledge to their advantage, threatening to lift their saris if their demands are not met. Interestingly, hijras also explicitly see their action as one of reclaiming respect or izzat. When I asked Munira the meaning of their practice, she said, "If people give us respect, then we are also respectful. But if they do not show us respect, then we also abuse them verbally and lift our saris. Then they bow their heads in shame and give us respect. It is like that."

In addition, the act of exposing themselves in itself conveys a potential curse to those who are subjected to the sight. There is a strong belief that by exposing their mutilated genitals, hijras can curse those present and render them impotent or infertile. In fact, as Serena Nanda (1990) notes, in highly orthodox families hijras were not allowed access to new brides for fear of their potential to contaminate the brides with their infertility (see Marriott 1976; O'Flaherty 1980; Daniel 1984; and Trawick 1990 for South Asian conceptions of "substance" transfer). By employing this strategy, hijras embrace this construction of them and use it to gain power.

This act is most often deployed during the explicitly public badhai performances. Almost every such performance ends with hijras haggling with the family of the bride or newborn child over the acceptable payment, and they often threaten to expose themselves if more money is not forthcoming. Even the threat of this action often produces results; to avoid the shameful exposure, the family often gives in to the hijra demands. As one South Indian neighbor of mine told me, "You just cannot get rid of [hijras] easily. They came to my house when my son was born, and, until we gave them what they wanted, they didn't leave. They started shouting obscenities, and they were even ready to lift their saris! So, to preserve our honor, we had to give them what they wanted."

One occasion when I witnessed this act was during the scene described in the previous section with the kandra hijras under the tank and the knife-sharpener. Not only did Sati start clapping her hands when the man did not stop his assertions regarding his masculinity, Shakuntala got up and, without warning, lifted her sari in front of him. Publicly shamed, the knife-sharpener immediately packed his things and literally ran from the tank. In recounting this incident to Munira later, Sati triumphantly told her, "When that *bhadva* [pimp] did not shut up, Shakuntala put her sari [*catla esindi*] on him."[15] This phrase—*catla esindi*—is used expressly for this action in koti terminology. As in this instance, it is used in a self-denigrating way but one that is paradoxically empowering at the same time. While Shakuntala's act of lifting her sari clearly focused attention on her stigmatized hijra identity, this action was simultaneously a statement that mocked male power and the procreative imperative. Much like the *nirvan* operation, this practice focuses attention precisely on the ascetic, non-reproductive gender liminality of hijras—a position that they embrace and use to their advantage.

Both these practices serve as unambiguous markers of muddied gender (as well as critical symbols of abjection and asceticism). Unlike the various accoutrements of femininity described earlier, these gender performances explicitly counter a reading of hijras as *merely* reinscribers of normative femininity. At the very least, by focusing attention on themselves as liminal figures both in terms of embodiment and gender ascription, hijras appear as potentially subversive agents, serving self-consciously to cause "gender trouble."

And yet, such an uncritical reading, which disregards their heartfelt desire to pass as women and does not view their embodied desires/practices as signifiers of more than merely muddied *gender* difference, is inadequate to any rigorous analysis of hijras' lives and the investments that are at stake for them. In many ways, these hijra practices and empowering stances encapsulate the limitations of a binary analysis that neither takes into account the imbrication of gender with/within the multiplicity of differences that constitute an individual's life, nor adequately captures what Margaret Trawick describes as the "intentional ambiguity of Indian life" (1990, 42). Such ambiguity, Trawick argues, is at the heart of all acts, persons, and relationships in India, a crucial quality in any understanding between human beings. As she elegantly puts it,

Intentional ambiguity, of the Indian variety, is more than just anomaly or unclassifiable otherness, more than something outside the structure that has somehow to be dealt with, more than just an ad-hoc way of getting from one category to another, and more than the kind of once-a-year chaos that is needed to keep some orders well-defined. Intentional ambiguity is not interstitial ambiguity, marginal, liminal ambiguity characteristic of what is dismaying or strange to people, but ambiguity at the heart of things, openly embraced where it is found, emphasized where it is hard to perceive, and created where it could not otherwise exist. (42)

As figures that simultaneously enact mutually exclusive interpretive frames and encode potentially discrepant presentations of self, hijras display such ambiguity in all its subtle, complex forms. They do not, in any simple way, *merely* subvert or reinscribe gender difference, but actively and intentionally court ambiguity in this regard. As "troubling" agents extraordinaire—for academics perhaps more so than for their own sense of self—hijra instantiations of ambiguity allow us to move beyond the aporia of the structure/agency debate undergirding much sociological and feminist analyses and to capture the fundamental, if elusive, quality of ambiguity—with respect to gender as well as religion, kinship, and class—that constitutes hijras' sense of self and relationship to wider society. Hijras, more than any gender theorists, are aware of this complexity and ambiguity. As Munira once said to me, "We are neither men nor women, but at the same time we are both. Hijras are *adha-bic* [half-in-the-middle] people, and that is why we are both feared and respected at the same time."

7

"Our People"

KINSHIP, MARRIAGE, AND THE FAMILY

In 1995, when I began my research, Saroja had just one cela (disciple), Madhavi, whom she appeared to be extremely fond of. Madhavi had been with Saroja for at least four or five years and had been an ideal cela in many respects. She looked after her guru (master) when she was ill, cooked and cleaned for her, bore all the expenses for her guru's frequent trips to her village, and supported Saroja when the latter did not feel like working. Although occasionally late in her daily payments to her guru, Madhavi never rebelled against this responsibility and was always respectful and considerate of her guru's well being. Saroja, on her part appeared to treat her cela with some consideration, giving her gifts of saris and even gold jewelry on one occasion. For all their power differentials, relations between the two seemed to be perfect.

A little over a year later, however, this situation was dramatically reversed. In December of 1996, Madhavi left to have her *nirvan* (emasculation) operation, despite Saroja's objection to this procedure, which had more to do with Saroja's resistance to relinquishing full control over her cela than with Madhavi's apparent unsuitability for the operation. When Madhavi got back about five days later, having successfully undergone the operation, she found herself without a home or support from any of her erstwhile "family" members. Madhavi had been physically thrown out from under the tank and was ostracized by her guru and all her extended hijra kin. She was extremely weak from the operation, in terrible pain, had nowhere to go, and none of her hijra kin would help her. Her guru had ordered all the hijras at the tank to abstain from helping Madhavi in any way, on pain of social ostracism. Nobody disobeyed this order. Madhavi was alone in her pain and misery, a fitting example of what would happen if a cela defied her guru, Saroja told me.

Thrown out from under the tank, Madhavi set up house on the opposite side of the road, on a little strip of vacant land overrun with weeds and cacti. Along with her panti—"[her] man" or "husband" as she otherwise referred to him—she cleared a bit of space on this land and constructed a little tent out of cardboard boxes, plastic wrappers, and whatever scraps of metal they could find. Husband and wife lived a somewhat self-sufficient, if precarious and dangerous life here, subject to the vagaries of the weather, policemen with eviction orders, and ruffians who wanted some quick and easy money. In addition to her husband, the only other person Madhavi interacted with on a daily basis was her (adoptive) hijra mother. Following her eviction from under the tank, Madhavi was adopted as the daughter of Kamala, another hijra who lived nearby. Kamala was not "related" to the tank hijras any more, although she used to live there in the past. She had changed her (hijra) house and was now living with her panti, selling illicit liquor and drugs for a living. Kamala helped Madhavi when she needed help most. To a large extent, as Madhavi herself acknowledges, Kamala was instrumental in keeping Madhavi alive and well during this trying period in her life.

About a month after her eviction from the tank, Madhavi told me gleefully that she had "[gone] and put the *rit* in the Sheharwala house."[1] Her new guru was a hijra named Renuka who currently lived in Chandigarh, a north Indian city. Madhavi's position as Renuka's cela located her three rungs below the senior-most leader or nayak of the house. As Madhavi recounts her story, she had been a cela of this same nayak before changing houses, from Sheharwala to Lashkarwala, about five years ago. Now, she was happy to accept a position in this same house, two rungs below that she had occupied just five years ago.

This vignette points to two important issues that I explore in this chapter. First, it references the importance of kinship, that is, social arrangements that organize the reproduction of material life, and the vital significance of these bonds for hijra identity. For Madhavi, it was inconceivable to remain without a kin network. She needed kin, whether it was her mother or her guru, and not just for material but also for social and symbolic reasons. One almost never hears of a hijra who lives and works alone. Despite incessant complaining about their burdensome obligations and the abuse meted out to them by their gurus, none of the hijras I interacted with said they would choose to live alone. Hijra authenticity and relatedness are evaluated in terms of belonging—having a *rit*, a guru, and extended hijra kin—factors that signal not just hijra identity, but also their difference and greater izzat (respect) relative to their fellow kotis.

Second, this incident showcases the variety of relationships in a hijra's life—guru, mother, and husband. Contrary to popular constructions of hijras as individuals without enduring kin ties,[2] hijras themselves repeatedly articulate the importance of these relationships in constructing their sense of identity. Their articulations also reveal the hierarchical arrangement of these relationships, wherein primary legitimacy is obtained through a *rit* in a hijra house and the guru-cela bond. Madhavi could have continued living an unencumbered life with her husband and mother. But such a life was not an "authentic" hijra life. In Madhavi's conceptualization, what legitimized and authenticated her hijra status—what in effect made her a "real hijra"—were the *rit* in the Sheharwala house and her relationship with her guru.

Time and time again over the course of my fieldwork, the *rit* was mentioned as a marker of difference and izzat. Those who had a *rit* in a hijra house were perceived to be of higher status than those who did not. The *rit* not only denoted membership in the wider community, but also hierarchized kotis along this axis of kinship. Those kotis who "had a *rit* in the house" were official kin, while "*bina ritwale*," or those without a *rit*, were, technically, not kin.[3] While this did not preclude the latter from identifying as kotis, as non-hijras, it placed them lower in the hierarchy of respect or izzat.

Why this privileging of kinship as a criterion of authenticity and status within the community? What is the meaning of kinship for these individuals, and how does their construction compare with dominant patterns of kinship in South India? How is kinship used as a status marker both within the koti community and outside of it? In this chapter, I address these questions using the axis of kinship as a key marker of self-crafting and the means whereby hijras and other kotis construct their identities and negotiate their izzat.

HIJRA KINSHIP AND FAMILY REDEFINED

Analyses of kinship in India have a long and distinguished history, dating at least from the time of Henry Maine (1822–88) and Lewis Henry Morgan (1818–81). Studies of the family and kinship in this region have ranged from comparative terminological analyses (Morgan 1970) to structural analyses of marital exchange in relation to governing "values" (Dumont 1983), the discerning of "indigenous ideas of relatedness"—what Schneider called the "code" and "substance" of kinship relations (Inden and Nicholas 1977; Ostor,

Fruzzetti, and Barnett 1982; Fruzzetti 1990), the logic of the caste system (Karve 1965; Mayer 1960), the purity of women (Yalman 1963), and the ideology of gift-giving in relation to kinship (Trautmann 1981; Vatuk 1975; Raheja 1988). In all of these analyses of kinship, marriage is the central and crucial variable. Problematic as Dumont's assertions might be regarding the ubiquity of the principle of alliance in South Indian as well as North Indian kinship (see Vatuk 1969, 1982; Madan 1975; Uberoi 1989), most scholars working on conceptions of the family and kinship in India have focused on marriage or alliance as the fulcrum of relatedness and the central institution of kinship relations. This is especially true of South India, where "every conceivable pattern of descent and form of marriage is represented" (Dumont 1983).

In fact, as Margaret Trawick notes in her book *Notes on Love in a Tamil Family* (1990), "[a]ny person trying to understand South Indian culture must eventually examine and comprehend [their] elegant patterns of kinship organization" (118). Trawick's ethnography is an elegant, "person-centered account of kinship" in South India, a cataloguing of the patterns of kinship that highlight the importance and fundamental ambiguity of love. Her book is a beautifully written account of the feelings of attachment between close kin in a Tamil family and the webs of signification they weave as they mediate between the texts and contexts of their lives, between an idealized system of kinship and the nature of desire in which the ideal can never be sustained.

Like many other South Indian kinship theorists, however, Trawick has as one of her goals in this book a better understanding of the logic and aesthetics of that fundamental model or ideal of kinship in South India—the practice of preferred or prescribed cross-cousin marriage. As she notes, "A key . . . feature in the pattern of Dravidian kinship is marriage." Without this ideal, "the organization of kinship terms and the basis of the system make no sense" (1990, 119). While Trawick, perhaps more than most other South Asian kinship theorists, acknowledges the significance of variation— "the plurality of wills and desires that make up actual human life"—her ethnography does not really address the specific kinship arrangements of groups such as hijras that do not explicitly acknowledge marital obligations and procreative kinship ideologies, are not moderated by the logic of the caste system and its concern with the "purity" of women (cf. Yalman 1963; Dumont 1983), and are unmediated by the soteriological imperative of the *kanyadana* (gift of a virgin) ideal (see Trautmann 1981; Fruzzetti 1990). Given this context, perhaps the most productive comparisons for purposes of better understanding hijra kinship structures are with those social groups that are similarly located with respect to the *non*-centrality of marriage and procreative kinship arrangements, that is, "subaltern" communities such as *devadasis*, so-called servants of god or "wives of the god-king" (Marglin 1985) and *tawa'ifs*, or courtesans—groups that challenge the "respectability" of marriage, explicitly or implicitly subvert gender roles, and encode an intricate guru-*sisya parampara* (teacher-disciple tradition) and household structure.

Devadasis, literally "servants of god," are women who are ritually dedicated, often before puberty, to service in Hindu temples. Prior to the early twentieth century, when it was "outlawed," this institution was far more common, although it continues to survive today in many parts of India, especially Orissa, Karnataka, Maharashtra, and Andhra Pradesh. *Devadasis* do not marry (mortal) men. Their dedication to temple service constitutes marriage to the deity Jagannatha, or the ascetic Jamadagni.[4] As Frederique Apfel Marglin notes, "[T]he *devadasis'* kinship practices were considered highly unusual among Hindu women, essentially because they do not marry. The *devadasis* on the other hand are also considered in some ways to represent the married state *par excellence*. Being married to [the deity] and hence never becoming widows, they embody the auspiciousness of the married state" (Marglin 1985, 46; emphasis in original). They are in effect *permanently* auspicious, *nityasumangali*, or ever-auspicious "wife-of-god/woman-with-no-(human)-husband" (Srinivasan 1984, 179; cf. Kersenboom-Story 1987; Meduri 1996; Allen 1997). At the same time, however, *devadasis* are considered impure; an impurity that derives from their engagement with dance and its association with sex work in nineteenth-century India. Subsequent to their "marriage" to the deity, legal marriage was proscribed for *devadasis*, but sex—with a selected patron, often either the king or members of his household, or temple priests—was not similarly proscribed. It is therefore this tension—between the auspiciousness and the impurity of *devadasis* stemming from their engagement both with forms of dance and nonmarital sex—that is particularly interesting in the context of a comparison with hijras.

In precolonial times, *devadasis* were primarily ritual performers, formally engaged in service to the temple. They were also temple dancers—trained and associated with Indian classical dance in the context of Hindu temple worship—an occupation that increasingly defined the understanding and representation of such women from the nineteenth century onward (Vatsyayan 1968; Gonda 1975; Eschmann, Kulke, and Tripati 1978; Bradford 1983; Srinivasan 1984, 1988; Marglin 1985; Meduri 1988, 1996). Women chosen for service as *devadasis* were trained from childhood in the arts of song and dance, and were renowned for their abilities.[5] Such was their repute, legend has it that when Rama, the eponymous hero of the epic *Ramayana* returned from exile with his wife Sita, his joyous brother explicitly instructed "all masters of musical instruments, and the *ganika* [*devadasi*] in full numbers" to "go out to behold the moonlike countenance of Rama" and welcome him home (Meyer 1971, 269).[6]

Historically, the vilification and subsequent decline in status of *devadasis* stems to a large extent from the association of dance with promiscuity—from an explicit construction of *devadasis* as "temple prostitutes" (Srinivasan 1984; Kersenboom-Story 1987; Meduri 1996; Allen 1997).[7] According to the well-known historian A. L. Basham, the institution of female temple dancers used to be a pan-Indian phenomenon, at least until the turn of the century (Basham 1959). The origins of what is today referred to as classical South Indian dance stem from just such a temple dance tradition (Erdman 1996). By the early twentieth century, however, this tradition had survived in only a few South Indian temples (Bradford 1983; Srinivasan 1984, 1985, 1988; Marglin 1985). It was at this period in Indian history, in the wake of the anti-*nautch* campaign and the restrictive prescriptions of (colonial) Victorian morality, that classical dance became domesticated, reformed, and "secularized"—in effect made "respectable" for middle-class consumption through its dissociation from (Hindu) temple complexes and, by extension, from the purview of "temple prostitution" and the *devadasi* community (Meduri 1996; Allen 1997; O'Shea 1998; cf. Reed 1998).[8] As the anti-*nautch* campaign declared, the association between *devadasis'* dance traditions and their engagement in "immoral" sex necessitated their denigration and subsequent outlawing.[9]

In addition to the reduced emphasis on the institution of marriage and the circulation of the dance/sex/stigma signifiers, the social structure of *devadasi* communities as well as many of their ritual enactments also resonate significantly with the rituals and social bonds established within contemporary hijra communities. According to Marglin, whatever the caste affiliation of *devadasis* prior to their joining the community, once they are initiated, "they are classified simply as *devadasis* who are said to have no rank or caste status" (Marglin 1985, 19), a classification beyond social boundaries that has obvious parallels with the hijra community. In addition, as several of these scholars maintain, the specific rituals involved in the *pottukattu* (initiation) and the *sadanku* (incorporation) ceremonies that *devadasis* undergo not only parallel Brahmin initiation and marriage ceremonies (Srinivasan 1984, 1988; Marglin 1985; Kersenboom-Story 1987), but also bear some resemblance to the various stages of hijra authentication, including the *rit* and *nirvan* ceremonies.

Further, the principal bond for *devadasis* is that with their mother (whether "real" or adopted). This bond is the key to the *devadasi* initiate's lineage, her social standing, and her well-being in the community, often determining her choice of dance guru as well as the basis of her relationship with her guru (Srinivasan 1984; cf. Meduri 1996). Despite the law of equal inheritance for sons *and* daughters in India (a rule that often favors sons over daughters in its "normative" practice), within the *devadasi* community, it is *daughters* through whom descent and inheritance are reckoned, and it is the mother-daughter relationship that forms the principal affective, material, and social bond. In fact, as Srinivasan (1984) informs us, a "telling Tamil proverb remarks upon seeing a dark and gloomy house or atmosphere: Why the mourning? It is as dark as though a boy has been born in a *dasi's* house" (193). Marglin notes that even the unmarried *devadasis* "along with their brothers and sisters-in-law, [form] a group which has no ties with patrilineality" (1985, 35). Such marginalization of marriage, "male issue," and patrilineality/patriarchy, the implicit or often explicit gender subversion apparent within the *devadasi* community, and the structural patterns of ritual and social organization among *devadasis*, make them a more useful comparison group for better understanding hijra social structures and meanings than affinal groups organized around procreative sexuality.

Another useful comparison group in this regard is that of the courtesans, or *tawa'ifs*, in the Muslim-dominated kingdoms of precolonial India such as Hyderabad and Awadh. These women were also associated with various forms of dance and sex work (Lynton and Rajan 1974; Oldenburg 1984, 1992). In one of the few detailed accounts of *tawa'ifs* that is both historical commentary and contemporary ethnography, Veena Oldenburg provides us with a glimpse of the world of *tawa'ifs* in Lucknow, noting that this world is "as complex and hierarchical as the society of which it was a part" (1984, 134; cf. Chandra 1973; Ruswa 1982).

From the end of the eighteenth century to the mid-nineteenth century, when Lucknow served as the capital of the kingdom of Awadh, nawabs were generous patrons of the *tawa'ifs* (or the honorific, *baiji*) in this city. Well-versed in the arts of dance, music, and entertainment, these *tawa'ifs* were "preservers and performers of the high culture of the court" (Oldenburg 1992, 30) and were highly respected both in the court as well as in society at large. As one scholar maintains, at the time, "it was said that until a person had associated with courtesans he was not a polished man" (Sharar 1975, 192), and Oldenburg notes that "young sons of the nobility [were] often sent to the best-known [*tawa'if* households] for instruction in etiquette, the art of conversation and polite manners, and the appreciation of Urdu literature" (Oldenburg 1992, 30).

There were several *tawa'if* households, or *kothas*, in Lucknow until the establishment of British suzerainty in the mid-nineteenth century. These households served to entertain—and were sponsored by—different nawabs and even the king himself. Each of these *kothas* was run by a chief courtesan, or *caudharayan*, often an older *tawa'if* now engaged in training younger celas or disciples in the arts of dance, music, and gendered *nakhre* (play or performance).[10] These celas were often talented daughters (and nieces) of the household—children of the *tawa'ifs* and their wealthy sponsors—as well as destitute or abused women who sometimes "chose" the freedom of the *kotha* over the confinement of their marital lives (Oldenburg 1984, 1992). In addition to this highly trained and prestigious core group of the *caudharayan*'s celas, the *kotha* also employed people to maintain this "high culture," including special chefs and musicians.[11] It also provided space for women less talented in the "high" aesthetics of pleasure, women called *thakahis* and *randis*, who were of a different class and training than the *tawa'ifs* and provided "chiefly sexual services" for the common man (Oldenburg 1992, 31). As Oldenburg emphasizes, these *kothas* not only provided refuge for many women abused by their husbands and affinal families, but the worldview, lifestyle, and practices of the *tawa'ifs*—primarily their gendered *nakhre* (performance) and their non-confrontational enactments of *capatbazi*, or lesbianism—were "self-consciously elaborated, subtle, and covert forms of resistance against patriarchal culture" (Oldenburg 1992, 23).

Only in the mid-nineteenth century, with the consolidation of British rule in India, did the reputation and prestige of the *tawa'if* tradition decline significantly, gradually becoming synonymous with common prostitution. This decline of their reputation and izzat was as much a response to Victorian morality and the pragmatic need to provide "healthy specimens" for European soldiers, as a result of a deliberate effort on the part of the British to "denigrate nawabi culture," according to the *tawa'ifs* interviewed by Veena Oldenburg (Oldenburg 1992, 33; cf. Ballhatchet 1980). In other words, for *tawa'ifs*, the golden age of their history preceded the British presence in India; their tradition, reputation, and izzat in society were tied to the history and patronage of the nobility in Muslim-dominated kingdoms like Awadh and Hyderabad, a kingdom to which many of them migrated after the exile of the Awadhi king, Wajid Ali Shah in 1856 (Oldenburg 1992).

Much like *devadasis* and *tawa'ifs*, hijras also see their "golden age" in the past, when they received the patronage of the nobility, both Muslim and Hindu, and were respected for their knowledge and performance of the arts (especially song and dance). Like *devadasis* and *tawa'ifs*, hijras predicate their identities on a subversion of "normative" marriage patterns and gender roles, are associated with a tension between sexual chastity and "promiscuity," and encode an intricate network of kin within their households. Their "houses" include gurus, mothers, and celas as the crucial kin bonds through which they constitute a lineage and reckon kinship and descent.[12] In addition, like those of *devadasis* and *tawa'ifs*, almost all the primary relationships of belonging and caring in hijras' lives center within the social and physical unit that constitutes their community.

Several scholars have noted this intricate network of kin within the hijra community (Opler 1960; Shah 1961; Sinha 1967; Salunkhe 1976; Pimpley and Sharma 1985; Sharma 1989; Nanda 1990, 1994; Cohen 1995b; Jaffrey 1996; Agrawal 1997). In none of these analyses do procreative kinship ideologies centered on the institution of marriage occupy the primary node of hijra relatedness. While the *idea* of marriage and marital relations might circulate as an important symbolic referent for hijras—as the moment of procreative potential that occasions their auspicious presence in the public domain and as the instantiation of desire that is always in conflict with the hijra ideal—the institution is clearly not the fulcrum of the hijra kinship structure. Ideally, marriage—to a man *or* a woman—is proscribed among hijras, and affinal kin are not significant in their kinship alignments. In fact, senior hijras explicitly invoke the rhetoric of asexuality and emphasize the renunciation of worldly ties, including especially marital ties and procreative sexuality. According to hijras in Hyderabad, the status and power of hijras is unequivocally linked to that of celibate sannyasis (ascetics). As Amir nayak said, "Real hijras are those who should have no mental or physical desire for men whatsoever. This is what is important." Thus, hijra identity is primarily indexed by asexuality and the absence of marital relationships with either men or women.

In addition, once they join the community, hijras are expected to cut off all ties with their natal families. Although most hijras were abandoned by their "own" or "blood" relatives (*sontham* or *rakta sambandam*) and remained bitter about this, in some instances hijras themselves, following the ideals of their community, renounced ties with their natal families. Given that the hallmarks of a sannyasi are celibacy and renunciation of family ties, hijras invoked their renunciation of natal family as a valued symbol and practice in this regard, in keeping with their sannyasi self-image.

These interdictions appeared to fundamentally structure hijras' conceptions of family and kinship. As they repeatedly stated, "family" for hijras was defined primarily in terms of other hijras, especially one's guru lineage; relationships with other hijras (and kotis), rather than natal family or "husbands" and their kin, constituted the most important relational bonds for hijras.[13] *"These* are our people now. It is only hijras who will look after us if anything happens," was the most commonly stated hijra sentiment. Any questions on my part regarding a hijra's relationship with her husband and the possibility of that tie being an enduring family bond was openly laughed at and dismissed outright. "How can they be our family? Family is *manollu* [our people], and they are the only ones who will take care of us when we get older," Shanti told me.

Central to this understanding of family is a notion of caring, indexed principally through a temporal (and spatial) dimension of "being there" rather than biogenetic connections (through "blood" and marriage). As with gay kinship ideologies in the United States, hijra and koti constructions of family appear to invert the association of biology with permanence, by presenting their "chosen" hijra/koti ties as the *"most* reliable and enduring of kinship relations" (Weston 1998, 63; emphasis in original). But while partners are an integral part of the enduring chosen family for lesbians and gay men in the United States, for hijras and kotis, their pantis or husbands are categorically *not* family. By definition, a husband or panti is not a koti and is therefore excluded from "family" categorization or the broader signifier of "our people."

Through such elaborations of belonging, not only do hijras and kotis potentially destabilize our "principles" of kinship—principles of descent and alliance, consanguinity and affinity that have been a staple of anthropological inquiry for decades (Radcliffe-Brown and Forde 1950; Lévi-Strauss 1969)—they also complicate our cultural understandings of "choice" in the context of kin relations. While the incorporation of "choice" in the definitions of family for the gay men and women of Weston's San Francisco "assigned kinship to the realm of free will inclination" (1991, 31), hijra and koti definitions of family do not appear to encode notions of idiosyncratic choice and egalitarian potential in quite the same way. In fact, aside from the *lack* of choice that some kotis articulated in their constructions of self and belonging, the central and only prescriptive bond in hijra conceptualizations of their family—the guru-cela bond—was not purely idiosyncratic, being more often assigned rather than chosen, and involved far more structured obligatory responsibilities than the gay familial relationships described by Kath Weston (1991, 1998).

To better understand hijra patterns of relatedness, we need to understand what, specifically, it means to identify as a hijra or koti in Hyderabad. What

are the particular historical and cultural contexts that mediate constructions of identity and kinship within these communities? And how are these
understandings of belonging, authenticity, and relationality tied to broader
constructions of self and the patterns of kinship in India? Understanding
why pantis do not constitute "family," and how relations of "koti-ness" operate through the particular networks of kin they incorporate is one aim of this
chapter. Much like the construction of gay relationships in Weston's United
States, "categories of permanence and transience" do indeed structure kotis'
relationships, but such temporality is indelibly inflected, measured, and
refracted through particular, culturally mediated understandings of love,
obligation, and service—that is, *caring* in the broadest sense of the term
(see Borneman 1997; Faubion 1997). If, as Kath Weston and others note,
individuals make their relationships not as they please but rather within
given historical and cultural circumstances, then we need to examine instantiations as well as potential inversions of "hegemonic" kinship ideologies in
terms of such specificities in order to better understand the lived meanings
of kinship for these individuals. For hijras and kotis therefore, we need
to study the specific interplay of history, meaning, and practice in their
structures of kinship and belonging—the tensions and fluid relationship
between their ideals and experiences, or what Trawick would describe as
the "intentional ambiguity" of love in "Indian culture" (1990, 41)—in order
to understand what it actually means to identify as a koti and the stakes
implicit in this process of subjectivation (see Foucault 1997). It is their affective bonds—of guru and cela, mother and daughter, husband and wife,
sister and *gurubhai*—in their historical, cultural, and gendered specificity
that we must pay attention to in order to appreciate the webs of significance
hijras and kotis weave as they constantly mediate between their longings
and ideals of kinship and their actual lived experiences.

In this chapter, I describe the various hijra kinship bonds that most hijras establish, such as the guru-cela relationship and the mother-daughter
relationship, as well as the supposedly prohibited relationships such as the
jodi (bond) with a husband, and the tie to the natal family. The tensions
between hijra desires, their structural patternings and "rules" of kinship,
and their lived experiences of these various affective bonds are crucial to
understanding the meanings of kinship and their resonance with normative kinship patterns. On the one hand, despite claiming nonprocreative
sexual identities and defying the perceived centrality of procreative sexuality to the definition of a family, hijras appear to reinscribe hegemonic
rituals and principles. This is evident in their ritualized rearticulation of the
marital bond and their mirroring of the consanguinal mother-child bond

(Lewin 1998b). Similarly, by establishing both obligatory, hierarchical relationships as well as those relatively more egalitarian relationships based on
affection, other self-identified kotis also appear to privilege "normative" familial alignments as significant for their identity and as a means whereby
they can acquire izzat. On the other hand, as Kath Weston cautions us,
"ostensibly similar formal features of kinship can carry conflicting meanings and embed subtle ideological shifts, allowing 'new' family forms to be
read simultaneously as radically innovative and thoroughly assimilationist.
In the end, they are intrinsically neither" (1998, 64). It is therefore through
the *complexity* of hijra/koti instantiations of kinship and family, that we can
understand (and potentially destabilize) the ideal and its often ambiguous
relation to lived experience—a goal the rest of this chapter strives toward
by describing the central affective ties in the lives of hijras and kotis.

LASHKARWALA/SHEHARWALA *RISTE*: HIJRA HOUSES, THE *RIT*, AND GURU-CELA RELATIONSHIPS

Sushmita and I were chatting in the shade of her hut. She had her legs
stretched out in front of her and was reclining against the side of the hut.
I was sitting a few feet away, on the same mat. It was quiet, about two in
the afternoon, siesta time at the tank. Most other hijras were either sleeping
or had gone for a movie. Suddenly, Yamini marched up to where we were
sitting and started shouting at Sushmita. She was obviously very upset about
something, and from what I understood the issue centered on Yamini's
cela, Palamma. Yamini was accusing Sushmita of negatively influencing
Palamma and encouraging her to run away from her guru. That morning,
Palamma had apparently decided that Yamini was too abusive and had
left for her natal village in Warangal. According to Yamini, Sushmita was
responsible for Palamma's decision, and she proceeded to abuse Sushmita,
using extremely harsh and crude language. "Was something poking you in
your ass, you *bhosrivala* [vagina-owner],[14] you *gandu-berupia*? You are an
andoli [orphan] kojja, and you think you can make trouble for us real kojjas!
We, me and my sisters are the real kojjas, not you.[15] Remember that! We
have a guru, unlike you ... " Yamini screamed at Sushmita. She continued
in this vein for a while. By this time, everyone who was at the tank had
woken up and come to see what the noise was all about. I had moved out of
Sushmita's hut, and was standing next to Surekha and Shanti, some distance
away. There were at least eight or nine hijras there, but none of them
lifted a finger or said a word to stop Yamini's tirade. Sushmita, who is

not particularly small or meek in other circumstances, was just sitting in a corner taking the abuse heaped on her with only murmurs of protest that she had nothing to do with Palamma leaving Yamini.

What this incident reveals, apart from the latent aggression in hijras' lives, is the importance of kin relatedness, or more specifically, the *rit* and guru-cela relationship in symbolizing membership within the hijra community. The other hijras "could not intervene" they said, because Sushmita was an *andoli* hijra. This term implies that she does not have a guru in the hijra community and therefore could be verbally abused by a "real" hijra. Sushmita had acquired a guru and put the *rit* in a hijra house as soon as she joined the community, ten years ago. But her guru had died a few years ago, and Sushmita had not chosen another guru since then. She was illegitimate in some respect—without an official kin network—and hence had to suffer in silence the shame of being abused by other *ritwale*, or "real," hijras.

As the opening vignette of this chapter and the incident above indicate, the *rit* is one, if not *the* most structured marker of hijra kinship. It is not so much an object as a symbolic act of initiation; it symbolizes a ritual enactment or "rite of passage," to use Van Gennep's (1960) phrase, which designates a hijra's formal membership within the community. The *rit* connotes belonging—to a hijra house specifically and to the community more broadly—and consequently indexes one of the most important criteria of authenticity and commitment to hijra identity.

Two hijra houses are represented in Hyderabad: the Sheharwala and the Lashkarwala houses. Their names literally denote their territorial domains, or *ilakas*—the "city" (*shehar*) and the "army camp" (*lashkar*), or Hyderabad and Secunderabad, respectively. The "city" of Hyderabad (what is now referred to as the old city) was the space where the Qutb Shahi kings and the Nizams ruled, while Secunderabad was the site of the British army encampment. The territorial domains of the two contemporary hijra houses, Sheharwala and Lashkarwala, are divided along the lines of this spatial history, with members of each house having the right to "ask" for badhai in Hyderabad and in Secunderabad, respectively. Thus, Lashkarwala or Sheharwala *riste* are the most important relationships for any hijra in Hyderabad and Secunderabad. Almost the first question asked of any hijra is either "Which house do you have the *rit* in?" or, "Who is your guru?" "Most important, if there is no guru and no *rit* with a hijra house, that person does not have izzat . . . and is not recognized as a hijra," Munira told me in no uncertain terms.

So what is the *rit*, how does one "put it," and how does it relate to the process of acquiring a guru and a wider kinship network? Second, how else is kinship elaborated? Third, what is the wider meaning of "putting the *rit*" in the context of the koti community, and how does it work both as a kinship marker and as a means to acquire status? Finally, what is the relationship between the patterns of kinship articulated within hijra and wider koti communities, and normative kinship patterning? In the following section, I address each of these questions, starting with a description of the ritual involved in acquiring membership in the community—putting the *rit* in a hijra house—before addressing the more abstract issues of its significance within the community and the importance of the guru-cela relationship in this kinship network.

The Ritual of the *Rit*

I witnessed the *rit* ceremony twice during my fieldwork. The first time I witnessed this important hijra rite, I had dropped in to see Irfan nayak one afternoon in October. I walked straight to her house, passing the larger Sheharwala house that is situated directly in front of it. Irfan nayak was at home along with her celas, Shahbaz and Rani, and another hijra I did not recognize. All of them greeted me very amiably, and, following the usual pattern, I sat down while Shahbaz began to make tea for everyone. After about half an hour of general conversation, during which I told the new hijra (a visitor from Delhi who was here for a few days) who I was and what I was doing, two other hijras I had not met earlier walked in. Both of them touched the nayak's feet saying "*paon padti hun*,"[16] and the older of the two greeted the other hijras present with "*salam aleikum*," a marked symbol of equality in status. She was another of Irfan's celas and thereby the other hijras' contemporary, or *gurubhai*. Her name was Saroja, I later learned. The other hijra with her was much younger and seemed utterly scared and awed in the presence of the nayak. Both of them appeared to be expected by Irfan nayak and her celas.

After the preliminary greetings, Saroja asked Irfan nayak "Where are the others?" in a fairly impatient tone of voice. Irfan replied, "They cannot come. Bala nayak has gone out to pay the municipal taxes, and Shafat nayak is not well. So let us not wait; let us do it now." I had no idea what they were referring to, but decided not to attract attention for fear that they would ask me to leave, a non-hijra not being privy to such privileged information. So I just sat quietly and watched.

They arranged themselves in a circle, covering their heads with the ends of their saris. In the center of the circle, they put a steel plate with some *paan* leaves and betel nut that they covered with a towel. Irfan then said, "We are meeting here because this hijra wants to put a *rit* in our house. What do you want your name to be?" she asked the young initiate, who appeared too scared to reply and just looked at Saroja. Saroja turned to Irfan and said, "Kaushal." Irfan then continued. "Kaushal, do you want to become the cela of Saroja?" Kaushal nodded. At this point, Saroja put four rupees and twenty-five paise on the plate, and Irfan said, "Kaushal is the cela of Saroja, who is the cela of Irfan of the Sheharwala house." All five hijras present, with the exception of Kaushal, then clapped loudly, saying "*din, din, din,*" three times.[17] Kaushal was told to touch the nayak's feet, then the feet of her guru, and then the feet of each of the other hijras in the room. "You are now a real [*asli*] hijra with a *rit* in the Sheharwala house. Don't forget that. And your guru, Saroja, you should serve her well because she is now everything to you—mother, father, husband, sister, everything," Rani said, while blessing her. Kaushal had now become a "real" hijra; she possessed the most important markers of hijra identity for an initiate—she had a guru who served as her immediate family and through whom she reckoned descent, and she had put the requisite *rit* in the Sheharwala house and, by extension, in the hijra community, whose rules she had now publicly acknowledged she would abide by.

While there are some differences between the ceremonies enacted here and the ritual as it has been described in the literature (Sharma 1989; Nanda 1990),[18] the fundamental meaning and structural grammar appears to be the same. Every hijra must have a guru, and initiation into the community—the acquisition or putting of the *rit* (*rit dalna*)—occurs only under the sponsorship of this guru. The guru-cela relationship is the most important bond among hijras and is necessarily central to hijra conceptions of family. It is a mutually beneficial, reciprocal relationship, entailing both social and economic obligations and responsibilities for both parties. Further, the *rit* signifies not only membership within the community as a whole but, more specifically, affiliation with a given symbolic hijra house, namely, that to which the guru belongs. Hijras in Hyderabad referred to the formal kinship bond between guru and cela that resulted from the *rit* in terms of the relationship associated with their symbolic house, as Lashkarwala or Sheharwala *riste* (bonds).

Guru-Cela Relationships

The centrality of the guru-cela relationship to hijra identity—its prescriptive quality and its importance for the initiate's acceptance and advancement in the community ranks—is undeniable. The initiate explicitly acknowledges the social and economic contractual obligations that are inherent in this acquisition of a new family. Although clearly hierarchical, with seniority among hijras (as a principle of both social organization and social control) being reckoned through the unequal power structure of gurus and celas, this relationship is a mutually beneficial, reciprocal one. Celas are expected to be obedient, respectful, and loyal, and to serve their gurus well by catering to all their domestic needs. In exchange for their celas' services and earnings, gurus are required to look after their health and well-being, treat them fairly, provide them with clothes and food, and give them the necessary training and knowledge about hijra customs and manners to permit their rise in seniority. The relationship between a guru and her cela is often highly idealized, with the guru being the cela's "mother, father, husband, sister, everything," to quote Rani. Hence the oft-repeated assertion, "This is our family now. It is only hijras who will look after us if anything happens."

As they repeatedly state, hijras consider only other hijras—or in wider social contexts, the koti community—rather than consanguinal or affinal kin, as their "family." And within this hijra family, it is the guru-cela bond, an iterative relationship,[19] that serves as the primary axis of kinship and genealogical descent.

Celas' responsibilities toward gurus include both economic and social obligations. As part of the initiation, a new cela has to pay a sum of one hundred and fifty rupees to her guru, to be distributed among the nayaks of that symbolic house. Although a cela can change her guru and house (Sinha 1967; Sharma 1989; Nanda 1990, 1994),[20] every time this occurs she has to pay twice the amount that she last paid for her *rit* ceremony. For instance, if a cela changes gurus and houses twice, she must pay her new guru six hundred rupees. By this process of accumulation, the amount paid by a hijra can be as much as the eighty thousand rupees recently paid by a hijra in Bombay, resulting in chronic debt and economic bondage. Why would someone agree to incur this debt and continue to serve as a cela? When I asked this question, I was greeted with incredulity at my naïveté. "It is because we need our gurus, our people, Gayatri," Madhavi told me patiently, the frequent changes being necessitated, in her opinion, by the abuse often meted out by gurus. Munira reiterated this when she said, "A hijra has to have a guru and a *rit* in a hijra house." Otherwise, as she noted earlier, "that person is not considered a hijra." So, whatever the price, one needs to pay the fee necessary to acquire a guru and a *rit* in a hijra house, even if it means paying a large amount because of frequent (perceived) abuse by multiple gurus.

This base amount, however, does not include the fines levied for the infraction of rules within the community. When I witnessed the *rit* ceremony the second time, it was when two kandra hijras, Srilakshmi and her guru, Rajeshwari, had gone to put a *rit* in the Lashkarwala house. Srilakshmi had recently run away to another city in a fit of anger and had affiliated with another hijra house in that city. In arguing her case with the nayak, Srilakshmi claimed that she had only been *living* with hijras belonging to another house, but had not in fact put the *rit* in that house. After a particularly vociferous transaction with the nayak, both Srilakshmi and her guru were asked to pay an amount totaling five thousand rupees, covering the cost of the *rit* as well as *dands* (fines) for the infraction of hijra rules, namely, not putting a *rit* quickly enough—"living like a *gandu*," as it was termed—and the nonchalant changing of house affiliations. This second act was not exactly an infraction of any rule, but it was frowned upon within the hijra community. The amount of the fine appeared to be fairly arbitrarily decided by the nayak, although it was subject to much loud, vituperative negotiation.

Celas not only incur a debt by virtue of the *rit* transaction, but are economically bound to their guru through the latter's control of their means of livelihood. This is especially true of badhai hijras. Given the nature of their ritual performances, group membership is absolutely vital to survival among this group. A new cela has to learn the songs and dances necessary to her trade, a knowledge base that can be imparted only by her seniors in the community. Further, whenever there is a badhai performance, it is left to the guru's discretion to take whomever she chooses with her. While the money thus earned is not retained by any one cela, those who are good singers and dancers (or are the guru's favorites) not only have an easier life in terms of everyday work, but also, as Vanitha informed me, "get more izzat... and acquire a name for themselves as good badhai hijras."

Earning a guru's displeasure can seriously damage a hijra's chances for promotion within the ranks and acceptance among one's peers, in addition to affecting such mundane but important issues as eating and sleeping patterns, household chores, discretionary budgets for a cela's other activities, and the amount of free time one can claim. Many kandra hijras with whom I spoke gave this reason as their justification for why they did not go live in their nayak's house, even though their presence was required or sometimes demanded: "If you go and live in the *chali* [nayak's house], then you don't have izzat there, and they make you do all the household work—cooking, cleaning, washing clothes, fetching things, pressing all their feet, everything. And then they don't even give you enough food to eat, because you have to eat whatever is leftover after all the elders have finished eating. You don't have money of your own to go buy food even! And anyway they will beat you if they know you have done that. I lived there for a few months, and I don't want to go back there right now. We'll see later," Shanti told me.

As mentioned earlier, the different hijra houses each have their own *ilaka*, or territorial boundary, within which they have the sole right to perform and earn money. All hijras are bound to their particular kin group and therefore territory, and any transgressions incur a severe beating and in some instances even death (Sharma 1989; Nanda 1990). Not only is there nowhere to perform as a single hijra, those who try to live and work independently often suffer social ostracism. Largely on account of this, most hijras did not see this as a viable or sensible option at all and, despite all the indignities, would rather stay with their gurus than try to live alone.

Further, making it on their own is made all the more difficult for celas because gurus have a vested interest in enlarging their own groups as much as possible. The cela's presence is required not merely to enhance a guru's prestige but also to defend a house's territorial boundaries, physically and symbolically. Until very recently, the Lashkarwala hijras in Hyderabad greatly resented their Sheharwala sisters, largely on account of the demarcation of *ilakas*, as well as the former's inability to defend their territory, for lack of a large enough pool of hijra members. Further, aside from their dancing and singing as a troupe, badhai hijras cannot afford to be solitary because they rely on their numbers to threaten and cajole their patrons into parting with money. "Single hijras I can easily deal with, but when they come as a group, that is when they are scary," my next-door neighbor told me.

While it is most pronounced for badhai hijras, the social and economic dependence of the cela on her guru is also evident among kandra (sex worker) hijras. For those living under the tank, every cela had to pay her guru a sum of fifty rupees every single day of the month, irrespective of her earnings for that day. This was greatly resented by the celas, but as Surekha said, "What can we do? We have to give them that money, otherwise they will throw us out or kill us." In addition, celas had to do all the household chores for themselves and their gurus: cooking, washing vessels and clothes, buying vegetables and rations, getting clothes ironed, and fetching odds and ends whenever required. Often but not always, a guru has two celas, permitting a splitting of the tasks and an easing of their individual burdens. Nevertheless, a guru can make life extremely trying for her cela. Some gurus are worse than others. For instance, one of the gurus at the tank, Yamini, can never retain any of her celas for more than a year because of her constant nagging as well as her physical and verbal abuse of them.[21] In the past, after suffering her for a while, these celas have either run away to another city and acquired a new guru, or gone back to their natal village to live their lives as non-hijra kotis.

Celas are at the beck and call of their gurus, and any delay in responding or inclination to be lazy is punished by either verbal or physical abuse. Further, although less pronounced relative to badhai hijras, kandra gurus also control the time and place of their cela's "working hours." Among the tank group, whose home was also their workplace, gurus retained the right to bring their customers back to their huts, while celas had to be content with performing out in the open or in stray train compartments across the railway tracks. While both gurus and celas engaged in sex work only during the evening and part of the night, gurus could contract with a customer during the day as well if they so chose, although this was rare. If a cela did the same however—especially if she had not fulfilled all her obligations to cook, clean, wash, and fetch—she was beaten by her guru for dereliction of duty. In addition, gurus control their celas' right to perpetuate the power structure by taking celas of their own. Hence, even though Shanti and Surekha had proven themselves "real hijras" by having had their *nirvan* operations and having served their gurus dutifully for more than five years, they were not permitted to take a cela because, as Munira, Surekha's guru, confided to me, this would weaken her (Munira's) control and lower her izzat in the eyes of her nati celas (cela's celas) who would be involved in sex work alongside her.

Seniority in the hijra community is measured both by time spent in the community (irrespective of the age of the hijra) and by the acquisition of celas. Ideally, having undergone the *nirvan* operation and proven oneself a real hijra, the next step would be to acquire a cela. The acquisition of a cela serves to signal "adulthood" in the community, and the ability, or *himmat* (strength), as Rohini once told me, to support another individual and continue the genealogical line. In reality however, there is some tension or ambivalence in allowing celas to acquire celas of their own. By permitting this act, gurus relinquish full control over their celas; they are acknowledging that celas have sufficient *himmat* and therefore must be given a certain amount of respect. Gurus, somewhat predictably, are ambivalent about this step.

Nevertheless, despite the apparently skewed nature of the guru-cela relationship, the fact remains that gurus, too, have a responsibility toward their celas. The guru is obligated to look after her cela in times of ill-health and misfortune, and to speak on her behalf at official hijra gatherings and ceremonies. She is expected to treat her cela as one would a daughter, showing affection and coming to her aid in times of difficulty. If ever there is an altercation involving the cela, the guru is expected to support her publicly, while recognizing that she alone reserves the right to reprimand her in private and even beat her if the need arises. At festivals and important hijra ceremonies, the guru is obligated to provide her cela with new clothes and money. In short, the guru is responsible for the health and happiness of her cela, and the latter's behavior reflects her upbringing, so to speak, and the izzat of her guru, as well as that of her house and the wider hijra family.

One of the guru's chief responsibilities is overseeing the cela's *nirvan* operation. Not only must the guru give permission for this act, she must also care for the cela (at least monetarily) after the operation while she is unable to work. At the end of the forty-day period of seclusion and rest following the operation, during which time it is often the hijra's mother, rather than her guru, who looks after her, it is the guru's responsibility to host the *dawat* (feast) that announces and celebrates the cela's newly acquired status as a *nirvan sultan*. This is one of the most important, and therefore potentially contentious, responsibilities that the guru discharges toward her cela.

Becoming a *nirvan sultan* appears to be a significant prerequisite to acquiring a cela. It is a significant economic burden, both in itself—because of the fees for the doctor, medicines, and food after the operation—as well as in terms of the potential loss of income for those days the cela is incapacitated and cannot "work." Although celas are made to pay back every rupee that is spent on them (at least among kandra hijras under the tank), they usually do so over a period of time. It is the guru's responsibility to advance the money that may be required in the meantime, although, judging from the experience of hijras under the tank, this responsibility is almost never met. Often, celas save up enough money for their expenses, which may be as much as ten to fifteen thousand rupees, before being permitted even to consider this step.[22] Although celas can and mostly do bear the cost of the *nirvan* operation on their own, taking this step without the social sanction of their guru is almost never done and has disastrous consequences, as the opening vignette indicates.

Despite all these hardships, kandra celas living under the tank continued to express ambivalence if not outright reluctance about going to live in the nayak's house. For the most part, they preferred to live their lives under the tank where there was more independence, access to money, the (relative) liberty to eat and sleep whenever they chose, as well as the freedom to satisfy their sexual desires. They chose this lifestyle even while recognizing that it had lower izzat both in the eyes of their community and the wider society. Under the tank, they had more autonomy and enjoyed the advantages of belonging to a distinct hijra community; stigmatized, but still acknowledged as a part of the larger hijra network across the country. For them, their somewhat precarious, violent, and dangerous life under the tank was preferable both to the constraints of living under the gaze of the nayak and to living as a social outcast without the support of a community.

As evident from the above, the guru-cela relationship is the cornerstone of the hijra kinship network. Ideally, it is a reciprocal bond that entails responsibilities and obligations as well as rights and benefits on the part of both gurus and celas. Without a guru, a hijra's very identity is called into question. She is a *gandu*, or at best, an *andoli* (an "orphan" and therefore an illegitimate) hijra, subject to severe abuse and derision. Likewise, without a cela, a hijra does not have izzat in the community. Acquiring a cela is a way of perpetuating the hijra lineage; in addition, it is a marker of the particular guru's standing in the community and a means of indicating both izzat and seniority. To quote Munira again, "without a *rit* and a guru ... that person is not considered a hijra."

The guru-cela relationship is a hierarchical obligatory relationship, as evidenced by the nature of the duties and responsibilities toward one another. In addition, in terms of its structural logic, it may be read as a marital or affinal bond. However, this is not how hijras themselves read this relationship. This reading is merely speculation on my part, based on the rituals they engage in and their symbolic meanings outside the hijra community. For instance, on the death of a guru, her cela is expected to enact the role of a Hindu widow, being referred to with the same label, *munda*, as well as being required to wear a white sari and break all her bangles in grief. Further, the *laccha*, or necklace that is tied by the guru on the occasion of her cela's official acknowledgment as a *nirvan sultan* (on the fortieth day after her operation), is also removed. According to some kandra hijras, the *munda* is expected to remain within the confines of her house, isolating herself from the community, although, after the requisite period of mourning, a *munda* hijra can become the cela of another hijra.

Despite the potential (structural) resonance of these rituals with Hindu rituals of mourning on the part of a widow, any questions on my part regarding an affinal or sexual relationship between two hijras elicited the most profound disgust and horror. "Haw, that can never happen! If any hijra did that, it would be disgusting," Surekha told me in answer to my explicit question. The apparent inappropriateness of this relationship was evident in the following incident relating to Srilakshmi's "marriage" to her panti.

Srilakshmi, a kandra hijra, was about to "get married" to her panti, Vijaybhaskar. However, for unavoidable reasons at the last minute, Vijaybhaskar, who lived in a different city, could not make it to Hyderabad on the day of his "wedding." All of the food and other arrangements had been made already. In addition, this was to have been a double wedding with another hijra, Savita, who would be marrying her panti, Suresh, at the same time. Since both the food and this other couple were ready and waiting, the "elders"—Srilakshmi's guru and her *gurubhais*—decided to go ahead with the ceremony. After Savita and Suresh had tied the knot, as it were (as the most important marker of this ceremony, the "husband" ties a *mangalsutra* [the necklace that serves as the Hindu marker of marriage for a woman] around the neck of his wife), it was Srilakshmi's turn to get "married." In the absence of her husband, and much to Srilakshmi's embarrassment, her hijra mother, Munira, tied the *mangalsutra*. I found it interesting that Srilakshmi's guru, who was also present, was not the one to do so. I had promised to take photographs for the two "wives," but when I raised my camera to take one of Munira tying the necklace, Srilakshmi told me that it was completely inappropriate and that I should not photograph it. Munira, however, enamored with the thought of being photographed, wanted me to take the shot, stating that, "it is not supposed to be this way; but take my photograph." I took the photograph. In the frame, Munira had turned her face completely toward the camera, while Srilakshmi had covered her mouth with her palm in an expression of embarrassment and horror.

If Srilakshmi's guru had tied the *mangalsutra*, would it have been any less inappropriate? The potential structural similarity between the *rit* and marriage rituals and relationships in terms of their prescriptive quality, their binding, obligatory nature, and the possibility (although frowned upon) of their dissolution, are intriguing avenues of future inquiry. Further, potentially mirroring a "traditional" husband-wife relationship, the cela is ideally proscribed from seeing her guru for forty days after her *nirvan* operation (until the *puja* [ritual or ceremony] to mark her transition), following which her guru ties the *laccha*, or necklace, on her cela, rather than her mother, who was the one who took care of her during this period. In addition, the rhetoric used to describe the operatee also appears to be significant in this respect. While getting Nagalakshmi ready for her *dawat*, Rajeshwari told me, "We make her up like a bride. A new sari, nice make-up, flowers in her hair—she should look just like a bride." After the *puja* that she performs, the operatee is taken ceremonially from her mother's house to her guru's, much like the bride who goes from her natal home to her affinal home. Further, like a *kanya* (unmarried girl), a hijra who has never put the *rit* in any house (*kori murat*) is more highly valued as a new member than one who has. In addition, it is through her guru that the cela establishes a lineage and is acknowledged as kin within her hijra house, much as with "hegemonic" patrilocal affinal relations.

Hence, although this "marital" contract between gurus and celas was not explicitly acknowledged by hijras and in actuality was overtly denied, the structural parallels between "normative" marriage rituals and those employed by hijras are interesting if not culturally significant.

What is the significance of such a rearticulation? Does the fact that hijra kinship alignments potentially mirror normative familial arrangements necessarily make these relationships merely derivative and therefore devoid of specific symbolic value? Or, as Judith Butler might argue, does this very fact, and the variety and complexity of these approximations, "trouble" the ideal of the normative family? By revealing the variety of kin relationships that obtain in the world, anthropologists and sociologists of kinship have established alternative forms and meanings of kinship (Schneider 1968; Stack 1974; Collier and Yanagisako 1987; Strathern 1988; Weston 1991; Stacey 1996; Franklin 1998). Such accounts necessarily question structuralist claims regarding the foundational imperative of heterosexual desire/ families, and implicitly highlight the role of such kinship alignments in producing individuated and gendered subjects (Butler 2000; cf. Lévi-Strauss 1969; Lacan, 1978). If the bases of kinship systems (and culture) are not always or only traceable to (structural) rules such as the incest taboo and the Oedipus complex, what then does this signify for "compulsory heterosexuality" as the defining "structure" of normative kinship? These are questions with no simple answers. By examining the variety of hijra/koti kin frameworks in their specific contexts of elaboration, we can begin to generate some answers to such questions and potentially retheorize the analysis of kinship. One such framework is that of love between (hijra) mothers and daughters—*pyar ke riste* (relationships/bonds of love), or Andhra *riste* as they sometimes refer to these relationships.

FURTHER NOTES ON LOVE

While the guru-cela bond is a necessary prerequisite for kinship within the hijra community, it does not appear to be a sufficient one. In addition to this highly valued bond, hijras forge other relationships—what they refer to as *pyar ke riste*, or relationships of love—with members of their community.[23] When asked about these relationships, many of them differentiated between the necessary guru-cela relationships (Lashkarwala or Sheharwala *riste*) and bonds of affection that were not obligatory—what they sometimes referred to as Andhra *riste*, relations of *pyar*, or love. Relationships characterized as Andhra *riste* were not as binding as those of the Lashkarwala or Sheharwala *riste*. They did not entail rigid responsibilities and obligations as the guru-cela bond did, nor were they restricted to members of one's own lineage or hijra house. The most common of such relationships were those between "sisters" (*behen*), and that between a "mother" and her "daughter" (*ma-beti* relationships).

The terms *dudh behan* and *dudh beti*, literally translated, mean "milk sister" and "milk daughter," respectively.[24] These terms are direct references to the nurturing bond between mother and daughter symbolized by the milk that a nursing mother feeds her daughter—milk that is shared by sisters, as daughters of the same mother. In addition to evoking images of affection and love, these terms also reference the very enactment of the ritual that forges *dudh* or *pyar ke riste*.

As Munira states, "Like a mother's milk that is given to her daughter and shared by all her children, who are then sisters," the individuals who are to become *dudh behans* or *betis* enact this nursing ritual. The *dudh ma* (mother) sits cross-legged and pulls up her blouse while holding her *beti* (daughter) in her lap, as any nursing mother would. She then pours some milk, using a cup held over her breast, into the mouths of the prospective *betis*, thereby sealing this relationship with "her" milk. To further seal the bond thus forged, each of the prospective *dudh behans* pricks her finger and lets a few drops of blood flow into the cup of milk, which is then shared by all of them, mother and sisters.

When I asked Rajeshwari why they adopted daughters, she told me it was to extend their kin relations, their *sambandam*. Daughters would more than likely be celas of other hijras with whom they could then form an alliance, she explained. Such relationships also serve *publicly* to strengthen ties between hijras, through a symbolic ritual enactment. By developing these bonds, each hijra is able to establish relationships with other hijras, thereby not only widening the kinship network but also cementing ties, as in Pierre Bourdieu's (1977) notion of "practical kinship." For instance, among kandra hijras, *dudh behans* would "exchange" celas, making these celas their respective *dudh betis*. This made for an extended, interconnected network of relationships between hijras living together. At the tank, for example, Rajeshwari and Munira were *dudh behans*, both daughters of Malamma. To further strengthen their bond, each made the other's cela her *dudh beti*—a symbolic act reinforcing the existing bonds between these hijras and serving as a mark of love and respect between the *dudh behans*.

Although not equivalent to the guru-cela bond either in terms of responsibilities or legitimacy, the mother-daughter bond has an important affective element that is not necessarily evident in the former relationship. The mother and daughter share a certain affection for each other, and this bond is often spoken of more tenderly than the obligatory but necessary kinship link between gurus and celas. Although there is some tension between these roles, in times of conflict, the guru's word is almost always more important and binding than that of a mother. For instance, Rajeshwari once told her daughter Aliya to accompany her to the market the following day to buy some clothes for an upcoming festival. That same evening however, Aliya's guru, Munira, told her that she had to go to Chowtuppal[25] in order to stock Munira's house there. There was absolutely no question as to which one of them Aliya would obey; she explained the situation to her mother and postponed the trip to the market.

Dudh betis are cared for by hijras like actual daughters. They are taken care of when ill, helped out of crises, given gifts for festivals, and may even be provided with a *kattanam*, or dowry, as happened, for instance, when Munira's daughter had her *nirvan* operation. The *betis* in turn are expected to cook, clean, and serve their mothers, but they are only so obligated if celas are absent. A daughter who did not perform this role would be cursed and derided for laziness but not penalized as a cela would be. Although daughters do not figure in the direct line of inheritance or genealogy, as do celas (i.e., they do not inherit property, wealth, or the nayak title), they are accorded respect and affection for their status as daughters.

Mothers often appeared to have greater affection for daughters than for their celas, even though there was no denying the greater significance and legitimacy of the guru-cela bond over the *ma-beti* one. For example, Munira's first daughter, Mary, had left the tank group about six years ago. It was rumored that she had gone back to her natal village and, having reverted to her "male appearance" (*mogarupam*) and lifestyle, had married a woman and was now "living as a panti."

In November of 1996, Mary returned to the tank. "She" was wearing pants and a shirt, had grown her beard, and looked exceedingly unlike a hijra. After the first welcomes, there was a heated discussion as to whether to accept Mary back into the community. Many of the senior hijras there—Rajeshwari, Vasundara, and Lekha—were against it because they believed that Mary had married a woman and was thereby no longer acceptable, despite her protests to the contrary.[26] Munira was the only hijra present who came to her defense, steadfastly believing in her daughter's "innocence." "First of all, I don't believe that Mary would have done that. If one supposes

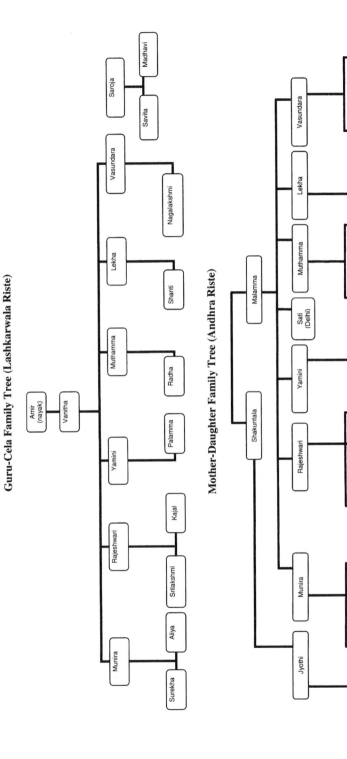

Family tree of tank hijras

she did, if she was my cela or anyone else's, that would have been a little different, but she didn't have a guru here. She is my daughter, and I am willing to take on the responsibility of looking after her. Let her stay here if she wants," Munira told them. Mary was allowed to live at the tank and was there until the day I left Hyderabad. There was an undeniable bond between the two, which in later conversations Munira would explicitly acknowledge and evaluate differently from the bond with her celas. This was a *rista* based not on obligatory responsibilities but on love—a *pyar ka rista*, as Munira emphasized.

These *pyar ke riste*, despite being significant components of hijra kinship, have not been noted by many of the scholars writing on hijras. In the literature, only Sinha (1967) mentions these bonds, and only in passing. The fact that they exist is significant, not only intrinsically, but also because they highlight the centrality of affective (mother-child) bonds in hijras' kinship network. The dramatic resonance between the consanguinal mother-child bond—symbolized by "breast feeding"—and the hijras' nursing ritual makes the parallel apparent. The very fact that these bonds are distinct from those with one's guru, with the marker of difference being affection, lends further credence to the potential significance of these relationships as natal or consanguinal ties. As Munira repeatedly informed me, the mother, not the guru, sometimes gives a *kattanam* (dowry) to her daughter, much as parents give a dowry to the bride on the occasion of her marriage. Munira had given Saroja, her daughter, a significant *kattanam*— "everything she might need . . . pots, pans, a mattress, a few good saris, some jewelry . . . just like a new bride," Munira said. Finally, after the establishment of the kin tie, the kinship terms used to refer to these family members are the same as those used by mothers for their daughters—*bidda/beti* and *amma/ma*, in Telugu and Hindi, respectively. Although I do not want to argue that these relationships are mere replacements or uncritical reflections of natal bonds, the resonance between non-hijra consanguinal relationships and hijra mother-daughter bonds is indeed remarkable, an instance of how, at particular moments, our socially produced worlds sometimes become naturalized into "new" forms of caring.

OTHER *RISTE*: THE *JODI* AND HUSBANDS

As noted earlier, one of the relational bonds that hijras explicitly did *not* recognize as characterizing "our people," yet nevertheless did establish and yearn for, was that between hijras and their pantis, or "husbands." Many of the hijras I knew in Hyderabad had pantis, especially the kandra hijras. And yet, if I asked them about this relationship and the possibility of this tie being an enduring familial bond, they would just laugh and dismiss it outright: "How can they be our family? Family is *manollu* [our people],[27] and they are the only ones who will take care of us when we are older," Shanti said echoing other hijras.

Almost the first question hijras would ask of me, no matter how well they knew me, was "When are you going to get married?" Without waiting for a reply, they would then dreamily imagine the scene: It would be a grand wedding with a big band, I would look very nice, dressed in a silk sari with flowers in my hair, and they would all come and dance at the wedding. Most important, my husband would be a handsome man who would not drink alcohol or beat me, who would take care of me and love me throughout my life. These imaginings highlight two issues in the lives of hijras. First, an idealization of marriage, a yearning for love and acceptance, or what Kakar (1989) refers to as the "desire for a *jodi* [bond]"; and, second, an ambivalence in their feelings toward men wherein the ideal of a non-drinking, kind man are set against the reality of physical abuse and alcoholism among their pantis.

Despite claiming nonprocreative sexual identities and defying the centrality of procreative sexuality to the definition of a family, hijras (especially kandra hijras) idealize marriage and the possibility of a long-term commitment with their pantis. While most kandra hijras in Hyderabad had pantis, those who did not would speak in longing terms of their ideal man: someone who would stay with them through thick and thin, someone with a regular job, who did not mistreat them, bought them gifts, and returned their love.[28]

A few hijras had been with their pantis for as many as ten or fifteen years. Munira and her panti, Zahid, for instance, had been "married" for thirteen years she said. She met him soon after she came to Hyderabad. As she describes it, she was standing in front of the station one evening, waiting for someone. She saw this man look her up and down, before walking into a sweet shop close by. She had noticed him but didn't follow him or react to his obvious interest in her.

I thought he was a ruffian [*goonda*] because he was hanging around with these other *goondas*. But he came back the next day, and this time he was alone. He asked me to go [sleep] with him, which I did. Like that, slowly, slowly we fell in love. We got married about one year after we met. I went to meet his family, and his grandmother [*dadi*] started saying we don't know if she is a real hijra or what. So, in a fit of anger, I lifted up my sari. I had become *cibri*. I was a *nirvan sultan* by that time, and I showed her. '*Arre*, this is a woman's body! This is a real hijra,' she said, and since then, no one has said anything to me. I go visit them once in two-three months, say *salam aleikum* and come back.

About three or four years after they were "married," Zahid married a Muslim woman at the insistence of his family. But as Munira tells the story, Zahid got remarried only after getting the approval of Munira and letting his affinal family know that he was "married to a hijra" as well. Zahid supposedly consented to the marriage only after he was reassured that they would accept his first (hijra) wife, Munira. Munira told this to me very proudly, as "proof" of her husband's faithfulness and respectability. Her co-wife has two children whom Munira often refers to as her own, and on whom she seems to lavish much affection and money. Her relations with her co-wife appear to be cordial; they call each other *aapa*, or sister, and share Zahid on seemingly unproblematic terms. This is, of course, Munira's version of the story. Nevertheless, Zahid does visit the tank at least three or four times a week, and appears to genuinely care for Munira. He brings her gifts on occasion, accompanies her on trips to Delhi and Ajmer, and even accepts verbal abuse from her without lashing out—a "good man" indeed.

Not all "husbands" are as caring or accommodating as Zahid. But many of them at least acknowledge their bond, and some do share a significant relationship with their hijra wives. Sati's husband came down with her to Hyderabad from Delhi, openly acknowledging his relationship with his hijra wife, both to the hijra community as well as to his natal family in Delhi. Similarly, Savita's panti visits almost every day, often bringing gifts for her from the shop that he owns in the old city. Surekha and her husband Rajesh also share a husband-wife relationship that is acknowledged by the hijras as well as all his friends. Every time he needs to bathe, have his clothes washed, or requires food or money, Rajesh comes to his wife Surekha, who gladly serves, cooks, cleans, and funds her husband. Hijras appear to perform these "wifely" duties gladly, in marked contrast to the way they care for their gurus. Not all of them live at the tank, as does Rajesh, but they are expected to visit as often as they can. As they approach, their wives are informed that their "man is here." Immediately, hijras stop what they are doing and, more often than not, go into their hut to greet their husbands in private.

There appear to be marked similarities in the gendered attitudes and responses of a hijra to her panti and the responses of a woman to her husband in middle-class India, especially with regard to internalized ideals of femininity and womanhood. Domestic responsibilities such as cooking, cleaning, washing, and sewing are clearly the wife's duties. A good wife, moreover, is likely to respect her husband, to avoid acting promiscuously in public when he is around (whatever her occupation or behavior outside of their relationship), and always to look after him and his needs, especially in times of trouble; in other words, she is expected to be a respectable, self-sacrificing, chaste woman. While hijras are not docile or submissive, they certainly are self-sacrificing and care deeply about how they are viewed by society in their capacity as "wives." Munira was extremely upset one day when she found out that Zahid had eaten at a hotel and slept with his friends on the road that night. She yelled at him when he came to see her the next day saying, "Don't you have a wife and house here? How will it look that you didn't come here? Won't people say she is probably not looking after him well?" Invariably, concern over what it will look like in the eyes of other people is the motive for chastising one's partner. Despite their marginality, concern for their izzat appears to motivate many of their actions. Surekha explicitly expressed this sentiment when she said, "Having a husband gives you some izzat [in the eyes of society]."

While "marriage" or maintaining a *jodi* appears to be a cherished ideal for hijras, it is clearly not without ambivalence. Hijras are officially discouraged by senior hijras from maintaining relationships with pantis. According to the hijra ideal of asexual identity and practice, official "family" does not include husbands or affinal kin. Senior hijras repeatedly deride "bad" or "false" hijras who openly maintain these relationships. "Real hijras" are those who are asexual, like ascetics; they look at neither men nor women, according to the nayaks. And yet, almost all hijras—including the nayaks—maintain such relationships, in their youth if not later in life.

Further, neglect, fickleness, and physical abuse on the part of these men toward their "wives" contribute significantly to hijras' ambivalent feelings toward their pantis, as is evident in the following statements. In response to a question about their relationships with pantis today, Shanti, a slightly older hijra, said, "It is a different thing. It is not desire any more. Now it is companionship and the hope that the person will be there for you later." She then added, "That never happens though. These men are all alike. They stay with you as long as you give them money and look after them. Then they are gone." Aliya echoed the same sentiments when she said, "Today men are not at all nice. They only want one thing [and] they take your money and go."[29]

On one occasion, when a hijra had asked me the question about marriage, Renuka, another hijra who was sitting close by, said "Why do you want to get married, Gayatri? Husbands only beat you, take your money. You waste all your strength and energy thinking and worrying about them. Don't get married." I later found out that Renuka had just broken up with her "husband" two days before we had this exchange. A few days later, however, I saw Renuka flirting with a man. She appeared very happy and introduced this man as her panti, whom she was going to marry soon. While this statement could be interpreted at face value, it could also be interpreted through the lens of hijras' often mocking attitude toward men. They would distance themselves from all pantis, especially their sexual "customers," and mock their intelligence or sexual perspicacity. "We make *ullus* [literally, "owls"; colloquially, fools] out of these men," Babu Rao told me proudly. "We say we will do *sis kam* [real work] and we do *kavdi* [false] sex.[30] They are in such a hurry and they don't know anything, so we can easily make *ullus* of them." Another time, Saroja said in obvious disparagement, "You just have to say 'ooh, ooh' two or three times, and these people [pantis] think that it is because of them, and they pay you more." Apparently, hijras distance themselves from pantis and use their effeminate role to play with and ultimately to mock supposed male knowledge and power.[31]

And yet, many hijras clearly love their pantis, sometimes to the point of distraction, even attempting suicide on their account. One hijra, a daughter of Mallamma's who lived in a city some distance from Hyderabad, actually did kill herself. She threw herself in front of a train because her panti had left her. While this was the only hijra I knew who had actually killed herself, almost every other hijra, especially among the kandra group, had attempted suicide at least once, more often than not on account of their pantis. Surekha said she had attempted suicide as many as three times because of her husband Rajesh's adultery. He was cohabiting with another hijra in Vijaywada. She was so upset by this development that she "did not see the value of living any longer" and swallowed a bottle of pesticide. She had to be rushed to the hospital and have her stomach pumped to save her life. Munira too had attempted suicide by swallowing insecticide at one point, she confided in me. Her husband Zahid had not come to visit her for a few weeks, and she was sure he was involved with someone else. "But, this was early in our relationship, Gayatri. It was only after learning how to deal with [this other] prostitute, being beaten by my man, after doing all that, that my man is with me now," Munira said. Shakuntala had slit her wrists on account of her panti, leaving scars that were visible seven years after the event. She was reluctant to explain how and why she had attempted suicide, but made it clear that it was because of her unqualified love for her panti.

As with other men and women in India, love or desire in all its intentionally ambiguous forms appears to animate hijra discourse and practice. "If it is at all legitimate to think of 'Indian culture' as an organic whole, a system that can be molded and described as such, then ambiguity must be a key component of that whole, a key feature of the communicative system by which that whole is maintained," writes Margaret Trawick (1990, 41). Perhaps, with regard to hijras' worldview too, it is intentional ambiguity that best describes their "paradoxical behavior." As with Trawick's Tamil family, if such ambiguity or "paradoxical behavior" could be explained at all, it was often in terms of love or desire (49).

OTHER *RISTE*: THE MATERNAL BOND

Yet another relationship that was ideally prohibited for hijras was the link with their natal families. As self-identified ascetics, or sannyasis, hijras are expected to cut off all ties with their "blood/own" (*sontham/rakta*) families when they elect to join their new hijra family. As many hijras repeatedly stated, it was other hijras (and in some instances, other kotis), but *not* their husbands or their natal kin, who were "their people" or "family" now. And yet, despite their explicit acknowledgment of these proscriptions, a few hijras continued to maintain ties with their natal families.

Some hijras had healthy, ongoing relationships with members of their natal families, most commonly their mothers. Many of them occasionally visit their mothers, and sometimes, though more rarely, their mothers visit them in return. As much of the Indian psychoanalytic literature emphasizes, the maternal bond appears to remain the strongest, and some hijras explicitly acknowledge this (see Kakar 1989; Kurtz 1992; Obeyesekere 1990; Ramanujan 1990). For instance, Munira told me that "as long as my mother is alive, I will go back home to visit and will be welcomed [there]. But once she is gone, then my brothers...I will never go back. All they care about is money." During the two-year period of my fieldwork, mothers of at least four of the thirty-odd hijras visited them at the tank.[32] Most of these visits lasted a few days at least, the mothers having traveled a considerable distance in many instances. While at least one of these mothers appeared to accept her son's decision[33] and did not try to talk him into returning with her to their natal home, others were still upset and extremely emotional regarding this issue. Although they could and did visit each other, there was an unambiguous (if not explicitly stated) acknowledgment on the part of both consanguinal mother and hijra child that the connection between them had irrevocably changed. Other hijras constituted the latter's family now, and while her tie to her mother would never be completely severed, there was no returning to her earlier life and natal family at this point.

Despite the retention of this strong link between natal mother and son in practice, such a relationship went against the ideal norms of the hijra community. The renunciation of natal kinship ties is a clear marker of hijra identity, serving to differentiate them from other kotis such as the zenanas, as the latter explicitly stated. "The hijras leave their mothers-fathers and live together in the *haveli* [house], but we don't do that," Rafat told me, pointing out the difference between hijras and zenanas. He also added that doing so required *himmat* (strength) and was an irreversible break that he was not willing to undergo at this point. Iqbal, one of the zenana *baijis* reiterated this difference. He also told me that it was his ties to his natal family that prevented him from joining hijras. His mother had recently passed away, he said, and now he was free to join the hijras and "go live in Irfan nayak's *haveli* [house]." Despite the fact that an absolute break with the hijra's natal family did not always occur, the ideal and its significance for hijra conceptualizations of family and kinship remain undisputed (Trawick 1990).

"*MANOLLU*": KOTI KINSHIP AND THE NEED FOR "OUR PEOPLE"

August 10, 1996, a lazy Saturday afternoon. Munira, Sushmita, Surekha, and Babu Rao were whiling away their time, playing *asta-camma* (a board game).[34] I was sitting with them, watching the progress of their game and chatting with Munira about everything from her conceptions of family to plans for the weekend. Shakuntala was sitting a short distance away, drying her just-washed hair. She seemed to be in a particularly foul mood, cursing someone or something under her breath. Srilakshmi and Kajal were eating their food a little distance away from the bathroom. Greatly involved in the game, Munira and others failed to notice the approach of two men toward Srilakshmi and Kajal. These men wore pants and shirts and seemed to approach without too much trepidation. They were standing and talking to Srilakshmi for a couple of minutes and were clearly intrigued by my presence. From their gestures and body movements, they were obviously asking Srilakshmi and Kajal who I was and what I was doing there. For some reason, this really seemed to irk Shakuntala. She started yelling at them, cursing them in the foulest language. She shouted at them, saying "what do you want here, *bhadvas* [pimps]? Get out of here; otherwise come and lick my ass!" Srilakshmi then piped up and said, "*Arre* Shakuntalanani, these are *our people* [*manollu*].[35] They are kotis from my village." Almost immediately, Shakuntala calmed down and, after composing herself, engaged them in a friendly conversation by asking what they were doing in Hyderabad. I turned quizzically to Munira, who said by way of explanation, "All kotis are our people.[36] We are one lineage [*kulam*]. But those who have the *rit*, only those [people] are the real thing [*asli ciz*]."

As the above vignette indicates, aside from the privileging of the *rit*, hijras adopt a shifting signifier in their demarcation of an insider/outsider boundary. For the most part, family for hijras refers to other hijras, and yet not all non-hijras are excluded from consideration: non-hijra kotis are also considered *manollu* (our people). The use of this term implies a wider, shared community of actors. It is a contextual signifier, dependent to some degree on the particular actors present. For hijras, *manollu* refers to the members of their own in-group—hijras—in the context of other kotis, but it refers to the *entire* koti community when the social context includes pantis (or narans). Similarly, members of the other koti groups, while recognizing kotis of their self-identified subgroup as their family, would extend this label to other kotis as well, in contexts where the reference group was either their natal families or their pantis.

What, according to its members, is shared by this wider community of actors? For hijras and other kotis, the "male" gender system is conceptualized in terms of pantis and kotis, with the latter identity being opposed to the former, both in sexual as well as everyday practice. Kotis are the receptive partners of pantis in sexual intercourse. In addition, kotis share behavioral norms and moral restrictions, and have their own lexicon, distinct from that of pantis or non-kotis (Hall 1995, 1997).

I was told by my zenana friend Salman, "You have to look at their hands. Kotis can be easily identified by the way their joints move, especially their wrist joints." The limp hand, seemingly unhinged at the wrist, along with the "way a man walks, stands, and looks at you," appear to serve as clearly defined koti identifiers. In addition, the use of what is often constructed in the public domain as "the hijra [hand] clap," is a clear symbol of divergent sex/gender identity. When used by non-hijra kotis, it serves unambiguously to align them with their more flamboyant, readily identifiable fellow kotis. Kotis appear to use this gesture to indicate not only their public allegiance to hijras, but also their knowledge and ultimate use of self-denigratory markers to mock male (heterosexual) power. By employing these gestures in the Public Garden, kotis acknowledge their deviance in the eyes of the public and, by embracing this perceived deviance, parody and potentially overturn the power differential.

All kotis appear to know and use their special vocabulary (Hall 1997). Whether they speak Telugu or Hindi, kotis used their vocabulary as an exclusionary device to communicate with fellow kotis and to set themselves apart from non-kotis. This coded lexicon was employed both to signify membership in the community at large and to distance themselves from the public and mock male power. For instance, in the garden, the most popular cruising and meeting spot for many non-hijra kotis, this code was invoked to make fun of the omnipresent plainclothes policemen. The koti term for these individuals, *ghodi* (mare), is used pejoratively by kotis to make fun of them and their supposed masculine power. Kotis use this term and make explicit fun of these *ghodis*, who appear unaware of this term of reference or the extent of kotis' disdain for them.

On one occasion when I was sitting with a group of zenanas in the garden, a *ghodi* walked up and sat down a short distance away, obviously intrigued by my presence in this all-"male" group. As he was approaching, one of the zenanas, Ahmad, announced to the others, "Hey, a *ghodi* is coming. Lets have some fun [with him]." He then turned to the policeman and staring directly at him, raised his eyebrows suggestively, running his tongue seductively over his lips while he did that. He then got up and walked a short distance away, swinging his hips in an exaggerated manner. The other zenanas were looking pointedly at the *ghodi* and laughing at his obvious discomfort. After a couple of minutes, the policeman got up and walked away. Ahmad made a clicking sound as if to say "Huh, these men!" as he shook his head in obvious disgust, before turning triumphantly back to the zenanas, who greeted his performance with whistles of approval.

All kotis, it seemed, whether hijras, zenanas, or kada-catla kotis, see themselves in opposition to pantis and use their perceived difference to signify their membership within the larger koti community as well as to mock the heterosexual imperative. For them, all kotis are *hamare log* or *manollu* (our people), in opposition to pantis who are "othered," both as objects of desire against whom kotis define themselves as well as subjects who instantiate the gender norm.

Aside from the ideational correlates among the various koti kin ties, there appear to be structural homologies as well. The kinds of *riste*, or relationships that zenanas, kada-catla kotis, jogins, and siva-satis develop resonate remarkably with the kinds of bonds described earlier among hijras. In addition to the *rit* with hijras (in a hierarchically lower position than hijra celas), zenanas had their own network of relationships within their own community. Of the four remaining zenana houses in Hyderabad, each had its own hierarchical structure with a head, or *baiji*, followed by his celas, who had celas of their own. Each zenana koti had a separate kinship bond with his respective zenana house—what they referred to as *man-pan*. The *man-pan* ritual was similar to that of the hijra *rit* ceremony. Much like the *rit*, the *man-pan* established guru-cela relationships among zenanas. The relationship between a zenana guru and his cela was also reciprocal and involved defined obligations and responsibilities. Given that zenanas did not live in one place together as a communal group, however, these guru-cela responsibilities were marginally different from those between a hijra guru and her cela. The performance of everyday domestic chores was not expected on the part of the cela. Nevertheless, whenever required, a zenana cela was expected to help his guru financially, emotionally, and, if necessary, physically. In turn, the guru was obligated to support his cela, both in public zenana contexts, as well as in times of need. Rafat for instance, felt compelled to lend his cela, Yusuf, some money to help out when the latter's wife fell ill and he needed money. He did so even though he was in no position to help and ended up borrowing money at an exorbitant rate of interest in order to help his cela. In addition, gurus were expected to pay for all their celas' functions and contribute gifts on ceremonial occasions. For all the trouble it entailed, having celas was nevertheless a measure of authenticity and izzat for the guru. It was a concrete kin link that both arranged social relationships within the community, and embodied seniority. As zenanas themselves noted, it was this aspect of their identity—the kinship link with hijras and the resonant relationships within the zenana community—that marked their difference from other kada-catla kotis and *berupias* and gave them more izzat vis-à-vis these other koti identities.

Although kada-catla kotis did not have either a *rit* or hierarchical ties structured in terms of guru-cela relationships, and explicitly disparaged the "traditional" ways of hijras and zenanas, there was an indisputable valence attached to kin that resonated through this community as well. Like *pyar ke riste* among hijras, kada-catla kotis also had structured mother-daughter relationships, sealed by a ritual in which both parties publicly declared their wish and then shared sweets, a practice akin to many non-koti celebrations as well. After announcing the *rista*, the "daughter" would feed her "mother," putting part of a sweet in her mouth and eating the other half, before sharing the box with the other kotis.

This ceremony was usually enacted in Gaudipet, a remote area some twelve or thirteen kilometers from Hyderabad, the koti *dawat* (celebration/feast) space. It was here, away from the public gaze, that kotis felt most comfortable meeting publicly and indulging in koti *nakhre*—joking and teasing each other mercilessly with lascivious speech and exaggerated feminine gestures and movements.[37] Following a particularly lewd comment by one of the kotis, I was told half-jokingly by Saroja, my hijra friend who accompanied me the first time I attended a koti *dawat*: "I told you, Gayatri. These people really use bad language and even we are embarrassed to listen to them."

These koti *dawats*, usually held on Sundays, would be attended by anywhere from fifty to two hundred kada-catla kotis, and on occasion, some zenanas and siva-satis. Apart from a chance to meet and catch up on gossip and news, these *dawats* also served as the forum to officialize kinship links within the community. On the occasion I was there with Saroja, the ostensible reason for the *dawat* was Viji's desire to make Mahesh his daughter. Unfortunately, we arrived too late to witness the ceremony, but I was told that it was nothing more than a declaration of intent, followed by a sharing of sweets and an exchanging of gifts, after which mother and daughter hosted a feast for their koti friends. The food—chicken curry and seasoned rice—was prepared right there with the help of all the kotis, amid much joking, teasing, and cavorting around. When I left at six in the evening, having been there since eleven in the morning, there were still at least fifty kotis there, eating, dancing, and gossiping with each other.

On the second occasion I attended a koti *dawat*, it was hosted by Avinash to celebrate his getting a new job. When I reached Gaudipet, he was sitting in the center of a circle of kotis, with his "mother" Moggu sitting next to him.[38] They were performing a ceremony to bless Avinash. The following is a description of this ritual from my field notes:

Moggu had set two steel plates in front of Avinash. One had a sari and material for a blouse, and the other had a pile of uncooked rice, two halves of a coconut, some turmeric, and *kum-kum* (vermilion powder). Moggu formally gave Avinash the clothes and, after putting them aside, took a pile of the rice in cupped hands and poured it onto the other plate. He then smeared some of the *kum-kum* and turmeric on Avinash's forehead, invoking a blessing for his daughter's continued good health and fortune. Avinash touched Moggu's feet as a mark of respect three times, each time touching his hands to his eyes. He then sat down. One by one, each of the kotis came up to him and performed the same actions (poured a handful of the rice, put a *bindi* on Avinash's forehead). He did not touch their feet though. After all of them had done this, Moggu, who was sitting by his daughter's side all along, asked for *kattanam* (dowry). He initiated this stage by waving an envelope of money over Avinash's head, before putting it on the plate. All the kotis followed suit, with Moggu announcing, as each koti came up, the amount each paid. Following this show of affection and regard, everyone was asked to sit and eat the food that Moggu, Avinash, and a few of his friends had prepared earlier in the day.

The "mother" is obligated not only to officiate at such ceremonies, but also to contribute both money and organizational help for such occasions. In turn, daughters are required to show respect, help out in times of trouble, and be considerate of their mothers' well-being. Deference is to be shown not just to one's mother but to all elders in the community. For instance, during a bantering conversation, Jayaprada (as one of the kada-catla kotis liked to call himself, after a popular Telugu film actress) had cursed his "aunt"—his mother's "sister"—calling him a *bhadva* (pimp).[39] Even though it was obviously meant in jest, Jayaprada was immediately reprimanded by the other elders and made to apologize to Hanumanth, a koti who was five years younger than he was. He apologized immediately without protest.

Given the centrality of desire to their identities, kada-catla kotis and zenanas (like many hijras), seemed extremely ambivalent about their husbands, who alternated between being the most important, loved individuals in their lives and being reviled and mocked for their licentiousness, insensitivity, and abuse. Despite incredible stories of abandonment and neglect, however, kotis continued to yearn for a significant relationship with their pantis, as shown by Frank's life-history, told in detail in the following chapter. Frank, a middle-aged, Christian man in his mid-forties, had suffered untold hardships for his pantis. He had sold his blood to a blood bank, and later his kidney, to earn enough money to satisfy his current panti. He had lost several jobs on account of "his man," been physically abused, and suffered ill health after the sale of his kidney. Nevertheless, he "loved [his] panti and was willing to do anything for him." After being beaten by his panti's relatives one day, Frank had this to say to me:

I told him these people came and hit me. I said who are these people to hit me? He was completely cold. He said you are a character who deserves to get a kicking. Then you tell me how I'll feel. I *loved* him a lot, Gayatri. I still love him. How can I forget him? Why, I ask god, why is god rude with me? I have not harmed anybody. I have not disappointed anyone in life, neither my friends nor the men. I loved somebody, and every man that came up to me in life has played a game. They played with me as much as they wanted to. They enjoyed sex as much as they wanted to, and then they booted me out. I adore you. I worship you [with reference to his panti]. I walked out of my house because of you. I left my house because of you, I left my family because of you, I left my friends because of you. Everybody I left because of you. I'm living *alone* because of you. My mother's last words were: "Frankie, you will be alone in this world. You will die alone. Nobody will come for your funeral. Not your friends, not Ravi [his panti]. In the end, the dogs will sniff you, or the MCH will throw you in the dustbin." My heart bleeds, but I can't cry anymore. I have no tears left. I used to wait for this man, Gayatri, from seven o'clock right up to one o'clock at night. And he would come at two and tell me the train was late, my cousin died. I came, you should be happy.

Avinash, another kada-catla koti, had a similar story. He too had sold his kidney for his panti, only to be abandoned after giving him the money. Iqbal, one of the zenana *baijis*, told me that he knew only one zenana who had a good relationship with his panti; every other zenana had suffered emotionally and physically on account of his panti. Other kotis told me stories of the physical and verbal abuse they suffered, about their pantis' insatiable appetite for money and gifts, the humiliation they had to swallow on account of keeping up appearances in public for their panti's izzat. Yet almost all of them told me that although "pantis would not support you when you need[ed] them in the same way as koti friends," they still wanted a perfect relationship with their pantis "more than anything else." Despite this overwhelming desire, pantis were clearly "other" in koti conceptualizations—arguably kin but not "family." They were the objects of desire but were hardly ever turned to in times of trouble or need. Kotis were acutely aware of their marginality and pantis' use and abuse of them. But, while they resented pantis for their apparent domination and lost no opportunity to mock male power, they "couldn't help loving them" and were "willing to do anything for [their] men."

"ALL KOTIS HAVE PANTIS": THEORIZING A NEED FOR KINSHIP?

Given the ubiquity of abuse, violence, and abandonment, as well as hijra/kotis' ambivalence toward men in general, why this strong desire for a social *jodi* (bond)? Why do kotis have such an overwhelming need for a loving husband? Scholars from various schools of thought have attempted to answer this question of relationality, or the structures of desire, in the context of broader processes of self-crafting in India, with psychoanalysts and psychological anthropologists providing perhaps the most elaborated theories.

The psychoanalytic literature in India attempts to answer this question in terms of the general "desire for fusion" and the subsequent modal resolution of the oedipal complex in India. In psychoanalytic understandings, this cultural theme of fusion manifests itself as "the unconscious fantasy of maintaining an idealized relationship with the maternal body" (Kakar 1989, 125). Although South Asian scholars differ in their characterizations of what constitutes the "maternal body" (Kakar 1981, 1989; Kurtz 1992), they appear to agree that the individual's goal is "integration, and not individuation" (Kurtz 1992, 30). In India, an individual's sense of self, they argue, is fundamentally connected to a desire for incorporation, for fusion with the (maternal) world, rather than a greater differentiation of self from others. According to these (male) authors, integration, in this context, more often than not implies the desire for an idealized relationship with one's mother (Kakar 1989).

Sudhir Kakar posits a "formidable consensus...for both men and women" regarding the ideals of womanhood (1981, 63; cf. Raheja and Gold 1994 for a valid critique of this position). This ideal is personified in the image of Sita—the pure, chaste, faithful heroine of the *Ramayana*, Kakar contends. The internalization of this ideal by all Indian women and their subsequent inability to challenge it and demand intimacy and recognition as women from their husbands, results in "aggressive, destructive impulses" directed toward the son. This results in ambivalent feelings toward the mother on the part of the son—she is both "nurturing benefactress and threatening seductress" (1989, 93). The modal resolution of this conflict is achieved through "lasting identification with the mother, which involves sacrificing one's masculinity" (1981, 102). Sudhir Kakar therefore claims that (for men) desexualization emerges as "the favored defensive mode in Indian fantasy" (1989, 144).

Gananath Obeyesekere (1990) makes a similar argument in his characterization of the unique resolution of the "Indian oedipal complex." Echoing A. K. Ramanujan (1983), he argues that the representation and consequent resolution of the oedipal complex in India follows from the particular cultural configuration of family relationships in this culture. The significance of the "erotic-nurturant bond that binds mother and son...and the patripotestal authority of the father" (Obeyesekere 1990, 81) results in the dominant Hindu form of the oedipal complex, which the son can resolve only though "submitting to the father's will and in effect castrating himself" (Goldman 1978, 363).

Since the "hegemonic narrative of Hindu culture as far as male development is concerned is that of the Devi, the great goddess, especially in her manifold expressions as mother in the inner world of the Hindu son" (Kakar 1989, 131), this form of oedipal resolution clearly allows for its realization. Hence, "if phallic desire was the violent and tumultuous 'way of the fathers,' genital abstinence, its surrender, provides the tranquil peaceful path back to the mother" (124). Given that "Indian myths constitute a cultural idiom that aids the individual in the construction and integration of his inner world"

(135), the myth of Goddess Parvati and her two sons, Ganesha and Skanda, clearly reflects this "hegemonic narrative" and its opposing wishes:

A mango was floating down the stream, and Parvati the mother said that whoever rides around the universe first, will get the mango. Skanda impulsively got on his golden peacock and went around the universe. But Ganesha, who rode the rat, had more wisdom. He thought: "What could my mother have meant by this?" He then circumambulated his mother, worshipped her, and said, "I have gone around my universe." Since Ganesha was right, his mother gave him the mango. Skanda was furious when he arrived and demanded the mango. But before he could get it, Ganesha bit the mango and broke one of his tusks. (136)

Ganesha seeks surrender and fusion with his mother at the cost of his masculinity (symbolized by the broken tusk), while his brother Skanda yields to the pull of individuation, which results in independence but exile from his mother's presence. As Kakar states, "that Ganesha's lot is considered superior to Skanda's is perhaps an indication of Indian man's cultural preference in the dilemma of separation-individuation" (1989, 137; cf. Kakar 1981; Obeyesekere 1984, 1990; Roland 1979; Kurtz 1992; Trawick 1990).

In this psychoanalytic formulation, it is integration with the mother (and subsequent emasculation) rather than individuation that constructs male desire and kinship relations. In a further elaboration of this "consensus," Sudhir Kakar (1989) accounts for gendered differences in the structure of fantasy by arguing that while "desire for fusion with the mother" is what constructs male fantasy, for women in India, it is the yearning for a *jodi* (bond) with the husband. Insofar as one can essentialize this interpretation of "Indian" relationality, therefore, hijras (and to some extent, kotis) would appear to have internalized and enacted both fantasies—male and female— in their desire for integration and in their subsequent bonds of kinship.[40]

In addition to this psychoanalytic interpretation and the ubiquity of the "desire for fusion" or "category mediation," as Margaret Trawick (1990) refers to a similar cultural theme, kotis' desire for kin bonds could reflect a culturally specific construction of self and other, a form of relatedness wherein Indian men and women primarily craft their identities within a relational/social context (Marriott 1976; Shweder and Bourne 1984; Ramanujan 1990; Trawick 1990; Shweder, Mahapatra, and Miller 1990).[41]

Every time I went to see the hijras, especially in the first few weeks of my acquaintance with them, I was questioned not so much about what I was attempting to accomplish and why, but who I was in terms of what my parents were doing, where they lived, how many siblings I had, whether I was married or not, and whether my siblings were married or not, among other questions. As most South Asian scholars or even casual visitors to India have noted in the past, the aspects of oneself that elicit most interest and commentary are not individual accomplishments but relational networks of hierarchy and exchange. Social relationships and the nature of one's obligations, in many respects, appear to define one's identity and status in India. In India, a person is who they are by virtue of their kin relations and the social context within which they locate themselves unlike Euro-American notions of the self or identity, these scholars maintain (Marriott 1976; Mines 1994; Roland 1979; Shweder and Bourne 1984).

The well-known anthropologist Clifford Geertz stated many years ago that "the Western conception of the person as a bounded, unique, more or less integrated motivational and cognitive universe, a dynamic center of awareness, emotion, judgment, and action organized into a distinctive whole and set contrastively both against other such wholes and against a social and natural background is, however incorrigible it may seem to us, a rather peculiar idea within the context of the world's cultures" (1975, 48). As some scholars would argue, the "peculiarity" of this notion is manifestly apparent in India, a nation where "individualism stirs but faintly and where the subordination of the individual to the superordinate family interests and relationships is a preeminent value," as Sudhir Kakar (1989) somewhat dramatically puts it.

However stigmatized and marginalized they may be in Indian society, might hijras too be constituted through and by such an ethic of relatedness? Why was it so inconceivable for hijras to strike out on their own and live independently? Madhavi was thrown out of her kin group, and, although she could have lived on her own, the thought of not "belonging" to the community was unthinkable. She was a "pariah" among the Lashkarwala hijras under the tank, as Rajeshwari told her, which led her to change her house and put the *rit* in the Sheharwala house, even if it was in a position lower than that she had held earlier.

Likewise, Tushar, a zenana koti, was from North India and did not really know anyone in Hyderabad. He used to come to the garden to find sexual partners as well as a social group and, after seeing the other zenanas on a few occasions, he struck up a conversation with them. On subsequent Sundays, when he came to Public Garden, he would join the zenana group and hang out with them until it was dark enough to look for sexual partners. Although zenanas did not appear to treat him differently despite his non-kin status, Tushar felt compelled to officially join the community. He became Rafat's cela in an informal ceremony (not the formal *man-pan* ceremony in the presence of the *caudhary* and *baijis*) conducted in the garden itself. Why this perceived need for kinship? What motivates kotis to establish kin ties, when they could often relate to their self-identified community just as well without these ties? Perhaps, as these scholars maintain, one of the reasons being alone—without a kin network—is so inconceivable in India is because identity is largely relationally constructed and context-dependent to a greater (and different) degree than it is in the West (Marriott 1976; Shweder and Bourne 1984; Ramanujan 1990; Shweder, Mahapatra, and Miller 1990).

This relational explanatory framework, however, much like the psycho-analytic one, leaves several questions unanswered. Aside from their problematic cultural and gendered essentialism, neither of these theorizations accounts for the more interesting patterns of relationship within the hijra and koti communities. Although the "desire for fusion" or "the cultural preference for integration" rather than individuation does address, to some extent, kotis' desire for kinship and perhaps the existence of certain significant bonds, it does not really explain why they adopt the specific kin and the rituals or practices they do, nor does it satisfactorily explain the power differentials evident in other relationships within the community. Likewise, the relational argument potentially accounts for the ubiquitous need for "our people," but it reveals nothing significant about the specific structures of caring and the particular constructions of kinship that I have described among hijras and kotis.

While it is difficult and to some extent pointless to *account* for kotis' need for kinship (or, for that matter, to account for such desires among non-kotis), the elaborations of relatedness within the community and the explicit statements highlighting the significance of such bonds confirm that kinship and elaborations of familial ties are *central* axes of hijra and koti identity. In a recent publication, Kira Hall notes that "the family is, after all, what distinguishes the hijra from most other members of Indian society, who are intimately involved in the extended families so instrumental to social organization" (1997, 444). This statement ignores the existence of the specific elaborations of hijra and koti kinship, the patterns of caring and relatedness within the community, and their fundamental resonance with broader mainstream societal patterns, structures, and sentiments. Joining the koti community obviously does not preclude the possibility of having an extended "family" and a social network much like "most other members of Indian society." The existence of the various koti relationships, patterned as they are on familial/affinal bonds, and the broader *need* for kinship that they express, appear to emulate rather than oppose or deny those of mainstream Indian society, while simultaneously throwing them into relief and challenging their very definitions of "normativity."

And yet, while there are clearly elements of mainstream ideologies and structures in hijra's articulation of kinship, it is perhaps too easy to analyze these patterns as either the workings of "power" or the apparent reactions to the contrary as "resistant" discourses/actions (see Foucault 1980; Anderson 1983; Williams 1989; Hobsbawm and Ranger 1992; Ginsberg and Rapp 1995). Seeing hijra and koti families as either necessarily counterhegemonic or necessarily assimilationist appears to be not just simplistic but uninteresting and counterproductive. Such understandings set hijra defiance of procreative and hegemonic definitions of "family" against their incorporation of such terminologies, rituals, and symbols. Instead, I would argue, understanding these options not as dichotomous ideological oppositions but as subtle tensions reflected through the various polysemic, affective bonds of hijras and other kotis is imperative. Ultimately, as Margaret Trawick notes, "The need to love is as important a force in human society as is the will to power. Power wants to destroy or consume or drive away the other, the one who is different, whose will is different. Love wants the other to remain, always nearby, but always itself, always other" (1990, 242). Hence, rather than understanding hijra and koti structures of caring and kinship, of self and other, through the framework of power and archetypes of resistance, as simple reflections of mythical mainstream patterns, it is more productive to see these kinship patterns as a complex web of significations, a web of emotional tensions between real people, fraught with ambiguous meanings—an "architecture of conflicting desires" as Trawick notes (152)—that fundamentally constitutes hijra/koti identity. If desire or love plays a central role in the lives of hijras and kotis, it is through the various, ambiguous, and conflicting patterns of kinship—the affective bonds of guru and cela, "milk" mother and daughter, sister and *gurubhai*, mother and son, husband and wife—that this love is made manifest. Only through understanding the relations between the idealized systems of kinship that hijras and kotis hold to, and the nature of desire and lived experience in which these ideals are often not sustained, can we *begin* to comprehend the "local pleasures and afflictions" and the cultural patternings of their lives (Nuckolls 1996). With this goal in mind, the next chapter allows hijras and kotis to speak for themselves and allows us to glimpse "what it means to make sexual difference matter" (Cohen 1995b, 277), revealing the multiplicity of ideals and the fundamental complexity of lived experiences.

8

Shifting Contexts, Fluid Identities

In an essay intriguingly titled "The Pleasures of Castration," Lawrence Cohen (1995b) poses two potentially antithetical analytic challenges for the construction of sexual difference. First, he argues for an analysis that "locates the body within a multiplicity of differences," rather than one which "reads the etiology of the sexed body in terms of the primacy of culture, political-economy, biology or psychology" alone (295). Second, and somewhat at cross-purposes, he emphasizes the "need to listen to the obviousness and necessity of sexual identities and embodiments, and not drain the corporeality of embodied experience by forcing it to stand for difference and difference alone" (295). Admittedly, both these analytic goals are significant and crucial challenges for any theory of sexuality. But how does one adequately address the "corporeality of embodied experience" without overemphasizing this aspect of difference while simultaneously paying attention to the multiplicity of differences within which it is embedded? Perhaps one way is to allow some of these individuals who have the most at stake to speak for themselves. In the following section, I recount the stories of two kotis I met in Hyderabad in the hope that these verbatim accounts capture something of the "local pleasures and afflictions" of their lives better than anything I could relate in the third person. Further, by juxtaposing these accounts, I hope to convey a sense of both the specificities of individual corporeal pleasures and embodied experiences as well as their complex embeddedness in a "multiplicity of differences."

SUREKHA'S STORY

Surekha is a twenty-six or twenty-seven year old hijra who has been living under the tank for about eight years. She was born as Sadgopal, in a village near the city of Warangal. Her mother died while giving birth to her, and she was raised, along with three stepbrothers, by her father and stepmother. Her family was Christian, she said, having converted a generation ago. Economically, her family would be classified as lower-middle-class, although she did not appear to want for any basic necessities as a child. I asked Surekha to tell me about her life: "How you became a hijra, why, about your family . . . all of that." In reply, Surekha said, "Come. I will tell you my story. It is a very sad story, but I will tell you. Other people should know, because then they can avoid the same mistakes." This is her story as she related it to me in the winter of 1995.

From when I was very small, [I was] friendly with girls. I would talk to them like a friend. From birth itself, I always liked to put *moggus*, play with girls, and help with the cooking and cleaning. I liked only men from that young age. I used to make up games where I was the wife, and this boy I liked was my husband, and I would make him do this and that to me. I tell the truth, Gayatri. No man spoiled me, like some of the other kojjas here say. When I did things, it was because I also wanted to do them. I also used to go to the station. The station was like the garden here, where all kotis meet. That is how I met Renuka, Kamala [other hijras]. Like that I lived for a couple of years, until I was fourteen or fifteen, at home.

[I was] studying in the tenth standard [grade] at the time. For the tenth standard exam, my father had given me money for my fees. What did I do with that? I wanted to learn dance, I wanted to learn *bharatnatyam* [a classical form of dance, popular in South India]; so the money that my father gave me, without paying the [exam] fees, I paid [that amount] for *bharatnatyam* fees. My cousin [father's elder brother's son] went and told my father. Saying, "Ah, you want to give stage programs, you want to become a cinema heroine," my father beat me up nicely. Even though he hit me, I didn't listen. I wanted to learn dance. I wrote the tenth standard exam, but I failed. My interest was not on studies. Studies were boring. [I wanted] to roam around, explore. My mind was not on one person. It was becoming very strange. I was only interested in doing things like a woman and roaming with men. I was not interested in studies. In the seventh [grade] I passed [my exam] first class. By the tenth [grade], I had become older, no? So all these mad thoughts and desires and words had surfaced.

After that, after I had failed the tenth, my father really wanted me to do well. I was the eldest in the house, no? My mother had died, right? That is why he really wanted me to do well. So, he put me [to work] in a cloth shop;

I didn't work. [He put me in] a lorry mechanic shop; I didn't work. He put me in a cycle shop; I didn't work. Again he paid the fees for my tenth standard exam. Even though he had paid the fees, I didn't write the exam. Why? When I don't have an interest in writing the exam, why should I do it? For their satisfaction alone? In the end, my father said, "Why were you born? Whose reputation were you born to spoil? Whose name were you born to spoil? [You should] die. You aren't finding a well [to throw yourself in] or poison to kill yourself, is it? Then at least fall under a train and die." He said this three times.

After he said that, I drank some pesticide medicine, but everyone made me vomit it out outside the house, and I survived. Having survived, I didn't want to continue living [in that house]. *Chi!* I don't want to live in this house anymore, [I thought]. Are my desires going to get any less as time goes on? No. In front of them, their izzat will go. I will not pass for a woman. My father used to say "Do not go out on the road. You will make me lose my izzat." Why should I make anybody lose his or her izzat? If I could just go somewhere and kill myself. I didn't want to live anymore. But I didn't come away *because* I wanted to live [among hijras]. I didn't want to wear saris. I didn't know *anything* about [hijras] here. I just wanted to go live far away from these people [my family]. When I appear so like this to these people, why should I live there? I don't have a mother. I don't have any real, immediate family. I don't have a real sister or brother, older or younger. Who do I have that I need to stay on for? Nobody is there who worries about me. *Chi!* I don't want to. I won't live there any more. Thinking that, I came away here [Hyderabad]. Renuka [and] another koti I knew in Warangal—Kennedy—had told me about his life here. Kennedy told me it was nice here, work in the morning, go to the garden in the evening, meet other kotis, "enjoy" with men in the evening, like that. He also told me that there were some kotis who lived in Secunderabad. That is why I got off the train here.

Here, you know Kamala, right? [Kamala is a hijra who used to live at the tank, but currently owns and operates a tea and sweet-stall about five hundred meters from the tank.] Well, her village and mine are close by—next to each other. When I arrived here I was wandering around at the station, hungry. I didn't know anyone [in Hyderabad]. I didn't know about these people [hijras], and I didn't come here to meet them. Anyway, Kamala was from the same village, right? I had only one rupee with me. With that one rupee I thought I would go and drink tea. So I went to a cart and I happened to go to her cart. She recognized me, asked how I was, what I was doing here. I said I was fine and that I had come to find work here.

[Gayatri: At that time you used to wear kada-catla clothes?]

Yes. I used to wear a pant-shirt. But I also used to wear a *bindi, katika* [eye-liner], and everything. I used to wear lipstick-wipstick and everything. But I used to wear a pant and shirt. [She was impatient to get back to her narrative, and shrugging off this line of questioning, continued with her story.]

"Okay, I will give you some work," Kamala said. "Will you work at my cart? You should wear a sari like this, and you can make a lot of money. Stay as long as you want, and then you can go to your parent's house whenever you want." I said okay. That day itself, I washed my hair, combed it properly, pulled out all the hair [on my face], and came to the tanki.

But then there was no tanki or anything. Then there was a room here. That was eight years ago, the time that I am talking about. Kamala brought me and introduced to me to all the people here. [She said,] "These people are your mothers and your sisters. You are the youngest here so you have to touch their feet." [Only] Munira, Kamala, Ramani, Sushmita, Vasundara, Jyothi, and Papamma were here, no one else. Even Rajeshwari [another senior hijra in this hierarchy] wasn't here at the time. I was introduced to all these people, and I said okay and stayed here. Then Kamala said, "Because it is the first day, I am taking all the money. I will give you three meals a day. From tomorrow, you give me twenty-five rupees." Like that, I was with Kamala for a month or two months. At that time, I met Rajesh [Surekha's husband]. I met him as a customer, first.

[Gayatri: Did he know that you were a kojja?][1]

Yes. He knew. Knowing I was a kojja, he brought some money and came to me. What do I know? Usually all these men come [to us]. The same way, he came too. Then he was much younger though. Even I was young then and didn't know very much. Wisdom, knowledge, all that I didn't have. So then both of us, you know. He gave me money. First he said he would give me twenty rupees, but he gave me only ten rupees. I started fighting with him. Then I felt sorry for him. [He said], "This isn't my place. I'm from a different place, Karnataka." So I said doesn't matter and let him go. Then after that, every day he would come up to me and wish me, saying, "*Namaste bhabhi*" [literally, "sister-in-law," but also a respectful form of address]. Look, whoever it is, I see to their stomach. Food. Whoever it is, I ask them if they've eaten, and if they have money. Otherwise I say "Here are ten rupees, go and eat." I think like this. Anyway after a week or two of his coming like this, I said, "See, you have no-one, I have no-one. *Chi!* I won't go to my father's house anymore. You are everything to me. Both of us will live together." He said fine. I was living with Kamala at the time. She became aware of this matter. After getting to know about it, she hit me and said, "No, don't do this. I got married and am suffering a lot. He has been hitting me. We have been fighting. Both of us belong to the same village. So, at least you [I hope] will remain well/fine. That is why you don't need this madness." Saying that, she fought with me. Either you want a husband or you want me [she said]. I thought "Why fight like this," so I took him and went to Bombay.

I went to Bombay, taking Rajesh. I stayed there for three months. I stayed with kojjas there. Bombay kojjas are there, aren't they? I stayed with them for two to three months. Went to the market and asked for money, asked for money here and there. Every day, whatever I earned, I would give to Krishna [a hijra from Andhra Pradesh, living in Bombay]. I was staying with her. For him [Rajesh] and me, all we need is a little shade to sleep. But who will give us this? If it was me alone, that would be one thing, but there is him too, his food, his *chai*. This is not our place, right? So I used to give away all the money. That Krishna also beat me up. If I didn't give them money every day, they would beat me. Can one make money every day, Gayatri? Even though I did everything there. I did this work also there [sex work], but less. As soon as it was time, I used to come home. He was there, right? So as soon as it was time, I used to come home. In the mornings what do we do sitting without any work? So we used to go ask for money in the marketplace. Here [Hyderabad], there is no asking for money in the market or anything. Everything is here only, on the tracks. In the evenings we go up [to the station platform] and then we come down. That is it.

I was in Bombay for three months, but I didn't like it there. This man [Rajesh], at his [young] age itself, he got drunk once. He cut himself [attempted suicide] once. I felt very bad. If I were to leave this man here, what would the people back there say? Wouldn't they say, "She went and left this poor boy who knows nothing at all there?" So I told him, "See, its not nice here. So both of us will go back to Hyderabad. Once we reach there, you can go wherever you want. But you should come back to Hyderabad with me. I took you to Bombay, so I should take you back to Hyderabad," I said. So we came back here. I gave them what little money I had, and I was looked after well. I was Kamala's daughter, right? And Kamala and Munira call each other *vadina-mardalu* [sisters-in-law]. So from then I was adopted as Munira's cela and looked after well, with love.

[Meanwhile] Rajesh had kept a woman. [She was] called Sapna. She was also like this. Meaning she was also involved in *vyabicaram* [sex work in Telugu]. She engaged in prostitution at the station too. Between the two of us, there were a lot of fights. She had a room in Lalaguda. If he came to me, she was angry, and if he went to her, I was angry. "So, have you gone and met the *kojjadi* [hijra thing] and come," she used to say. I used to say,

"So have you gone and met the *lanjadi* [crude word for prostitute]." But even between the two of us, Rajesh and me. To me he says, "Continue practicing *dhanda* [work or prostitution in hijra terminology]," and to her he says, "Don't do it," and takes her home. Will I like that? Because I didn't like it, I would fight. Because of the fights, in the end she went away. After she left, Muniramma said, "All this is not nice; so if we marry the two of you, each of you will be afraid of the other and you will remain together." Saying this, Muniramma took me to Chowtuppal [a town forty-odd kilometers from Hyderabad, where Munira and a few other senior hijra sex workers rent rooms where they can get away for the week-ends], and made him her son. Saroja [Munira's daughter in the hijra kinship network] made him her younger brother, and Rajeshwaramma [Munira's sister] made him her son. After that, they performed our marriage, with a *mangalsutra* and everything. So I became their daughter-in-law. After that I lived like that. There were big fights. I hadn't had any "operation-geeperation" then. We were fighting a lot, and he would beat me everyday. See; see all these bumps [on my head]?

But, we continued living like that, because I loved him, Gayatri. I continued doing this work, this tank work, giving him my money. He used to come at night. Then in the morning, we both happily ate what I cooked, he had a bath, I washed his clothes, like that. Then, there was a system, Gayatri [said ruefully]. At seven I go up [to the railway station for "work"], and at ten I have to come and sit aside. In the morning I can't see anyone's [any man's] face or talk to anyone near the platform. I cannot put flowers in my hair; I cannot put any powder on my face in the mornings. Now he is making the other person—you know the one I told you about earlier [a few months ago, Rajesh had started seeing another hijra in the city of Vijaywada] go according to this system. If [I] wear a nice sari, he says "*Chi*, take it off." Like this he acts now. Seeing all this, these people [hijras] also used to shout at me: "Look at him! He doesn't work, he just eats and roams around and eats your money.[2] Leave him!" If he hits me, he hits me; if he shouts at me, he shouts at me. But later I know he feels bad. "I don't have anyone. How can you leave me and go, Surekha?" he used to say. So how can I leave him? I stayed here.

Then, a few months later, I had my operation. I had decided to become *cibri* before only, but then one day I had gone to the market to buy some things. When I was there, I decided to earn some extra money, so I went to the shopkeepers to ask for money, even though it was not the Lashkarwala territory.[3] When I walked up to one shopkeeper though, maybe because he didn't recognize me, he said "Show me that you are a real kojja." I was still *akkva* [not operated on] then. Having completely lost respect and feeling ashamed, I quietly came back. After that, I decided to become *cibri* [operated on], and after a few months I went for my *nirvan* [operation].

I took Rajesh with me for the operation, because he was about to be arrested here. You know that drunkard next door, Rajesh [another Rajesh who lives in the neighboring colony]? My Rajesh became friends with him and started roaming around with him. See, whoever one roams around with, people consider them together. That Rajesh is a *goonda* [ruffian]. People say he has killed at least one person, and done other bad things. This man ["my Rajesh"] was also caught with him, and the police were going to take him away. So I took him with me to Vijaywada. See, whichever person [hijra] gets the operation done for me, then tomorrow they will say, "We did it for you, we looked after you, we did this, we did that, we took so much trouble." So I told Rajesh, "See, so many days you have been with me right? So you only should see to me, whether I'm happy or unhappy. You have to look after me. That's your headache. If I get the operation done too, it is your headache," I told him. Saying that, I took him with me to get the operation done. I took him to the hospital, but then he was scared, so I sent him away. He came back to Hyderabad, and the police caught him and put him in jail. So, instead of him, Vasundara looked after me [after the operation].

I was in hospital [in Vijaywada] for eight days. From the hospital I was brought here. Gayatri, what can I tell you! Hot, hot water, after boiling it until it was very hot, they threw it [on the wound]. Muniramma thrashed me, on the wound. She pulled me and thrashed me with a *lota* [metal jug]. [She hit me] on the wound and it opened. "Without telling any of us, taking her husband and getting [the operation] done!" she said. She was very angry and said all kinds of things. God knows all that. I won't say it with my mouth. I didn't say anything to them. I thought, these people have got it done, so they know everything about it. Even if I opened my mouth, they would shout at me and say "Keep quiet, you don't know anything." In this bathroom itself—where we have a bath—they hit me. Blood was just flowing down. They said "Ha! It doesn't matter. If all that dirt and maleness comes out, then the swelling will decrease, and then it will be good." I thought maybe that is true. Then they took me to Chowtuppal. In the morning Munira and Saroja came there. Again they held me against the wall and beat me. They hit me on the eighth day, they hit me on the ninth day, they hit me on the tenth day, and by the eleventh day, there was a big hole there, enough for a hand to fit in. You could see the flesh inside. Then they all thought I was going to die, and Lekha and others started crying. Surekha will not live anymore [they thought]. I needed to be taken to a doctor. Who was going to look after me? This man was in jail. I didn't have any money. So I went to Muniramma and said, "If I have to die, you kill me, and if I have to live, you have to keep me alive." I asked her to take me to the hospital. So she took me there, spoke to the doctor, and completely, said I have to be made completely well. Every day I was given injections and pills, injections and pills. My hands had become really hard from taking all these injections. But slowly, I began to get well. Everyone came back here [to Hyderabad]. They left me alone there [in Chowtuppal] to get well.

[Meanwhile] in front of the house—you have seen Munira's house, right? Remember the house just in front of her house? I got to know a boy in that house. "Know" meaning. See Gayatri, I didn't have any bad intentions. That boy also had a wife and children. He didn't have any such intentions either. But the two of us, no one was at home, right? So for "time-pass," I used to go and talk to them, carry their children. I used to call them *akka* [sister] and *bava* [brother-in-law]. When it is necessary, one needs someone, no? So I got to know this man. That man never had any bad intentions. Only I used to make fun saying, "*Bava*, I don't have a husband. He is in jail. Won't you marry me? Do this, do that." This was just for "time-pass." That is all. I didn't think like that.

After forty days, [the hijras] did a big *dawat* [feast] for me. [They] sacrificed a goat, put up a big tent, put "sound-boxes." They all came. Rajeshwaramma gave me a sari. All the expenses were borne by my guru only, Muniramma. Kabir tied anklets on my feet. [It was] very nice. How much ever they did though, I cried a lot because Rajesh wasn't there. Tell me, Gayatri, at such a happy time if he isn't there? I cried and cried. Seeing me crying this way, the people opposite—the husband and wife—asked why I was crying like this. "Oh! It is because her husband isn't here with her," they told them. That night I went to their house. Wearing flowers in my hair, a new sari, like a bride, I went to their house and [saying] "*Bava* [brother-in-law]," I touched his feet. He poured a huge amount—this many coins—into the *kongu* of my sari. Then I went home. Muniramma and others told me to rest here for a few days before coming back to Hyderabad because my health was still not so good. Saying this, they left me in Chowtuppal and went back to Hyderabad.

The next night, [seeing as] I had just had the operation, someone took me to have some drinks, some *kallu* [toddy]. I came back home, to Munira's house. I had taken off my clothes. I had taken off my sari and put it aside and lay down in my petticoat. I went to sleep. In the middle of the night, that boy came and lay beside me. I didn't know. When I woke up in the middle of the night, I found him next to me. If I make a racket, his house is right opposite. If I make a racket, whose reputation is ruined? Only mine. But his reputation will also be spoiled [tarnished]. So why do it [I thought], and I kept quiet. With that boy I did this work first, after my operation.

After doing it with this boy, then I came and met Rajesh in jail. He said, "When I come out of jail, if I know that he has spoilt you, I will kill him." So I said, "*Chi*, there is nothing like that." What should I have done, Gayatri? Before this happened, he had met that person in Vijaywada. Before my operation itself, he had gone and met her once. So I thought, this man, even if he stays for two days, he will go away. Whereas that man in Chowtup- pal, he told me to stay back there and not go to Hyderabad. "You stay in my house. My wife will make a little food, so you stay with us," [he said]. So I thought "Why should I come to this tank, get involved with all these fights?" But his wife, any wife would feel that way of course, if one's husband is thinking of another woman. She said something in anger to him. So I said, "Why say anything to him, sister? It isn't his fault." She said, "It is my husband, so I will say what I want. Who are you to say anything?" When she said this, when she got angry, I said, "Am I chasing your husband because I don't have one? I have a husband too," I said. So in fifteen days, I saved three thousand rupees and got him [Rajesh] out of jail. Nobody else helped me. I myself saved the money and got him out. We lived together quite happily for a while.

But when this man [Rajesh] came out of jail, everyone, all the hijras told him. They told him that I did this and that in Chowtuppal. So this man used to hit me *every day*. After hitting me and hitting me, he thought, "I will kill her if I continue hitting her," and he started his trips to Vijaywada. He used to go, she used to come. It used to go on like that. Me, after many years, I went home the other day. Both of us went, to my mother's house for Dussehra [an important Hindu festival]. You know what happened when both of us went? He said, "I'll get a lot of money selling fruit, so you go ahead, and I will join you soon." So I said okay and went ahead. He then took all his money and my money and went to Vijaywada, to her. Then with her, he came to my house. There was a lot of tension in my house. My people knew that we were married. Then, if he brings someone else, how will it look? So I didn't want to stay. So the next morning we left, and then he took me to her house. Then he says, "You should stay together. You are like her and she is like you. What will you do if I take a woman tomorrow? You will be company for her and she for you." What does she want though? She wants him all the time. He shouldn't have anything to do with me. How can I live with a person like that? He also wants that. When [I] asked him, he said, "It has been many years with you. You have become old now. If she is feeling passionate, let it be." How can I agree to that? All these years we were both together, and now that I am a little older, he says, "I don't want to be with you anymore." How will I feel? Anyway, for fifteen days—I wasn't here, remember? I thought, let us even try living like this and see. So I went [to Vijaywada] and we lived together to see how it was. That one, she looked after me all right. But she didn't give me anything, and I didn't give her anything. We both earned our individual incomes, and both of us gave it to him only. Between the two of us, everything was fine, but the problem arose when we went to bed. How will he sleep with both of us? If he talked with me, she was angry; if he talked to her, I was angry. But because she was new, he preferred her too. Then I would be in between both of them, right? So in the middle of the night, I left. Without their knowing it, I came away. But then, after coming halfway, I turned and went back. *Chi!* Here also I couldn't live easily. If I could live with the Chowtuppal man, I thought. But he also has a wife and children. If he roams around with me, it is improper for him, isn't it, Gayatri? It is wrong, isn't it? If he didn't have children, and if I didn't have this station work, I could go with him. Poor things, his wife and children. I try and understand everybody Gayatri, but there is no one who tries to understand me. I give my fifty rupees [to my guru], get up, wash my clothes, I mind my own business. [I also want] things from life, [even] I want a child, I want a husband. I want to make a life for myself. [But] this man is like this, that woman is like that. Between the two of them, I want to go away somewhere. Everywhere it is the same life though. Also, if I go away, it is as if I were afraid isn't it? [But] what is this life worth, if it is the same as death?[4]

Not only does Surekha's narrative reveal the incredible pathos of her life, an aspect that is not emphasized by other accounts of hijras, it also highlights what appears to be one of the most important current preoccupations of several hijras: their relationships with the significant men in their lives. Almost all kandra hijras' accounts of their desires, motivations, and life trajectories were overwhelmingly focused on their relationships with their pantis, the abuse they suffered on account of these relationships, and, in several cases, their ultimate abandonment by these men. Although they would begin their narration with how they were "like this from birth, [we] liked to do women's work," catalog their sexual "dysfunction" ("our bodies did not work"), subsequent "desire for men," and the furtive attempts to gain sexual pleasure, most of their narratives would shift to often abusive, unrequited but "necessary" relationships with men, events that clearly shaped their desires and identities. This emphasis on relationships with pantis is evident not just in hijras' narratives, but in those of several other kotis as well. Below, I present excerpts from Frank's story, in which his overwhelming desire for "[his] man" and how much he is willing to suffer on account of this relationship are apparent.

FRANK'S STORY

Frank is a self-identified "Anglo" (Anglo-Indian) man in his late thirties or early forties. He was obviously handsome in his youth but has "let [himself] go" recently, after "selling [his] kidney for [his] husband." I met him at one of the *dawats* (feasts) hosted by kada-catla kotis in Gaudipet. He was one of the few self-identified kotis who spoke English, and we struck up a conversation soon after we were introduced. He gave me his number at work (a warehouse for sanitary products), and we planned on meeting at his house, a tiny, one-room apartment near the station, where he said he would tell me his story. We met a week or so later. Although I tried to ask him about his life as a child and about how he "got into this line," as he phrased it, he was extremely reluctant to talk about these issues, not so much for reasons of embarrassment or confidentiality, I think, as because he didn't think them interesting or important enough. One topic that he never tired of however, was his "husband," returning to it on each of the ten or so times I interviewed him. Frank told me his story in English, unlike the other hijras and kotis, who spoke to me in Hindi or Telugu. Here are excerpts from Frank's story.

From when I was very small, Gayatri, I used to like going with men. I never went with a woman, unlike some of these other kotis. Even in my school, I used to look only at the boys. They also knew that. And I used to play games, flirting with them and all. I had sex with another boy then. After that I used to have [it] quite frequently. Run off after school, roam the streets, like that. My father, uncles, everybody used to get very angry and beat me at home. But I didn't stop. I couldn't stop. How could I? I enjoyed only like this. Sometimes I used to put on a little makeup—steal my sister's, you know—and go to see men like that. Then after school, I didn't finish my school because, like this. But I got a job, a very good job in the airport because of my English and all [he maintained a stall at the airport which sold everything from books to pharmaceuticals]. No one could speak like me so well. And I used to talk nicely to the customers. "What can I get you, sir, madam," like that. Even the airhostesses used to like me so much and get me perfume and all when they came back from abroad. I used to earn nicely, but everything I gave to my man.

[Frank and "his man" Ravi met one night, about nine years ago, in 1989. As Frank tells the story, he was] walking back from work one day. It was quite late in the night. When I came to the station, I met Vinod. She is my childhood friend.[5] We saw this man standing at a distance, and I told Vinod that I wouldn't mind having that man, for a go. So, then Vinod talked to this man. And then this man told Vinod, "Why don't you introduce me to this person." Vinod said, "Okay, she's my very close friend. I will introduce you." I told you no? That time I was very attractive. I was the center of attraction, Gayatri. I am not saying with pride, but I was *very* center of attraction. When I used to walk on the road, people, guys used to whistle to me, and all those things. I used to take all that. Actually, some time back this Ravi had seen John [another friend of Frank's] and me many times. He followed us also, I believe. So, then this man told me, he said, "*Anytime, anywhere*, I'm all yours," and all that. Then, we didn't do anything immediately. We used to meet, have tea, go to the [toddy] compound together, like that. But we didn't do anything. He used to give us tea and all these things, talk to us. Then, in the same year, it was in the month of May, in the first week of May. Ravi, he said "Come, we'll go and have toddy." So, we used to go to this compound, na? Where they have toddy. Myself, Ravi, Vinod, and Mugga, we four of us went. And while we were drinking, Vinod asked that guy [Ravi], "You would like to marry somebody?" Actually, at the time, he was another [koti] character of mine's friend, boyfriend. She [this other koti] also cared for him, but that bitch wanted money. Every time he used to give her money. He used to take her to the house, sleep, have sex, give her rations and all those things, but she is more fairer and good-looking. Her name is Shailesh. Then what happened, in the compound, Vinod asked him [Ravi], "Why don't you marry somebody?" He said, joking, "What ma, I must marry you, huh?" he asked. "No, no! Not me. Marry my sister, that is, Frankie here. She is alone and it would be a good match," she said. So we discussed everything. He said okay, "I will get married to her." That was on a Saturday. Next Saturday, fourth of May, we planned to go. He said, "We will meet at Jubilee bus-stop, we will get all the things, and we will go to Yadigirigutta" [a popular Hindu pilgrimage spot a hundred kilometers or so outside Hyderabad]. So we met there. He bought a black-bead *mangalsutra* [the necklace that is tied by the bridegroom on the bride, a marker of the marital bond in Hindu marriages]. It was only costing fifty rupees. Vinod told me you have to buy a real-gold ring. I bought a ring. Then we went. Fifth May was the wedding. May fifth, around 11:30 or 12 P.M. we got married, *legally.* Legally in the sense, he tied the *mangalsutra* and all. Before tying everything, we gave it to the *pujari* [priest] to keep it near the god's feet. Then the *pujari* gave it in the temple premises itself. While he was tying the *mangalsutra*, the wedding band was playing outside. Somebody else was getting married. So that band was hearing [heard] in the temple itself, so that sound was affecting us. So it was like my marriage only, legally. Then, he put the *mangalsutra* [and] I put the ring. That night, we had sex. Everything, everything, very sweetly it went off and all these things. We came back to Hyderabad. He was very nice to me. [With] his mother's pension he bought me a new watch and all that. Everything was going on smooth and soft. Every day it was going on like this, meeting and everything. He was working. I was working, coming back. He used to wait for me. I used to bring him rations and all those things and give him. Everything he used to take and go. Then I went and met his wife, his children. He is a married man having three children, you know. Everything was going smoothly.

Then, a few years ago, I caught him having sex right here—in my room—with another character. This character, another koti, is a friend of mine. You know her also, Sashank. Right here, Gayatri! How should I feel? I went and drank poison. I collapsed. Then he left me. He didn't want to come and see me even. But Vinod made him come. He came to my house. I was living at home with my sisters and all then. This Mahakali *puja* is there, no? That day he came to my house. My brother-in-law told me. My brother-in-law knows I have a boyfriend. My brother-in-law told me, "I don't want any scene in front of the house. Just wear on your clothes, go sit in the auto, and go *away* with that man! Because, see, a scene, anything takes place in this locality, there will be nothing else. Your sister will die," and all those things. So I left my family, my house, and came to live here.

Vinod and Mugga, they told me, "Leave him off. You don't want him." But then I said "No. How can I leave my man after I got married to him?" I *cannot* do that. Then, after marriage also, five years I controlled myself. It was only that one man. After five years, Vinod told me, "What is this Frankie? You have sacrificed your life in such a way. You are a person that used to have five, five a day, five men a day!" "Then what you want me to do?" [I said]. She said, "I'll get you another." But still I said no. Actually, Ravi, he always used to tell me that he loved me. He never loved me, Gayatri. He *never* loved me. It was only one-sided love. He only loved me for my money. And every time we used to meet after my marriage, he used to tell me, "My house is mortgaged, I need money, I need money." I had no other sources. Then I planned it in such a way, I planned three months in advance, and I sold my kidney, for the cost of sixty-five thousand rupees. Then I gave him the full money for him. [I] told him to go release his house. After releasing his house also, he had only debts. I thought if he releases his house, he won't have any debts [and] he will help me also. But he was not in the helping stage; he was in the taking stage. He was in the taking spree. *Every day* he wanted money. Okay, I loved him. I gave him the money. I gave him my hard-earned money. I never duped anybody, neither I robbed any money. Everything was my own money, which I saved up in the bank, and which I earned with my own earnings, and I worked for the money. I never said no to him. Everything. Even when he wanted money sometimes, and I didn't have, I sold my blood. One bottle cost eleven [rupees and] sixty [paise]; two bottles at a time I gave him. So this was just continuing like this. Every time he would just fight with me and leave me off. And every time, he will give me one time, he will never come [at that] time. Every time he used to treat me very rude. Anybody comes to my room, he will doubt them. Talk at the back of me, never tell anything in front of my face. *Accha*, not only am I buying *his* clothes, he will want for his family. Okay, his wife, his children, his young brother, his mummy! Then you tell me what you want me to do? Rations I supply. They say must not give and then tell. But if he keeps on leaving you and goes, then what do you want me to do?

I tried to take him to my home. But they didn't like him. I know my sister didn't like him. I think he was trying to get her once. They told me not to bring him and come. I said okay, fine. Then once, my full family went off to some place. Only then he came and stayed with me for full twenty-one days. We used to eat, drink, *enjoy* sex to the *maximum* limit. Sex was no bar. The love-making was, no couple has enjoyed I think, in their maximum life. Now you tell me. At the age of forty, he doesn't want to have sex with me. He says I'm dummy. I don't want, I don't want to have sex with you. I'm fed up of you. I used to tell him, "Okay, you don't want [me]; I'll go with somebody else." "Go ahead! Who will want you?" [he said]. I used to tell him, if I give five rupees, a ragpicker will come and fire me. "Get fired! What do I care?" These are the words he spoke to me last. How will I feel, Gayatri?

When his mother was very sick, I gave him ten thousand rupees once. I gave five thousand once, then two thousand once. See your mother is cured. Your mother is my mother. I couldn't help my mother, but your mother? I'm having the money to help her. Get her cured. Her arm and leg fell off. He didn't tell me. Then I went and saw her. She cried in the hospital. I said don't worry. I'll get you the best of treatment. He used to take the money, but I didn't know. He put her in the Railway hospital [a government hospital].

And when she died, he didn't tell me, Gayatri. Today, tomorrow, I think he is going to come. Forty days he didn't come, Gayatri. How do you *think* I will face life? How do you *think* I will go through it? For days I went without food, worrying when he didn't turn up. Twelve days I starved. After twelve days, do you think a person will have any strength left? Remaining days, only tea, coffee, tea, coffee. Finally, you know Avinash [another koti friend]? He met her by accident and told her that his mother had died. Then she came and told me. Twenty-sixth December, 1994. I met him in the compound. He started crying, I consoled him. I said, "Take this money." I forgave him. I took him back.

One day, his wife caught us red-handed when we were doing sex. Then she was also against me. After that she told me not to come, not to put my foot in her house. But, my money was genuine to them. My things, my gifts were very genuine to them. And I am one of the eldest son's guardians in the school. I put him in Seventh-Day Adventist School. Now he is in the fourth standard, and he comes first in class. I didn't have to give any donation. He wanted the child to study in a Catholic school. Because I'm an Anglo, I could get him in. Then, his own brother-in-law came and hit me in my own house. Why did you give Ravi that money? Where did you get the money? What is the relationship between you and this man? My elder sister came out, and she said, "I'll slipper you all! Get out of here! I don't know who are you all, and I don't know who is Ravi. If you all don't go, I'll call the police." Only then they went off. Then, the same day I went. I created a big scene in front of his house. I told him, "You bastard!" I called him [that]. I said, "You are a bastard!" I said, "These people came and hit me." I said, "Who are these people to hit me?" Then also he took it lightly. He took it cool. He said, "You are the kind of character to get a kicking." Then you tell me how you think I'll feel? I *loved* him a lot, Gayatri. I still love him. How can I forget him? Come on, you show me a way. I told him, "You want to leave me, go. But show me my way." "Why? Why should I show you a way? Go get fucked! By some Tom, Dick, or Harry." He told Vinod and Raju, "I don't want him. I can't come with him. The society doesn't want him. I don't want him now. I can't." On the birthday, on the third day after [my] birthday, he tells me, "If I bed with you, I'll get AIDS. I won't bed with you."

As a husband, as a Telugu man, I married him in the Telugu rites no? As an Anglo-Indian, I went into Telugu rites. I became a Hindu. I married him in that custom, and all the Telugu lawful rites I have done. And still, lawful rights I behave with him. After all that I have been through, why? Why, I ask god, why is god rude with me? I have not harmed anybody. I have not disappointed anybody in life—neither my characters [implying other kotis], nor the men. I loved somebody, and every man that came up to me in my life has played a game. They played with me as much as they wanted to. They enjoyed sex as much as they wanted to, and they booted me out. In such a way, in a very rude manner, that I can't describe it. And this man, he has crossed all the limits, all the bounds. Vinod even told him, "See, son, you can't leave her [Frank] in this stage. She's in agony in the garden. Any day she will collapse." "Even if she is dead, don't come and inform me. I don't want to come for her funeral," he said. "I adored you, I worshipped you," I said, "you are my god. My people know, but my people are not proud of you. Okay, I walked out of my house because of you. I left my house because of you. I left my family because of you. I left my friends because of you, I left my neighbors because of you, I left my cousins, my aunties, my uncles, *everybody* I left because of you. I'm living *alone*, because of you." My mother's last words were "Frankie, you will be alone in this world. You will die alone. Nobody will come for your funeral, not your friends, not Ravi. Last, the dogs will sniff you, or the MCH [Municipal Corporation of Hyderabad] will throw you in the dustbin. These are your mother's words—take it or forget it." Tell me what you want me to do? My heart bleeds, but I can't cry any more. I have no tears left.

I used to wait for this man, from seven o'clock right up to one o'clock at night. And he comes at two-thirty and tells me "The train was late, my cousin died. I came. You should be happy." He tells me, "the people that you have borrowed money from, I want to see that they strip you and give you a kicking." I changed his dressing style, Gayatri. I changed the way he lived. I made him into a modern husband. I gave him the world's best things, the world's love. No doubt I didn't have it, but I begged, borrowed, I worked for it; I never robbed, neither did I steal, but I gave it to him. Matching color shoes, matching color socks, the clothes which I chose, I liked. The sari that I liked for his wife, I bought, costing three thousand seven hundred, four thousand two hundred, two thousand seven hundred, two thousand five hundred, each sari! I just loved him, Gayatri. I still love him. I can't forget him. I just can't. But god said no, there is an ending, there is a beginning? I must think it is an ending, Gayatri. I just loved him. I still love him. How *can* I forget him? You won't believe. See, when I come to this room, and I find the room empty. How I feel? How happy you feel, when your man is here. I die for him to kiss me, you know. I die [for] one kiss! It's costing me one crore rupees; one kiss, one crore rupees, Gayatri. Just a touch on my lips, my lips are not even wet. How do you think I feel? I used to tell my sister. She said, "Frankie, you have to bear it up. You have accepted him, but he didn't accept you. You have to." My friends say, "You forget him, Frankie. You *have* to forget him in this life." Vinod says, "You forget him now. I'll get you another fellow. He may sleep with you and go, but he won't love you." How can I get? When you have somebody in your heart, how can I get another fellow? He will forget me because he is having wife and children. Who am I having? Who am I having in this world? Nobody Gayatri. I gave my life for these men, and now there is nobody to help me.

TRAUMAS OF BECOMING: KOTI NARRATIVES OF PLEASURE/PAIN

Clearly, these two narratives resonate in certain respects. Whatever their life trajectories, both these individuals appear to have had similar adolescent experiences, made similar sacrifices, and experienced analogous feelings of jealousy, hopelessness, and despair. According to Surekha's chronicle of her life, she became a hijra quite by chance. As she stated, she could just as easily have lived her life as a kada-catla koti, not having had the "desire to wear saris, . . . have the operation or anything." Like Frank, she knew that "she liked only men," and this, in addition to a desire to "do women's work" is what occasioned both the abuse at home as well as her decision to come to Hyderabad and join the kotis under the tank. Further, the intense longing, extreme generosity, repeated abuse and suffering at the hands of the men they loved, and ultimate feeling of loneliness despite the existence of their respective communities, seem remarkably resonant across the two narratives. In fact, over and over again during my fieldwork, I heard the same wrenching pathos in several kotis' narratives. I heard about the wretchedness of their lives, the stigma associated with being "in this line," the traumas of unrequited love and abandonment, of physical abuse at the hands of pantis and other men, and of betrayal by friends, almost at the same time as I heard exultant accounts of how they could "enjoy sex to the maximum" with their partners, the remarkable strength of their friendships with some of the other kotis, and the intense, if fleeting pleasures they derived from their sartorial and corporeal inclinations—similar stories across the koti spectrum that spoke of embodied desires and pleasures as well as disappointments and frustrations in their lives.

Several kotis, including Surekha and Frank, spoke of similar childhood experiences: the brief moments of pleasure playing furtive games with boys; the early desire to do "women's" tasks—cooking, cleaning, and putting *moggus*—stealing their sisters' makeup and clothes for the brief pleasure of dressing up before they were thrashed by their parents and siblings; the joy of snatching clandestine moments in their schoolyards, public restrooms, bus and railway stations, and later the Public Garden to flirt with men; their dreams of having sex with the most handsome boy in their neighborhood or school; and, often, the reality of physical abuse, parental expectations and obligations to the family, and the responsibility of hiding their "real" desires, knowing them to be deviant and socially unacceptable.

The extraordinary violence that each of them suffered appeared almost ubiquitous in all their lives. Several koti narratives would date their entry into "this line" from the point in their lives when they were "spoiled" by their friends, neighbors, and teachers. As Suresh, a kada-catla koti told me quite calmly and matter-of-factly, "I entered this line first when I was 'raped' by my teacher in school.[6] I was nine or ten years old, and my teacher told me that he wanted to talk to me after class. Then he 'raped' me. I didn't know anything at that time about 'homosex,' or kotis, or anything. I didn't enjoy at all that time, but slowly, slowly I began to enjoy, and now I am a 'homosex' person only." On a different occasion, Raju, another kada-catla koti, had the same story to tell. "I was spoiled by my brother's friend first. I didn't know anything ... I was only eight years old. After that I began to 'enjoy' only 'homosex.'"[7] In the next section, I tell the story of Vikas who "got into this 'homosex' line" by virtue of being "spoiled" by his neighbor, a tough navy serviceman.

Several hijra narratives also mention this act of "spoiling," which serves as the point of origin for their subsequent choice to become hijras. Munira, Nagalakshmi, Kajal, Lekha, and several others subscribed to the theory of "spoiling" as the source of the weakness in their body (penis). "If you do like that, from the back you know. If other people do like that to you, then slowly, slowly your body becomes weak, and you cannot do anything after that. You become a koti or a hijra. It was like that for me," Kajal told me in a somewhat embarrassed tone. "First, this neighborhood *goonda* [ruffian] spoiled me. He took me to the fields and he spoiled me, first. Then, when he told other people, then they also spoiled me, and slowly my body had no more strength," she added, avoiding my eyes as she said this. While the notion of being "spoiled" could be a convenient retrospective starting point for many of these narratives, the violence of the act itself is indisputable and can hardly be ignored.

Likewise, many kotis made bodily sacrifices for "their men." Frank's selling of his kidney, mentioned earlier, is an example of the extent to which he and others would go to appease or satisfy their "husbands." In addition, I heard innumerable accounts of suicide attempts by several kotis. Frank, like Surekha, had "drunk poison" in a bid to kill himself. Munira's narrative echoes this violent act. When her family rejected her for her effeminate ways, she swallowed a whole bottle of pesticide. Again, when her husband Zahid misbehaved with another woman, Munira drank poison in another abortive suicide attempt. Almost every hijra at the tank had scars on her wrists and hands, which they said reflected their attempts to kill themselves. I also heard stories about zenanas who threw themselves under trains and were maimed, while others slit their wrists, all on account of their pantis. Such violence appears to be widespread across the various kotis' narratives.

And yet these narratives differ as well. While Frank and Surekha, both Christians, obviously suffered similar patterns of intense longing and violence on account of their "husbands," Frank was neither "a bitch who takes money" nor would he ever consider becoming a hijra. The notion of physically emasculating himself both appalled and disgusted him. For Frank, the particular sartorial, familial, and corporeal embodiments that constituted hijra identity from his perspective were manifestly different from the specificities of his own pleasures and desires as a koti. As he stated, "Whatever it is, I like to have anal sex and all. But I could never have this operation and wear these clothes and all that things. I don't believe in this *rit-wit*, baba! I go for these koti *dawats* when they call me, I talk nicely to them, sometimes we even go to the garden together, but I don't want to do all of these things—put the *rit*, wear saris all the time, have this operation and all." Like some of the other kada-catla kotis, it was sexuality or "homosex" rather than gendered practice that appeared to condition Frank's identity and desire. Further, Frank would not consider himself a prostitute, even though he used to "turn tricks" with a number of men—at least "five in one day" as Vinod stated—and sometimes even for money, to help pay the rent or provide for his husband. For the most part, sex, aside from defining the basis of their identity, was "for enjoyment and pleasure," unlike those "bitches who take money."

For their part, hijras believed that kada-catla kotis, defined as they were by their unquenchable sexual desire, were offensive for this reason. When I first asked hijras to clarify the difference between themselves and kada-catla kotis, the first thing they said was, "Those *gandus*! They are only interested in chasing men all the time," in a highly disgusted tone of voice. "We just do *kavdi* [false sex] and take these pimp's money, but those kada-catla kotis, they do *sis* [real] work with everyone. *Thu!*" Lekha once told me. Precisely because hijras ostensibly did not gain pleasure from these encounters and instead exploited the men for money, sex was more respectable for them.[8] In addition, as Surekha's story reveals, the ability to experience shame and act on it was what finally led her to have her operation performed. By resisting the impulse to undergo this procedure, kada-catla kotis and zenanas are revealing not only their unbridled lust but also their essential shamelessness, according to hijras.

Then again, there are gay-identified men who also *ghumo* (cruise) in the garden, but for whom the terms *sis* and *kavdi* are just as meaningless as they were initially to me. Many of them do not know the customs and rituals of hijra life, nor do they especially care to find out about them. Instead, they have weekly meetings in the garden attended by other upper-middle-class, English-speaking, homosexual men, to discuss the latest news regarding gay activities in cities such as Bombay and Delhi, to sell and distribute copies of *Bombay Dost* (the most popular English-language gay magazine in India), and to function as a support group. For hijras, who lived as a community and supported each other through their various crises, the notion of a support group that met once a week to "just talk about [their] experiences" seemed perfectly ludicrous. And while many of these gay men did not see themselves as kada-catla kotis, not even recognizing the term, hijras saw no difference between the two groups. According to hijras, all kada-catla kotis were *gandus*, whose bad language, overt *lacak-matak* (hip-swinging) mannerisms without the "appropriate" sartorial and gendered desires, and excessive sexuality defined them and thereby separated them from themselves.

According to other kotis like jogins and siva-satis, the single most important difference between them and the hijras was religion. "We are all Hindus, unlike those [hijra] people who are all Musalmans," Lakshmana, one of the jogins told me. "We don't have the *khatna-watna* [circumcision] done, like those people. We are Hindus," another jogin added. Interestingly, it was not divine possession, the fact that the god or goddess "comes onto [their] bodies" that jogins emphasized as the difference between themselves and hijras, but circumcision. And while religion was acknowledged to be one of the differences between jogins and zenanas, what Akbar, one of my zenana friends, chose to highlight was not circumcision but the fact that zenanas ate *halal* meat while jogins did not. Clearly, even similarly construed axes of difference evoke manifestly different interpretations of embodied knowledge and practice.

Evidently, people have different corporeal, moral, religious, economic, political, and cultural investments at stake. To posit a unidirectional narrative for all so-called third-sexed individuals that obliterates these differences in an attempt to read their bodies and desires as primarily sexual, and then marks their identity and difference solely on the basis of this sexuality, is limited, if not misleading. Although the spectrum of desires and pleasures appears to be similar for several of these kotis, what is at stake in their lives, the multiplicity of differences—including class, caste, region, generation, occupation, and education—within which their lives are embedded, and their situated constructions and interpretations of desire, embodiment, and pleasure are very different. To reiterate Cohen's phrase, "all thirdness is not alike" (1995b, 277).

And yet, what happens to this attempt to trouble the project of gender fluidity when one can apparently "switch" (in a manner of speaking) one's sex/gender identity? Several zenanas and kada-catla kotis had wives and children at the same time as they identified as kotis. While there was some moral indignation associated with this fluid subjectivity, as revealed, for instance, by Frank's statements that he "never went with women, unlike some of these other kotis," this was clearly an established practice among some kotis. Several zenanas and kada-catla kotis I spoke to acknowledged their alternative life to me. While "this line" of homosociality was separate from "that line" of heterosexuality, apparently the divide was not always clearly marked.

While such fluidity existed among hijras as well, it was associated with far more disapprobation. I constantly heard rumors about various hijra sex workers who had been "married" and had had children before joining the community—*berupia-gandus*, as they were disparagingly referred to. These rumors were loudly denied before the hijra concerned bounced the *berupia* insult onto someone else. The rumors were never confirmed, but they were frequently used either to surreptitiously deride particular hijras or as an insult in the heat of an argument. Clearly, crossing this sexual/gender divide was one of the more serious transgressions for a hijra. A case in point is that of Mary. When I first saw Mary, "she" had a thick moustache and beard, short hair, and was wearing pants and a shirt. I assumed she was a kada-catla koti who was visiting her friends at the tank. When I next saw her, a few days later, she was wearing a sari and had plucked out or shaved her beard. She told me shyly that she had just come from her village, but she used to live here (under the tank) a few years ago. In fact, she was Munira's first daughter, she said proudly, and had now returned to the tank because she wanted to rejoin the group. When Mary was called away to perform some task, Lekha, another fairly senior hijra, pulled me aside to tell me Mary's story. "Mary used to live here you know. But then he ran away—went back to his village and married a woman. I believe he even has children! *Thu!* That *berupia*. He shouldn't be allowed to return here," she said vehemently.[9] I asked Munira about this rumor. "I know everyone is saying that Mary went back to her village and became a panti. But I don't believe it. She could not do such a thing, my Mary." In fact, as I outlined in an earlier chapter, this issue resulted in a particularly contentious debate among the senior hijra sex workers, who argued about whether to allow Mary to remain at the tank. Munira stood up for her daughter on that occasion and convinced the others to let Mary rejoin the hijra fold.

Needless to say, nayaks and other senior badhai hijras were constantly decrying the current hijra *zamana* (period, or age). "These people, who knows if they are real hijras, or *berupias*, or what they are! Here, we do not allow whoever wants to become a hijra for two minutes to come into the house. But these 'tanki' [sex work] people, *berupias*, and all these people come and go as if it is their parent's house!" Amir nayak said in total annoyance. As Munira and others pointed out however, it is not as if the nayaks are truly concerned about the ostensible past of their nati celas. "As long as you give the money when you are putting the *rit*, they don't ask at that time if you are a *berupia* or anything. All they care about is the money. And then they talk!" Munira said in reply to my question. Whatever the apparent proscriptions or taboos, it is possible (though reprehensible by hijra standards), to switch between sexual roles. Yet, despite the apparent blurring of the "lines" of sexuality, none of the kotis would ever explicitly refer to themselves as pantis or overtly acknowledge their *berupia* status, even when referring to their past. Despite the fluid scale of gendered identities within the koti spectrum, such fluidity hardly ever crosses the koti/panti divide.

Over the course of my fieldwork, there appeared to be constant movement and flux, as I perceived it, between the various koti "identities"—kada-catla koti, zenana, hijra, jogin, and siva-sati. I encountered several kotis who had gone from one to another koti identity without apparent discomfort. Vikas was one such koti. I first met Vikas at his kada-catla koti "mother's" house in Koti, a locality in Hyderabad. He had just arrived from Bombay for a brief visit, he said. Vikas then proceeded to tell me the story of his life. He was born in a small village a few hundred kilometers from Cochin, in the southern state of Kerala. Vikas was the last of seven children and was thereby greatly indulged by his parents and siblings. He remembers his childhood as extremely happy and carefree, spent largely in the company of his mother (a factor that contributes to the development of homosexuality, in his opinion). But all this changed with the arrival of their new neighbor, a navy serviceman. "I still remember the day he came to our village," Vikas said. "It was a Saturday. We did not have school on that day, and so I was playing in the garden. I saw this man on the road. He was wearing a very smart uniform and he looked so handsome, I cannot tell you! He looked at me straight, and my heart was going *dhud-dhud*. I was very much scared. I ran inside the house after that." Over the next couple of years, as Vikas grew to late adolescence, the navy serviceman and he "became good friends." One day, his friend invited Vikas into his house, and "spoiled" him. He then quickly added, "I should not say that I did not enjoy. I also enjoyed. But once you enjoy like that, once you enjoy 'homosex,' you cannot go back. Because of this man first, I became a *gandu*," Vikas said very matter-of-factly and seemingly without rancor. After a few years, Vikas came to Hyderabad to look for work and was employed as a "bearer" in a private club. "I became a full-time kada-catla koti then. Every evening, after work, I used to go to PG [Public Garden] and enjoy with other men," Vikas added. This continued for at least ten or twelve years, until he "began to worry about who would look after me in old age." Last year, he went to Bombay with Srinivas, one of his friends, and "became a hijra" in the Dhongriwala house. He "put the *rit* and everything" and is now a "full-time" hijra in Bombay. "But when I come to Hyderabad, I am a kada-catla koti again, and enjoy freely in PG like before I used to," Vikas said (in English).

Vikas's friend Srinivas, with whom he went to Bombay, had a somewhat similar life trajectory. Srinivas was a zenana before he became a hijra in Bombay, and during the week of his visit to Hyderabad, hosted a *dawat* (feast) at the Yellamma temple in Balkampet. I attended this *dawat* and was surprised to see not just zenanas, but also several jogins and siva-satis. Before becoming a zenana, Srinivas was apparently a siva-sati. Despite vehement statements to the contrary regarding the importance of categorical rigidity, no one present appeared to object or even question Srinivas's multiple identities. When I saw Srinivas next, he was in the garden, cruising for partners with Vikas and his zenana friends.

Akbar, my zenana friend, told me that for some four years he lived as a hijra, in his hijra *dad-guru*, Pasho nayak's house. While I am not sure that Akbar's statement was true (based on other zenanas' statements), such temporary residence appeared to be a theoretical possibility, as I witnessed in Irfan nayak's house. Likewise, one of the zenana *baijis*, Iqbal, reiterated his resolve to leave this zenana-life and "become a hijra" in his guru Irfan nayak's house. Irfan nayak's other celas, Rani and Shahbaz, were both siva-satis before they became badhai hijras. So was Lata, one of Bala nayak's senior celas. All three of them continued to attend the *bonalu* festival at the Yellamma temple in Balkampet to meet their erstwhile gurus and friends, despite its explicit proscription within the hijra community. Another former siva-sati, referred to simply as Sati, stopped being possessed by the goddess when she became a hijra sex worker. Bhabhi, a good friend of Shanta's (Vikas's "mother"), was a kada-catla koti, and while he "did not put the *rit*" and become a hijra, he used to go "practice [his] *dhanda* [sex work]" with hijras, and was formally adopted by one of the hijras (Vasundara) as her daughter. Likewise Bala Rao, a kada-catla koti who used to roam around (*ghumo*) for men in the garden for the last ten or fifteen years, decided last year to join the hijra community. He has not put the *rit* and has no intention to do so, he said, but he continues to live and "work" with hijra sex workers at the tank. Bala Rao is a married man with two children, a fact that hijras do not seem to be aware of. I only found out through his former friends in the garden, fellow kada-catla kotis who asked me to prevail upon him not to "ruin his life, wearing those clothes and going with hijras" and instead, to "go back to his wife and children and lead a decent life," albeit a life that did not preclude cruising in the garden with his kada-catla-koti friends. Bala Rao was obviously not alone in this respect. Several other kotis were married and led a similarly surreptitious, dual life. This was one reason why kada-catla kotis had their *dawats* outside Hyderabad, they told me, so no one they knew would see them "enjoying like this."

Not only can one switch identities across the koti spectrum, but a certain degree of flexibility is allowed within the hijra subcategory itself. As I noted in an earlier chapter, hijras can officially change their hijra house. After her expulsion from the tank, Madhavi immediately changed her house from Lashkarwala to Sheharwala. Likewise, Vanitha, Amir nayak's cela, changed houses from Sheharwala to Lashkarwala a few years ago. Kajal, one of the hijra sex workers at the tank, belonged to the Bullakhwala house in Bombay but was planning to become Rajeshwari's cela in the Lashkarwala house now that she had moved to Hyderabad. The kinship network apparently allows for a certain degree of mobility, even though frequent changes are frowned upon.

Similarly, although hijras state that only certain individuals are allowed to become hijras, this rule is often relaxed, as in the case of the "American hijra." While I have never met her, I was told by Irfan nayak that someone— an "Amrikan"—had approached the hijra community in Delhi and asked to be allowed to join. As Lawrence Cohen and later Serena Nanda informed me, this was Anne, a male-to-female American transsexual (pers. comm.). Anne currently lives in California and is an "official" hijra in one of the hijra houses in Delhi.

What does one make of this degree of flexibility? How does one reconcile the "different stakes" that each of these individuals has with their apparent ease of transition from one category of "thirdness" to another? Can it be that some differences matter more than others, making for different degrees of permeability? Or is this further proof that sexual identity is not and cannot be the only baseline for comparison. Perhaps this fluidity is possible precisely because each subject-position is variously determined: different axes of inequality, lived experiences, and interpretations of desire, pleasure, and morality construct each of these "sexual" identities. Far from repudiating the differential stakes that each individual has, the potential for mobility across these categories highlights the complicated nature of each of these subject-positions. In other words, no easy correlations exist between ideals, embodied desire/praxis, and sexual identity. The fluidity of perceived self-presentation precludes any easy reading of difference as merely sexual or gendered. Axes of identity and their salience in an individual's life shift and interconnect, not just spatially, but categorically and temporally as well, with different configurations of identity emerging at different points along a person's life. Significantly, however, it is lived experience that provides the key to understanding this phrase. Not only is the body located within a multiplicity of differences but, what is more important, it is the *embodied experience* of the individuals concerned that should serve as the ultimate basis for theorizing and understanding difference/identity. As Adrienne Rich states in *Of Woman Born*, "Perhaps we need a moratorium on saying 'the body.' ... When I write 'the body,' I see nothing in particular. To say 'the body' lifts me away from what has given me primary perspective. To write '*my* body' [on the other hand] plunges me into lived experience, particularity" (1986, 215; emphasis added). Likewise, perhaps the koti narratives should lead us to avoid theorizing on the basis of disembodied knowledge and instead compel us to look closely at kotis' "local pleasures and afflictions," at their ideals and lived experiences, in order to discover what is *really* at stake for them.

9

Crossing "Lines" of Subjectivity

TRANSNATIONAL MOVEMENTS AND

GAY IDENTIFICATIONS

It was early evening in Hyderabad, and the Public Garden was gradually coming to life. I was sitting on a low wall adjoining the tea-stall, having a cup of *chai* with Suresh, a young, self-identified gay man, when we had the following conversation. "Is it true that in America there is a book that tells you specific locations across the country where you can find other 'gays'?" Suresh asked me eagerly. "Where did you hear that?" I asked. "This friend of mine went for a 'homosex' party in Bombay, and there was a 'gay' man who had just come from abroad. He told my friend," Suresh replied. "It would be so great if there was one like that for India also, because then easily we could go enjoy with other people in this 'line,'" he added wistfully.[1]

In this chapter, I focus on the two somewhat related images or notions circulating in this modern Indian gay narrative. The first is the construction of sexual subjectivity implied by the usage of the term *gay* in Hyderabad. Despite the differences between the nineteenth-century episteme of "homosexuality" uncovered by Foucault, and the newer, twentieth-century episteme of "gay" identity, both epistemes tend to elide the receptive/penetrative sexual distinction so common in parts of Latin America and Asia (Jackson 1989, 1997; Carrier 1995; Lancaster 1988, 1992, 1995; Parker 1991, 1999; Murray 1995; Kulick 1997, 1998; Green 1999; Seabrook 1999; Carillo 2002). This elision appears to be in marked contrast to the constructions of identity by hijras/kotis.[2]

The second image refers to the transnational links invoked by Suresh and the people he referred to as being "in this line," and the particulars of their narratives and subject-positionings stemming from these perceived connections. I want to highlight the apparent difference in the dynamics of this self-construction in urban India vis-à-vis the protracted, internal process of disciplining and dividing that produced Foucault's "modern" homosexual in the West.

I highlight these images by addressing the relationship between two apparently different models or archetypes of same-sex sexuality that are currently deployed in Hyderabad. Following a brief overview, I sketch the ideal outlines of these two models—what one of my koti friends referred to as the "modern gay" model and the "traditional koti" model—before problematizing their depiction either as coherent definitional fields or as mutually exclusive markers of tradition and modernity. In particular, I point to two issues that highlight this disjuncture. First, rather than a Foucauldian understanding of modern homosexuality in terms of a *superimposition* of one "apparatus" (sexuality) over that of another (alliance), I argue that in Hyderabad, the mutually coexisting nature of the "traditional" and "modern" paradigms and the potential interactions between them belie such a "universal narrative of supercession" (Sedgwick 1990).[3] Second, I maintain that the *translocal* nature of "gay" subjectivities in India argues against both a coherent, universal "global gay identity" (Altman 1997, 2001; cf. Warner 1999) and an explicitly local particularity. Ultimately, what I emphasize is the complexity of the cultural production of homosexual identity in the interactions of the West and the non-West, local cultural systems, and global politico-economic forces.

EXPLORING THE CONTEMPORARY TERRAIN OF HOMOSEXUALITIES

In the now famous passage from the *History of Sexuality*, Michel Foucault states,

As defined by the ancient civil or canonical codes, sodomy was a category of forbidden acts; their perpetrator was nothing more than the juridical subject of them. The nineteenth-century homosexual became a personage, a past, a case history, and a childhood, in addition to being a type of life, a life form, and a morphology, with an indiscreet anatomy and possibly a mysterious physiology.... The sodomite had been a temporary aberration; the homosexual was now a species. (1980, 43)

According to Foucault, this instance of subjectivation in the West, resulted from an epistemic disjuncture in the nineteenth century in which sexual identity was produced by the disciplining knowledge of the sexual sciences and the dividing practices of modern states. Foucault's historical method focuses on unearthing epistemic ruptures that occur across the passage of time in one spatial unit, namely the West. But what happens if we take into account the genealogy of knowledge/subjectivity across *space* as well as time, as Donald Donham (1998) asks? Quite apart from the fact that Foucault did not take into account the potential importance of the colonial relationship in the production of current Western notions of homosexuality—a point Ann Stoler (1995, 1997) eloquently makes—he also did not address the potential impact of the rapid transnational flow of knowledge, commodities, persons, and narratives, and its role in the formation of notions of sexuality in regions not "in the western part of the world" (Foucault 1980, 11).

Further, as Eve Sedgwick (1990) points out,[4] recent historical work in gay/lesbian studies, following Foucault's initiative and pointing out ever more precise datings and narratives of the development of homosexuality implicitly "underwrite[s] the notion that 'homosexuality as we conceive of it today,' itself comprises a coherent definitional field rather than a space of overlapping, contradictory, and conflictual definitional forces" (45). Instead, contemporary notions of "homosexuality" can be effectively denaturalized and better understood only by exploring the "gaps between minoritizing and universalizing . . . gender-transitive and gender-intransitive understandings of same-sex relations" (47), especially in varied "sites of desire" in the contemporary transnational world (see Manderson and Jolly 1997).

A recent body of literature that appears to address these transnational flows of sex/gender signs and commodities advocates what I shall refer to as the "global gay" narrative (see Altman 1996, 1997, 2001). The premise of this narrative is the "emergence of a 'Western' style homosexuality" in non-Western regions of the world, characterized by a "modern invention, namely, the creation of an identity and a sense of community based on (homo)sexuality" (Altman 1997, 423). With the increased transnational traffic in signs and narratives, this "modern invention," which developed as a result of particular historical specificities in the West, has apparently diffused to emerge as a variant of a universal, "global gay" identity in non-Western regions, including Asia. Although proponents of this view obviously recognize that this pattern is not a simple diffusion from West to East, replacing "traditional" or "indigenous" sex/gender formations in a "linear genealogy" (Altman 1996, 79), such formulations inadvertently perpetuate the somewhat sterile and culturally marked binarisms of gay/West/modern versus indigenous/non-West/traditional. For instance, Dennis Altman states, "On the one hand, Asian gay men, by stressing a universal gay identity, underline a similarity with westerners. Against this, on the other hand, the desire to assert an 'Asian' identity . . . may undermine a similarity with westerners" (1997, 418). In another section, he states that the "claiming of lesbian/gay identities in Asia . . . is as much about being western as about sexuality" (1997, 430).

No doubt the gay identities and practices of 1990s Asia are, in certain recognizable terms, different from earlier sex/gender configurations. The construction of a gay identity primarily around homoerotic sexuality does in fact appear to be a recent development. And while such identity config-urations are to a large extent tied to the emergence of global networks of communication between gays and lesbians worldwide, this is by no means a simple instantiation of a coherent, universal gay identity. What I point to in this chapter is the complexity of these transactions and the subsequent pro-ductions of identity (or identities). I hope to provide some understanding of this local terrain of "(homo)sexuality" by juxtaposing the sex/gender di-chotomies of so-called traditional koti and modern gay identity. My ultimate goal is to highlight the complex, negotiated nature of contemporary sexual identity in Hyderabad, interrogating in this process notions of sexuality, identity, culture, and modernity.

TRADITIONAL SUBJECTIVITIES: KOTI SEXUAL ARCHETYPES

First, I want to recapitulate the outlines of the koti model of same-sex sexu-ality I have outlined earlier (that hijras also subscribe to)—the classificatory grid *against* which the gay model is seemingly crafted. For the purposes of highlighting their apparent difference from the gay model, I briefly sum-marize these criteria again as follows:

First, all sexually active or adult individuals are categorized into three identities, kotis being one of these, with the other two being narans and pantis. While narans are women—an undifferentiated category based pri-marily on anatomy and gendered practice, kotis are defined by their public expression and enactment of gendered desire—liking to "do women's work" and desiring the receptive position in same-sex encounters with other men. Pantis, in this sex/gender system, are the partners of kotis and/or narans, bounded not merely by the form of their penetrative sexuality but also *against* the constellation of "female" practices and desires openly embraced by these other identities.

Second, there is a range of koti identities—of which hijras are just one group—differentially positioned along a hierarchy of authenticity and re-spect. In the eyes of the hijras, the most important criteria that garner this respect are kinship, sexual desire (or its lack), and the degree of visibil-ity and respect in the public sphere. One of the most important of these criteria, repeatedly mentioned by hijras in their attributions of authenticity, is kinship. Very briefly, kinship is defined in this context as affiliation and social obligation to one of the hijra houses or lineages in the community. By deploying the marker of kinship, or the *rit*, individuals signify their membership in that house as well as within the wider community of hijras and kotis. The *rit* not only denotes membership in the wider community but also hierarchizes kotis along this axis of kinship. There are kotis who are "officially" kin (those who "have a *rit* in the hijra house") and those who are not (*bina ritwale*, or those without a *rit*). While this does not prevent the latter from identifying as kotis, it clearly places them lower in the koti prestige hierarchy.

In addition to the *rit*, all hijras define themselves in opposition to the overly licentious and much disparaged kada-catla kotis, or *gandus*, as hijras more commonly (and pejoratively) refer to them. According to hijras, *gandus*, or men who enjoy anal sex, are defined not only by the *form* of their sexual desire, but more importantly, by its *excess*. As such, *gandus* are disparaged by *all* hijras, both the supposedly asexual hijras as well as those who are sexually active. These hijra "prostitutes" not only employ a life-cycle rhetoric of sexual prostitution progressing to asexual ritual practice, but also profess a dislike of indiscriminate sexual desire and practice. According to hijras, excessive sexual desire is a marker of inauthenticity that both defines *gandus* and by that token separates them from the supposedly authentic, asexual hijras. An active symbol of hijras' essential *a*sexuality that is deployed for this purpose is the physical excision of their genitalia, or the *nirvan* operation. Apparently, having this operation not only signals respect within the koti community and indicates possession of the *himmat*, or strength, necessary to acquire seniority, but it also provides a measure of izzat in the outside world. One becomes resolutely and irrevocably a "real hijra" following this operation. In hijra constructions, this corporeal symbol instantiates their greater authenticity and respect, serving simultaneously as an indictment of their more libidinous fellow-kotis.

MODERN SUBJECTIVITIES: GAY SEXUAL ARCHETYPES

Against this koti/hijra model of same-sex desire and identity is the model delineated by self-identified gay individuals such as Suresh in the opening vignette. The classificatory grid that these gay individuals outline not only creates an identity based primarily on sexual object choice, but this reconfiguration of identity apparently involves different criteria from those employed by the koti sexual paradigm. Although this model of same-sex sexuality was clearly not beyond contestation, by and large the contours of this grid conform to certain rules.

For one thing, much like the production of the homosexual as a distinct species of person in the nineteenth-century West, gay men in Hyderabad see themselves in opposition to the heterosexual population, with the boundary defined explicitly by their sexual orientation rather than anatomical sex or gendered (feminine) practice. In Suresh's wistful fantasies, "this line" of homosex/sociality was squarely opposed to "that line" of heterosexuality. In this modern sensibility, sexual identity is construed in the idiom of consumption, as a function of object choice and of practice defined in those terms. Rather than accept the penetrative/receptive koti/panti model described above, both partners in this modern same-sex relationship are reconfigured as gay, a move that elides the focus on public displays of femininity that apparently define "lower-class" koti identity.

A case in point is Pratap, a handsome, middle-class man who prided himself on straddling both worlds—that of self-identified gay men and that of kada-catla kotis. During my fieldwork in Hyderabad, I heard frequent rumors that Pratap was the partner or panti of at least one kada-catla koti. In fact, Bala Rao, the kada-catla koti who had recently joined the hijra sex workers, claimed that Pratap was her panti before he abandoned her. Given kotis' gender-differentiated world, wherein pantis are clearly separate from kotis, how is Pratap's dual identity reconciled within this domain? When I asked Pratap about the rigidity of the division, he answered, "Not like that. It is not fixed like that. It is not that pantis cannot become kotis and vice versa. After all, we are all 'gays.'" Other gay men I spoke to articulated similar beliefs, even if they did not use koti terminology. "You know like top/bottom or bottom/top, as some people say? The same way the active partner can sometimes be the passive partner and sometimes be the active. It depends on various things you know," Rajeev told me in a conspiratorial whisper, not wanting to be caught divulging these embarrassing details to a woman.

Given the classificatory grid I outlined earlier, this is not a notion that appears to sit easily with other kotis. For them, kotis are defined by their publicly acknowledged enactments of "female" desires/practices—including being receptive partners in male same-sex intercourse with pantis being the exclusively penetrative partners. However, as Kishore, a self-styled gay spokesman, told me, "Those are all different, old-fashioned ideas—this koti, panti, and all this top/bottom business. It is not fixed like that. Some like to do this way, some like to do another way. But we all like to go with another man. That is the difference. Only those hijras and people talk in that koti/panti language like that. Here, we are all just 'homosexuals' or 'gays,' you know," he added with a smile. In this scenario, "this line" of homosexuality, marked by its "modernity" as compared to the "old fashioned" subject-positions of hijras and other kotis, is defined in opposition to "that line" of heterosexuality.

Further, the criteria of membership for this subject-position requires neither official kinship in the manner prescribed for hijras nor any rhetoric or public display of either femininity or asexuality. Identifying the pattern of desire—that is, occupying the gay public space of gardens and bus stations in Hyderabad—and acknowledging a desire for other men makes all such individuals *equally* gay, as Kumar implied, without the hierarchical positionings that are so vital to hijra community structure. In addition, within this sexual paradigm, the very definition of the players seemingly centers explicitly on their *sexuality* or sexual object choice rather than other aspects of identity such as gendered practice, ritual performance, hierarchical kinship, or asexuality, as with hijras.

A new class of individuals appears to have been created, for whom sexuality indeed seems to have replaced gendered practice as a marker of self-identification (see Altman 1997; Balachandran 2001). Two events hastened the creation and acceptance of this sexual paradigm in India. One was the establishment in 1990 of the first magazine for alternative sexualities, *Bombay Dost,* and the public gay persona of its chief editor, Ashok Row Kavi. Following the public recognition of an "AIDS crisis" in the 1990s, this in turn inspired the establishment of several sexual health/gay advocacy groups in India—at least twenty by 2002, including two in Hyderabad.

The second event was the liberalization of the economy that was initiated in the early 1990s in India. This move not only heralded the entry of multinational companies, greatly increasing the transnational traffic in persons, signs, and images, but also reformed import policies and introduced foreign-based satellite television, such as the Rupert Murdoch-owned Star TV network—with its accompanying baggage of soaps, sitcoms, and Hollywood movies—into India. These changes facilitated the emergence of an increasingly wealthy upper-middle and middle-class populace who not only had access to these previously out-of-reach objects and narratives but, for the first time, could also afford them. As Edward Gargan noted in a *New York Times* article written shortly after the first "legal" issue of *Bombay Dost* was printed for circulation, "Most of the homosexuals [in Bombay] are young professionals who work in this city's expanding private sector and whose standard of living is well above the national average." This point is key to the "evolving gay culture" in India, according to Ashok Row Kavi. "There have always been opportunities for gay sex," he stated to the reporter, "but the point is that it is now a movement, that it is an evolving gay culture." This commitment to gay identification and the political liberation premised on a notion of "gay culture" does appear to be somewhat different from earlier conceptualizations of sex/gender difference and identity. But, as I argue in the following section, these differences are far more complex and cannot be neatly dichotomized along the axes of modernity and geography, as some theorists of the global gay school of thought argue.

THE FLUIDITY OF ARCHETYPES

While the coexistence of these two somewhat different sexual paradigms was immediately apparent to me, obviously the picture was far more complex. These "traditional" and "modern" models were *not* consistently or evenly adopted. Neither, as I gradually realized, were they mutually exclusive. For one thing, the evolution of this "gay culture" in urban India, despite its transnational origins and ongoing connections, is not isomorphous with its international label. Some of the casual partners of these gay individuals do *not* acknowledge themselves as gay, being more comfortable with "traditional" labels such as panti or kada-catla koti. In addition, it is polysemic images of the *yaar*, or the *dost* (very loosely translated as "friend") that condition the quest of many gay individuals for relationships with other men. In February of 1999, for instance, a "conference of gays in the country,"[5] entitled Yaarian 1999, was held in Hyderabad.[6] One of the self-conscious aims of this conference was to "try to identify an indigenous, or *desi*, terminology for the concept of gay." As one of the participants quipped, future conferences should be referred to as "Yaarian-Sari/an," to include a broader spectrum of gender identities and practices specific to India. In fact, as one theory for the history of the koti construct indicates, the "rift" between koti and gay identities is an artificial one, apparently created by "foreigners, no less," interested in dividing the indigenous community on the basis of class. Prior to this globalized power play, these terms and their multiple meanings were somewhat more fluid lexical codes that indexed playful (and campy) language rather than a compartmentalized code for fundamentally different identities. The very construction of the koti category in this understanding is a product of the modern matrix of politics and class/global privilege, reflecting neither a categorical rift on the ground, nor a hierarchy of authentic sexual practice or identity.[7]

For every transnationally received symbol of gayness in India, there is one that self-consciously emphasizes an Indian aspect of identity. While this is most evident in the concerns of the Indian diasporic gay community, it is also apparent in the resident gay population of urban India.[8] In the 1998 anniversary issue of *Bombay Dost* for instance, alongside articles such as "A Stonewall Inn Collection," an exhibit of photographs of white, male actors by "renowned photographers" such as Costa and Bianchi, are articles that attempt to self-consciously reclaim "our thousand-year heritage of homoeroticism," as one anonymous author maintains. The Yaarian 1999 conference also occasioned the creation of a national collective named LGBT India—for lesbian, gay, bisexual, and transgender support groups of India—until such time as a "more creative, more inspiring...more *desi* [native to the country] name could be determined."

On the one hand, some people are attempting to carve out a unique space on the transnational gay platform by claiming local self-referential labels and invoking culturally inflected images of the *dost* (friend) in their self-fashioning as gay *Indians*. On the other hand, some, like Suresh in the opening vignette, are given tantalizing glimpses of this modern sexuality but do not embrace this "alternative sexuality" in its upper-middle class form. This "class" of people who refer to themselves as both gay and kada-catla koti draws on globally circulating narratives of gayness, while its members simultaneously construct themselves within local networks of meaning and traditional subject-positions within the hijra/koti model. Suresh has friends who frequent the "homosex" New Year bashes in Bombay, apparently attended by "gay men from [various cities across India], as well as those from San Francisco, New York, and London" as he informed me, while his other friends are "adopted" into hijra kinship networks as daughters and disciples in their hierarchical community structures. Bhabhi, for instance, was officially Vasundara's daughter in the hijra kinship network, while simultaneously constructing himself both as a kada-catla koti and gay in the Public Garden of Hyderabad. Likewise, Vikas, although now a "full-time hijra" in Bombay, considered himself a kada-catla koti in Hyderabad, actively cruising for male partners with his "'homosex' friends," as he stated it, in the Public Garden.[9] Similarly, Srinivas, his friend and fellow Bombay hijra, hosted parties for self-identified gay men, in addition to jogins, zenana, and kada-catla kotis—his "previous forms" as he stated—every time he returned to Hyderabad for a visit.

To further complicate the discursive production of a stable and coherent "global gay identity," one can point to the differences apparent within the so-called modern gay community in India. As a recent vituperative exchange on the LGBT_india online listserv between two South Asian self-identified "gay" activists revealed, there were not only radical differences in their respective constructions of what it means to be gay in India, whether one should "come out" and confront one's family, and how one should go about doing so, but also differential investments in a "globalizing" rhetoric and "need for recognition" by the international gay community. As one of the participants in this debate disparagingly stated, possessing even "a modicum of nationalism" would obviate the necessity for global recognition, a priority for the gay community in India according to the other activist. Likewise, the ideological differences between the two gay advocacy/sexual health groups in Hyderabad in their constructions of gay identity, and the meanings of Indian "tradition" and "modernity," quite apart from the politics and practice of activism, militate against the emergence of a universal "western-style...homosexuality in Asia" (Altman 1997, 421). "To see oneself as 'gay' is to adhere to a distinctly modern invention, namely the creation of an identity and a sense of community based on (homo)sexuality," Altman states (1997, 423). But clearly, identifications and differences between similarly positioned actors are not as coherent or stable as a global gay identity would presume.

Conversely, on my last visit to Hyderabad, I was entrusted with the task of finding out more about the medical clinic that was apparently established by "one of our kotis [living] in [a] foreign [country]," as hijras described a well-known, London-based gay activist. "Last month, one of my 'customers' from Saudi [Arabia] told me about it. I believe this clinic is only for us—kotis here and in the garden," Shanti, my hijra friend, explained to me, including in her lexical label both her fellow-hijras living in Secunderabad, as well as the gay-identified men frequenting the Public Garden. Later that week, when I spoke to some of these self-identified gay men in the garden, I was reassured that indeed, the clinic was for "all gays...but please tell hijras to come only on Sundays." On further inquiry, I was told that this was because their izzat was at stake: "If hijras come during the day, what will people think? Everyone will know this is a 'homosex' clinic then, and our izzat will go. You can understand how this will look...So you tell them," Rakesh told me, somewhat apologetically. In the same discursive move, hijras are being included as a recognizable, gay-identified subjectivity/community on the one hand, while simultaneously differentiated by the apparently traditional koti criterion of izzat and (sartorial) visibility, on the other hand. Interestingly, this differentiation is posited as one that someone like me, perceived by Rakesh as a straight woman "[outside] this line," could easily appreciate and thereby convey to others "in this line." Clearly, "lines" of identification/difference are not merely sexual but can shift along local frames of reference, revealing varying alignments of sociality.

Finally, not only are the particular articulations of the Indian gay male refracted through different lenses, but so-called traditional subject-positions such as hijras also construct themselves creatively within this apparently modern matrix. For instance, when an Indian cosmonaut went into space along with a Soviet crew in the 1980s, the president of a hijra organization in Delhi wrote to Indian and Soviet leaders, requesting that in the interests of parity, the "sexually underprivileged" such as themselves be sent into space in future ventures ("Clapping Demand" 1994). Likewise, a hijra making a bid for Parliament in 1996 ran under the slogan "You don't need genitals for politics. You need integrity," explicitly highlighting hijras' inability to produce children, thereby making them perfect antidotes to the rampant corruption and nepotism of modern Indian politics. In the past few years, at least six hijras have run for local office and won their elections on this platform.[10] The mainstream political parties, including the Congress and Bharatiya Janata Party (BJP), are now actively courting hijras as the new "sexual" minority, and Uma Bharati, the controversial spokesperson for the BJP, apparently indicated in a recent interview that her party is extremely open to the idea of fielding hijras as candidates in future elections ("Voting in a Gender-Bender" 2000).

DISJUNCTURE AND DIFFERENCE: NOTES TOWARD A CONCLUSION

Eve Sedgwick and others have criticized Michel Foucault's early work on the formation of sexual identity as a "unidirectional narrative of supercession" (Sedgwick 1990, 46; Butler 1993; Morris 1994). As Sedgwick contends, we need to relinquish the narrative of rupture that has sustained the discourse on sexuality in the wake of Foucault. As she states, "Issues of modern homo/heterosexual definition are structured, not by the supercession of one model and the consequent withering away of another, but instead by the relations enabled by the unrationalized coexistence of different models during the times that they do coexist" (Sedgwick 1990, 47). The present seems to be one of those times in India when apparently different systems cohabit in a single social field. The simultaneous presence of these "different" sexual classificatory grids in India and their varying emphases on modernity illustrate the fluid constructions of sexual subjectivity in this region.

Further, as I argue in this chapter, the "unrationalized coexistence" of these so-called traditional and modern models—the "paradoxical unity . . . of disunity," as Berman (1982) describes it in a different context—not only questions the facile dichotomies between these terms, calling for a historicization of *both* koti and gay identities, but also blurs the boundaries that define gay identity, both in India and in the imaginary location of the "West." Clearly, the refraction of "this line" in Hyderabad to reveal several competing paradigms of sociality, with the concurrent deployment of "sexuality," "alliance," corporeality, and respect, among other bases of identification, militates against an epistemic disjuncture of any one "line" or model in favor of another.

10

Conclusion

"In the Kaliyuga, we [hijras] will become kings and rule the world.[1] That is what Rama decreed thousands of years ago when he blessed us," Shanti told me proudly. We were sitting under the water tank and talking about her future, as well as the future of hijras more generally. "When is that time going to come?" I asked. "That time will come very soon. You see, that time will come very soon," Shanti replied, nodding sagely.

Perhaps "that time" is now. Although hijras have not become kings, they are rapidly gaining visibility in the South Asian mainstream, whether in the media, the courts, or in everyday life. Following the 1936 decision to give them the right to vote, hijras won the right to run for local political office in 1977 and most recently, in 1994, gained the hard-won right to vote as women in the national elections ("Clapping Demand" 1994).[2] For the first time in Indian politics, hijras are not only standing for election to local, state, and even national office, they are also being actively courted by mainstream political parties for these positions. They are entering this domain of the public sphere *as hijras*, explicitly highlighting their identity as emasculated individuals who cannot reproduce. Hijras, in other words, are transforming themselves in the public imaginary from objects of ridicule and repositories of shame to ideal citizens of the modern nation-state (Reddy 2003).

A hijra recently ran for public office under the campaign slogan "You don't need genitals for politics. You need integrity." Explicitly constructing themselves as politicians without the encumbrances of a family, and thereby freed of the motive for nepotism, hijras are declaring themselves as the perfect antidotes to the rampant corruption and immorality of Indian politics. More important, by recasting themselves as embodiments of respect and morality, they are, in that very attempt, making the body central to constructions of gender, authenticity, and modernity. It is precisely the lack of genitals that allows hijras to be "neutralists"—the term they adopted when urging the president of India to invite them, as people beyond the in-group fighting typical of "men and women," to form a government in Gonda district of Uttar Pradesh in northern India (Hall 1997). In other words, it is their embodied state that not only constructs their authenticity as "real hijras," but also provides their transcendent morality as people beyond the factional politics of men and women.

In this book, I have articulated a relatively simple point: that hijra (and koti) identity should be understood in terms of a multiplicity of differences, including those of sexuality, religion, gender, kinship, and class. Against an essentialized vision of the third sex, I have argued that hijras and kotis in Hyderabad construct, experience, and enact their individuality through each of these forms of hierarchical social difference. Implicit in this con-struction is the role of the body in constituting the materiality of gender and subjectivity. In negotiating these axes and their relative izzat, it is corporeal pleasure and practice that reveals what is ultimately at stake. By pulling up their saris and revealing their postoperative site, hijras are not only "recre-ating through their gesture the very violence of that moment of becoming" (Cohen 1995b, 298) but also indicating their authenticity as "real" hijras who have "paid the necessary price to transform gendered dominance into intergendered, auspicious, and playful thirdness" (298), unlike the "false" kotis and *berupias*.

Such idioms of "realness" and "falseness" employed by hijras strikingly emphasize the concept of authenticity. In a recent article, Bradd Shore notes that "authenticity is indefinable and ineffable, a moving target shifting with context. . . . And like certain other terms (such as 'real'), authenticity comes forward into consciousness only when it is felt to be in trouble" (1997, 2). Hijras' employment of the idiom of authenticity exemplifies this statement. As we have seen, Hyderabadi hijras' invocation of a third sex or gender did not always institute itself in opposition to the binary gender framework. That is, in many contexts, hijras in Hyderabad adopted cultural symbols and practices that were either feminine or a combination of masculine and fem-inine, rather than positing themselves categorically as a third alternative—"neither man nor woman." Often, their thirdness, and more generally the authenticity of their particular construction of identity, was posited only in opposition to those they considered to be false kotis/men, a point reiter-ated by Lawrence Cohen and others, who maintain that hijras often frame themselves within a binary language, only invoking their thirdness with reference to other ambiguous categories such as zenanas (Cohen 1995b; see also Agrawal 1997).

Whether constructing themselves within a binary, tertiary, or "half-in-the-middle" (*adha-bic*) sex/gender framework, hijras and kotis explicitly invoked embodied practice as the medium for the construction of their notions of identity and authenticity. Corporeality, in other words, is integral to hijras' constructions of the various axes of their identity, including sexuality, religion, gender, sartoriality, kinship, and class. Looking back through this study, we see that it is embodied practice—whether in terms of performative (sexual) acts/positions (chapter 3); emasculation (chapter 4); enactments of religious difference through circumcision, clothing style, and eating practices (chapter 5); plucking of one's facial hair, practices of clapping one's hands threateningly and pulling up one's sari to reveal the "proof" of emasculation (chapter 6); ritual affiliation with lineage houses (chapter 7); or their individualized "pleasures and afflictions" (chapters 8 and 9)—that is central to the constructions of hijra and koti identity. The markers of hijra identity and social relations more generally are inscribed onto and configured through the body.

Each of these axes, as well, is enlisted in crafting more than merely a corporealized *sexual* identity. The *nirvan* operation, for instance, paradoxically appears to increase hijras' izzat at the very moment that categorical identification with this label stigmatizes them in the eyes of the mainstream public. The very construction of authenticity both within the hijra community and in wider societal evaluations also marks hijras as potential repositories of shamelessness. By exposing their genitalia—by which act they are construed as shameless—they act as purveyors of this stigma to the public, for which potential they are feared. Interestingly, hijras themselves see this action as one of reclaiming respect. Recall my hijra friend Munira commenting, "If people give us respect, then we are also respectful. But if they do not ... then we also abuse them verbally and lift our saris. Then they bow their heads in shame and give us respect. It is like that."

At the same time as emasculation serves as the absolute marker of stigmatized hijra identity, evoking horror and fear in the public, it also serves as a symbol of their religious authenticity and by this token, increases their izzat. Hijras are the chosen vehicles of the (Hindu) goddess through whose auspices they sacrifice their genitalia and their sexual desire, and thereby receive the power to confer fertility on others. Through this operation, they invoke this axis of religion in yet another way as well. Rather than signaling the lack of sexual desire, some hijras referred to the *nirvan* operation as an extension of circumcision, an act that all Muslims—as hijras in Hyderabad identify themselves—are obligated to perform. As Munira once said to me only half-jokingly, "We are even more Muslim than Muslims. They cut off only so much, and we cut off the whole thing." Clearly, corporeal symbols of identity are enlisted in crafting more than merely hijra's sexual identity.

Further, by deploying the formal marker of kin affiliation—the *rit*, the conferring of which involves an elaborate ritual and active sponsorship by the hijra community—individuals signify their membership in a hijra house and in the wider community of hijras and kotis. Ideally, this ritual is preceded by circumcision (*khatna*) which indicates, as one nayak informed me, the intensity of the potential hijra's desire, that is, "whether they really want to join the hijras or not," aside from its religious referent. Moreover, this ritual is often seen as the first step toward the ultimate "proof" of hijra authenticity—their genital excision.

Significantly, hijras have also established alternative modes of relationship—much like Pierre Bourdieu's (1977) "practical kinship" in a sense—which accommodate non-*rit* individuals within their fold. Perhaps the most important of these alternatives are the genealogical relations—what they refer to using the Hindi term for milk, or *dudh*—relationships embodied through the ritual of mothers "suckling" their daughters, or as "sisters," sharing their blood with one another. Among hijras, kinship is yet another way in which social relations are inscribed onto the body—through blood, milk, and other (bodily) "traumas of becoming" (Cohen 1995b, 296).

In recent years, not only has the notion of sex as a biological "fact" been seriously questioned if not virtually denounced (Weeks 1981; Foucault 1980; Laqueur 1990; Stolcke 1993; Moore 1994), but with the resurgence of interest in embodied "practices" (Bourdieu 1977, 1984; Giddens 1979, 1984; Ortner 1984; Knauft 1996), all social constructions of sex—given their articulation by embodied actors—are seen as grounded in the body's corporeality (see Merleau-Ponty 1962; Csordas 1990, 1994). In this ethnography, I extend a Foucauldian understanding of sex and sexuality to encompass other aspects of hijra identity.[3] I have argued here for a corporeal understanding of this notion of socially constituted sexuality as itself rooted in a multiplicity of other differences. It is embodied practice that marks and inscribes hijra identity. But if the body is the medium through which they enact their individuality, izzat is the currency through which they construct it.

Izzat, therefore, emerged as one of the primary criteria that motivated hijra action and according to which they evaluated their behavior and constructed their identity. Across the various axes of their identity, hijras crafted their individuality by evaluating their relative izzat both within the context of the hijra community, as well as against other kotis, AC/DCs, *berupias*, and the Hyderabadi public more generally. In other words, izzat was the currency through which identity and authenticity was measured. Following Mattison Mines's contention that "Indians know their society in terms of who people are" (1994, 2), an understanding that is in turn mediated by what they do—their "reputation, individual responsibility, trust, control, agency and eminence" (23)—hijra individuality was constructed in large part by negotiating their respective izzat. As was well known among hijras, certain practices—the *nirvan* operation, the denial of sexual desire and abstention from sexual practice, establishment of a *rit* in a hijra house, growing their hair, wearing saris, refraining from shaving their beards, saying *namaz*, celebrating *muharram*, among other enactments[4]—were fundamental to inscribing and revealing their agents' superior *himmat* (strength/agency) and izzat, constituting in that very move their heightened "reputation . . . responsibility . . . control, agency and eminence" (23). In the calculus of izzat, these practices not only authenticated hijras but also increased their spatial network of kin and their reputation in their community and, through it, their reputation with the wider public in whose households they "performed" their blessing.

Notably, hijras asserted and reclaimed izzat through the operation of the body. In hijra conceptualizations, not only did the operation—as the "violent embodying of the truth that phallic power is not uniformly distributed" (Cohen 1995b, 298)—serve to differentiate "real" from "false" hijras/kotis, but it simultaneously served to locate them unambiguously in the public imaginary. As Munira insightfully points out, not only does the operation authenticate them as real hijras, but revealing this corporeal violence also serves to reclaim respect from society. Recall that when she lifted her sari and showed her "in-laws" that she had "nothing there," they were apparently satisfied not only about her authenticity as a hijra, but also her legitimacy as an acceptable "daughter-in-law."

In this context, frameworks of identity and meaning are produced through the constant negotiation between ideals or desires and lived experiences. As Margaret Trawick reminds us, there is an inseparable, "fluid relationship between ideal and experiences in India," with each related to the other as "food and spirit, feeling and flesh," each "constantly being transformed one into the other" (1990, 23). Perhaps, if hijra constructions of gender, individuality, and relatedness (and the anthropological endeavor to understand them) teach us anything at all, it is that notions of culture, self, and meaning can only be comprehended through the unresolved tensions between such desire and experience, between individuals' ideals and practices. To quote Trawick again, in our quest for understanding, we "have to come to terms with the fact that 'meaning' cannot be pinned down, is always sought but never apprehended, is never this and never that, never here nor there but always in between, always inherently elusive and always inherently ambiguous" (Trawick 1990, xix), a viewpoint that hijras would readily endorse.

In 1994, the year before I began fieldwork, one of the first mainstream Hindi films to focus expressly on a hijra's life was released. *Tamanna* (wish/desire) tells the apparently true story of Tiku, a hijra who adopts and raises a child. As in other Bollywood films, the premise of the plot is relatively simple: Tiku finds a girl-child abandoned in a dumpster (because of her gender, as we later find out) and decides to adopt the child and raise her "himself," as her adopted "father." He names her Tamanna presumably to symbolize not only his aspirations for her, but also his own thwarted desires. Contriving to keep the knowledge of his "hijra-ness" from Tamanna, and at great financial and emotional cost, Tiku sends her to boarding school. In true Bollywood style, after the usual twists and turns in the plot, Tiku's love and goodness ultimately triumph. He is reunited with his daughter, who realizes the value of his strength of character and the purity of his love. Too late, in a teary scene at the end, Tamanna expresses her love and respect for him, before Tiku dies in her arms. When I asked one of the hijra nayaks what she thought of this film, she brightened and said, "Ah! *That* is how they should show hijras in films. There are also good people among us [hijras]. Look at Tiku. That is a person you can respect in life." Apparently, despite the marginalization and subtle vilification of the hijra community in the film, the reclamation of izzat that resulted from Tiku's various trials and tribulations and his "successful" negotiation of this value in the wider society is what ultimately matters.

I conclude this chapter with the words of two of my koti friends in Hyderabad. The first is Munira, who became my closest hijra friend. When I first asked her what the difference was between hijras and kada-catla kotis, she said, "There is a lot of difference, Gayatri. We are people with izzat. We put the *rit* and we have other customs [*rit-riwaz*]. Not like these king by day, queen by night *gandus*." A few months later, when I asked Vijay, a kada-catla koti, the same question, he replied, "We don't go around wearing saris and doing all these *rit-wit* things like the hijras. We work every day, and we have some izzat." To invoke Lawrence Cohen's phrase once again, "all thirdness is not alike," a position that these individuals with the most at stake would clearly appreciate. And yet, even though these kotis would disagree on the value attached to their embodied authenticity, the value itself is couched in similar terms, using the idiom of respect as the primary marker of difference. Or, as my koti friends would say in typical Hyderabadi

Everyday life at the tank, 1997

Hindi, *"Aise-ich hain. Yeh sub izzat ka sawal hain"*—"It is like that only. All of this is a matter of respect."

POSTSCRIPT

There are two ways I might end this ethnography. On the one hand, whether intentionally or not, hijras are being incorporated into a wider, transnational, gay world. The intensity of their engagement with this world appears to have increased, even if their actual experiences of modernity may not have changed significantly.[5] Not only are self-defined gay groups attempting to incorporate hijras into their political agendas, hijras too are adopting idioms of modernity in recrafting their identities for a transnational world. One reading of hijras' lives would highlight their engagement and articulation with this world and the possibilities it suggests for constructing their individuality and "emancipating" themselves in the public domain. The other reading, however, has to take into account the violence inherent in their lives and the fact that, sadly, today, many hijras are suffering and dying from AIDS.

Under the tank, 2000

In the summer of 2000 I returned briefly to my home, my field. I had not seen my hijra friends in about two years and was eagerly anticipating my visit with them, looking forward to catching up on all their news. A couple of days after I reached Hyderabad, I went to visit them under the tank. I took the bus and walked the last hundred meters or so to the tank, smiling to myself at the thought of my hijra friends' surprised expressions. I got to the tank and found, to my horror, that all their painstakingly built huts had been ripped apart. The entire area under the tank was overgrown with weeds and strewn with bricks, garbage, and pieces of plastic sheeting that once covered their huts. There were no hijras there.

I ran over to some of the non-hijra neighbors in the bordering housing colony, people I had gotten to know fairly well over the course of my fieldwork. I had grown especially close to one of these neighbors, Rukeya, a young Muslim woman who lived with her children and mother in one of the houses nearby and earned her living by selling strings of jasmine flowers for hijras to put in their hair. Rukeya was at home, and, after exchanging a few preliminary greetings, I asked after the hijras. She replied fairly matter-of-factly that the police had finally razed their huts and evicted them for good from this plot of government land that they had been squatting on for at least ten years. She did not sound either particularly surprised or upset, but seeing my expression, quickly added, "But they still come here in the evenings. So don't worry, you can still see them."

That evening, I returned to the tank. It was around 6:00 P.M. There was still some light, and as I walked up to the tank, I saw Munira and Aliya walking in from the other side. I was absolutely overjoyed to see them. We sat down amid the remnants of their huts and talked. Even though it had been two years since I had last seen them, it felt like I had never left. I could not wait to hear about their lives and started bombarding them with questions. In retrospect, I should have known something was wrong as soon as I began to ask after various hijras. Every question I asked about specific hijras drew only a vague response, a subdued mumbling that that individual was not here now, was in Bombay, or was just "gone." In my enthusiasm, I did not immediately pick up on their hesitation or discomfort. It was only about an hour later, when I was alone with Munira, that she told me that four hijras from under the tank had died these past two years, and at least two of them from AIDS.

One of them was her daughter, Saroja, another of my close friends at the tank. I had had absolutely no idea that she was even ill. The last letter I had received from hijras under the tank was one she had written and mailed almost a year ago. She did not mention her sickness at all in the letter. Clearly, Saroja's death was still a painful topic for Munira. Battling with Munira's grief, though, was another emotion—anger. "I'm not scared of saying the word. Saroja died because of AIDS *bimari* [illness]," she told me defiantly. "And these *bhadvas* [pimps] here, they wouldn't even look at her when she was dying, Gayatri. What kind of hijras are they, these *randis* [crude word for prostitutes] here," she spat in utter disdain. "I am going to leave this 'tanki' and this work and go live somewhere else in Hyderabad. What is the point of being a hijra if these people—our people—won't look after you when you need it?" she added in absolute indignation. "I have been saying for a long time that I will go live on my own. Now I am going to do it, you see."

I went back to the tank the next few evenings, but I never saw any hijras again. I was leaving Hyderabad the following week and wanted, at the very least, to say goodbye. But that was the last I saw of my hijra friends from the tank. Saroja used to call me at my father's apartment from a pay phone, taking great pleasure from this simple act. She would set up a time to call me in the morning or late in the evening after I got home, anticipating with both excitement and dread the possibility of my father's picking up the phone. "What will he say if he picks it up?" she would ask, giggling.

"Will he just put the phone down? What will he think when he knows a hijra is calling you!" she would continue. I am going to really miss hearing Saroja's voice over the phone. Her wonderful, wry sense of humor and her mischievous teasing manner almost always succeeded in getting a rise out of the other hijras, not only contributing greatly to my "data," but also making my fieldwork experience as enjoyable and rewarding as it was—my form of therapy for coping with the rigors of fieldwork at home, as I once joked. I wish I could end on a different note, but I hope this ethnography will serve as a tribute to the strength and resilience of Saroja as well as other hijras and kotis and, despite the hardship of their lives, to their hospitality, humor, warmth, and generosity in the face of tremendous odds.

Except for the last character, all of these names are pseudonyms.

MUNIRA Senior tank hijra; from North India; about thirty-six years old; loud, likes to appear fierce and belligerent but is actually quite gentle; foul-mouthed, warm, generous, with a self-deprecating sense of humor; somewhat vain, worried about remaining poor and losing her looks; extremely loyal, generous, adventurous; a charmer; extremely patient and always willing to spend time with me; sees herself as my protector and benefactress at the tank; my closest friend.

RAJESHWARI Munira's sister; from Andhra; about thirty-two years old; educated, middle-class (natal) family; soft-spoken, even-tempered, confident, somewhat aloof but extremely polite, dignified, fair; the real authority at the tank, mediator extra ordinaire. Passed away in 2001.

SUREKHA Munira's cela and Rajeshwari's daughter; from Warangal; about twenty-eight years old; extremely warm, generous to a fault, open, idealistic, somewhat naïve, eager to please, often taken advantage of and teased mercilessly; educated through tenth grade, intelligent, keen to learn about new things; a romantic, devoted to her husband, Rajesh.

SAROJA Munira's daughter; from the Telangana coast; approximately thirty years old; beautiful and knows it; extremely wry sense of humor, always ready to tease, make fun of others; somewhat selfish; calculating, very observant, quiet, wary of strangers but completely accepting, thoughtful, and considerate once she warms up. Passed away in 1999.

ALIYA Munira's cela and Rajeshwari's daughter; from a town a few hours distant; about twenty-seven years old; the only hijra born to Muslim parents among the tank group; very masculine musculature, quite striking to look at, bright-eyed, full of energy; extremely hard-working, extremely responsible, kind-hearted, a realist; resentful of her guru's verbal abuses, frequently complaining behind her back.

SHANTI Lekha's cela and Vasundara's daughter; about forty years old, from Telangana; balding and extremely conscious of it; proud, defensive, loyal, generous, somewhat moody; believes she has been unfairly treated; smart, knowledgeable. Passed away in 2000.

MADHAVI Used to be Saroja's cela; from Nizamabad; twenty-six years old; warm, extremely generous, prone to exaggeration; self-identified benefactress of the marginalized, eager to please; sees herself as an iconoclast, martyr, my protector.

NAGALAKSHMI Vasundara's cela and Rajeshwari's daughter; from coastal Andhra; about twenty-seven years old; short, stocky, quiet, funny, idealistic, sometimes aloof, responsible; avoids the limelight.

SRILAKSHMI Rajeshwari's cela and Munira's daughter; from Warangal; approximately twenty-four years old; muscular, coarse-featured, responsible, hard working, considerate, generous; somewhat distant but always polite, extremely shy.

SUSHMITA Not officially related to anyone at the tank but a frequent visitor for a year or two at a time; from coastal Andhra; older than many of the tank hijras, approximately forty-two; very gentle, shy, unassuming; has a drinking problem; educated through the tenth grade; warm, extremely generous, hopeless with money.

AMIR NAYAK Munira and her sisters' grand-guru (guru's guru); leader of one of the Lashkarwala households; migrated years ago from Karnataka; somewhat portly or matronly-looking; kind, generous, hospitable, warm, non-confrontational, quiet, well-respected, open; not bound by rigid rules of etiquette.

IRFAN NAYAK Leader of one of the Sheharwala households; native of Secunderabad; thin, tall, dark, bespectacled; grave, generous, kind, worried about her health, nonjudgmental; good to her celas. Passed away in 2000.

FRANK A handsome, middle-aged man; about thirty-six years old; a nonpracticing Catholic; articulate, dramatic, extremely warm and generous, somewhat egotistic, a martyr; very direct, sometimes manipulative. Untraceable in the last three years, and, sadly, rumored to have passed away in 1999.

ARIF KHAN A zenana *baiji*, native of Hyderabad, going on a hundred years; glorious head of hair, warm, twinkling eyes, open, generous, wonderful sense of humor, wise; has seen too much to take things terribly seriously, loves his extended family and especially his grandchildren.

GAYATRI Living in America; born in Hyderabad; thirty years old; upper-middle-class; thin, frail-looking; convinced she would get malaria in the field but never did; short-haired; looks younger than her age; bespectacled; soft-spoken, sometimes naïve, open to new experiences, constantly asking silly questions; photographer, inveterate note-taker.

CHAPTER ONE

1. Fab India is the name of a well-known, somewhat elite, clothing store in New Delhi that retails a distinctive style of clothing.

2. The term *sex/gender* was first used by Gayle Rubin (1975) in her now famous essay "The Traffic in Women: Notes toward a 'Political Economy' of Sex." I use the slashed term in this book to highlight the intricate but labile connections between the terms *sex* and *gender*, biology and culture. At the most simplistic level, often, when the term *sex* is used in this book, it refers to the empirical category of biological sex (keeping in mind that even this meaning is inherently unstable, given the potential disjunctures between the chromosomal, anatomic, and secondary sex attributes associated with this term). *Gender* in this construction refers to how we think about and enact sex on an everyday basis; what we make of our classifications as male or female. When used in conjunction with the term *system*, this phrase references the ideological uses of the sexed/gendered body. I follow Epstein and Straub's definition of this phrase: "Sex/gender systems . . . are historically and culturally specific arrogations of the human body for ideological purposes. In sex/gender systems, physiology, anatomy, and body codes (clothing, cosmetics, behaviors, miens, affective, and sexual object choices) are taken over by institutions that use bodily difference to define . . . gender identity" (1991, 3).

3. This definition of hijras is vastly oversimplified and will become more complicated by the end of this ethnography. Also see Nanda (1990, xix–xxi) for the disjunctions inherent in hijras' lives. It is important to note that although the majority of individuals in this community are phenotypic men (for lack of another phrase) with a variety of sexual dysfunctions and homoerotic desires who subsequently excise their genitalia, a minority are intersexed individuals, or people born with ambiguous genitalia, whatever their chromosomal and hormonal makeup. Clearly the term *hijra* includes individuals with a wide range of desires, practices, anatomical features, and psychological dispositions.

4. This recent focus on filmic representations of hijras does not mean that they were never depicted in Hindi or vernacular-language films prior to this global

interest; their presence in the popular Hindi film *Sadak* is a case in point. But, arguably, it is only in the past six or seven years that attention has focused so directly and intentionally on hijras in middlebrow films. This is evidenced by recent Hindi films such as *Tamanna*, *Dayra*, and *Darmiyan*, which, paradoxically, hijras both deride as vilification and recommend as providing authentic images of themselves. The most recent film in this genre, directed as much to Western as to Indian audiences, is *Bombay Eunuch*, currently playing to critical acclaim in many U.S. cities.

5. Zia Jaffrey's book *The Invisibles: A Tale of the Eunuchs of India* (1996) comments on just such a change in the decade between her first visit with Hyderabadi hijras and her second in 1994.

6. Independent corroboration of this case proved extremely difficult owing to the passage of time before I learned of it—hijras didn't tell me about it until several months into my fieldwork—and the unwillingness of police to show me their files or acknowledge this incident (they all claimed ignorance). Given the police's willingness to malign hijras in personal conversations with me, their intransigence in this matter was particularly noteworthy and perhaps explained by their reluctance to reveal the names and addresses of the other, non-hijra party involved. However, given that hijras themselves sometimes fabricate these accusations to perpetuate the myths associated with them and instill a sense of fear among non-hijras (see chapter 3), this abduction story may not be true and should not necessarily be read as such.

7. Although they are separate (though contiguous and closely related) cities, in everyday conversations, references to Hyderabad implicitly include Secunderabad. Given Hyderabad's status as the capital of the state (of Andhra Pradesh) and its longer and more vivid history, most residents—even if, like me, they *lived* in Secunderabad—identify as "Hyderabadis." "Secunderabadi" is not a common epithet.

8. As the Andhra Pradesh tourist brochures proudly proclaim, Hyderabad is one of the few cities in contemporary India that still maintains a "unique blend of Hindu and Muslim cultures" reflecting its history as a Muslim principality as well as its present-day large Muslim population (36 percent according to the most recent statistics [*Manorama Yearbook* 2002]). Given India's majority Hindu population (82 percent, with Muslims accounting for only 11 percent of the country's population), very few Indian cities, and certainly no other South Indian cities, have a similar religious constituency of Hindu/Muslim.

9. The eight kings of the Qutb Shahi dynasty were rulers of the kingdom of Golconda between 1518 and 1687 CE. Muhammad Quli Qutb Shah, the founder of the city of Hyderabad, was the fifth king of this dynasty, ruling from 1580 to 1612. The invasion by the Mughals (from north India) and the subsequent capture of Golconda in 1687 ended the rule of the Qutb Shahi dynasty. However, after the death of the Mughal emperor Aurangzeb in 1707, the supremacy of the northern

empire gradually eroded. At the time, a viceroy, or *subedar*, of the Mughal emperor, Nizam-ul-Mulk Feroze Jung Asaf Jah, administered the Deccan, or the southern part of the country. He quickly established his supremacy in the Deccan and in 1724 became the first Nizam and the founder of the Asaf Jahi dynasty. Hyderabad under the Nizams was the largest princely state in India. The seven Nizams of this dynasty ruled the kingdom of Golconda/Hyderabad for nearly 225 years until 1948, when the Hyderabad state became a part of the Indian Union. In 1956, the map of India was redrawn into linguistic states, and Hyderabad became the capital of Andhra Pradesh, the first state to be demarcated according to this criterion (Alam 1986; Prasad 1986; Ray 1988; Ali Khan 1991; Seshan 1993; Luther 1995).

10. This location is currently marked by the famous sightseeing attraction of Charminar. This monument, indelibly associated with images of Hyderabad, is situated in the heart of the old city. It was constructed by Muhammad Quli Qutb Shah between 1591 and 1593, and derives its name from the four minarets on its corners (*car* means "four") that frame a two-story structure, including a mosque on the second floor. Although built to commemorate the end of a plague epidemic, popular mythology constructs it as a symbol of Muhammad Quli's love for his wife Bhagmati (or Hyder Begum).

11. Other large cities in the south, such as Madras and Bangalore, also have significant hijra populations, although I am not sure how extensive hijra genealogies are in these other cities or whether their numbers were as large a generation or two ago.

12. The term used most often to refer to hijras in Telugu, the local language of Andhra Pradesh (the state of which Hyderabad is the capital), is *kojja*. Perhaps this term is derived from *khoja*, itself a derivative of *khwaja*, "real master" (from *khwajaseras*): those who "decorated" the real master in royal Muslim households. In early (British) colonial accounts, *khojas* were differentiated from hijras, with the former being a gloss for hermaphrodites, and the latter denoting the less-respected eunuchs (Ebden 1855; Crooke 1896; Thurston 1909; Russell, Bahadur, and Lal 1916). For the most part, when referring to themselves, hijras I spoke to altered their lexical label according to whether we were speaking Telugu or Hindi. They referred to themselves as kojjas when speaking Telugu and as hijras when speaking in Hindi. For purposes of coherence and convenience, I use just one term—*hijras*, the more familiar and widely used term in the rest of the country—to refer to these individuals. *Hijra* is an Urdu word, though its etymology is traceable to Persian, either from the root word *hiz*, meaning "effeminate," or from *hich*, for a person who is *hichgah*, nowhere (Jaffrey 1996, 148).

13. See chapter 4 for hijras' version of their history in relation to the story of Rama; also see Nanda 1990 for a similar account.

14. The other hijra lineages in the country, according to much of the literature and hijras' own accounts, are Lallanwala, Bhendi Bazar/Bullakhwala, Dhongriwala, Mandirwala, and Chatlawala (cf. Nanda 1990), although the exact number of lineages

in the country and the particular names of these lineages in the different cities are debatable.

15. The *ilakas*, or territorial boundaries of the respective lineages, appear to have been a major source of conflict. About four or five years ago, a fairly serious disagreement occurred between the two lineages regarding the Secunderabad *ilaka* and whether or not hijras from one lineage had exclusive territorial rights in this area. As narrated to me (by Lashkarwala hijras), by sheer brute force, Sheharwala hijras wrested the right to *mamgo* (lit. ask; obtain their ritual payment, or *badhai*) in Secunderabad, and ever since there has been a virtual war between the two lineages. Even visiting between members of the two houses was proscribed, this proscription being enforced by a fine for transgression. In addition to the question of *ilakas*, Vanitha (one of the Lashkarwala hijras) caused much tension by changing her house from Sheharwala to Lashkarwala. Only in 1997 were the two lineages reunited—a rapprochement made possible largely by the death of one of the senior leaders of the Lashkarwala lineage in July of that year.

16. I realize, of course, that in spatializing "the field" in this way, I go against the grain of recent anthropological cultural critique (Gupta and Ferguson 1997). However, I do so consciously, to underscore the artifice not just of fieldwork and the text, but also the authenticity of the native ethnographer. To quote Gupta and Ferguson in a somewhat different manner than they intended, perhaps "home" is, after all, "from the start a place of difference" (1997, 33), generative of new tensions and exchanges between the authentic other and the authentic anthropologist (cf. Narayan 1993; Weston 1997).

17. *Tanki* in this instance refers to the concrete water tank—a huge circular tank at least thirty feet wide that is built on stilts, rising to the height of a three-story building. The English word *tank* (modified to *tanki*) was used to refer to this structure both by hijras and non-hijras.

18. *Neither Man nor Woman: The Hijras of India* (Nanda 1990). A second edition of this book was published in 1999. In explaining my agenda, I pointed to the book and said that I wanted to write a book about hijras in Hyderabad much like this book about hijras in Mumbai and "Bastipore." In addition to the text, the book contained photographs of hijras Nanda had written about. As it turned out, hijras in Hyderabad were sufficiently intrigued by the book, of which they had had no knowledge, to entertain my early efforts at fieldwork.

19. *Bidis* used to be unfiltered, inexpensive cigarettes smoked by the poor, available only in India. Now they are being sold in the United States as an "ethnic" product and cost ten times what they sell for in India.

20. I use feminine pronouns to refer to hijras, following their own usage and preference.

21. Almost everyone in Hyderabad speaks Telugu, the official state language, although most people also speak a smattering of Hindi or "Hyderabadi Hindi"—a bastardized mix of Hindi and Urdu, with a few words of Telugu thrown in for good measure.

22. Hijras living under the tank also belonged to the same symbolic houses as hijras in the old city. Most hijras who lived under the tank were sex workers and belonged to the Lashkarwala lineage, a fact that the Sheharwala lineage used explicitly to indicate their greater symbolic capital.

CHAPTER TWO

1. I am aware that such a narrative strategy—a separation of ethnographic setting from theoretical framework—creates an artificial divide between theory and ethnography, implying that they are mutually exclusive, unitary categories of thought and narrative. I retain this artificial division not out of any desire to make a theoretical/ methodological point, but merely for reasons of expediency—as a pragmatic response to the length of these chapters, and for the convenience of lay readers disinclined to engage in the (sometimes abstruse) debates within academic literatures.

2. Following the periodization (and disclaimers) of Ruth Vanita and Saleem Kidwai (2000), I use the terms *ancient* and *medieval* somewhat broadly to denote periods between the Vedic (ca. 1500 BCE) and the eighth century, and from the eighth century until the establishment of British rule in the eighteenth century, respectively. As Gyanendra Pandey (1989) and others have noted, this form of periodization, with its use of religious categories as distinguishing markers—an ancient Hindu and a medieval Muslim era—is a colonialist reading of history. While I do not intend to perpetuate this understanding, I am limited to some extent by the paucity of published Indian historical material relating to hijras and to categories of gender and sexuality more generally. Thus, in following the available historical record, this account of hijra history depends more than I would like on what I must call Hindu and Muslim texts and analyses for the so-called ancient and medieval periods, respectively.

3. This premodern construction of sexuality has obvious and interesting implications for Michel Foucault's contention regarding the nineteenth-century birth of the "homosexual . . . species" and the concept of sexuality more generally in Western Europe (Foucault 1980; cf. Weeks 1981; Greenberg 1988; Halperin 1990; Winkler 1990). However, while there may be no disputing the antiquity of conceptions of sexuality, a "third nature" and prescriptions for sex with individuals belonging to such a category in ancient India, as well as the meanings attached to these various words are by no means stable and unitary, glossed unproblematically as either "eunuch" or a "third sex." We must keep in mind the disjunctures and potential slippage among these terms when reading this section.

4. Perhaps the best known sex change story is that of the *Mahabharata*'s Amba/ Sikhandini/Sikhandin, in which the abducted and thereby "defiled" princess Amba, rejected by both her affianced partner and her (celibate) abductor, Bhishma, prays to Shiva for the "boon of manhood," to avenge Bhishma's thwarting of her "duties as a woman" (Vanita 2002, 31; see also chapter 4 of this book for hijras' invocation of Sikhandin). Another transsexual transformation invoked by hijras is the myth of

Aravan, wherein Aravan agrees to sacrifice himself in battle as long as he marries and makes love to a woman first. As no woman was willing to be widowed in this manner, the god Krishna takes the form of a woman, marries Aravan, makes love to him, and is subsequently widowed. After a brief period of mourning, Krishna assumes his male form. Hijras and other kotis engage annually in a ritualized enactment of this myth at the Koothandavur festival in Tamil Nadu (Shetty 1990; Nanda 1990; cf. Handelman and Shulman 1997; Doniger 1999; Vanita and Kidwai 2000). See also the myth of Ila, destined to be a *kimpurusha* (literally, "what man"), alternating between being a man for one month and a woman for the next (Doniger 1999; Vanita 2002).

One of the best-known same-sex procreation stories is that of the embrace of Shiva and Vishnu (as Mohini), elaborated in the Puranas (Vanita 2002, 69–71), as well as variations of this myth in these and later texts that document the birth of a child from Siva's seed, variously identified as Ayyappa, Skanda, Hanuman, or Hariharaputra, the child of two male gods—Hari/Vishnu and Hara/Shiva (O'Flaherty 1973; Hiltebeitel 1988; Shetty 1990; Doniger 1999; Vanita and Kidwai 2000). Also note the myth of Bhagiratha, believed to be born of sexual intercourse between two women (Roy 2000).

5. The relationship between these two understandings of gender—pertaining to the sex of an individual and grammatical gender—and the necessity for further clarification of their potential link is exemplified by the changing meaning of *linga* at this time. Originally referring only to a "characteristic mark or sign" (Nirukta 1.17; quoted in Zwilling and Sweet 1996, 372, n. 26; J. Flueckiger, pers. comm.; see also O'Flaherty 1973; Doniger 2000), the term later came to refer to "sexual characteristic" in general, and "penis" in particular.

6. The position that gender is characterized by the presence or absence of the primary and secondary characteristics is presented straightforwardly in the third-century Brahmanical text *Mahabhasya* 4.1.3: "[Q:] What is it that people see when they decide, this is a woman, this is a man, this is neither a woman nor a man? [A:] That person who has breasts and long hair is a woman; that person who is hairy all over is a man; that person who is different from either when those characteristics are absent, is neither woman nor man [*napumsaka*]" (quoted in Zwilling and Sweet 1996, 372, n. 27).

7. This debate was central to the subsequent division of Jains into two orders—Svetambara and Digambara. See Dundas 1992 for the history and delineation of Jain sectarian differences. Also see Jaini 1979 for a more detailed account of Jain doctrines.

8. These same two characteristics were used to describe *mollis* in Greco-Roman literature (Halperin 1990).

9. For literature explicitly relating to same-sex love, eroticism, and the ubiquitous themes of divine love, bridal mysticism, and celibacy in the Bhakti and Sufi traditions during this period, see Vanita and Kidwai 2000.

10. In one interpretation of the Hadiths, or Islamic texts, Prophet Muhammad is believed to have disavowed castration, stating, "The one who castrates himself does not belong to my religion. In Islam, chastity takes the place of castration" (quoted in Jaffrey 1996, 30). As a result, eunuchs were *necessarily* imported from outside, given the interdiction against the creation of eunuchs in Muslim courts.

11. In addition to Mecca and Madina (usually spelled Medina, but I follow Shaun Marmon's spelling in this discussion), the "eunuchs of the Prophet" also existed as powerful societies at the tombs of the Sultans in Cairo, the Haram al-Sharif Mosque (commonly known as the Dome of the Rock Mosque) in Jerusalem, and at the tomb of Abraham in Hebron, in addition to other sacred tombs in Najaf among other cities at the height of the Mamluk Sultanate. In 1990, however, the societies at Mecca and Madina were the only surviving societies, with seventeen eunuchs still serving in Madina, and fourteen in Mecca (Marmon 1995, ix). In a fifteenth-century record of these societies, reference is made to eunuchs from several ethnic groups, including "Hindi" (from the Indian subcontinent), who make up the majority of eunuchs at Madina during this period (39).

12. This attribution has interesting echoes in the recent claims by hijra contenders for political election in India (see the conclusion of this book and Reddy 2003).

13. While many of the eunuchs of the Prophet were slaves of the Mamluk sultans, others among them had gained their freedom after serving in the Cairo Citadel (Marmon 1995).

14. As Srivastava (2001) notes, the conjoining of various "unnatural" groups— tribals, Muslims, and eunuchs—in the colonial imagination and subsequent efforts to control them through legislation is noteworthy. In discussions preceding the enactment of the Criminal Tribes and Acts Bill, not only was there an official motion to include eunuchs within the rubric of such other "criminal castes," but stereotypes about the "unnatural" sexual promiscuity (and implicit interchangeability) of eunuchs and Muslims abound—evidenced in part by their apparent role, as "debauched castes," in outbreaks of venereal disease (Ballhatchet 1980, 20). According to correspondence directed at the Government of India Legislative Office just prior to the passing of the Criminal Tribes and Castes Bill, "It is probable that in the three towns of Farrackabád . . . there are not less than 1,500 persons of the hijra and *zánána* [non-castrated transvestite] classes. Their condition arises from immemorial usage, and degrading as it is, their practices are . . . sanctioned by public opinion of all Mussulmans" (cited in Srivastava 2001, 4).

15. This focus on hijras' labor, in terms of its sexual nature and its ritual, performative elements, was to resurface in early post-colonial accounts as well (see Carstairs 1957; Opler 1960).

16. More recently, coercion as a form of recruitment, against overwhelming ethnographic evidence to the contrary, has been the explicit focus of debate on hijra origins (Allahbadia and Shah 1992).

17. See Kuefler 2001 for an account of the centrality of reclaimed masculinity in the Roman Christianity of late antiquity.

18. It is important to note that despite Gandhi's brilliance in subverting colonial conceptualizations of masculinity and bringing women, both ideologically and physically, into the forefront of colonial resistance, his obsessive, if personal, preoccupation with the "problem" of male sexual desire and the repudiation of such desire (often upholding patriarchal privileges at the cost of women, who served merely as either the vehicles of incitement or "proof" of success) are problematic for the analysis of women's sexual freedom (Lal 1995).

19. Another noteworthy ethnography of hijras in this genre is Zia Jaffrey's somewhat impressionistic account of hijras in Hyderabad, *The Invisibles: A Tale of the Eunuchs of India.* Jaffrey tells the story of her initial interest and subsequent quest for information on hijras, revealing more about herself and the people who helped her gain access to the community in Hyderabad than about hijras themselves. Spanning a decade from her first visit to Hyderabad in 1984 to her second, and somewhat unsuccessful, last visit in 1994, the book is engaging and eminently readable, but it exemplifies Mattison Mines's (1994) contention about socially contextualized individuality in India: It highlights the importance of "knowing people," rather than a nuanced understanding of hijras and their everyday lives in Hyderabad.

20. Also noteworthy in this regard is the recent article by Anuja Agrawal (1997).

21. These analyses range from a critique of Dumont's overreliance on holism to critiques of purity and pollution as the singular principles of caste order and Dumont's orientalizing structural dichotomies, among other issues (e.g., see Tambiah 1972; Marriott and Inden 1977; Morris 1978; Berreman 1979; Daniel 1984; Appadurai 1986; Das and Uberoi 1971; Béteille 1987; Dirks 1987, 2001; Jaer 1987; Madan 1987; Raheja 1988; Mines 1994; Kapadia 1996).

22. I am grateful to Lawrence Cohen for highlighting this point and clarifying my thinking in this regard.

23. For other (nonstructuralist) historical and cultural analyses of renunciation and the iconic value of the *sannyasi,* see Farquhar 1918; Ghurye 1964; O'Flaherty 1973; Carrithers 1979; Obeyesekere 1981; Ojha 1981; Parry 1982; Thapar 1982; Burghart 1983; Narayan 1988; van der Veer 1989; Olivelle 1993; Basu 1995; Khandelwal 1997, 2001; Phillimore 2001; and Srivastava 2001.

24. See Burghart 1983 and van der Veer 1989 for a critique of this rigid dualism.

25. This is a different form of sexual renunciation from that employed by wrestlers. The latter is a form of control invested with particular moral meanings, while the former is a radical abstention, which, from the wrestler's point of view, might require different, and maybe less, moral fortitude. Nevertheless, the iconic value and moral significance of sexual renunciation is common to both ideologies.

26. This trope and, more generally, the meanings of religious identification/iconography assume particular significance in light of Hyderabadi hijras' generic Muslim identification, a point I elaborate in chapter 5.

27. I am not arguing here for the primacy of the Mediterranean notion of honor that only subsequently "diffused" to other regions. It is conceivable that the notion of honor as it is constructed in South Asia, for instance, was *constitutive* of the idea that has since become the essence of the Mediterranean region. However, I have no data to support this notion, nor is it my primary analytic question.

28. See Jeffery 1979; Papanek and Minault 1982; and Mandelbaum 1988 for ethnographic accounts of *purdah* morality; see also Karlekar 1986, 1991; Mani 1986, 1998; Chatterjee 1989, 1997; and Sinha 1995 for similar analyses of the materiality of the "women's question" within Indian nationalist discourse in the colonial context.

29. According to McHugh (1998), the Nepali word *ijjat* is a transformation of the Hindi/Urdu term *izzat*, which in turn derives originally from Farsi.

CHAPTER THREE

1. I use the term *cartography* somewhat ironically to indicate the differential mappings of identity as well as to highlight the overlapping, sometimes contradictory terrains of identity-construction and politics among these groups (see Weston 1993, 1998). I borrow the term *sex/gender* from Gayle Rubin (1975, 1984).

2. In this book, I use the terms *hijra* and *kojja* almost synonymously, following Hyderabadi hijras' usage. By and large, the Hindi/Urdu term *hijra* is used more often in the north of the country, whereas the Telugu term *kojja* is more specific to the state of Andhra Pradesh, of which Hyderabad is the capital. For consistency I use the more common term *hijra* rather than *kojja* when referring to the community in Hyderabad, regardless of their linguistic context of use.

3. In Kira Hall's work among hijras in north India, this vocabulary is referred to as Farsi (Hall 1995, 1997). Although I did not come across this usage in my own fieldwork in Hyderabad, hijras' use of this term is interesting for its potential invocation of historical and religious legitimacy—as an identity/vocabulary deriving from (Islamic/Shi'a) Persia or Iran, where the Farsi language (which, incidentally, bears no clear etymological relationship to this hijra/koti vocabulary) was and is spoken to this day.

4. The word *koti* does exist in Telugu; it means "monkey." Initially, when I asked hijras whether their use of the term had any connection with this meaning, they just laughed and dismissed it outright. They could not tell me the etymology or history of their word, however. The term *koti* probably has no discernable relation to the commonly used Telugu term, although some maintain that its usage in this context alludes to someone who swings from branch to branch with multiple partners, much like a monkey or koti. More plausibly, the meaning derives from a Kannada term for dancer (K. Nagaraj, pers. comm.), and in general terms implies an effeminate man in koti vocabulary.

5. I use the feminine gender when referring to hijras because that is what they usually prefer and use.

6. I use masculine pronouns to refer to these kotis largely because of their self-referential terms (to me), but also because the feminine pronoun was used by these

kotis (unlike hijras) only in some contexts (e.g., when referring to fellow kotis or in the context of bantering conversations in collective koti gatherings).

7. Open acknowledgment of relations with men was taboo among hijras; only hijra sex workers disclosed such information to me. Men who were hijras' pantis, however, were apparently not stigmatized by non-hijra society on account of their sexual relationships. Not only was engaging in sex with a hijra seen as equivalent to any other extramarital sexual experience, but it might also be invested with a certain amount of pride. As one of these men told a male acquaintance of mine, "[having sex with a hijra] is a different kind of excitement [*masti*]. You should try it at least once."

8. In one case, however, I was explicitly asked to intervene by "talking sense into" one koti (BR), who had abandoned his wife and children and temporarily joined the hijras. The other kotis—BR's friends—told me to try to get BR to "live a decent life and go back to his wife." It was significant that only after BR joined the hijras was he believed to be leading an indecent life. Prior to this, he had been cruising the park with his other koti friends for at least ten years. Even though he had been married all this time, the koti lifestyle was not considered transgressive in the same way as his current (proto) hijra lifestyle.

9. In the rest of the chapter, I use the term *pantis* to refer to these individuals rather than to exclusively heterosexual men.

10. It may not be a defining criterion at all; see chapter 4 in this context for an elaboration of another embodied axis of identity/difference.

11. Hijras often earn only half or a third of what female sex workers in the same area earn.

12. I explore kinship relations in chapter 7.

13. It is difficult to talk of class and to place hijras in a particular class based on income, the "traditional" parameter for this differentiation (e.g., see Béteille 1982; and Dickey 1993 for a problematization of this criterion). In terms of actual income, hijras probably qualify as upper-middle-income or at least middle-income people, which ordinarily connotes a very different lifestyle—equivalent to that of a semiaffluent middle-class—than the one they live. Judging by their lifestyle, they would probably be classed as low-income/lower-class.

On a different note, the similarity in solvency (Rajesh's poverty and Surekha's income/earning potential) and patterns of caring between hijras and their "husbands" and between *travestis* in Brazil and their partners—as detailed by Don Kulick in *Travesti* (1998)—is striking. Equally striking is the difference in the degree of abjection between hijras and *travestis*. In these relationships, *travestis* appear to be able to hold their own or maintain their izzat better than hijras. Why this might be so begs analysis, but I lack the space to go into it here.

14. The etymology of the term *naran* probably derives from *nari*, the Hindi term for women.

15. Despite my attempts to negate the various linguistic and sartorial markers of class, I was undoubtedly perceived as an upper-middle-class woman, invoking

potential class barriers to communication (see Kumar 1992 for a different interpretation of class and gender difference, and its impact on communication).

16. There appeared to be class differences on this issue. While self-identified gay men in Hyderabad, who generally had a higher socioeconomic status, had heard about and interacted in a few instances with lesbian women, this was obviously not the case with hijras (see chapter 9 for an elaboration of these differences).

17. I hesitate to use the term *category* because, first, kotis cannot be neatly packaged into isolated, hermetically sealed categories, and, second, I describe them as ideal types within a given subgroup; no single individual subscribes to all of the criteria of membership all of the time. Nevertheless, the term does capture some degree of closure, which I think is essential not only for theoretical purposes, but also, and more importantly, for how they think of themselves in given contexts. Most individuals would situate themselves as being a certain type of koti, opposed to other kotis in a given situation, but this identification was understood to be fluid to some extent and did not proscribe the crossing of koti lines in a different context.

18. Another common term for hijras is *na-mardi*, otherwise translated as "without maleness."

19. Circumcision was mentioned by badhai hijras as yet another difference between themselves as "real" hijras and kandra hijras (who did not rigidly enforce circumcision as a criterion of membership) as "false" hijras. Kandra hijras, according to this reckoning, were inauthentic on various levels, not merely sexual but also religious.

20. Until recently, they had to vote as men and were listed accordingly in the government census. In 1994, they won the right to vote as women if they chose (Hall 1997). In the last few years, they have also successfully stood for election—and in at least one instance won—from seats reserved for women. However, this electoral win was disputed in the courts for precisely this reason—hijras' putative sex or gender. Kamla-jan's opponent in the election is contesting her electoral win on the grounds that hijras are not in fact women but (impotent) men, a position that has won support in the lower courts and the Madhya Pradesh High Court, and is to be appealed in the Supreme Court.

21. All of these are either large metropolitan cities that serve as major centers for in-migration, or erstwhile Muslim principalities (prior to Indian independence).

22. See chapter 1 for a list of these houses. I expand on the meaning and significance of a hijra house in chapter 7.

23. I use masculine pronouns to refer to zenanas because this is how hijras refer to them and in most instances, how zenanas refer to themselves.

24. A pathan suit is the dress originally associated with Pathans (from Afghanistan) in the popular imagination—a long shirt to the knees, worn over a loose-fitting *salwar*, or pajama. See Lawrence Cohen (2002) for an elaboration of the relationship between Pathans, "staple of the colonial homoerotic" and current conceptualizations of homosexuality (153).

25. "This line" refers to the (little) line of sex between men in opposition to the (big) line of sex between men and women (see Cohen 1995a, 2002).

26. Again, I use masculine pronouns to refer to kada-catla kotis because that is how they refer to themselves (in most contexts) and how hijras and most other kotis refer to them.

27. See chapter 9 for an elaboration of this issue.

28. These individuals would perhaps be referred to as AC/DCs by hijras, even if gay men might not refer to themselves in this way.

29. Since the conclusion of my fieldwork, another nongovernmental organiza-tion—Mithrudu (also meaning "companion" or "friend" in Telugu)—has been estab-lished in Hyderabad. The tension between these organizations in terms of their os-tensible class-base, their "authenticity" in speaking for the (alternative sex/gendered) public, their sources of funding, and the personal friction between their founders, reveals the different stakes and refractions implicit in this project of gay identi-fication.

30. Since the conclusion of my fieldwork, Sathi has acquired office space and a telephone line, and its community outreach efforts have far greater appeal and a much wider impact than when I originally conducted my fieldwork.

31. Each issue costs fifty Indian rupees, or approximately one dollar.

32. I use feminine pronouns in referring to Frank, following his own usage. My conversations with Frank were mostly in English.

33. I use masculine pronouns when referring to jogins and siva-satis, following their usage as well as that of hijras.

34. This appears to be a Telugu-derived word from the roots *kshemam* (good), and *arti* (propitiation of the deity).

35. The suffix *ollu* refers to "people." For transliterative purposes, I use the term *jogins* when rendering the plural of this category, and *jogin* when rendering the singular.

36. *Puttuka* means "birth" in Telugu. The index of birth or biological embod-iment was yet another axis of (naturalized) authenticity along which "real" and "not-as-real" kotis (including hijras) were sometimes identified and differentiated.

37. While goddess possession is the most common form of divine possession, an important variant is possession by one of the various incarnations of Siva and Vishnu (including Koothandavur, the god whose festival in Tamil Nadu is commonly referred to as the "hijra festival" in the popular press, owing to the number of sari-clad men in attendance). Significantly, it is not only men who get possessed by the goddess/god, but also women, further complicating the jogin "category" by the inclusion of individuals (narans) who are not kotis.

38. In recent years, articles in the popular press have reported increasing friction between "real" and "fake" hijras, leading in many instances to violence and police arrests. As Sanjay Narad reported from Bhopal, eight hijras (including one recently elected local politician) were recently arrested for forcibly emasculating a man they claimed was a "fake" hijra who was stealing their rightful income by impersonating

hijras. This act was the culmination of a protracted quarrel between these two groups of "real" and "false" hijras (Narad 2003; cf. Meghdoot 2000).

39. This understanding perhaps overly reifies the distinction between sex and gender. However, there was a discernable difference in hijras' reactions to *berupias* and to AC/DCs, a difference not entirely attributable to the economic factor of income-generation or "stealing."

CHAPTER FOUR

1. Throughout this chapter, I use the terms *sex work* or *prostitution* to refer to sex in return for money. While I recognize that sex work or prostitution can be variously constructed (White 1990; de Zalduondo 1991; Schoepf 1995; Manderson and Jolly 1997; Turshen 1998), hijras use these terms to imply engaging in sex in return for money fairly consistently across various contexts. I adopt their usage in this chapter.

2. This is one of the two symbolic houses in Hyderabad; see chapters 3 and 7, where I elaborate on the meanings and symbols associated with these houses.

3. As mentioned in the introduction, hijras' alignment with an ascetic image did not appear to have any *explicit* anticaste potential in the manner of Khare's (1984) Lucknow Chamars, although such alignment could be interpreted as an *implicit* critique of the hierarchies of caste, class, and religion.

4. Not until about three months into my fieldwork did hijras—celas and gurus—openly acknowledge their engagement in sex work.

5. Not surprisingly, hijras emphasize desire rather than the exchange of money, even though the latter is what differentiates current kandra hijra activities from their predecessors' enactment of sexual desire.

6. Presumably, in this context, the "bad work" in question is not merely enacting sexual desire but doing so *publicly* in return for money.

7. See Cohen 1995b for "alternative" (non-hijra) frameworks of thirdness, predicated on the semiotic potential of terms such as *saheli* (girlfriend).

8. Interestingly, when Amir nayak initially used the phrase "*naqli* [false/rogue] sannyasis," she was not referring to the difference between the badhai and kandra hijras. Instead, it was in the context of indicating that *all* hijras were one step better than sannyasis because, unlike these potentially false sannyasis, hijras were really celibate, having no physical or mental desire. My subsequent question regarding the role of kandra hijras in this framework was what occasioned the response quoted earlier.

9. Even though hijras identified as Muslims after joining the community (see chapter 5), most Hyderabadi hijras were not Muslims at birth. For the most part, hijras in Hyderabad were born as Hindus and grew up surrounded by Hindu myths, symbols, and iconography (see Knipe 1975 and Kakar 1981 for accounts of a "Hindu world image"). However, it is important to note in this context that a "Hindu world image" or "tradition," despite the essentializing potential of such terminology, is not a single tradition but a "mosaic of cults, sects and deities...constituted

through plurally authored, multiply motivated myths which must be read not only as alterations and reinterpretations but also as appropriations and contestations" (Pathak and Sengupta 1995, 288).

10. In this chapter I have adopted Olivelle's (1993) translation of *tapas* as asceticism. Further, although recognizing that asceticism and renunciation (*sannyasa*) could evoke marginally different meanings, I have used the two terms synonymously here. Thus, asceticism is also referred to as *sannyasa*, and its proponents as *sannyasis* or *sannyasins* (male) and *sannyasinis* (female).

11. This is obviously not a complete description of Hinduism nor does it take into account the impact of other movements that emphasize devotion to god (*bhakti-marga*) rather than asceticism or paths to salvation such as knowledge (*jnana-marga*) and good acts (*karma-marga*). Explicitly challenging the dominance of Vedic sacrificial religion and the caste, linguistic, and gender exclusions implicit in these paths, *bhakti* (devotion), as the term implies, emphasized *personal* religious experience and intimacy with one's deity (especially with Shiva and with Vishnu in his earthly incarnations of Krishna and Rama), incorporating a radically new form of religious expression as well as social protest. The earliest proponents of *bhakti* can be traced to South Indian (Alvar and Nayanar) hymnists in the seventh and eighth century CE, although it wasn't until the fourteenth century or so that this *marga*, or path, spread to the north and became an increasingly popular movement and acknowledged form of religious expression, one that inspired a plethora of musical traditions, art forms, and poetry that live on to this day (e.g., see Lele 1981; Hawley 1984, 1988; Eck and Mallison 1991; Lorenzen 1995; Anand 1996; Narayanan and Cutler 1996).

During this same period, Sufism also prospered—the mystical Islamic tradition that emphasizes direct personal experience of God as the path toward the "truth" of divine love and knowledge, and the veneration of a *pir* (teacher) or charismatic Sufi figure. Although the founders of the most important Sufi lineages, such as Chisti, Naqshbandi, Suhrawadi, and Qadiri, were central and west Asian in origin, they flourished in the Indian subcontinent, especially during the fifteenth through the seventeenth centuries, alongside the various *bhakti* movements of the time (see Schimmel 1976; Eaton 1978; Desiderio 1995).

12. The potential association between the means by which "ascetic heat" is generated, that is, bodily manipulation, and hijras' corporeal asceticism is especially noteworthy.

13. As indicated by this myth, *tapas* is not only creative but also potentially disruptive, threatening the order of the universe; hence the necessity of distracting the (male) sannyasin by sending a woman. However, in other Indian myths and philosophies, it is female power that is transcendent and responsible for the creation of the universe. In this context, as Margaret Trawick notes, there is a potentially fascinating "magnetism" or confluence between Samkhya cosmology and Jacques Lacan's semiotic/psychoanalytic theories: the "notion that the rupture of a transcendent male consciousness into the primeval maternal equilibrium causes the world to be created." In all of these analyses, including present-day Indian "folk"

wisdom, desire is recognized as both a "painful but creative activating process in the world" (Trawick 1990, 146).

14. These were "solutions" offered most readily to men. For women, of course, the ultimate ideal is *pativrata*—being a chaste wife and serving one's husband—through which one could potentially attain liberation. But as Ojha (1981) and Khandelwal (2001) note, women do in fact become renouncers, or sannyasinis, without necessarily "becom[ing] men in order to gain legitimacy as renouncers" (Khandelwal 2001, 158). Also see Khandelwal 1996 and 1997 for excellent analyses of the complex gendered ideologies mediating (female) sannyasinis' accounts of themselves and the tradition of renunciation.

15. The origin and history of this fourfold *asrama* system remains a subject of much debate (see Dumont 1960; O'Flaherty 1973; Kakar 1981; Heesterman 1982; Olivelle 1993).

16. Some theorists argue against the *asramas* as stages of life, preferring to view them as voluntary vocations (Olivelle 1993).

17. While recognizing that the Brahmanical theory of the four *asramas* "brought asceticism into conventional custom by making it the last stage of a man's curriculum," Thapar views ascetics as social *dissenters* expressly because of their rejection of the *grhasta asrama*, or the householder stage, that is, their "negation of the family as a basic unit of society ... and insistence on celibacy" (1978, 73). Inherent in this "act of opting out of the existing lifestyle and substituting a distinctively different one ... [is that] the characteristics of the new lifestyle [are] seen as a protest against the existing one" (84). "But," she adds, "the element of protest was muted by the wish, not to change society radically, but to stand aside and create an alternative system" (86).

18. Drawing on the relationship between the androgyny of Siva and the goddess in various forms, David Shulman posits an argument for understanding gender as an infinite, concentric regression. As he says, "The goddess always has the male inside her, while she is somewhere inside of him. . . . If one gender is thus effectively wrapped inside the other, largely deriving from the other, we could perhaps do better to think of gender generally as an infinite concentric regress, male within female, within male within female ... " (Shulman and Handelman 1997, 157–58).

19. As the story (somewhat simplified) is popularly understood, Sikhandi was the reincarnated form of Amba, a woman slighted by Bhishma. Amba then swore revenge on him and finally, after a period of *tapas*, achieved her goal by becoming the charioteer of Arjuna in the final battle between the Kauravas and the Pandavas in the *Mahabharata*. Recognizing Sikhandi as Amba reincarnated, Bhishma could not fire an arrow at him/her. In the time Bhishma took to hesitate, Arjuna, shielded by Sikhandi, shot the fatal arrow that killed Bhishma. Of the various mythological figures that hijras associated themselves with, this was one of the few that was not *simultaneously* a man and a woman, that is, a non-differentiated entity.

20. As mentioned earlier, the term *nirvan* means rebirth and indexes Hindu/ Buddhist understandings of rebirth through enlightenment. This construction also

potentially invokes particular appropriations of birth, differentiating spiritual from physical birth. As Kumkum Roy notes in a different context, spiritual birth (often defined as masculine) often takes precedence over physical birth, as in those initiation ceremonies where upper-caste Hindu boys are "reborn" from their spiritual teachers (1995, 15–16).

21. For more details on this topic, see Nanda 1990; a whole chapter is devoted to the ritual and significance of this operation.

22. This article was given to me by a kada-catla koti who thought I "might be interested in this story," but presumably also to underline his moral superiority as a koti who "doesn't do these sorts of things"; see chapter 9 for potential tensions between hijras and kada-catla kotis.

23. Rumors circulated long after the article was printed that this initial recounting was a slight exaggeration. The eager reception of this account, however, merely highlights the mainstream public's fascination with these stories about hijras (and *tawa'ifs*, according to Oldenburg 1992) and is perhaps one more instance of the generation of ambivalence at the boundaries of respectability (Goffman 1963). More generally, such incidents (and their coverage by the media) are deeply implicated in wider issues of sex trafficking, fueling various global moral panics (Vance 2003).

24. This begging for alms from shop owners is a contemporary hijra occupation that is both accepted and even legitimized by references to sannyasis (ascetics) and mendicants who beg for a living.

25. A version of this story was related to Serena Nanda as well; see Nanda 1990, 31–32.

CHAPTER FIVE

1. Of the thirty hijra sex workers living under the water tank, only two were Muslim at birth; two were Christian (including the speaker here, Surekha), and the rest were Hindu before they joined the hijra community. I am not as certain about the natal religious affiliations of badhai hijras because many of them claimed to have been born as Muslims, although this was refuted by other hijras. Of the fifteen badhai hijras I got to know fairly well, only one was born to a Muslim family.

2. There is a strong commitment to a common set of normative *practices* in Islam (Prindle 1988). In this context, Cantwell Smith (1957) points out that there is no word for *orthodox* in any Islamic language, suggesting that it may be more appropriate to refer to Islamic *orthopraxy*, or commonality of practice, rather than *orthodoxy*, or commonality of belief. As he states, "The word usually translated as 'orthodox,' actually means rather 'orthoprax,' if we may use the term. A good Muslim is one . . . whose commitment may be expressed in practical terms that conform to an accepted code" (1957, 28).

This is not to imply that there is a disjuncture between praxis and mythology/symbolic iconography in India, one being associated strictly with Islam and the other with Hinduism. Rather than indicating a divergent model of identity-formation, hijras' deployment of religious symbols and practices highlights the intricate imbrication of Hinduism with Islam in India and simultaneously questions an oppositional relationship between religious praxis/ideology by pointing to the flawed logic of divergence implicit in these assumptions.

3. Although it seemed completely self-evident to hijras, I did not know about their self-identified Muslim affiliation until a few months after I began fieldwork. Much to my surprise, *all* hijras in Hyderabad claimed to be Muslim, although they were not necessarily devout practitioners. While this could be an artifact of the cultural/regional context, as mentioned in the introduction (i.e., Hyderabad is 36 percent Muslim, unlike many other Indian cities), the fact remains that, whatever their natal religion, all hijras in this city identified as Muslim, if not in creed then at least in many of their practices.

4. This aspect of their lifestyle is well known and frequently noted in the literature on hijras (Salunkhe 1976; Nanda 1990), and often commented upon by non-hijras.

5. Hyderabadi Muslims are primarily Sunnis, although there is a significant Shi'ite minority, especially in the old city (Pinault 1992). The Qutb Shahi dynasty—the founders of the Golconda/Hyderabad kingdom—were Shi'as. Their successors, the Asaf Jahi dynasty—the seven Nizams of Hyderabad—were Sunnis, although they continued their predecessors' sponsorship of public Muharram processions and Shi'ite shrines in the city. While Hyderabadi hijras did not explicitly identify as Shi'a Muslims, the fact that they celebrate Muharram suggests that they are more likely to identify as Shi'a than as Sunni. Note, however, that Sunni Muslims in Hyderabad have been known to incorporate elements of Shi'a ritual and imagery in their ideology and practice of Islam.

6. I am extremely grateful to Lawrence Cohen for pushing me to extend my analysis here and for pointing me toward this line of reasoning.

7. This term has been variously translated as "Islamic tradition" (Ahmad 1980), the "practices of the Prophet" (Ewing 1988), and the "ritual involved in individual practices such as circumcision" (Mehta 1996). Hijras in Hyderabad used the term in the latter sense, and that is how I employ it in this chapter.

8. This village is about four hours from Hyderabad in the same state, Andhra Pradesh. The name of the village has been changed to protect the anonymity of the hijra.

9. In a recent article, Deepak Mehta (1996) discusses the constitution of the male body through and by the ritual of circumcision. In this article, he distinguishes between the two terms *khatna* and *musalmani*, as used by the Ansari Muslims of Uttar Pradesh (in northern India) to refer to circumcision. In my own fieldwork, I did not come across the latter term. Further, while he states that the use of the terms *khatna* and *sunnat* reflect a class difference, I did not find this to be true among hijras in Hyderabad.

10. The term *bijli* refers to electricity in Hindi. This was Shanti's chosen "work" name, with Shanti being her more commonly invoked hijra name. Baksh is the

suffix or appellation given to all members of this particular hijra house, a term that implies "to give" in Urdu/Farsi.

11. Women can make this pilgrimage, but they must be accompanied by a guardian (*mahram*)—their husbands, fathers, brothers, or sons (all of whom hijras "officially" lack). Women are prohibited from going unescorted. Relatively few Muslim women from India actually go on the Hajj, however (Sharif 1975 [1921]; Ahmad 1980). The word *mahram* translates as "forbidden," that is, in the context of sexual morality, one who is "forbidden" sexually (by virtue of consanguinity) and is thereby "permitted" morally.

12. Although *namaz* is incumbent on both women and men, women cannot perform this act if they are menstruating, postpartum, or have not completed their ablutions before prayer, as is the case with many householder women.

13. This was the rule for Lashkarwala hijras. I am not certain if this rule applies to all hijras.

14. Nowadays, Sunnis in India may also celebrate this occasion, and it appears to serve more to demarcate Muslims from non-Muslims than to signify the rift between the two Muslim sects.

15. An *asurkhana* is the shrine where *alams*—the crests that symbolize the battle-standards of the Karbala martyrs—are stored, and where the annual Muharram liturgies, or *majalis*, are held. *Matam* refers to the expression of grief or loss and, in the Shi'ite context, describes the ritual lamentations mourning the death of those killed during the battle of Karbala in the seventh century. The most common form of *matam* is repeated breast-beating, either with one's hand or, in more extreme forms, with razors or knives (Pinault 1992).

16. In the past, many Hindus (including senior officials in the Nizam's court) used to accompany these processions. This is less common today, and participation in the procession is becoming more of a religious marker in the politicized climate of religious/ethnic conflict in present-day Hyderabad.

17. This was true in Hyderabad. Prior to Ijaz nayak's death, there was a long-standing dispute between the Lashkarwala and Sheharwala houses, with virtually no contact between them. Visiting or interacting with hijras from the other house incurred a stiff fine if the nayaks discovered it. Only the death of Ijaz nayak and the impending *roti* stimulated the settlement of this acrimonious, six-year dispute.

18. Also referred to as Bedhraj Mata (deriving from the location of the temple dedicated to her, Bedhrajpur in Gujarat), or Murgi (chicken) Mata, from the vehicle/animal she is depicted as riding.

19. Serena Nanda was told a version of the same myth by hijras she interviewed; see Nanda 1990, chap. 3.

20. It is noteworthy that Hindus form the bulk of hijras' clientele. Although I am not sure why, it is perhaps not coincidental that among Hindus, hijras see the Sindhi community—people originally from the northwest region of the country where the hijra's temple now stands—as being their most lucrative and respectful clients.

21. For opposite views, including the contention that the principles of Islam did not affect Hinduism as a whole and vice versa, see Panikkar 1963.

22. *Karma* implies the self's past determining the present and denotes an ethic of responsibility; *talavrata/talaividi*, as the terms imply (in Telugu and Tamil respectively), refer to one's fate inscribed on one's forehead at birth, without any necessary relation to prior actions (Keyes and Daniel 1983).

23. The simultaneous deployment of these enactments potentially troubles the very categories "Hindu" and "Muslim," pointing to historically and contextually constructed meanings of these referents.

24. I do realize that the historical and the cultural, insofar as one can artificially separate them, are not mutually exclusive bases of analysis, but I address them as such merely for reasons of clarity.

25. This region—the Deccan plateau—came under Muslim domination in the fourteenth century, with the establishment of the Bahmani kingdom by Hasan Gangu, an erstwhile official in the north Indian kingdom of the Delhi Sultanate. As legend has it, Hasan Gangu claimed descent from the Sassanid ruler, Bahman ibn Isfandiyar of Iran and thereby adopted the title of Bahman Shah after which the kingdom was named. However, as a popular legend has it, his name (and the name of the kingdom he established) derives from a corruption of the word *brahman*. Apparently, on his journey south, Hasan fell asleep one afternoon under the shade of a tree. A Hindu *brahman*, or priest passing by noticed to his astonishment that, much like the representation of the Hindu god Vishnu reclining under the hood of a cobra, Hasan was also protected by a cobra. Impressed, the priest waited till Hasan woke up and offered to become his servant, under the condition that his name be added to Hasan's. Hasan agreed and, following the establishment of his kingdom, named it after the Brahmin. Following the disintegration of the Bahmani kingdom in the early sixteenth century, the Qutb Shahis emerged as a prominent dynasty who staked their claim—and eventually established their suzerainty—over what was to be known as the kingdom of Golconda.

As an aside, although I did not personally come across the term *Farsi* in reference to hijra/koti "language," the fact that this term—analogous to the language spoken in Persia/Iran—was used by hijras in Banaras to refer to their distinctive vocabulary/language is at least interesting and potentially significant (see Hall 1995, 1997).

26. The city was modeled after Persian cities such as the garden city of Isfahan, where Mir Momin—the prime minister of Muhammad Quli Qutb Shah, who was entrusted with the task of planning the city—grew up. It was planned as a city "unparalleled anywhere in the world and a replica of heaven on earth" (Kakar 1995, 5; cf. Luther 1995). If traveler's accounts are to be believed, it was indeed a great and beautiful city, renowned for its cuisine, patronage of the arts and other hedonistic pleasures, and the graciousness of its people—a cultural legacy that lingers in the collective memory of Hyderabadis today. Further, despite the Perso-Islamic

domination and explicit patronage of Shi'ism by these rulers, it was a time of religious tolerance as well. Several non-Muslims—including Hindus—were appointed to administrative positions and shared political power at court, as noted by travelers such as Jean-Baptiste Tavernier and Francois Martin, who visited the city in the seventeenth century (Tavernier 1995 [1676]; Martin 1983).

27. Again, the potential slippage between the contemporary hijra category and that of eunuch slave, and the sometimes problematic inclination to read present realities into past texts/histories must be kept in mind.

28. A variation of this story that was related to me was that Mahbub Ali Pasha was not in Hyderabad at the time of his son's birth and summoned the hijras to Aurangabad where he was currently stationed. Heeding his summons, the hijras could not return to Hyderabad in time to bless Osman Ali Khan's son.

29. See Ahmed and Singh 2002 for a potential exception in this regard.

30. Such communal violence in India came to a head a decade ago during the Babri Masjid crisis. This crisis refers to the 1992 destruction by Hindu *karsevaks*, or workers of right-wing Hindu organizations in India, of a mosque in Ayodhya that was built in the sixteenth century by the Mughal emperor, Babur. The *karsevaks* maintained that the mosque was apparently built on the premises that marked the exact birthplace of Rama, the eponymous hero of the epic *Ramayana*. The destruction of the mosque resulted in widespread rioting and communal violence, in which thousands died all over the country, including in Hyderabad.

31. The popularity and subsequent spread of the Urdu language (and even its etymology) derives from these polyglot armies. The term itself is a Turkish word meaning "camp" (which also shares the root for the word "horde" in English), and the language is a mixture of Turkish, Persian, and Hindi—the languages spoken by the various soldiers recruited in these armies.

32. By *communalism*, these secularists do not mean a civic sense or responsibility, as the term is commonly used in the United States, but a specifically local, South Asian meaning that derives from affiliation with one's religious, ethnic, linguistic community, often to the active exclusion of other communities that share the same social and geographic space (see Ludden 1996).

33. Recall Munira's statement that "we are even more Muslim than Muslims" (by virtue of the operation).

CHAPTER SIX

1. In other words, become "reborn" as a hijra, having undergone excision of the male genitalia.

2. Most trains in India have an enclosed compartment reserved for women. Some hijras, like Munira, said they traveled only in these compartments for fear of getting harassed by men. While hijras are supposedly allowed to travel free on any form of public transportation in the subcontinent, especially trains, Munira and a few others took pride in not doing so. Instead, they bought their tickets like every other passenger. On a tangential note, on this same occasion, there was much

consternation because Aliya had mistakenly been identified as a man on her ticket. Before setting off, they wanted me to go to the railway reservation office with them and get this rectified. My presence, they felt, would invoke a linguistic (English) and class privilege that would get the job done more quickly than if they were to go by themselves, and they were probably right.

3. In addition to such practices, hijras also inscribe their understandings of gender through and onto their relationships with pantis, an issue I explore further in chapters 7 and 8.

4. Jogins and siva-satis also used these *cimtes*, as Nicholas Bradford (1983) noted during his research with *jogappas* in the neighboring state of Karnataka. In Bradford's account, the instrument *jogappas* used was referred to as *darsan*, while hijras use that term for the beard and the act of using the instrument to pluck one's beard.

5. While I do not know the specific etymology of the term *paonbattawala*, the word *paon* means "feet" in Hindi, *batta* means "cloth" in Telugu, and *wala* refers to a person (male). According to hijras, *paonbatta* was their (koti) word for marriage.

6. It is interesting that fairness is invariably conflated with femininity. Although the issue of race does not have the emotionally valenced meanings in India that it does in the United States, the color of one's skin is nevertheless a potent signifier. For hijras, fairer skin is associated with enhanced beauty and femininity. This relationship of whiteness or race/coloniality to gender appears to be metonymic rather than metaphorical. Passing as a woman is not *like* passing as white; rather, whiteness is a *part of* femininity (and possibly vice versa [L. Cohen, pers. comm.]). Hence hijras' construction of my appearance: to them, my fairness was less a reflection of class status than of femininity itself. See O'Flaherty 1980; Daniel 1984; Trawick 1990; and Alter 1992 for excellent analyses of the significance of color in relation to gendered identifications in India. In seeming contrast, however, at the mythic level, white is associated with Siva, while dark (red or black) is associated with Siva's consort, Sakti in many of her forms. As Trawick points out, "The black-white contrast is a symbol of the male-female contrast, the purity of Siva and the fertility of Sakti" (1990, 31). Whitening therefore also seems to be semantically tied to this red-white distinction, especially in its association with female and male sexual fluids (see Daniel 1984; Doniger 2000).

7. As Margaret Trawick comments, "South Indians take skin color very seriously" (1990, 31). This sensitivity, she argues, is partly attributable to the hierarchical social relations between north and south Indians, partly to the history of being colonized by the (white) Europeans, and partly a reflection of class and caste hierarchies, given the darker coloring of those (often of low caste/class) who toil outdoors in the sun.

8. I was surprised by how few hijras were bald or even had receding hairlines, given the timing of emasculation in their respective sexual histories, which was almost always after the development of secondary sexual characteristics. Of the hijras I knew in Hyderabad, only three were balding.

9. The extent to which intentionality or motivation does or does not go to construct resistance and the enlistment of hijras in this debate is an interesting issue. As Cohen (1995b) warns, however, it is important not to read the "etiology of the sexed body" in terms of the primacy of any *one* explanatory idiom, but to locate it within a multiplicity of differences.

10. The importance of a surgically constructed vagina contrasts interestingly with the apparent disavowal of the centrality of the *nirvan* operation, highlighting the complex stakes of embodiment and gendered difference in relation to hijra identification.

11. The same story was told by the Bastipore hijras to Serena Nanda (1990, 19), although the hijra was not named in that case.

12. According to the hijras, Ajmer Baba was a holy man living on the outskirts of the city of Ajmer in North India, a seer who was widely believed to be able to grant people's boons.

13. This is especially true of Butler's early work, such as *Gender Trouble* (1990); the argument is perhaps less applicable to her later work, including *Bodies That Matter* (1993).

14. In an interesting if problematic twist in the past couple of years, this hijra potential—the potential to threaten, disrupt, and shame—has been capitalized upon by credit card companies. These companies, including the pioneer in this regard, aptly named Unique Recoveries, have begun to employ hijras to threaten debtors and ensure that they pay their dues; see http://news.bbc.co.uk/1/hi/world/south_asia/332173.stm.

15. The term *catla* is the koti or Farsi term for sari, while the term *esindi* means "to put" in Telugu.

CHAPTER SEVEN

1. The term *rit* literally translates as "custom" or "tradition." In this context, it refers to hijras' acquiring or "putting" a "tradition" in a particular hijra lineage. Whether speaking in Hindi or Telugu, the term is conjugated with the verb "to put" (*dalna, esudu*). Hijras "put a *rit*" in a house and by that act, acquire an extended network of kin as well as certain social obligations and rights.

2. This is an understanding that hijras themselves sometimes play with and perpetuate in the public domain. When hijras ran for public office in North India, for instance, their electoral platform explicitly highlighted their lack of kin ties: without "family," there was no danger of nepotism and corruption (see the conclusion of this book as well as Reddy 2003).

3. Although a *rit* was an ideal prerequisite for kinship, it was not a wholly restrictive one. Kotis with a *rit* were clearly "family," but even those without a *rit* could and occasionally would be referred to as kin in the context of "other" individuals, i.e., pantis or narans.

4. The Goddess Yellamma and all of her "sisters" who possess (literally "come onto the bodies" of) jogins are also "married" to Jamadagni (Bradford 1983).

5. Women (or girls) became *devadasis* in several ways. Women "chosen" for the initiation were often the daughters of existing *devadasis* or related through affinal kin, thereby inheriting their position. Others might have been "given up to a deity by a family in trouble [*kadata*]" or even, as Nicholas Bradford (1983) notes, given up to a deity so as to continue the family's line of descent and gain in status through this act, since *devadasis'* children are believed to be children of God.

6. This narrative resurfaces in hijra mythology as well, wherein hijras, like *devadasis*, are believed to play a role in welcoming Rama and Sita back to Ayodhya (see conclusion of this book and Reddy 2003 for more details). See also Srinivasan 1984 and 1988; Kersenboom-Story 1987 and Meduri 1996 for analyses that trace the historical transformation of the *devadasi* from her precolonial practice as temple ritual performer to her naming, in the nineteenth-century, as temple "prostitute" and finally, in the twentieth-century, to emblem of the nation.

7. According to Frederique Marglin, "the association between dance and sex is very strong. The dance ritual [for *devadasis*] is also known to stand for the last 'm' in the five m's offering of the tantric *sakta* ritual. This last 'm' is *maithuna*: sexual intercourse" (1985, 95).

8. The roots of this disassociation stemmed in large part from the politicization of *nac*, or dance, in colonial India. Starting in the 1890s, several educated Hindus, brahman and nonbrahman alike, started a movement widely known as the anti-nautch (an Anglicization of the Sanskrit *nac*) campaign. A social reform movement, the anti-nautch campaign advocated several measures for the "upliftment" of women, including and especially the eradication of those practices "injurious" to their well-being such as temple dancing, a practice that was indelibly associated with prostitution and thereby immorality in such constructions. As Amrit Srinivasan notes, "articulated ostensibly as a move to boycott dance both in the temple and in elite homes, it was the *devadasis*—the 'caste' of women who performed it—against whom such reform action was primarily aimed" (1984, 9). Coupled with the eventual legislation of such boycotts and the gradual erosion of royal patronage, the *devadasi* temple "tradition" declined significantly and was almost completely eradicated by the time India gained independence from the British.

These reform efforts, however, were accompanied by a significant revival effort, since *devadasis* at the time were often the sole practitioners of these "classical" dance forms. Realizing that these dance traditions would die with the institution of *devadasis* without some intervention, "revivalists" argued (successfully) for the separation of dance from temple service and a relocation of such classical dance training in secular dance academies set up in different parts of the country. As Allen (1997) argues, the domestication and resanctification that constituted the revival of such classical dance obscures many processes, which he identifies as repopulation (the appropriation of a practice by one community from another), reconstruction (changing elements of the repertoire and choreography), renaming (from *nautch* to *bharata natyam*), resituation (from temple to the stage), and restoration (the reinvention of a seemingly ancient practice); see Allen 1997, 63–64; cf. Srinivasan

1984, 1988; Marglin 1985; Kersenboom-Story 1987; Meduri 1996; cf. Erdman 1996; Reed 1998.

9. Another reason given for the decline of the "morality" or chastity of *devadasis* is the role of Muslims, specifically the ascendance of the Muslim court vis-à-vis the declining importance of the Hindu temple. As one of the active proponents of the revival movement states, "Due to the successive Muslim invasions and weak political authority, there must have been moral degradation on the part of the *maharis* [*devadasis*]. . . . [I]t is from this period that the *maharis*, who were originally intended for temples and Gods alone, came to be employed in royal courts as well. From [then] on, the *maharis* ceased to be respected as *dasis* of the Lord and came to be associated with concubinage" (Patnaik 1971, 56).

10. Note the similarity in terminology between the *tawa'ifs* and the zenana kotis, namely, the terms or labels for their leader, *caudharayan* and the honorific title *baiji*. Interestingly, in Hyderabad, one version of the zenana genealogical story attributes their apparent superiority in dance and musical performance vis-à-vis hijras to the fact that the latter "stole" the zenanas' profession from them.

11. Many of these musicians belonged to the most famous lineages, or *gharanas*, of the time, and much of the late nineteenth-century North Indian (Hindustani) classical music was invented and refined in these *kothas* (Neuman 1980; Manuel 1987; Rao 1990; Oldenburg 1992).

12. In all of the various Hindu sects and nonsectarian movements, such as the Ramakrishna (Kripal 1995; Roy 1998), Sai Baba (Babb 1986; Srinivas 1999, 2001), the International Society for Krishna Consciousness (ISKCON), and Rajneesh (Palmer 1994) movements (this is by no means an exhaustive list of movements or scholarship on such movements), the historico-mythical *guru-sisya parampara* (teacher-disciple tradition) is reproduced; that is, gurus impart their knowledge to their students or *sisyas*. Traditionally, more in myth than in real life, there appeared to be an ethic of renunciation—*sisyas* were supposed to go serve their masters exclusively and renounce their kin ties, at least temporarily, until they had acquired what knowledge they could from their guru. However, contemporary gurus such as Sai Baba, Rajneesh, and others, neither expect nor demand renunciation of sexuality or normative kinship bonds as a condition of learning and membership.

In this regard, another potential parallel with hijra social structure is the Islamic *guru-sisya* tradition—that of *piri-muridi* (Schimmel 1975; Gilmartin 1984; Digby 1984; Combs-Schilling 1989; McDaniel 1989; Ewing 1990, 1997; Ansari 1992; J. Flueckiger, pers. comm.). Muslim *pirs*, or Sufi "saints," spiritual guides and healers, and their *murids* (disciples) constitute a parallel tradition of non-kin-based knowledge transference. Although this model does not require an ethic of asceticism (i.e., the *pir* and his *murids* are often householders), it does require *seva*, or service, performed by *murids* for their master, much like a guru-cela relationship among hijras.

13. Depending on the language spoken (i.e., Hindi or Telugu), the terms used most commonly for "family" were *kutumbam*, or *khandan/parivar*, respectively.

On one or two occasions, hijras used the term *kulam* (lineage) to refer to other hijras, specifically those in their own hijra house.

14. When used among non-hijras (between men primarily), this term implies that the referent, although male, has been demasculinized. When used among hijras, paradoxically, this term seems to refer not so much to demasculinization as to hyper-masculinization, and it is a highly pejorative term (see Hall and O'Donovan 1996).

15. While it may be significant that Yamini used the term *kojja* rather than *hijra* in this context, she probably used this term because, unlike many of the other hijras under the tank, Yamini was not comfortable in Hindi and always spoke in Telugu. As noted earlier, the term for hijra in Telugu is *kojja*. In this particular incident, Yamini's entire monologue was in Telugu.

16. Translated, the phrase means "[I] touch your feet." It is a greeting reserved for those higher in status than oneself among hijras, in contrast to *salam aleikum*, a common Muslim greeting that indexes equality among hijras.

17. The term *din* signifies duty in Urdu. I am not sure what the specific significance of this term is in this context, and hijras themselves were unable to clarify this for me.

18. Ideally, the presence of all nayaks is required, and part of the ceremony involves the nayaks' seal of approval: a tossing of their rings in the air, over the head of the prospective cela, before clapping their hands and shouting *din*. Further, a record of the cela's *rit* is recorded in a book for future reference, I was told by many hijras, although I never did get to see this document.

19. The nayak's celas are the gurus of their own celas; these celas in turn have celas of their own for whom they serve as gurus in an iterative relational pattern.

20. As Serena Nanda (1990) notes in her ethnography, hijras can change their guru and, by extension, their house affiliation, when they have a grievance with their existing kin. Ideally, the cela decides to sever these ties. Often, however, the cela does not have this option, since the validity of guru-cela disagreements is mediated and decided by the senior members of the household, including, sometimes, the less-than-objective guru's contemporaries, or *gurubhais*.

21. She never actually officialized any of her celas by putting a *rit* on them in the presence of the Lashkarwala nayak. Thereby she avoided the costs, both economic and in terms of status, that this pattern would incur in the normal course of events. Had the nayak known that she was retaining celas without official sanction or that they were leaving her often enough to elicit comment, Yamini would have been severely reprimanded.

22. These costs include five thousand rupees up front to the doctor for performing this illegal operation, at least five thousand rupees for medicines and food after the operation, and the remainder for the *dawat* at the end of the period of seclusion.

23. Hijras use this phrase, *pyar ke riste*, to refer to relationships with their husbands, to indicate the foundation of the relationship—love, *pyar*, or *mohabbat* (see Reddy 1999). However, the phrase has also been used by non-hijras to refer to a variety of so-called fictive relationships, most notably sibling and parent-child

relationships (Freed 1963; Vatuk 1969). Such relationships are premised on notions of volition or choice, in contrast to immediate consanguinal (and affinal) ties. The use of the term *fictive* to refer to such relationships, however, has increasingly been criticized, given the presumptions of authenticity and, implicitly, heterosexual normativity that underlie such constructions (see Weston 1991, 1998).

24. This ritual and terminology appear to reflect a Muslim practice of surrogacy, a multiply valenced practice that also structures affinal relations. "Milk" mothers are surrogate mothers who have nursed a child or children. Subsequently, all "milk" relations—"brothers" and "sisters"—are proscribed as potential affinal kin. I am grateful to Sylvia Vatuk for directing me to this practice and its significance.

25. Chowtuppal is a small town on the outskirts of Hyderabad, about two hours distant, where some senior kandra hijras had rented houses as weekend retreats.

26. This accusation—marriage to a woman—was the most reprehensible and stigmatized accusation within the hijra community. It was often considered "proof" of inauthenticity if an individual was rumored to have married a woman before joining the hijra community.

27. This term variously refers to hijras or the broader community of kotis, depending on the context.

28. They were the only hijras who openly acknowledged this bond and whose pantis could and would visit them at "home." Badhai hijras also had pantis, but they were not allowed into their house; in addition, there was a clear rhetoric of asexuality and denial of this relationship among these hijras. Nevertheless, the fact that even nayaks (apart from other badhai hijras) have pantis, or certainly had them at some time in the past, seems indisputable.

29. For an excellent account of the commodification of desire in the context of modernity, see Knauft 1997; see also Mines 1994. To what extent these statements by hijras reflect a *class* sentiment, given that many lower-class women also articulate similar statements rather than (or in addition to) a uniquely gendered sentiment, remains to be determined.

30. In koti terminology, *sis* (real) sex refers primarily to anal sex when used in juxtaposition with *kavdi*, which implies "false sex" or frottage (sex between the thighs). They do, however, have another term that refers explicitly to anal sex.

31. See also Oldenburg (1984, 1992) for a similarly mocking sentiment toward men on the part of *tawa'ifs* or courtesans in Lucknow.

32. The disparaged kandra hijras openly retained their natal links. I am not sure if badhai hijras did sever their links completely, but they made no explicit reference to their natal families; if anything, their rhetoric appeared to reinforce the ideal image of the ascetic renouncer who cut off all ties with the social world.

33. The mothers continued to use the masculine gender to refer to their sons and, in most contexts, used their male "birth" names.

34. This is a fairly common board game played between two or more players. The hijras draw their "board"—a boundary enclosing twenty-five evenly spaced squares—on the ground with charcoal. They use tamarind seeds instead of dice,

scraping one side against a rough surface to produce two different kinds of surfaces. The objective is to move through a defined series of squares by rolling the "dice" to arrive at the center of the board, killing the opponent's pieces along the way. For a couple of months, hijras at the tank were obsessed with this game, playing it several times a day for monetary stakes (which gradually increased from one rupee to as much as ten rupees for each game lost).

35. The Telugu term *manollu* derives from the root words *mana*, or "our," and *ollu*, which is the plural suffix for "people."

36. We were speaking in Hindi, and she used the phrase *hamare log* (our people) rather than the Telugu term, *manollu*. These two terms appeared to be interchangeable in their contexts of meaning, the choice depending on the particular language being spoken.

37. Although indexing a slightly different connotation and context, Lucknow *tawa'ifs* also explicitly invoked *nakhre* (exaggerated pretense/play) as a form of embodied action, as much to perform "femininity" as to ensnare unsuspecting men (Oldenburg 1992).

38. This was a familiar name rather than his real name. It indexes the designs made on the ground (primarily by the women of a household). Apparently Moggu was given this name by his koti friends because of his love for making these designs as a child.

39. As mentioned earlier, kotis (other than hijras) usually used the masculine pronoun when referring to each other, unless expressly making a point of their "feminine" proclivities, a practice I follow in this book.

40. In an important extension of such a psychoanalytic formulation, Margaret Trawick points out that in this process of self-crafting—of defining the self in relation to the other—"as life proceeds, often, what happens to the self is neither individuation nor internal integration, but rather a continuous *de*crystallization and *de*individuation of the self, a continuous effort to *break down* separation, isolation, purity, as though these states, left unopposed, would form of their own accord and freeze up life into death" (1990, 243; emphasis in original).

41. Both of these lines of inquiry address the issue of relationality in India—in effect, the *need* for interactional social relationships and the particular structures of self/desire that are produced in this process. They do not necessarily address why it is that, within these relationships, or rather in order to remain in them, kotis suffer so much abuse and pain. To a certain extent, the answers to such questions may derive from the gendered nature of individual and institutionalized "domestic violence." The embodiment of dominant forms of masculinity and femininity through and by violence not only allows for the *constitution* of particular gendered selves, but also perpetuates gendered patterns of violence that in turn reinforce and strengthen these problematic understandings of gender in a circular pattern of reasoning. Hence, kotis' desires and constructions of gender/self are deeply implicated within these patterns of gendered violence and abuse, often with devastating consequences for their lives.

CHAPTER EIGHT

1. This question was in reference to a statement Rajesh had made to me. He had told me that he thought Surekha was a woman the first time he met her.

2. Even Rajesh acknowledged that during their six or seven years together, Surekha must have spent "over two lakhs" (two hundred thousand rupees) on him, a fairly substantial amount by any economic standard.

3. See chapters 1 and 7 regarding territorial boundaries between hijra houses.

4. In 1996, Rajesh slept with another hijra sex worker at the tank—an older hijra who was the equivalent of Surekha's grandmother in the hijra kinship network. He also continued to visit the hijra in Vijaywada, despite Surekha's protests. Needless to say, Surekha was extremely upset at these developments. Finally, in April of 1997, Rajesh went back to his village in Karnataka to marry his niece, according to "tradition." Surekha claimed to have brokered this alliance. She attended the wedding there, and was clearly happy and hopeful that Rajesh would settle down now, "have children, get a job, earn well," and lead a decent life. When I left the city in 1997 (at the end of fieldwork), Rajesh was to come back to Hyderabad accompanied by his wife, and Surekha was looking forward to welcoming her newly acquired "sister." On a subsequent visit I learned that Rajesh did in fact come back to Hyderabad with his wife, and for a brief period before he went back to his village, he lived with his wife *and* Surekha in a small room in Secunderabad.

5. I have retained the gendered pronouns exactly as related by Frank.

6. Our conversation was in Telugu, but he used the English words *rape* and *homosex.*

7. The English term *homosex* was used, as was the term *enjoy.*

8. And yet, it was sexual desire that defined kandra hijras and distinguished them from badhai hijras in the latter's view.

9. Interestingly, the same stories were circulating about Lekha—that she had been married as a young man before she joined the hijra community. Also note Lekha's use of the masculine pronoun when referring to Mary in this context.

CHAPTER NINE

1. Our conversation was in Telugu but for a few English words noted by single quotation marks.

2. See Nanda 1990. I want to make two caveats here: First, I realize that a vast body of literature addresses itself explicitly to the differences between "homosexuality as we know it today," and previous arrangements of same-sex relations (Weeks 1981; Halperin 1990; Sedgwick 1990). Although recognizing that the terms *homosexual* and *gay* may refer to distinct periods in the history of this phenomenon, I use the terms interchangeably, drawing primarily on my informants' articulations. Second, I realize that the axes of subjectivity and behavior respectively, as the basis for a differentiation between Foucault's nineteenth-century "homosexual" and contemporary "third sex" categories, is a flat, simplistic, and overly crude characterization.

Nevertheless, I retain this distinction on the basis of my informants' repeated differentiation between homosexual or "gay," and hijra/koti identities.

3. As Michel Foucault notes, "Particularly from the eighteenth century onwards, Western societies created and deployed a new apparatus which was *superimposed* on the previous one," namely, the "deployment of sexuality," which, like the "deployment of alliance . . . connects up with the circuit of sexual partners, but in a different way" (Foucault 1980, 6).

4. "Axiom 5: The historical search for a Great Paradigm Shift may obscure the present conditions of sexual identity" (Sedgwick 1990, 44).

5. This was the second national "conference of gays in the country"; the first was in Bombay in 1994.

6. This term refers to the plural of *yaar*, or "friend."

7. This is neither the only "theory" relating to the history of the category/lexical label of koti, nor is this particular construction devoid of political maneuvering. The potential rifts or identity politics within the self-identified gay community in India are well-known, speaking both to the refraction of a unitary gay (or koti) identity, as well as the multiple, positioned nodes in the crafting of modern sexual identities, both gay and koti. In this context, further research is necessary to explore the emergence and contextual deployments of *both* gay and koti signifiers, given their increasingly complex and fluid circulations within the semantic fields of AIDS and sexual rights discourses. In this chapter, I have attempted to demonstrate the hybridity of gay and koti sex/gender systems. But perhaps, as Lawrence Cohen suggests, future iterations of this argument and further research on these issues need to go beyond merely highlighting fluidity and challenge the "adequacy of viewing koti and gay as different systems, however interlinked" (pers. comm.).

8. I lack space to explore the potential differences/identifications between the gay men and women of the "diaspora" and those in Hyderabad in this study. For thoughtful analyses relating to diasporic constructions of history and sexuality, see Gopinath 1996; Puar 1998; Shah 1998; also see issues of *Trikone* magazine.

9. The politics of location and space in the construction of (sexual) identity is a topic of obvious significance in this context (see Soja 1989; Lefebvre 1991; Colomina 1992; Bleys 1996; Brown 1998).

10. As noted earlier, in the one instance when a hijra stood for election as a woman (i.e., from a seat reserved for female candidates), the lower courts of the Indian judicial system deemed her election invalid on the grounds that she was not in fact a woman, but an (impotent) man. Seemingly, the positions hijras can legitimately claim in the modern public sphere remain gendered, even if their electoral platform explicitly highlights their status beyond gender.

CHAPTER TEN

1. The Kaliyuga, literally the "period of Kali," is "one of the 'terrible names' for the goddess, Siva's wife," as Madeleine Biardieu (1994, 181) translates Kali. Kaliyuga

is the fourth *yuga*, or cosmic period, and represents the lowest depth of *dharmic* degradation of all of the *yugas*.

2. In 2003, however, BBC news reported that the high court in the state of Madhya Pradesh ruled that hijras were in fact men, not women, and therefore could not run for office in those constituencies that were reserved for women (accessed online at http://news.bbc.co.uk/1/hi/world/south_asia/2724321.stm).

3. For Foucault, sex or sexuality is not an inherent quality of the body, but instead, a way of fashioning the self "in the experience of the flesh," which is itself "constituted from and around certain forms of behavior" (1980, 36).

4. Perhaps the most ambiguous in this respect was their relationship with their pantis. On the one hand, any expression of sexual desire was inimical to the practice of "real hijras." Extending this trope of authenticity, hijras explicitly defined kada-catla kotis and gay men in the park by their excessive desire. On the other hand, the desire for a "husband" and "someone to take care of you forever" was one of the hijras' most ubiquitous and potent yearnings.

5. Although their incorporation within compendia of gay and lesbian readers as well as their engagement with lesbian/gay/bisexual/transgendered, or LGBT groups in India and abroad are fairly recent occurrences, this does not imply that hijras have had no links with "foreign" lands, peoples, and commodities. In fact, many of the sexual customers of hijras living under the tank were men from "Saudi"—a generic label that includes all men living or currently working in the several countries in the Middle East. Hyderabad, with its numerically significant Muslim population, has a long history of extensive traffic—of people, goods, and services—between the city and these countries for economic and religious reasons, among others.

GLOSSARY

Hindi and Telugu words have been transliterated with diacritics only here in the glossary. Established conventions have been followed to render these words in Roman script. Hindi transliteration follows the standard Oxford Hindi-English dictionary (1993) edited by R. S. McGregor. Telugu transliteration follows the conventions of the Telugu-English dictionary by J. P. L. Gwynn (1991). Proper nouns, whether personal or place names, have not been italicized or provided with diacritical marks.

Extended vowels (i.e., drawn out, as for a dotted note in music) have been shown with a macron: *ā* as in *father*; *ī* as in *machine*; *ū* as in *rule*. With respect to consonants, attention is drawn to the following: *c* as in the *ch* of *church*, *ś* as in *sugar*, *ṣ* as in *shun*. Further, a distinction has been made between dental and cerebral consonants: *t* (as in *ethical*), *d* (as in *the*), in contrast to *ṭ* (as in *toast*), and *ḍ* (as in *dot*). Aspirated consonants have the letter *h* added to them: *kh*, *gh*, *ch*, *th*, *dh*, *ṭh*, *ḍh*, *ph*, *bh*. Finally, the use of English words in a Hindi or Telugu sentence is indicated with single quotation marks.

AC/DC	a man who is both a "passive" and an "active" partner in same-sex intercourse
acchā	good; indicative of affirmation
ādāb	discipline/training or proper behavior; also a form of (Muslim) greeting
ādhā-bīc	literally, "half-in-the-middle"
akkva	not operated; a hijra who has not had the *nirvan* operation
ālam	the crest symbolizing the battle standards of the Karbala martyrs
āṇḍoli	an orphan; a hijra who does not have a guru
apadharma	conduct that is specified for an emergency
ardhanārīśvara	half man/half woman
ārti	religious invocation
aslī	real; often used to indicate authenticity

aslī sannyāsi	real ascetic
āśrama	ideal fourfold stages of life in Hinduism
badhāi	the payment made to hijras for their performance at weddings and the birth of a (male) child
badhāi hijṛā	one who engages in the "ritual" practices of singing and dancing and gets a (badhai) payment
badmāś	wretched fellow
bāiji	head of household among zenana kotis
bāl-kumārī	young, unmarried girl
bandāram	turmeric
baṛe hijṛe-log	the older/respected hijras
bastī	neighborhood
behenjī	sister
berūpia	a man who impersonates a hijra without formally inscribing any of the markers of hijra identity
beśarm	lacking or without shame
betī	daughter
bhaḍvā	pimp
bindī	mark on forehead; traditionally a symbol of a Hindu married woman but increasingly used for aesthetic purposes; also referred to as *bottu* in Telugu
binā rītwāle	without a *rit* or kinship link with a hijra house
boḍi	bald
bonālu	pots
brahmacārya	first stage in the *asrama* stages of life; also refers to abstinence from sexual intercourse as religious self-restraint
burā	bad
burqā	the long, black dress worn by Muslim women that covers their bodies from head to foot; worn to maintain respectability/honor or izzat, but also seen as a cloak of power by some women
cāl-calan	gestures and movements
capaṭbāzi	lesbianism (derived from captī = vulva [colloq.])
cāṭla	sari or female clothing
cāṭla esindī	put her sari on (someone); phrase commonly used by hijras to refer to the practice of lifting the sari to embarrass and shame others
ceḍu/ceḍugoṭṭu	to spoil; spoiling
celā	disciple of a teacher (guru)
chātī	bosom; chest
cībri	operated; a hijra who has undergone the *nirvan* operation

cīmṭe	tweezer
caudharāyan	chief courtesan; similar to term of reference for chief zenana or *caudhary*
caudhary	leader or head of all zenanas in Hyderabad
dāiamma	midwife
dāiamma cībri	one who had been operated by a hijra *daiamma* or midwife
dādi	paternal grandmother
daṇḍ	fine; often imposed for the transgression of a rule
dargāh	mausoleum
darśan	literally, a ritual viewing/blessing of the god/goddess; beard or the act of plucking one's beard in koti usage
dāwat	celebration/feast
deḍh tālī	one-and-a-half clap; a hijra practice that signals the onset of a particular discursive performance for the benefit of the public
deś/ūr	the place of one's birth or one's spatial orientation
devadāsi	female servant of god; temple dancer
dhandhā	work; often used by the hijras to refer to prostitution
dharm	religion
dīn	duty; also piety
dūdh behan	milk sister
duniyādāri	person of this world; householder
esindī	to put
esuḍu-theesuḍu	putting in and taking out; another form of (pejorative) reference to an AC/DC or "double-trick *gandu*"
gāṇḍū	one who uses his ass (*gand*); faggot
ghasl	a washer of the dead; related to the Arabic term for ritual purification of the body
ghoḍī	literally, "mare"; policeman in koti usage
ghūmo	roam; cruise
girāki	customer
golī	pill
goonḍa	ruffian
grhasta	householder
grhastya	second, householder stage of the *asramas* or life-stages in Hinduism
guru	teacher or spiritual guide; hijra senior
guru-śiṣya paramparā	teacher-disciple tradition

gurubhāi   contemporary; a form of address to refer to contemporaries in the hijra hierarchy

halāl   that which is allowed, permitted, or permissible; meat from animals that have been ritually sacrificed

hamāre log   our people; similar to Telugu term *manollu*

harīm   the private or domestic sphere; semantically linked to notions of sanctity and the forbidden (female domain)

himmat   courage/strength

ijjat   honor or respect in Nepali

ilāka   territorial boundary

inām   gift (of land) by erstwhile ruler

intīriam   semen

izzat   respect or honor

jāti   caste

jātra   pilgrimage

joḍi   bond; often marital bond

jogin   a (Hindu) worshipper possessed by one of the forms of the Devi, Siva or Vishnu; often this person is ritually "married" to the goddess and wears female clothing thereafter; also referred to in text as *jogappa/jogollu*

kabarstān   cemetery

kaḍā   cross-over in Tamil

kaḍā-cāṭla   male clothing, or pants-shirt in koti terminology

kaḍā-cāṭla kōti   a koti who wears male clothing, does not have an official kinship link with hijras, and does not have the *nirvan* operation

kām   work

kāma   love/desire

kāndra   sex work

kāndra hijṛā   hijra who engages in sex work

kanyā   unmarried girl; virgin

kanyādāna   gift of a virgin

kaṭṭanam   dowry

kavḍī   false; usually with reference to sex

khatnā   circumcision

khwājasera   chief eunuch

kojja   hijra in Telugu

komaṭ   oral sex in koti terminology

korī mūrat   hijra who has never put a *rit* in a house; virgin initiate

koti	a "female-identified" man who desires and engages in receptive (same-sex) intercourse and adopts "feminine" mannerisms of discourse and practice
kulam	lineage
kuṭumbam	family; also *parivār, khāndān* in Hindi
lacak-maṭak	hip-swinging
lacchā	necklace
laśkar	army camp
linga	phallus
lungī	wrap-around cloth
majalis	annual Muharram liturgies
mangalsūtra	necklace that is tied by a bridegroom on a bride; a marker of the marital bond in Hinduism
mān-pan	the ritual and marker of kinship that signifies allegiance to a zenana house
manollū	literally, "our people"; from *mana* (our) and *ollu* (people) in Telugu
mārga	path
mard	man
mardāna	area of household set aside for men
masjid	mosque
matam	ritual lamentation mourning the deaths of the Karbala martyrs
mayyat	viewing of the deceased
mogarūpam	maleness, male appearance
moggu	rice-flour or colored powder designs drawn on the ground, typically by women
mohalla	neighborhood
mokṣa	enlightenment; liberation from the cycle of rebirth
muṇḍā	widow in koti usage; literally, bald
murīd	disciple
nakhre	play or performance; sometimes refers to coquetry in speech and mannerisms
namāz	daily prayers prescribed for a practicing Muslim
nāna-dādi	grand-gurus
nānī	grandmother
naqlī	false
nāyak	the hijra leader in each of the symbolic houses
nāran	anatomical woman
nātī celā	cela's cela; grand-cela
nīrjī	semen in koti vocabulary

nirvān — literally, "spiritual rebirth"; used among hijras to connote the physical excision of male genitalia

nirvān sultān — hijra who has undergone the *nirvan* operation

panti — a man who is the penetrative (rather than receptive) partner in same-sex intercourse; also refers to the husbands of hijras

paonbaṭṭawāla — an ostensibly "heterosexual," married, non-sari-wearing man in koti terminology

paon padtī hūn — literally, "I touch your feet"; hijra greeting for those senior in rank to the speaker

parivār — family

paruvu — respect in Telugu

pedda maniśī — big/respected person

peś — lifestyle

pīr — teacher/saint

Pīr panḍuga — festival of the saints (*pirs*); a colloquial Hyderabadi usage for the Shi'a Muslim festival of Muharram

pūjā — ritual of worship in Hinduism

purdah — veil worn by Muslim women; also curtain

puruṣa — man

pyār ke riśte — bonds/relationships of love

rakta sambandam — blood relationships

raṇḍī — a crude word for prostitute

riśtā — relationship/bond; plural: *riste*

rīt — the formal marker of kinship that signifies allegiance to a hijra house or lineage

rīt-riwāz — kinship custom/tradition

roṭī — funeral/death ceremony in koti usage; literally, food

sahelī — girlfriend

śaitān — devils

salām āleikum — common Muslim greeting

salwār kurtā — dress worn by young women

sannyāsa — final stage of the fourfold Hindu *asrama* stages of life

sannyāsi — ascetic; renouncer

śarm — shame

sauram — false hair; typically an attachment used to add volume and length to hair

sīpo — vagina in koti terminology

sīs — real in koti terminology; often in reference to the act of sexual intercourse

śiva-sati	a Hindu-identified person possessed by Siva, the god of destruction; a member of the koti "family," defined by "desire for men"
sontam	own; often referring to natal family in kinship contexts
strī	woman
sūdi	injection
sunna	certain ritual observances and a programmatic code of behavior that is an approximation of the Prophet Muhammad's
sunnat	circumcision
sūrma	kohl (used as eyeliner)
talaiviḍi/talavrāta	literally, "writing on the forehead"; popular understandings of the Hindu concept of destiny
tapas	asceticism; ascetic heat
tawā'if	courtesan
taziya	symbolic representations of the tombs of the Karbala martyrs that are carried during Muharram
tālī	clap
vānaprasta	third stage of the fourfold *asrama* stages of life
vyabicāram	prostitution in Telugu
zenāna	a male (koti) dancer who adopts "feminine" gestures and mannerisms; wears female clothing only when performing; has a kinship network distinct from that of hijras. Also, the domestic space reserved for women.

REFERENCES

Abu-Lughod, L. 1985. Honor and the Sentiments of Loss in a Bedouin Society. *American Ethnologist* 12:245–61.

———. 1986. *Veiled Sentiments: Honor and Poetry in a Bedouin Society*. Berkeley and Los Angeles: University of California Press.

Abu-Zeid, A. M. 1966. Honor and Shame among the Bedouins of Egypt. In Peristiany 1966.

Agrawal, A. 1997. Gendered Bodies: The Case of the "Third Gender" in India. *Contributions to Indian Sociology*, n.s., 31 (2): 273–97.

Ahmad, I., ed. 1976. *Family, Marriage, and Kinship among Muslims in India*. Delhi: Manohar Press.

———. 1980. *Ritual and Religion among Muslims in India*. Delhi: Manohar Press.

Ahmed, M., and D. Singh. 2002. *Myself Mona Ahmed*. Zurich: Scalo Press.

Alam, S. M. 1986. *The Growth of Hyderabad City: A Historical Perspective*. Hyderabad: Azad Oriental Research Institute.

Ali Khan, R. 1991. *Hyderabad: 400 Years, 1591–1991*. Hyderabad: Zenith Services, Asia Publishing House.

Allahbadia, G. N., and N. Shah. 1992. Letter. India: Begging Eunuchs of Bombay. *Lancet*, Jan. 4, 48–49.

Allen, M. H. 1997. Rewriting the Script for South Indian Dance. *Drama Review* 41 (3): 63–100.

Almaguer, T. 1994. Chicano Men: A Cartography of Homosexual Identity and Behavior. In *The Lesbian and Gay Studies Reader*, ed. H. Abelove et al. New York: Routledge.

Alter, J. 1992. *The Wrestler's Body: Identity and Ideology in North India*. Berkeley and Los Angeles: University of California Press.

———. 1997. Seminal Truth: A Modern Science of Male Celibacy in North India. *Medical Anthropology Quarterly* 11 (3): 275–98.

Altman, D. 1996. Rupture or Continuity? The Internationalization of Gay Identities. *Social Text* 48 (3): 77–94.

_____. 1997. Global Gaze/Global Gays. *GLQ: A Journal of Lesbian and Gay Studies* 3:417–33.

_____. 2001. *Global Sex*. Chicago: University of Chicago Press.

Anand, S. 1996. *The Way of Love: The Bhagavata Doctrine of Bhakti*. Delhi: Munshi Manoharlal Publishers.

Anderson, B. 1983. *Imagined Communities: Reflections on the Origin and Spread of Nationalism*. London: Verso.

Anderson, M. 1990. *Hidden Power: The Palace Eunuchs of Imperial China*. Buffalo, NY: Prometheus Books.

Ansari, S. 1992. *Sufi Saints and State Power: The Pirs of Sind, 1843–1947*. Cambridge: Cambridge University Press.

Appadurai, A. 1986. Is Homo Hierarchicus? *American Ethnologist* 13:745–61.

_____. 1988. Putting Hierarchy in Its Place. *Cultural Anthropology* 3 (1): 136–49.

_____. 1996. *Modernity at Large: Cultural Dimensions of Globalization*. Minneapolis: University of Minnesota Press.

Arnold, D. 1985. Crime and Control in Madras, 1858–1947. In Yang 1985.

Artola, G. 1975. The Transvestite in Sanskrit Story and Drama. *Annals of Oriental Research* 25:56–68.

Asano-Tamanoi, M. 1987. Shame, Family, and State in Catalonia and Japan. In Gilmore 1987.

Austin, I. 1992. *City of Legends: The Story of Hyderabad*. New Delhi: Viking Press.

Ayalon, D. 1999. *Eunuchs, Caliphs, and Sultans: A Study in Power Relationships*. Jerusalem: Magnes Press, Hebrew University.

Ayres, A. C. 1992. A Scandalous Breach of Public Decency: Defining the Decent—Indian Hijras in the Nineteenth and Twentieth Centuries. B.A. honor's thesis. Harvard University.

Babb, L. A. 1981. Glancing: Visual Interaction in Hinduism. *Journal of Anthropological Research* 37:387–401.

_____. 1986. Sathya Sai Baba's Miracles. In *Redemptive Encounters: Three Modern Styles of the Hindu Tradition*. Berkeley and Los Angeles: University of California Press.

Balachandran, C. 2001. A Preliminary Report on Emerging Gay Geographies in Bangalore. *South Asia: Journal of South Asian Studies* 24:103–18.

Balaji, M., and Malloy, R. L. 1997. *Hijras: Who We Are*. Toronto: Think Asia.

Ballhatchet, K. 1980. *Race, Sex, and Class under the Raj*. New York: St. Martin's Press.

Balse, M. 1976. *The Indian Female: Attitudes Toward Sex*. New Delhi: Chetana Publishers.

Barnett, S. A. 1976. Coconuts and Gold: Relational Identity in a South Indian Caste. *Contributions to Indian Sociology*, n.s., 10:133–56.

Barthes, R. 1972. *Mythologies*. Trans. Annette Lavers. New York: Hill and Wang.

Basham, A. L. 1959. *The Wonder That Was India*. New York: Grover Press.

Basu, A. 1995. Feminism Inverted: The Gendered Imagery and Real Women of Hindu Nationalism. In Sarkar and Butalia 1995.

Bean, S. 1989. Gandhi and *Khadi*: The Fabric of Indian Independence. In *Cloth and the Human Experience*, ed. A. B. Weiner and J. Schneider. Washington, DC: Smithsonian Institution Press.

Beck, B. E. F. 1972. *Peasant Society in Konku: A Study of Right and Left Subcastes in South India*. Vancouver: University of British Columbia Press.

Berman, M. 1982. *All That Is Solid Melts Into Air: The Experience of Modernity*. New York: Penguin.

Bernier, F. 1891. *Travels in the Mughal Empire*. Reprint, London: Willin Pickering, 1934.

Berreman, G. 1979. *Caste and Other Inequities: Essays on Inequality*. New Delhi: Manohar Books.

Béteille, A. 1982. *Marxism, Pluralism, and Orthodoxy*. Dehradun: Indian Renaissance Institute.

———. 1986. Individualism and Equality. *Current Anthropology* 27 (2): 121–34.

———. 1987. *The Idea of Natural Inequality and Other Essays*. Delhi: Oxford University Press.

Bhimbai, K., ed. 1901. Pavayas in Gujarat Population: Hindus. *Gazetteer of the Bombay Presidency*. Bombay: Government Central Press.

Biardeau, M. 1994. *Hinduism: The Anthropology of a Civilisation*. 2nd ed. Delhi: Oxford University Press.

Blair, C. 1961. *Heat in the "Rig Veda" and "Atharva Veda": A General Survey with Particular Attention to Some Aspects and Problems*. American Oriental Society Publication No. 45. New Haven, CT: American Oriental Society.

Bleys, R. 1996. *The Geography of Perversion*. London: Cassell.

Blok, A. 1981. Rams and Billy-Goats: A Key to the Mediterranean Code of Honor. *Man*, n.s., 16:427–40.

Blunt, W. S. 1909. *India under Ripon: A Private Diary*. London: Cassell.

Bobb, D., and C. J. Patel. 1982. Eunuch: Fear Is the Key. *India Today*, Sept. 15, 84–85.

Bordo, Susan. 1992. Social Construction, Sexuality, and Politics. *Women and Politics* 12 (1): 73–78.

Borneman, J. 1997. Caring and Being Cared For: Displacing Marriage, Kinship, Gender and Sexuality. *International Social Science Journal* 154 (Dec.): 573–84.

Bourdieu, P. 1966. The Sentiment of Honor in Kabyle Society. In Peristiany 1966.

———. 1977. *Outline of a Theory of Practice*. Cambridge: Cambridge University Press.

———. 1984. *Distinction: A Social Critique of the Judgement of Taste*. Trans. Richard Nice. Cambridge, MA: Harvard University Press.

Bradford, N. 1983. Transgenderism and the Cult of Yellamma: Heat, Sex, and Sickness in South Indian Ritual. *Journal of Anthropological Research* 4:307–22.

Brandes, S. 1980. *Metaphors of Masculinity*. Philadelphia: University of Pennsylvania Press.

Brown, J. N. 1998. Black Liverpool, Black America, and the Gendering of Diasporic Space. *Cultural Anthropology* 13:291–325.

Burghart, R. 1983. Renunciation in the Religious Traditions of South Asia. *Man,* n.s., 18:635–53.

Burton, R. 1993 [1913]. *Personal Narrative of a Pilgrimage to Al-Madinah and Mecca.* Vol. 2. London: Dover.

Butalia, U. 1998. *The Other Side of Silence: Voices from the Partition of India.* New Delhi: Penguin.

Butler, J. 1990. *Gender Trouble: Feminism and the Subversion of Identity.* New York: Routledge.

———. 1993. *Bodies That Matter: On the Discursive Limits of "Sex."* New York: Routledge.

———. 2000. *Antigone's Claim: Kinship between Life and Death.* New York: Columbia University Press.

Caplan, P. 1989. Celibacy as a Solution? Mahatma Gandhi and Brahmacharya. In *The Cultural Construction of Sexuality.* New York: Routledge.

Carillo, H. 2002. *The Night Is Young: Sexuality in Mexico in the Time of AIDS.* Chicago: University of Chicago Press.

Carrier, J. 1995. *De Los Otros: Intimacy and Homosexuality among Mexican Men.* New York: Columbia University Press.

Carrithers, M. 1979. The Modern Ascetics of Sri Lanka and the Pattern of Change in Buddhism. *Man,* n.s., 14:294–310.

Carstairs, M. G. 1956. Hinjra and Jiryan: Two Derivatives of Hindu Attitudes to Sexuality. *British Journal of Medical Psychology* 29:128–38.

———. 1957. *The Twice-Born: A Study of a Community of High-Caste Hindus.* London: Hogarth Press.

Castoriadis, C. 1987. *The Imaginary Constitution of Society.* Cambridge, MA: MIT Press.

Chakravarti, U. 1985. Of Dasas and Karmakaras: Servile Labor in Ancient India. In *Chains of Servitude: Bondage and Slavery in India,* ed. U. Patnaik and M. Dingwaney. New Delhi: Sangam Books.

Chandra, M. 1973. *The World of the Courtesan.* Delhi: Vikas Publishing House.

Chatterjee, I. 1999. *Gender, Slavery, and Law in Colonial India.* New Delhi: Oxford University Press.

———. 2002. Alienation, Intimacy, and Gender: Problems for a History of Love in South Asia. In *Queering India: Same-Sex Love and Eroticism in Indian Culture and Society,* ed. R. Vanita. New York: Routledge.

Chatterjee, P. 1989. Colonialism, Nationalism, and Colonialized Women: The Contest in India. *American Ethnologist* (Aug.): 622–33.

———. 1997. *The Nation and Its Fragments: Colonial and Postcolonial Histories.* Delhi: Oxford University Press.

Chowdhury, I. 2001. *The Frail Hero and Virile History.* New Delhi: Oxford University Press.

Claiborne, W. 1983. India's Eunuchs Have Fallen in Esteem. *Washington Post*, April 7, 4.

Clapping Demand. 1994. *Hindustan Times*, Nov. 7.

Cohen, L. 1993. The Aesthetics of Castration. Paper presented at American Anthropological Association Meetings, November 15, Washington, DC.

————. 1995a. Holi in Banaras and the Mahaland of Modernity. *GLQ: A Journal of Lesbian and Gay Studies* 2 (4): 399–424.

————. 1995b. The Pleasures of Castration: The Postoperative Status of Hijras, Jankhas, and Academics. In *Sexual Nature, Sexual Culture*, ed. P. Abramson and S. Pinkerton. Chicago: University of Chicago Press.

————. 1999. *No Aging in India: Alzheimer's, the Bad Family, and Other Modern Things*. Berkeley and Los Angeles: University of California Press.

————. 2002. What Mrs. Besahara Saw: Reflections on the Gay Goonda. In *Queering India: Same-Sex Love and Eroticism in Indian Culture and Society*, ed. R. Vanita. New York: Routledge.

Cohn, B. S. 1987. *An Anthropologist among Historians and Other Essays*. Delhi: Oxford University Press.

————. 1989. Cloth, Clothes, and Colonialism: India in the Nineteenth Century. In *Cloth and the Human Experience*, ed. A. B. Weiner and J. Schneider. Washington, DC: Smithsonian Institution Press.

Colapinto, J. 2000. *As Nature Made Him: The Boy Who Was Raised As a Girl*. New York: HarperCollins.

Collier, J., and S. Yanagisako, eds. 1987. *Gender and Kinship: Essays toward a Unified Analysis*. Stanford, CA: Stanford University Press.

Colomina, B. 1992. *Sexuality and Space*. New York: Princeton Architectural Press.

Combs-Schilling, E. M. 1989. *Sacred Performances: Islam, Sexuality, and Sacrifice*. New York: Columbia University Press.

Cooper, Anderson. 1999. India's Modern-Day Eunuchs. 20/20 Downtown. ABC News Service, New York, Oct. 14.

Crooke, W. 1896. *The Tribes and Castes of North-Western India*. Reprint, Delhi: Cosmo Publications, 1974.

Csordas, T. 1990. Embodiment as a Paradigm for Anthropology. *Ethos*, March 18, 5–46.

————, ed. 1994. *Embodiment and Experience: The Existential Ground of Culture and Self*. New York: Cambridge University Press.

Daniel, E. V. 1984. *Fluid Signs: Being a Person the Tamil Way*. Berkeley and Los Angeles: University of California Press.

Daniel, S. 1983. The Tool-Box Approach of the Tamil to the Issue of Moral Responsibility and Human Destiny. In *Karma: An Anthropological Inquiry*, ed. C. Keyes and V. Daniel. Berkeley and Los Angeles: University of California Press.

Das, V. 1977. *Structure and Cognition: Aspects of Hindu Caste and Ritual*. Delhi: Oxford University Press.

—————, ed. 1990. *Mirrors of Violence: Communities, Riots, and Survivors in South Asia*. Delhi: Oxford University Press.

—————. 1995. National Honor and Practical Kinship. In *Critical Events: An Anthropological Perspective on Contemporary India*. Delhi: Oxford University Press.

Das, V., and J. P. Uberoi. 1971. The Elementary Structure of Caste. *Contributions to Indian Sociology*, n.s., 5:1–81.

Davis, J. 1977. *People of the Mediterranean: An Essay in Comparative Social Anthropology*. Cambridge, MA: Schenkman.

Desiderio, P. 1995. *Piri-Muridi Relationships: A Study of the Nizamuddin Dargah*. New Delhi: Manohar.

de Zalduondo, B. O. 1991. Prostitution Viewed Cross-Culturally: Toward Recontextualising Sex Work in AIDS Intervention Research. *Journal of Sex Research* 28 (2): 223–48.

Dickey, Sara. 1993. *Cinema and the Urban Poor in South India*. Cambridge: Cambridge University Press.

Digby, S. 1984. Qalandars and Related Groups: Elements of Social Deviance in the Religious Life of the Delhi Sultanate of the Thirteenth and Fourteenth Centuries. In *Islam in Asia*, ed. Y. Friedmann. Boulder, CO: Westview Press.

Dirks, N. 1987. *The Hollow Crown: Ethnohistory of an Indian Kingdom*. Cambridge: Cambridge University Press.

—————. 2001. *Castes of Mind: Colonialism and the Making of Modern India*. Princeton, NJ: Princeton University Press.

Donham, D. 1998. Freeing South Africa: The "Modernization" of Male-Male Sexuality in Soweto. *Cultural Anthropology* 13 (1): 3–21.

Doniger, W. 1999. *Splitting the Difference: Gender and Myth in Ancient Greece and India*. Chicago: University of Chicago Press.

—————. 2000. *The Bedtrick: Tales of Sex and Masquerade*. Chicago: University of Chicago Press.

—————. 2003. Third Nature in the *Kamasutra*: The Asymmetry of Male and Female Homoeroticism. Gender Studies Distinguished Faculty Lecture, May 21, University of Chicago.

Doniger, W., and S. Kakar. 2002. Introduction. *Kamasutra*. Oxford: Oxford University Press.

Dubois, A. J. A. 1959 [1918]. *Hindu Manners, Customs, and Ceremonies*. London: Oxford University Press.

Dumont, L. 1960. World Renunciation in Indian Religions. *Contributions to Indian Sociology* 4:33–62.

—————. 1970. *Homo Hierarchicus: The Caste System and Its Implications*. Chicago: University of Chicago Press.

—————. 1983. *Affinity as a Value: Marriage Alliance in South India*. Chicago: University of Chicago Press.

Dundas, P. 1992. *The Jains*. London: Oxford University Press.

Eaton, R. 1978. *Sufis of Bijapur, 1300–1700: Social Roles of Sufis in Medieval India.* Princeton, NJ: Princeton University Press.

Ebden, H. 1855. A Few Notes, with Reference to "the Eunuchs," to be Found in the Large Households of the State of Rajpootana. *Indian Annals of Medical Science* 3:520–25.

Eck, D. 1981. *Darsan: Seeing the Divine Image in India.* Chambersburg, PA: Anima Books.

Eck, D., and F. Mallison., eds. 1991. *Bhakti Traditions from the Regions of India: Studies in Honor of Charlotte Vaudeville.* Groningen: Egbert Forster.

Eco, U. 1975. *A Theory of Semiotics.* Bloomington: Indian University Press.

Elliot, C. A. 1892. *Laborious Days.* Calcutta: J. Larkins.

Engels, D. 1996. *Beyond Purdah? Women in Bengal, 1890–1939.* Delhi: Oxford University Press.

Engineer, A. A. 1980. *The Bohras.* Delhi: Vikas Publishing House.

———. 1989. *Communalism and Communal Violence in India: An Analytical Approach to Hindu-Muslim Conflict.* Delhi: Ajanta Publications (India), Ajanta Books International.

Enthoven, R. E. 1922. *The Tribes and Castes of Bombay.* Reprint, New Delhi: Asian Educational Services, 1990.

Epple, C. 1998. Coming to Terms with Navajo Nadleehi: A Critique of Berdache, "Gay," "Alternate Gender," and "Two-Spirit." *American Ethnologist* 25 (2): 267–90.

Epstein, J., and C. Straub, eds. 1991. *Body Guards: The Cultural Politics of Gender Ambiguity.* New York: Routledge; London: Chapman and Hall.

Erdman, J. L. 1996. Dance Discourses: Rethinking the History of "Oriental" Dance. In *Moving Words: Re-writing Dance.* London: Routledge.

Eschmann, A., H. Kulke, and G. C. Tripati, eds. 1978. *The Cult of Jagannatha and the Regional Tradition of Orissa.* New Delhi: Manohar Press.

Ewing, K. 1988. Ambiguity and Shari'at. In *Shari'at and Ambiguity in South Asian Islam,* ed. K. Ewing. Berkeley and Los Angeles: University of California Press.

———. 1990. The Politics of Sufism: Redefining the Saints of Pakistan. In *Pakistan: The Social Sciences' Perspective,* ed. A. S. Ahmed. Karachi: Oxford University Press.

———. 1997. *Arguing Sainthood: Modernity, Psychoanalysis, and Islam.* Durham, NC: Duke University Press.

Faridi, F. L., ed. 1899. Hijdas. *Gazetteer of the Bombay Presidency.* Bombay: Government Central Press.

Farmer, P. 1992. *AIDS and Accusation: Haiti and the Geography of Blame.* Berkeley and Los Angeles: University of California Press.

———. 1998. *Infections and Inequalities: The Modern Plagues.* Berkeley and Los Angeles: University of California Press.

Farmer, P., M. Connors, and J. Simmons, eds. 1996. *Women, Poverty, and AIDS*. New York: Common Courage Press.

Farquhar, J. 1918. *Modern Religious Movements in India*. New York: Macmillan.

Faubion, J. D. 1997. Introduction. In *The Essential Works of Michel Foucault, 1954–1984: Aesthetics, Method, and Epistemology*, xi–xxxv. New York: W. W. Norton.

———. 2001. Introduction: Toward an Anthropology of the Ethics of Kinship. In *The Ethics of Kinship: Ethnographic Inquiries*, ed. J. D. Faubion. New York: Rowman and Littlefield.

Fear Is the Key. 1982. *India Today*, Sept. 15, 84–85.

Filliozat, J. 1964. *The Classical Doctrine of Indian Medicine*. Delhi: Oxford University Press.

Flueckiger, J. B. 1996. *Gender and Genre in the Folklore of Middle India*. Ithaca, NY: Cornell University Press.

Forbes, L. 1998. *Bombay Ice: A Novel*. New York: Farrar, Strauss, and Giroux.

Foucault, M. 1980. *The History of Sexuality: An Introduction*. New York: Vintage.

———. 1995. *Discipline and Punish: The Birth of the Prison*. New York: Vintage Books.

———. 1997. Technologies of the Self. In *Essential Works of Michel Foucault*. Vol. 1. *Ethics: Subjectivity and Truth*, ed. P. Rabinow. New York: New Press.

Franklin, S. 1998. Incontestable Motivations. In *Reproducing Reproduction: Kinship, Power, and Technological Innovation*, ed. S. Franklin and H. Ragone. Philadelphia: University of Pennsylvania Press.

Freed, S. A. 1963. Fictive Kinship in a North Indian Village. *Ethnology* 2:86–103.

Freeman, J. 1979. *Untouchable: An Indian Life History*. Stanford, CA: Stanford University Press.

Freitag, S. 1985. Collective Crime and Authority in North India. In Yang 1985.

Friedrich, P. 1977. Sanity and the Myth of Honor. *Ethos* 5:281–305.

Fruzzetti, L. 1981. Muslim Rituals: The Household Rites versus the Public Festivals in Rural India. In Ahmad 1980.

———. 1990. *The Gift of a Virgin: Women, Marriage and Ritual in a Bengali Society*. Delhi: Oxford University Press.

Fuller, B. 1910. *Studies of Indian Life and Sentiments*. London: John Murray.

Gait, E. A. 1911. *Census of India: Standard Forms Prescribed in Connection with the Census of 1911*. Calcutta: Census Commission of India.

Gandhi, L. 1998. *Postcolonial Theory: A Critical Introduction*. Delhi: Oxford University Press.

Gaul, N. 2002. Eunuchs in the Late Byzantine Empire, c. 1250–1400. In *Eunuchs in Antiquity and Beyond*, ed. S. Tougher. London: Duckworth and the Classical Press of Wales.

Geertz, C. 1975. *The Interpretation of Cultures*. Chicago: University of Chicago Press.

Gellner, E. 1969. *Saints of the Atlas*. Chicago: University of Chicago Press.

Ghurye, G. 1964. *Indian Sadhus*. Bombay: Popular Prakashan.

Giddens, A. 1979. *Central Problems in Social Theory: Action, Structure, and Contradiction in Social Analysis*. Berkeley and Los Angeles: University of California Press.

————. 1984. *The Constitution of Society: Outline of a Theory of Structuration*. Berkeley and Los Angeles: University of California Press.

Gilmartin, D. 1984. Shrines, Succession, and Sources of Moral Authority. In Metcalf 1984.

Gilmore, D. 1980. *The People of the Plain: Class and Community in Lower Andalusia*. New York: Columbia University Press.

————. 1982. Anthropology of the Mediterranean Area. *Annual Review of Anthropology* 11:175–205.

————, ed. 1987. *Honor and Shame and the Unity of the Mediterranean*. Special Publication No. 22. Washington, DC: American Anthropological Association.

Ginsberg, F., and R. Rapp, eds. 1995. *Conceiving the New World Order: The Global Politics of Reproduction*. Berkeley and Los Angeles: University of California Press.

Goffman, E. 1963. *Stigma: Notes on the Management of Spoiled Identity*. Englewood Cliffs, NJ: Prentice-Hall.

————. 1973. *The Presentation of Self in Everyday Life*. Woodstock, NY: Overlook Press.

Goldman, R. P. 1978. Fathers, Sons, and Gurus: Oedipal Conflict in Sanskrit Epics. *Journal of Indian Philosophy* 8:325–92.

————. 1993. Transsexualism, Gender, and Anxiety in Traditional India. *Journal of the American Oriental Society* 113:374–401.

Gonda, J. 1975. *Ascetics and Courtesans*. Vol. 4 of *Selected Studies: History of Ancient Indian Religion*. Leiden: E. J. Brill.

Gopinath, G. 1996. Funny Boys and Girls: Notes on a Queer South Asian Planet. In *Asian American Sexualities*, ed. R. Leong. New York: Routledge.

Green, J. 1999. *Beyond Carnival: Male Homosexuality in Twentieth-Century Brazil*. Chicago: University of Chicago Press.

Greenberg, D. F. 1988. *The Social Construction of Homosexuality*. Chicago: University of Chicago Press.

Gupta, A. 1998. *Postcolonial Developments: Agriculture in the Making of Modern India*. Durham, NC: Duke University Press.

Gupta, A., and J. Ferguson, eds. 1997. *Anthropological Locations: Boundaries and Grounds of a Field Science*. Berkeley and Los Angeles: University of California Press.

Hall, K. 1995. Hijra/Hijrin: Language and Gender Identity. PhD diss. University of California, Berkeley.

————. 1997. Go Suck Your Husband's Sugarcane! Hijras and the Use of Sexual Insult. In *Queerly Phrased: Language, Gender, and Sexuality*, ed. A. Livia and K. Hall. New York: Oxford University Press.

_____. N.d. *Intertextual Sexuality: Parodies of Class and Identity in Liminal Delhi.* Unpublished paper.

Hall, K., and M. Bucholtz, eds. 1995. *Gender Articulated: Language and the Socially Constructed Self.* New York: Routledge.

Hall, K., and V. O'Donovan. 1996. Shifting Gender Positions among Hindi-Speaking Hijras. In *Rethinking Language and Gender Research: Theory and Practice,* ed. V. Bergvall, J. Bing, and A. Freed. London: Longman.

Halperin, D. M. 1990. *One Hundred Years of Homosexuality.* New York: Columbia University Press.

Handelman, D. 1995. Guises of the Goddess and Transformation of the Male: Gangamma's Visit to Tirupati and the Continuum of Gender. In *Syllables of Sky: Studies in South Indian Civilization,* ed. S. S. Shulman and V. Narayanaravu. Delhi and New York: Oxford University Press.

_____. 1997. *God Inside Out: Siva's Game of Dice.* New York: Oxford University Press.

Hassan, M. 1997. *Legacy of a Divided Nation.* Boulder, CO: Westview Press.

Hawley, J. S. 1984. *Sur Das: Poet, Singer, Saint.* Delhi: Oxford University Press.

_____. 1988. *Songs of the Saints of India.* New York: Oxford University Press.

Hebdige, D. 1991. *Subculture: The Meaning of Style.* London: Routledge.

Heesterman, J. C. 1982. Householder and Wanderer. In Madan 1982.

Herdt, G, ed. 1994. *Third Sex, Third Gender: Beyond Dimorphism in Culture and History.* New York: Zone Books.

Herzfeld, M. 1980. Honor and Shame: Problems in the Comparative Analysis of Moral Systems. *Man,* n.s., 15:339–51.

_____. 1984. The Horns of the Mediterraneanist Dilemma. *American Ethnologist* 11:439–54.

Hiltebeitel, A. 1980. Siva, the Goddess, and the Disguises of the Pandavas and Draupadi. *History of Religions* 17 (2): 147–74.

_____. 1988. *The Cult of Draupadi.* Vol. 1, *Mythologies: from Gingee to Kuruksetra.* Chicago: University of Chicago Press.

Hiltebeitel, A., and B. Miller, eds. 1998. *Hair: Its Power and Meaning in Asian Cultures.* Albany: State University of New York Press.

Hobsbawm, E., and T. Ranger. 1992. *The Invention of Tradition.* Cambridge: Cambridge University Press.

Hollister, J. N. 1989. *Islam and Shia's Faith in India.* Delhi: Taj Publications.

Hopkins, K. 1978. *Conquerors and Slaves.* Cambridge: Cambridge University Press.

Hutton, J. H. 1931. *Census of India, 1931.* Reprint, Delhi: Gian Publishing House, 1986.

Hyam, R. 1990. *Empire and Sexuality: The British Experience.* New York: St. Martin's Press.

Ibbetson, D. C., et al. 1911. *A Glossary of the Tribes and Castes of the Panjab and North-West Frontier Province.* Lahore: Civil Gazette Press.

Inden, R. 1986. Orientalist Constructions of India. *Modern Asian Studies* 20 (3): 401–46.

————. 1990. *Imagining India*. Oxford: Basil Blackwell.

Inden, R., and R. Nicholas. 1977. *Kinship in Bengali Culture: A History of Caste and Clan in Middle-Period Bengal*. New Delhi: Vikas Publishing House.

Jackson, P. 1989. *Male Homosexuality in Thailand: An Interpretation of Contemporary Sources*. New York: Global Academic Publishers.

————. 1997. Kathoey><Gay><Man: The Historical Emergence of Gay Male Identity in Thailand. In Manderson and Jolly 1997.

Jaer, O. 1987. The Ideological Constitution of the Individual: Some Critical Comments on Louis Dumont's Comparative Anthropology. *Contributions to Indian Sociology* 21 (2): 353–62.

Jaffrey, Z. 1996. *The Invisibles: A Tale of the Eunuchs of India*. New York: Pantheon Books.

Jaini, P. S. 1979. *The Jaina Path of Purification*. Delhi: Vikas Publishing House.

Jeffery, P. 1979. *Frogs in a Well: Indian Women in Purdah*. London: Zed Books.

John, M., and J. Nair, eds. 1998. *A Question of Silence: The Sexual Economies of Modern India*. New Delhi: Kali for Women Press.

Kaelber, W. O. 1989. *Tapta Marga: Asceticism and Initiation in Vedic India*. Albany: State University of New York Press.

Kakar, S. 1981. *The Inner World: A Psychoanalytic Study of Childhood and Society in India*. Delhi: Oxford University Press.

————. 1989. *Intimate Relations: Exploring Indian Sexuality*. New York: Penguin Books.

————. 1995. *The Colours of Violence*. New Delhi: Viking Publishers.

Kalliat, P. 1990. *Jareena: Portrait of a Hijda*. Third World Newsreel. VHS video recording, 25 min. New York: Visionova.

Kapadia, K. 1996. *Siva and Her Sisters: Gender, Caste, and Class in Rural South India*. Boulder, CO: Westview Press.

Karlekar, M. 1986. Kadambini and the Bhadralok: Early Debates over Women's Education in Bengal. *Economic and Political Weekly: Review of Women's Studies* (April): 25–31.

————. 1991. *Voices from Within: Early Personal Narratives of Bengali Women*. Delhi: Oxford University Press.

Karve, I. 1965. *Kinship Organisation in India*. Bombay: Asia Publishing House. (Orig. pub. 1953.)

Kersenboom-Story, S. 1987. *Nityasumangali: Devadasi Tradition in South India*. Delhi: Motilal Banarsidass.

Keyes, C., and V. Daniel, eds. 1983. *Karma: An Anthropological Inquiry*. Berkeley and Los Angeles: University of California Press.

Khan, N. S. 1994. Identity, Violence, and Women: A Reflection on the Partition of India, 1947. In *Locating the Self: Perspectives on Women and Multiple Identities*, ed. N. S. Khan, R. Saigol, and A. S. Zia. Lahore: ASR Publishers.

Khan, S. 1999. Through a Window Darkly: Men Who Sell Sex to Men in India and Bangladesh. In *Men Who Sell Sex: International Perspectives on Male Prostitution and HIV/AIDS*, ed. P. Aggleton. Philadelphia, PA: Temple University Press.

———. 2000. Males Who Have Sex with Males in South Asia. *Pukaar* 12–13 (Oct.): 22–23.

Khandelwal, M. 1996. Walking a Tightrope: Saintliness, Gender, and Power in an Ethnographic Encounter. *Anthropology and Humanism* 21 (2): 111–34.

———. 1997. Ungendered Atma, Masculine Virility, and Feminine Compassion: Ambiguities in Renunciant Discourses on Gender. *Contributions to Indian Sociology* 31 (1): 79–107.

———. 2001. Sexual Fluids, Emotions, Morality: Notes on the Gendering of Brahmacharya. In *Celibacy, Culture, and Society: The Anthropology of Sexual Abstinence*, ed. E. Sobo and S. Bell. Madison: University of Wisconsin Press.

Khare, R. 1984. *The Untouchable as Himself: Ideology, Identity, and Pragmatism among the Lucknow Chamars*. New York: Cambridge University Press.

Kidwai, S. 1985. Sultans, Eunuchs, and Domestics: New Forms of Bondage in Medieval India. In *Chains of Servitude: Bondage and Slavery in India*, ed. U. Patnaik and M. Dingwaney. New Delhi: Sangam Books.

———. 2000. Medieval Materials in the Perso-Urdu Tradition. In *Same-Sex Love in India: Readings from Literature and History*, ed. R. Vanita and S. Kidwai, 107–25. New York: St. Martin's Press.

Kitts, E. J. 1885. *A Compendium of the Castes and Tribes Found in India*. Bombay: Education Society's Press.

Kleinman, A., V. Das, and M. Lock. Social Suffering. Special issue, *Daedelus* 125 (1): 261–83.

Knauft, B. 1996. *Genealogies for the Present in Cultural Anthropology*. New York: Routledge Press.

———. 1997. Theoretical Currents in Late Modern Cultural Anthropology: Toward a Conversation. *Cultural Dynamics* 9:277–300.

Knighton, W. 1855. *The Private Life of an Eastern King. By a Member of the Household of His Majesty, Nussir-u-Deen, King of Oude*. New York: Redfield.

Knipe, D. M. 1975. *In the Image of Fire: Vedic Experiences of Heat*. Delhi: Motilal Banarsidass.

Kosambi, D. D. 1975. *An Introduction to the Study of Indian History*. Bombay: Popular Prakashan.

Kripal, J. 1995. *Kali's Child: The Mystical and the Erotic in the Life and Teachings of Ramkrishna*. 2nd ed. Chicago: University of Chicago Press.

Krishmaswamy, R. 1998. *Effeminism: The Economy of Colonial Desire*. Ann Arbor: University of Michigan Press.

Kuefler, M. 2001. *The Manly Eunuch: Masculinity, Gender Ambiguity, and Christian Ideology in Late Antiquity*. Chicago: University of Chicago Press.

Kulick, D. 1997. The Gender of Brazilian Transgendered Prostitutes. *American Anthropologist* 99 (3): 574–85.

———. 1998. *Travesti: Sex, Gender, and Culture among Brazilian Transgendered Prostitutes*. Chicago: University of Chicago Press.

Kumar, N. 1992. *Friends, Brothers, and Informants: Fieldwork Memoirs of Banaras*. Berkeley and Los Angeles: University of California Press.

Kurtz, S. 1992. *All the Mothers Are One*. Chicago: University of Chicago Press.

Lacan, J. 1978. *The Four Fundamental Concepts of Psychoanalysis*. Ed. J-A Miller. Trans. A. Sheridan. New York: W. W. Norton.

Lal, V. 1995. The Mother in the "Father of the Nation." *Manushi: A Journal of Women and Society* 91 (Nov.–Dec.): 27–30.

Lancaster, R. 1988. Subject Honor and Object Shame. *Ethnology* 27 (2): 111–25.

———. 1992. *Life Is Hard: Machismo, Danger, and the Intimacy of Power in Nicaragua*. Berkeley and Los Angeles: University of California Press.

———. 1995. That We Should All Turn Queer? Homosexual Stigma in the Making of Manhood and the Breaking of a Revolution in Nicaragua. In *Conceiving Sexuality: Approaches to Sex Research in a Postmodern World*, ed. J. Gagnon and R. Parker. London: Routledge.

Laqueur, T. 1990. *Making Sex: Body and Gender from the Greeks to Freud*. Cambridge, MA: Harvard University Press.

Lawrence, W. R. 1928. *The India We Served*. London: Cassell.

Lefebvre, H. 1991. *The Production of Space*. Trans. Donald Nicholson-Smith. Oxford: Blackwell Press.

Lele, J., ed. 1981. *Tradition and Modernity in Bhakti Movements*. Leiden: E. J. Brill.

Leonard, K. I. 1978. *Social History of an Indian Caste: The Kayasths of Hyderabad*. Berkeley and Los Angeles: University of California Press.

Lévi-Strauss, C. 1969. *The Elementary Structures of Kinship*. Rev. ed., trans. J. Bell and J. von Sturmer. London: Eyre and Spottiswoode.

Lewin, E. 1998a. Wives, Mothers and Lesbians: Rethinking Resistance in the U.S. In *Pragmatic Women and Body Politics*, ed. M. Lock and P. Kaufert. New York: Cambridge University Press.

———. 1998b. *Recognizing Ourselves: Ceremonies of Lesbian and Gay Commitment*. New York: Columbia University Press.

Lingat, R. 1973. *The Classical Laws of India*. Berkeley and Los Angeles: University of California Press.

Lopez, D. S., Jr., ed. 1995. *Religions of India in Practice*. Princeton Readings in Religions. Princeton, NJ: Princeton University Press.

Lorenzen, D. N., ed. 1995. *Bhakti Religion in North India: Community Identity and Political Action*. Albany: SUNY Press.

Ludden, D., ed. 1996. *Making India Hindu: Religion, Community, and the Politics of Democracy in India*. Delhi: Oxford University Press.

Luther, N. 1995. *Hyderabad: Memoirs of a City.* Hyderabad: Orient Longman.

Lynch, O. 1969. *The Politics of Untouchability.* New York: Columbia University Press.

Lynton, H. R. 1993. *My Dear Nawab Saheb.* Hyderabad: Orient Longman.

Lynton, H. R., and M. Rajan. 1974. *The Days of the Beloved.* Hyderabad: Orient Longman.

Mackie, J. L. 1977. *Ethics: Inventing Right and Wrong.* Harmondsworth, UK: Penguin Books.

Madan, T. N. 1975. Structural Implications of Marriage in North India. *Contributions to Indian Sociology,* n.s., 9 (2): 217–43.

―――, ed. 1982. *Way of Life: King, Householder, Renouncer: Essays in Honor of Louis Dumont.* Paris: Edition de la Maison des Sciences de L'Homme.

―――. 1987. *Non-renunciation: Themes and Interpretations of Hindu Culture.* Delhi and New York: Oxford University Press.

―――, ed. 1995. *Muslim Communities of South Asia: Culture, Society, and Power.* Delhi: Manohar Press.

Mandelbaum, D. 1988. *Women's Seclusion and Men's Honor: Sex Roles in North India.* Tucson: University of Arizona Press.

Manderson, L., and M. Jolly, eds. 1997. *Sites of Desire, Economies of Pleasure: Sexualities in Asia and the Pacific.* Chicago: University of Chicago Press.

Mani, L. 1986. The Production of an Official Discourse on Sati in Early Nineteenth-Century Bengal. *Economic and Political Weekly: Review of Women's Studies* 21 (April): 32–40.

―――. 1998. *Contentious Traditions: The Debate on Sati in Colonial India.* Berkeley and Los Angeles: University of California Press.

Mann, P. 1992. *Season of the Monsoon.* Sydney: Pan Press.

Manorama Yearbook. 2002. Kottayam, Kerala: Malayala Manorama Press.

Manucci, N. 1907. *Mogul India, 1653–1708.* London: John Murray.

Manuel, P. 1987. Courtesans and Hindustani Music. *Asian Review* 1 (Spring): 12–17.

―――. 1989. *Thumri in Historical and Stylistic Perspectives.* Delhi: Motilal Banarsidass.

Marcus, M. A. 1987. Horsemen Are the Fence of the Land: Honor and History among the Ghiyata of Eastern Morocco. In Gilmore 1987.

Marglin, F. A. 1985. *Wives of the God-King: The Rituals of the Devadasis of Puri.* Delhi: Oxford University Press.

Marmon, S. 1995. *Eunuchs and Sacred Boundaries in Islamic Society.* Oxford: Oxford University Press.

Marriott, M. 1976. Hindu Transactions: Diversity without Dualism. In *Transaction and Meaning: Directions in the Anthropology of Exchange and Symbolic Behavior.* Philadelphia, PA: Ishi Press.

―――. 1989. Constructing an Indian Ethnosociology. *Contributions to Indian Sociology,* n.s., 23 (1): 1–39.

Marriott, M., and R. Inden. 1977. Toward an Ethnosociology of South Asian Caste Systems. In *The New Wind: Changing Identities in South Asia*, ed. B. Kapferer. The Hague: Mouton.

Martin, F. 1983. *Memoirs of Francois Martin (1670–1694)*. Vol. 1. Trans. L. Vardarajan. Delhi: Manohar Press.

Mauss, M. 1967. *The Gift: Forms and Functions of Exchange in Archaic Societies.* New York: W. W. Norton.

———. 1985. A Category of the Human Mind: The Notion of Person, the Notion of Self. In *The Category of the Person: Anthropology, Philosophy, History.* Cambridge: Cambridge University Press.

Mayer, A. 1960. *Caste and Kinship in Central India: A Village and Its Region.* London: Routledge and Kegan Paul.

McDaniel, J. 1989. *The Madness of the Saints: Ecstatic Religion in Bengal.* Chicago: University of Chicago Press.

McHugh, E. 1998. Situating Persons: Honor and Identity in Nepal. In *Selves in Time and Place: Identities, Experience and History in Nepal*, ed. D. Skinner, A. Pach III, and D. Holland. New York: Rowman and Littlefield.

Meduri, A. 1988. Bharatnatyam: What Are You? *Asian Theatre Journal* 5 (1): 1–22.

———. 1996. Nation, Woman, Representation: The Sutured History of the Devadasi and Her Dance. PhD diss. New York University.

Meeker, M. 1979. *Literature and Violence in North Arabia.* Cambridge: Cambridge University Press.

Meghdoot, S. 2000. Eunuchs in Surat Face Cut in Business. *Indian Express*, Dec. 9. Accessed online at www.indian-express.com/ie/daily/19981209/34351174.html.

Mehta, D. 1996. Circumcision, Body, and Community. *Contributions to Indian Sociology*, n.s., 30 (2): 215–43.

Mehta, V. 1977. *Mahatma Gandhi and His Apostles.* London: Andre Deutsch.

Mencher, J. 1974. The Caste System Upside Down, or the Not-So Mysterious East. *Current Anthropology* 15:469–93.

Menon, R. 1997. Reproducing the Legitimate Community: Secularity, Sexuality, and the State in Post-Partition India. In *Appropriating Gender: Women's Activism and Politicized Religion*, ed. A. Basu and P. Jeffrey. New York: Routledge.

Menon, R., and K. Bhasin. 1998. *Borders and Boundaries: Women in India's Partition.* New Delhi: Kali for Women Press.

Merleau-Ponty, M. 1962. *Phenomenology of Perception.* New York: Humanities Press.

Merton, R. 1957. *Social Theory and Social Structure.* New York: Free Press.

Metcalf, B., ed. 1984. *Moral Conduct and Authority: The Place of Adab in South Asian Islam.* Berkeley and Los Angeles: University of California Press.

Meyer, J. J. 1971. *Sexual Life in Ancient India.* Delhi: Motilal Banarsidass.

Minault, G. 1998. *Secluded Scholars: Women's Education and Muslim Social Reform in Colonial India.* Delhi: Oxford University Press.

Mines, M. 1988. Conceptualizing the Person: Hierarchical Society and Individual Autonomy in India. *American Anthropologist* 71 (6): 1166–75.

———. 1994. *Public Faces, Private Voices: Community and Individuality in South India*. Berkeley and Los Angeles: University of California Press.

Misra, S. 1964. *Muslim Communities in Gujarat*. Bombay: Asia Publishing House.

Mitamura, T. 1970. *Chinese Eunuchs: The Structure of Intimate Politics*. Trans. C. A. Pomeroy. Tokyo: Charles. E. Tuttle.

Moffat, M. 1979. *An Untouchable Community in South India: Structure and Consensus*. Princeton, NJ: Princeton University Press.

Mohan, C. 1979. The Ambiguous Sex on the War-Path. *Hindustan Times Weekly*, 8.

Moore, H. 1994. *A Passion for Difference: Essays in Anthropology and Gender*. Bloomington: Indiana University Press.

Morgan, L. H. 1970. *Systems of Consanguinity and Affinity of the Human Family*. Oosterhaut, Netherlands: Anthropological Publications.

Morris, B. 1978. Are There Any Indians in India: A Critique of Dumont's Theory of the Individual. *Eastern Anthropologist* 31 (4): 365–77.

Morris, R. 1994. Three Sexes and Four Sexualities: Redressing the Discourses on Gender and Sexuality in Contemporary Thailand. *Positions* 2 (1): 15–43.

Mujeeb, M. 1967. *The Indian Muslim*. London: George Allen and Unwin.

Murray, S. O. 1995. *Latin American Male Homosexualities*. Albuquerque: University of New Mexico Press.

Naim, C. M. 1979. The Theme of Homosexual (Pederastic) Love in Pre-modern Urdu Poetry. In *Studies in the Urdu Ghazal and Prose Fiction*, ed. M. U. Menon. South Asian Studies Publication Series. Madison: University of Wisconsin Press.

Nanda, S. 1990. *Neither Man nor Woman: The Hijras of India*. New York: Wadsworth. (Second ed. published in 1999.)

———. 1994. Hijras: An Alternative Sex and Gender Role in India. In Herdt 1994.

Nandy, A. 1983. *The Intimate Enemy: Loss and Recovery of Self under Colonialism*. Delhi: Oxford University Press.

Nandy, A., and V. Das. 1985. Violence, Victimhood, and the Language of Silence. *Contributions to Indian Sociology*, n.s., 19 (1): 26–42.

Narad, S. 2003. Eunuchs, Corporator Held on Castration Charge. *Sifynews*, May 29. Available at www.sifynews.com.

Narayan, K. 1988. *Storytellers, Saints, and Scoundrels: Folk Narrative in Hindu Religious Teaching*. Philadelphia: University of Pennsylvania Press.

———. 1993. How Native Is a "Native" Anthropologist? *American Anthropologist* 95:671–86.

Narayanan, V., and N. Cutler, eds. 1996. *Gods of Flesh/Gods of Stone: The Embodiment of Divinity in India*. New York: Columbia University Press.

Neuman, D. M. 1980. *The Life of Music in North India: The Organization of an Artistic Tradition*. Detroit, MI: Wayne State University Press.

Newton, Esther. 1972. *Mother Camp: Female Impersonators in America*. Chicago: University of Chicago Press.

Nigam, S. 1990. Disciplining and Policing the "Criminals by Birth." *Indian Economic and Social History Review* 27 (2): 131–64.

Nikhilananda, S., ed. 1953. *Vivekananda: The Yogas and Other Works*. New York: Ramakrishna-Vedanta Center.

Nuckolls, C., ed. 1993. *Siblings in South Asia*. New York: Guilford.

———. 1996. *The Cultural Dialectics of Knowledge and Desire*. Madison: University of Wisconsin Press.

Obeyesekere, G. 1981. *Medusa's Hair: An Essay on Personal Symbols and Religious Experience*. Chicago: University of Chicago Press.

———. 1984. *The Cult of the Goddess Pattini*. Chicago: University of Chicago Press.

———. 1990. *The Work of Culture*. Chicago: University of Chicago Press.

O'Flaherty, W. D. 1973. *Asceticism and Eroticism in the Mythology of Siva*. London: Oxford University Press.

———. 1980. *Women, Androgynes, and Other Mythical Beasts*. Chicago: University of Chicago Press.

Ojha, C. 1981. Feminine Asceticism in India: Its Tradition and Present Condition. *Man in India* 61 (3): 254–85.

Oldenburg, V. 1984. *The Making of Colonial Lucknow, 1856–1877*. Princeton, NJ: Princeton University Press.

———. 1992. Lifestyle as Resistance: The Courtesans of Lucknow. In *Contesting Power: Resistance and Everyday Social Relations in South Asia*, ed. D. Haynes and G. Prakash. Berkeley and Los Angeles: University of California Press.

Olivelle, P. 1993. *The Asrama System: The History and Hermeneutics of a Religious Institution*. New York: Oxford University Press.

Opler, M. E. 1959. Review of G. M. Carstairs's *The Twice-Born: A Study of a Community of High-Caste Hindus*. *American Anthropologist* 61:140–42.

———. 1960. The Hijara (Hermaphrodite) of India and the Indian National Character. *American Anthropologist* 62:505–11.

Ortner, S. 1984. Theory in Anthropology Since the 1960s. *Comparative Studies in Society and History* 26 (1): 126–66.

O'Shea, J. 1998. "Traditional" Indian Dance and the Making of Interpretive Communities. *Asian Theatre Journal* 15 (1): 45–63.

Ostor, A., L. Fruzzetti, and S. Barnett, eds. 1982. *Concepts of Person: Kinship, Caste, and Marriage in India*. Cambridge, MA: Harvard University Press.

Palmer, S. J. 1994. *Moon Sisters, Krishna Mothers, Rajneesh Lovers: Women's Roles in New Religions*. Syracuse, NY: Syracuse University Press.

Pandey, G. 1989. The Colonial Construction of "Communalism": British Writings on Banaras in the Nineteenth Century. *Subaltern Studies VI*, ed. R. Guha. Delhi: Oxford University Press.

Panikkar, K. M. 1963. *The Foundations of New India*. London: George Allen and Unwin.

Papanek, H., and G. Minault, eds. 1982. *Separate Worlds: Studies of Purdah in South Asia*. Delhi: Chanakya Publications.

Parekh, B. 1989. *Colonialism, Tradition, and Reform: An Analysis of Gandhi's Political Discourse*. New Delhi: Sage.

Parker, R. 1987. Acquired Immunodeficiency Syndrome in Urban Brazil. *Medical Anthropology Quarterly* 1 (2): 155–75.

———. 1991. *Bodies, Pleasures, and Passions: Sexual Culture in Contemporary Brazil*. Boston: Beacon Press.

———. 1999. *Beneath the Equator: Cultures of Desire, Male Homosexuality, and Emerging Gay Communities in Brazil*. New York: Routledge.

Parry, J. 1982. Death and Cosmogony in Kashi. In Madan 1982.

Pastner, C. 1988. A Case of Honor among the Oasis Baluch of Makran. In *Shari'at and Ambiguity in South Asian Islam*, ed. K. Ewing. Berkeley and Los Angeles: University of California Press.

Patel, G. 1997. Home, Homo, Hybrid: Translating Gender. *College Literature* 24 (1): 133–50.

Pathak, Z., and S. Sengupta. 1995. Recasting Women. In Sarkar and Butalia 1995.

Patnaik, D. N. 1971. *Odissi Dance*. Cuttack: Goswami Press.

Peirce, L. 1993. *The Imperial Harem: Women and Sovereignty in the Ottoman Empire*. New York: Oxford University Press.

Peristiany, J. G., ed. 1966. *Honor and Shame: The Values of Mediterranean Society*. Chicago: University of Chicago Press.

Phillimore, P. 2001. Private Lives and Public Identities: An Example of Female Celibacy in Northwest India. In *Celibacy, Culture, and Society: The Anthropology of Sexual Abstinence*, ed. E. Sobo and S. Bell. Madison: University of Wisconsin Press.

Pimpley, P. N., and S. K. Sharma. 1985. Hijras: A Study of an Atypical Role. *Avadh Journal of Social Sciences* 2:41–50.

Pinault, D. 1992. *The Shiites: Ritual and Popular Piety in a Muslim Community*. New York: St. Martin's Press.

Pitt-Rivers, J. A., ed. 1963. *Mediterranean Countrymen: Essays in the Social Anthropology of the Mediterranean*. Paris: Mouton.

———. 1977. *The Fate of the Shechem*. Cambridge: Cambridge University Press.

Prasad, A. H., and M. Yorke. 1991. *Eunuchs: India's Third Gender*. Video recording, 50 min. Kas Moviemakers, British Broadcasting Corporation Television Service.

Prasad, D. 1986. *Social and Cultural Geography of Hyderabad City*. New Delhi: Inter-India Publications.

Preston, L. W. 1987. A Right to Exist: Eunuchs and the State in Nineteenth-Century India. *Modern Asian Studies* 21 (2): 371–87.

Prindle, C. 1988. Occupation and Orthopraxy in Bengali Muslim Rank. In *Shari'at and Ambiguity in South Asian Islam*, ed. K. Ewing. Berkeley and Los Angeles: University of California Press.

Puar, J. 1998. Transnational Sexualities: South Asian (Trans)nation(alism)s and Queer Diasporas. In *Q&A: Queer in America*, ed. D. Eng. Philadelphia, PA: Temple University Press.

Pugh, J. 1988. Divination and Ideology in the Benares Hindu Community. In *Shari'at and Ambiguity in South Asian Islam*, ed. K. Ewing. Berkeley and Los Angeles: University of California Press.

Radcliffe-Brown, A. R., and C. D. Forde, eds. 1950. *African Systems of Kinship and Marriage*. London and New York: Oxford University Press.

Radhakrishna, M. 1989. The Criminal Tribes Act in the Madras Presidency: Implications for the Itinerant Trading Communities. *Indian Economic and Social History Review* 26 (3): 269–95.

Raheja, G. G. 1988. *The Poison in the Gift: Ritual, Prestation, and the Dominant Caste in a North Indian Village*. Chicago: University of Chicago Press.

Raheja, G. G., and A. Gold. 1994. *Listen to the Heron's Words: Reimagining Gender and Kinship in North India*. Berkeley and Los Angeles: University of California Press.

Rahman, T. 1990. Boy-Love in the Urdu Ghazal. *Annals of Urdu Studies* 7:1–20.

Ramanujan, A. K. 1983. *Poems of Love and War from the Eight Anthologies and Ten Long Poems of Classical Tamil*. Delhi: Oxford University Press.

———. 1990. Is There an Indian Way of Thinking? An Informal Essay. In *India through Hindu Categories*, ed. M. Marriott. Delhi: Sage.

Rao, V. 1990. Thumri as Feminine Voice. *Economic and Political Weekly*, April 28, 9–14.

Ray, B. 1988. *Hyderabad and British Paramountcy*. Bombay: Oxford University Press.

Raychaudhuri, T. 1989. *Europe Reconsidered: Perceptions of the West in Nineteenth-Century Bengal*. Delhi: Oxford University Press.

Reddy, G. 1999. Bonds of Love: The Desire for Companionate Marriages among the Hijras of Hyderabad. Paper presented at the meeting of the American Anthropological Association. Washington, DC, November.

———. 2000. Constructions of Sexuality in the Context of HIV/AIDS in Hyderabad, India. Masters thesis in Public Health. Emory University.

———. 2003. "Men" Who Would Be Kings: Celibacy, Emasculation, and Reproduction of Hijras in Contemporary Indian Politics. *Social Research* 70 (1): 163–98.

Reed, S. A. 1998. The Politics and Poetics of Dance. *Annual Review of Anthropology* 27:503–32.

Reeves, P. D., ed. 1971. *Sleeman in Oudh: An Abridgement of W. H. Sleeman's "A Journey Through the Kingdom of Oudh in 1849–50."* London: Cambridge University Press.

Rich, A. 1986. *Of Woman Born: Motherhood as Experience and Institution*. New York: W. W. Norton.

Ringrose, K. 1994. Living in the Shadows: Eunuchs and Gender in Byzantium. In Herdt 1994.

Roland, A. 1979. *In Search of Self in India and Japan*. Princeton, NJ: Princeton University Press.

Rose, H. A. 1919. *A Glossary of the Tribes and Castes of the North Western Frontier Provinces and the Protected Territories of the North West Frontier Provinces*. Reprint, Delhi: Amar Prakashan Publishers, 1980.

Roy, A. 1983. *The Islamic Syncretic Tradition in Bengal*. Princeton, NJ: Princeton University Press.

Roy, K. 1995. Where Women Are Worshipped, There the Gods Rejoice. In Sarkar and Butalia 1995.

————. 2000. Krittivasa Ramayana: The Birth of Bhagiratha (Bengali). In *Same-Sex Love in India: Readings from Literature and History*, ed. R. Vanita and S. Kidwai. New York: St. Martin's Press.

Roy, P. 1998. As the Master Saw Her: Western Women and Hindu Nationalism. In *Indian Traffic: Identities in Question in Colonial and Postcolonial India*. Berkeley and Los Angeles: University of California Press.

Rubin, G. 1975. The Traffic in Women: Notes on the "Political Economy" of Sex. In *Toward an Anthropology of Women*, ed. R. Reiter. New York: Monthly Review Press.

————. 1984. Thinking Sex: Notes for a Radical Theory of the Politics of Sexuality. In *Pleasure and Danger*, ed. C. S. Vance. New York: Routledge and Kegan Paul.

Russell, R. V. 1916. *The Tribes and Castes of the Central Provinces of India*. London: Macmillan.

Russell, R. V., R. Bahudur, and H. Lal. 1916. Hijra, Khasua. In *Tribes and Castes of the Central Provinces of India*. Vol. 3. London: Macmillan.

Ruswa, M. M. 1982. *Umrao Jan Ada*. Trans. K. Singh and M. A. Husaini. Madras: Sangam Books.

Saletore, R. N. 1974. *Sex Life under Indian Rulers*. Delhi: Hind Pocket Books.

Salunkhe, G. 1976. The Cult of the Hijadas of Gujarat. *American Anthropologist* 61:1325–30.

Sanghvi, M. 1984. Walking the Wild Side. *The Illustrated Weekly of India*, March 11, 25–28.

Sarkar, T. 1995. Heroic Women, Mother Goddesses: Family and Organization in Hindutva Politics. In Sarkar and Butalia 1995.

Sarkar, T., and U. Butalia, eds. 1995. *Women and the Hindu Right: A Collection of Essays*. New Delhi: Kali for Women Press.

Schact, J. 1974. *Shorter Encyclopedia of Islam*. Ed. H. A. R. Gibb and J. H. Kramer "Shari'a." Leiden: E. J. Brill.

Schimmel, A. 1975. *Mystical Dimension of Islam*. Chapel Hill: University of North Carolina Press.

————. 1976. *Pain and Grace: A Study of Two Mystical Writers of Eighteenth-Century Muslim India*. Leiden: E. J. Brill.

_____. 1980. *Islam in the Indian Subcontinent*. Leiden: E. J. Brill.

Schneider, D. 1968. *American Kinship: A Cultural Account*. Englewood Cliffs, NJ: Prentice-Hall.

Schneider, J. 1971. Of Vigilance and Virgins. *Ethnology* 10:1–24.

Schoepf, B. 1995. Culture, Sex Research, and AIDS Prevention in Africa. In *Culture and Sexual Risk: Anthropological Perspectives on AIDS*, ed. H. Brummelhuis and G. Herdt. Australia and United States: Gordon and Breach.

Seabrook, J. 1999. *Love in a Different Climate: Men Who Have Sex with Men in India*. London: Verso Press.

Sedgwick, E. K. 1990. *Epistemology of the Closet*. Berkeley and Los Angeles: University of California Press.

Seshan, K. S. S. 1993. *Hyderabad–400: Saga of a City*. Hyderabad: Association of British Council Scholars, A. P. Chapter.

Shah, A. M. 1961. A Note on the Hijadas of Gujarat. *American Anthropologist* 63 (6): 1325–30.

Shah, N. 1998. Sexuality, Identity, and the Uses of History. In *Q&A: Queer in America*, ed. D. Eng. Philadelphia, PA: Temple University Press.

Sharar, A. H. 1975. *Lucknow: The Last Phase of an Oriental Culture*. Trans. and ed. E. S. Harcourt and F. Hussain. London: Paul Elek Printers.

Sharif, A. 1975 [1921]. *Islam in India: The Customs of the Musalmans in India*. Trans. G. A. Heklots. Delhi: Oriental Books Reprint Corporation.

Sharma, S. K. 1989. *Hijras: The Labelled Deviants*. New Delhi: Gian Publishing House.

Sharma, U. 1990. Public Employment and Private Relations: Women and Work in India. In *Women, Employment, and the Family in the International Division of Labour*, ed. J. P. Stichter. London: Macmillan.

Shetty, K. 1990. Eunuchs: A Bawdy Festival. *India Today*, June 15, 50–55.

Shiva, A., S. MacDonald, and M. Gucovsky. 2000. *Bombay Eunuchs*. Film. Gidalya Pictures, New York.

Shore, B. 1997. Authenticity, an Exploration: A Cultural Trends Analysis for the Doblin Group. Report presented at Emory University, Atlanta, GA, August.

Shweder, R., and E. J. Bourne. 1984. Does the Concept of a Person Vary Cross-Culturally? In *Culture Theory: Essays of Mind, Self, and Emotion*. Cambridge: Cambridge University Press.

Shweder, R., M. Mahapatra, and B. Miller. 1990. Culture and Moral Development. In *Cultural Psychology: Essays on Comparative Human Development*, ed. J. W. Stigler, R. A. Shweder, and G. H. Herdt. Cambridge and New York: Cambridge University Press.

Shyamsundar, A. 1996. Producing Sex Was His Business. *Crime and Detective*, July 8, 16–23.

Sideris, G. 2002. "Eunuchs of Light": Power, Imperial Ceremony, and Positive Representations of Eunuchs in Byzantium. In *Eunuchs in Antiquity and Beyond*, ed. S. Tougher. London: Duckworth and the Classical Press of Wales.

Singer, M. 1972. *When a Great Tradition Modernizes: An Anthropological Approach to Indian Civilization*. New York: Praeger.

Sinha, A. P. 1967. Procreation among the Eunuchs. *Eastern Anthropologist* 20:168–76.

Sinha, K. 1993. *The Third Sex: A Novel*. Trans. N. Mukherjee. Bombay: India Book Distributors.

Sinha, M. 1995. *Colonial Masculinity: The "Manly Englishman" and the "Effeminate Bengali" in the Late Nineteenth Century*. Manchester, UK: Manchester University Press.

Smith, C. W. 1957. *Islam in Modern History*. New York: New American Library.

Soja, E. 1989. *Postmodern Geographies*. London: Verso.

Srinivas, M. N. 1965. *Religion and Society among the Coorgs of South India*. New York: Asia Publishing House.

———. 1987. *Social Change in Modern India*. New Delhi: Orient Longman.

Srinivas, S. 1999. The Brahmin and the Fakir: Suburban Religiosity in the Cult of Shirdi Sai Baba. *Journal of Contemporary Religion* 14 (2): 245–61.

———. 2001. The Advent of the Avatar: The Urban Following of Sathya Sai Baba and Its Construction of Tradition. In *Charisma and Canon: The Formation of Religious Identity in South Asia*, ed. V. Dalmia, A. Malinar, and M. Christof-Fuechsle. Delhi: Oxford University Press.

Srinivasan, A. 1984. Temple "Prostitution" and Community Reform: An Examination of the Ethnographic, Historical, and Textual Contexts of the Devadasi of Tamil Nadu, South India. PhD diss. London: Cambridge University.

———. 1985. Reform and Revival: The *Devadasi* and Her Dance. *Economic and Political Weekly* 20 (44): 1869–76.

———. 1988. Reform or Conformity? Temple "Prostitution" and the Community in the Madras Presidency. In *State, Community, and Household in Modernizing Asia*, ed. B. Agrawal. New Delhi: Kali for Women Press.

Srivastava, S. 2001. Introduction: Sexual Sites, Seminal Attitudes. In *Sexual Sites, Seminal Attitudes: Sexualities, Masculinities and Culture*. Special issue, *South Asia* 24:1–24.

Stacey, J. 1996. *In the Name of the Family: Rethinking Family Values in the Postmodern Age*. Boston: Beacon Press.

Stack, C. 1974. *All Our Kin: Strategies for Survival in a Black Community*. New York: Harper and Row.

Stewart, F. H. 1994. *Honor*. Chicago: University of Chicago Press.

Stolcke, V. 1993. Is Sex to Gender As Race Is to Ethnicity? In *Gendered Anthropology*, ed. T. del Valle. London: Routledge.

Stoler, A. L. 1995. *Race and the Education of Desire: Foucault's History of Sexuality and the Colonial Order of Things*. Durham, NC: Duke University Press.

———. 1997. Educating Desire in Colonial South East Asia: Foucault, Freud, and Imperial Sexuality. In Manderson and Jolly 1997.

Strathern, M. 1988. *The Gender of the Gift: Problems with Women and Problems with Society in Melanesia*. Berkeley and Los Angeles: University of California Press.

Sweet, M., and L. Zwilling. 1993. The First Medicalization: The Taxonomy and Etiology of Queerness in Classical Indian Medicine. *Journal of the History of Sexuality* 3 (4): 590–607.

Tambiah, S. 1972. Review of *Homo Hierarchicus: An Essay on the Caste System*, by Louis Dumont. *American Anthropologist* 74:832–33.

Tarlo, E. 1996. *Clothing Matters*. Chicago: University of Chicago Press.

Tavernier, J. B. 1995 [1676]. *The Six Voyages.* London: Macmillan Press.

Thapan, M., ed. 1997. *Embodiment: Essays on Gender and Identity*. Delhi: Oxford University Press.

Thapar, R. 1978. *Ancient Indian Social History*. New Delhi: Orient Longman.

———. 1982. Householders and Renouncers in the Brahmanical and Buddhist Traditions. In Madan 1982.

Thurston, E. 1909. *Castes and Tribes of Southern India*. Madras: Government Press.

Tolen, R. 1991. Colonizing and Transforming the Criminal Tribesman: The Salvation Army in British India. *American Ethnologist* 18 (1): 106–25.

Tougher, S. 1999. Images of Effeminate Men: The Case of Byzantine Eunuchs. In *Masculinity in Medieval Europe*, ed. D. M. Hadley. London: Addison-Wesley/Longman.

———. 2002. In or Out? Origins of Court Eunuchs. In *Eunuchs in Antiquity and Beyond*, ed. S. Tougher. London: Duckworth and the Classical Press of Wales.

Trautmann, T. R. 1981. *Dravidian Kinship*. Cambridge: Cambridge University Press.

Trawick, M. 1990. *Notes on Love in a Tamil Family*. Berkeley and Los Angeles: University of California Press.

Tsai, S. H. 2002. Eunuch Power in Imperial China. In *Eunuchs in Antiquity and Beyond*, ed. S. Tougher. London: Duckworth and the Classical Press of Wales.

Tsing, A. L. 1994. *In the Realm of the Diamond Queen: Marginality in an Out-of-the-Way Place*. Princeton, NJ: Princeton University Press.

Turshen, M. 1998. The Political Ecology of AIDS in Africa. In *The Political Economy of AIDS*, ed. M. Singer. Amityville, NY: Baywood.

Uberoi, P. 1989. Review of L. Dumont: Homo Hierarchicus and Affinity as a Value. *Contributions to Indian Sociology*, n.s., 23 (2): 273–75.

———, ed. 1993. *Family, Kinship, and Marriage in India*. Delhi: Oxford University Press.

———, ed. 1996. *Social Reform, Sexuality, and the State*. New Delhi: Sage.

van Buitenen, J. A. B. 1973. *Mahabharata*. Vol. 3. *The Book of Virata*. Trans. and ed. J. A. B. van Buitenen. Chicago: University of Chicago Press.

Vance, C. 2003. The Sex Panic: Useful Knife or Hysterical Tool? Paper presented at American Anthropological Association Conference, November 20, Chicago, IL.

van der Veer, P. 1989. The Power of Detachment: Disciplines of Body and Mind in the Ramanandi Order. *American Ethnologist* 16:458–70.

————. 1998. *Religious Nationalism: Hindus and Muslims in India.* Delhi: University of Oxford Press.

Van Gennep, A. 1960. *Rites of Passage.* Chicago: University of Chicago Press.

Vanita, R., ed. 2002. *Queering India: Same-Sex Love and Eroticism in Indian Culture and Society.* New York: Routledge.

Vanita, R., and S. Kidwai, eds. 2000. *Same-Sex Love in India: Readings from Literature and History.* New York: St. Martin's Press.

Vatsyayan, K. 1968. *Classical Indian Dance in Literature and the Arts.* New Delhi: Sangeet Natak Academy.

Vatsyayana, M. 2002. *Kamasutra.* Trans. Wendy Doniger and Sudhir Kakar. New York: Oxford University Press. (Orig. produced in the third century.)

Vatuk, S. 1969. Reference, Address, and Fictive Kinship in Urban North India. *Ethnology* 8:255–72.

————. 1975. Gifts and Affines in North India. *Contributions to Indian Sociology* 3:94–115.

————. 1982. Forms of Address in the North Indian Family. In Ostor, Fruzzetti, and Barnett 1982.

Voting in a Gender-Bender. *Indian Express,* February 28, 2000.

Vyas, S., and D. Shingala. 1987. *The Life Style of the Eunuchs.* New Delhi: Anmol Publications.

Warner, M. 1999. *The Trouble with Normal: Sex, Politics, and the Ethics of Queer Life.* New York: Free Press.

Weber, M. 1958. *The Religion of India.* Glencoe: Free Press.

Weeks, J. 1981. *Sex, Politics, and Society: The Regulation of Sexuality since 1800.* London and New York: Longman. (Orig. pub. 1977.)

————. 1986. *Sexuality.* New York: Tavistock.

Weston, K. 1991. *Families We Choose: Lesbians, Gays, Kinship.* New York: Columbia University Press.

————. 1993. Lesbian/Gay Studies in the House of Anthropology. *Annual Review of Anthropology* 22:339–67.

————. 1997. The Virtual Anthropologist. In Gupta and Ferguson 1997.

————. 1998. *Long Slow Burn: Sexuality and Social Science.* New York: Routledge.

————. 2002. *Gender in Real Time: Power and Transience in a Visual Age.* New York: Routledge.

White, L. 1990. *Comforts of Home: Prostitution in Colonial Nairobi.* Chicago: University of Chicago Press.

Wikan, U. 1984. Shame and Honor: A Contestable Pair. *Man,* n.s., 19 (4): 635–52.

Williams, R. 1989. *Culture and Society.* New York: Columbia University Press.

Winkler, J. J. 1990. *The Constraints of Desire: The Anthropology of Sex and Gender in Ancient Greece.* New York: Routledge.

Wyatt-Brown, P. 1982. *Southern Honor.* New York: Oxford University Press.

Yalman, N. 1963. On the Purity and Sexuality of Women in the Castes of Ceylon and Malabar. *Journal of the Royal Anthropological Institute* 93 (1): 25–58.

Yang, A, ed. 1985. *Crime and Criminality in British India*. Tucson: University of Arizona Press.

Zajovic, S. 1994. Women and Ethnic Cleansing. *Women against Fundamentalism* 5 (1): 30–48.

Zwilling, L. 1992. Homosexuality as Seen in Indian Buddhist Texts. In *Buddhism, Sexuality, and Gender*, ed. J. Cabezon. Albany: SUNY Press.

Zwilling, L., and M. J. Sweet. 1996. "Like a City Ablaze": The Third Sex and the Creation of Sexuality in Jain Religious Literature. *Journal of the History of Sexuality* 6 (3): 359–84.

Zysk, K. G. 1991. *Asceticism and Healing in Ancient India: Medicine in the Buddhist Monastery*. New York: Simon and Schuster.

INDEX

AC/DCs, 54, 72, 226. See also *gandus*
Agrawal, Anuja, 242n20
AIDS. *See* HIV/AIDS
Ajmer Baba (holy man), 256n12
akkva (non-operated) hijras, 72, 134
Ali Khan Asaf Jah II, 11
Alter, Joseph, 38–39
Altman, Dennis, 213, 220
Amba (princess), 239n4, 249n19
ambiguity: active courting of by hijras, 141; of Indian culture, 141, 173; of ithyphallicism, 87; of love in Indian culture, 152
ambivalence, 250n23; of author about undertaking this project, 3–5; in feelings of hijras toward men, 169; of hijra-panti relations, 171–73; of Indian sexuality, 55, 80; of koti-panti relations, 179
"American hijra," 209
anal sex, 260n30
Andhra Pradesh, 71, 146
Andhra riste, 164–68. *See also* hijra kinship
andoli (orphan) hijra, 154, 162
Appadurai, A., 41
Aravan, myth of, 239n4
ardhanarisvara (half man/half woman), 89
Arjuna-Brhannala, 89–90, 91
"artificial eunuchs," 28

asceticism: and eroticism, in Vedic literature, 87; Hindu ideal of, 84–91, 97; and power to create, 97; privileging of, 80. *See also* sannyasi (ascetic/renouncer) lifestyle; *tapas*
asexuality, as mark of "real" hijra, 48, 83, 84, 89, 150, 247n8
asli (real) hijras, 56, 83, 84. *See also* "real" and "false" hijras, distinction between
asrama (life-stages) system, 87, 89, 91, 249n15, 249n16; *brahmacarya*, 39, 88; *grhasta asrama* (householder stage), 35, 37–38, 88, 249n17; *vanaprasta*, 88
Aurangzeb (emperor), 6, 115, 236n9
authenticity. *See* hijra authenticity
Ayalon, David, 23

Babb, Lawrence, 126
badhai hijras (ritual practitioners), 79, 89, 245n19; aggressive behavior, 159; asexuality as mark of "real" hijras, 83; circumcision, 103; economic dependence upon guru, 158; izzat of, 56, 81, 84; natal religious affiliations, 250n1; and pantis, 260n28; patronage of Nizam, 83; in relation to sexual desire and practice, 81, 84
badhai performances, 13, 78, 79, 97–98; singing at weddings, 56; threat of bodily exposure, 140